WHERE'S THE MEERKAT?

WHERE'S THE MEERKAT?

ILLUSTRATED BY PAUL MORAN,
STEVE WILTSHIRE AND SIMON ECOB

WRITTEN BY JEN WAINWRIGHT

DESIGNED BY ANGIE ALLISON AND ZOE QUAYLE

Michael O'Mara Books Limited

A Meerkat Adventure

Prepare to embark on an adventure that will take you all around the globe. You're about to meet a family of mischievous meerkats who are going on the trip of a lifetime, and have invited you along for the ride.

Your Challenge ...

All you have to do is spot ten meerkats in each picture. Sounds simple, right? Be warned, this family is expert at blending in with a crowd, so you'll need your sharpest searching skills. If you get stuck, the solutions can be found at the back of the book.

Really eagle-eyed searchers can use the special 'Spotter's Checklists' at the back of the book, where there's more fun stuff to find in every picture and tick off.

Bon voyage and happy searching ...

Meet The Family

Now it's time to meet the meerkats and find out more about the crazy critters in this fantastic family.

Back row (left to right): Miranda, Florian, Albert, Raoul, Sofia, Matthew
Front row (left to right): Frankie, Maxwell, Samson, Hannah.

Lives in:
Sandy Warren, Africa

Likes:
Travel, adventure, mischief, fancy dress

Favourite Music:
The Beetles, MeerKaty Perry

Favourite Films:
An American Meerkat in Paris, Meerkat On A Hot Tin Roof

Favourite Books:
Termites And Men by John Steinbeck, The Burrowers by Mary Norton

Favourite quotations:
'You must be the change you want to see in the world' – Meerkatma Gandhi.

Individual Profiles

Read on to discover more vital information about each member of the family.

Miranda:
As the maternal figure of the group, Miranda is practical, sensible and never without a clean hanky. She also knows the lyrics to every James Bond theme by heart.

Florian:
This chirpy chappy makes a mean banana milkshake, and has recently started learning folk dancing. He also has an unrivalled back catalogue of mongoose-themed jokes.

Albert:
Albert is mostly known as 'Grampy' to the others in the group. He's a dignified and sprightly old gent with a vast collection of vintage baseball cards.

Raoul:
Raoul dreams of being a rock star. He plays the bassoon (badly), but has written an epic rock ballad, which he hopes will get airtime on *Scorpion FM*.

Sofia:
The highlight of Sofia's life has been her nomination for 'Miss Meerkat' – a prestigious beauty pageant. She point-blank refuses to travel anywhere without her fur straighteners.

Matthew:
Here comes trouble. Matthew can usually be found exactly where he shouldn't be. His special skills include being able to fit six biscuits in his mouth at once.

Frankie:
Frankie's the baby of the bunch. She's also a feisty tomboy, who particularly enjoys infuriating Sofia by hiding her beauty products up trees and in holes.

Maxwell:
Always full of bright ideas, Maxwell has almost perfected his designs for the 'Meerkat-O-Matic' – a device that's part predator alarm, part jet-pack.

Samson:
Samson is a bit of a dark horse. He may be a bookworm with a keen interest in botany, but he's also a karate black belt with a spectacular roundhouse kick.

Hannah:
Hannah is a true artist. She's always painting and sculpting, but her recent series of 'cubist family portraits' has not been greeted with tremendous enthusiasm by her siblings.

Rio De Janeiro, Brazil

The family have landed in Rio and they're ready to party! They are headed straight for the Sambadrome – a huge concrete stadium, where as many as 50,000 musicians and performers parade wearing elaborate costumes in front of cheering crowds.

Hannah and Sofia are excited about dancing the night away, and have been practising their best samba steps. The parties and parades often continue until sunrise, so there will be some sleepy meerkats tomorrow ...

New York, USA

While the grown-ups in the family want to see the Empire State Building and the Statue of Liberty, for Frankie and Raoul it's all about Times Square. They're dazzled by all the cool neon signs, called 'spectaculars'.

1.6 million people pass through Times Square every day, so it's easy to get lost in the crowds. But Frankie and Raoul have promised that they'll meet the others at Toys 'R' Us. With a giant, moving T-Rex, a Ferris wheel and a two-storey dolls' house, it's the place they're most excited about going on this whole trip.

Innsbruck, Austria

The Winter Olympics have been held in Innsbruck twice, so the meerkats have decided it's the perfect place to try out their skills on the slopes.

Albert has surprised everyone by showing some real flair. He's even been brave enough to try out a couple of the snowboard jumps. Poor Samson has had much less success and, after a couple of embarrassing falls, he would really like to skip the skiing and head straight to the city to visit the castle and the Imperial Palace.

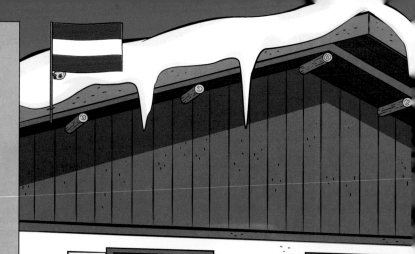

Paris, France

Ever since she was a pup, Sofia has dreamed of visiting Paris. She has been driving everyone mad with her constant talk about the shopping, the fashion, the shopping, the romance, the shopping, the pastries, the shopping and ... the shopping.

As well as hitting the chic boutiques along the Champs-Elysées, she plans to climb the Eiffel Tower at night, all 324 metres of it, including the antennae on top – ouch! She wants to see why Paris is known as 'The City of Lights.' Ooh la la!

BOULANGERIE

Moscow, Russia

As the snow begins to fall, a crowd gathers in Moscow's famous Red Square for the start of the military music festival. Miranda is feeling in fine voice and can't wait to join in with the singing and the parades.

Even though Albert is cold and rather crotchety, he's amazed by how beautiful St Basil's Cathedral looks at night. With its nine separate chapels, and brightly coloured 'onion domes', it looks like something straight out of the pages of a fairy tale.

The Great Wall, China

The Great Wall of China stretches for a massive 8,851.8 kilometres. Florian's eyes nearly fell out of his head when Albert suggested they tackle all of it!

Hannah loves the legend of Meng Jiang Nu, which tells of a beautiful young woman who cried so much when she heard that her husband had died while building the wall, that a whole section of it came tumbling down. Hannah thinks this is so romantic that she's not even complaining about her paws hurting from all the walking.

Easter Island, South Pacific

Gadget-mad Maxwell was convinced that Easter Island would be 'well boring'. But, actually, he's finding it fascinating – even though there's not much in the way of mobile phone signal.

The giant statues, known as 'Moai', are scattered all over the island, some of them weighing up to about 80 tonnes. Lots of them were carved over 1,000 years ago. Maxwell is busy trying to work out how the enormous objects were moved across the island in the days before machinery was used.

Sydney, Australia

As an art and music lover, Hannah couldn't wait to arrive in Sydney to see the famous Opera House. But she's surprised to see that up close, the tiles covering the World Heritage Site are actually almost yellow, not white like she'd expected.

Despite being told not to, Matthew's climbing Sydney Harbour Bridge before you can say 'tasty termite'. Known by locals as 'the coat hanger', it's the largest steel arch bridge in the world.

London, UK

Florian has fallen in love with London in the short time that the family have been here. He has bought an enormous Union Jack flag, and some commemorative Royal Wedding plates and mugs showing Prince William and Catherine, Duchess of Cambridge, to decorate the warren back at home.

Today, it's the changing of the guard at Buckingham Palace, and the crowds have gathered to watch the soldiers marching in their uniforms and tall bearskin hats.

Venice, Italy

When it's Carnival time in Venice, the streets and canals come alive. Everywhere you look there are musicians, jugglers and revellers wearing elaborate and beautiful masks.

After having created his very own pizza, with all the toppings that the restaurant could manage to find, Matthew has now decided to try his hand as a gondolier, using a pole to push the sleek, black boats along the canals. Let's hope he doesn't get 'canal-sick'!

Giza, Egypt

The Great Sphinx of Giza is a truly impressive sight. The enormous statue has the body of a lion, and the head of a man, although Raoul thinks it would look much better with the body of a dragon and the head of a meerkat.

Raoul has learned that the Ancient Egyptians would mummify their dead by wrapping them in bandages. Before this could happen, they removed the dead person's brain through their nose. He is now threatening to do this to his sisters whenever they annoy him, which is most of the time.

Bangkok, Thailand

The floating markets near Bangkok are a feast of smells, colours and sounds. After a long journey, Frankie is starving, and she's spoilt for choice with the mounds of tropical fruit, vegetables, meat and hot, local delicacies for sale from the boats.

The sellers paddle their boats along the canal – called a 'khlong' – shouting to customers and selling their wares. By the end of their visit, Frankie is feeling so stuffed that she can't possibly eat another thing.

Kyoto, Japan

Miranda has been quietly looking forward to this visit for ages. The Shinto shrines of Japan are known as places of calm and tranquility, and she can't wait to take some deep breaths and absorb some of the peace and quiet among the blossoming cherry trees.

The beautiful building is a shrine to the 'kami' – the sacred spirits of the Shinto religion. Kami aren't always gods and goddesses, they can also be forces of nature, such as thunder and tornados, or parts of the natural world, such as lakes and trees.

Santa Cruz, USA

The meerkats have decided to relax for a while on the beach at Santa Cruz in the warm California sun. While Sofia struts her stuff on the boardwalk, Raoul is having a go at surfing, with hilariously mixed results.

Later, the family plan to go to the funfair. Hannah and Samson can't wait to go on the Giant Dipper, the iconic wooden roller coaster that opened in 1924, but Albert has decided he's getting too old for this sort of thing. He'll sit back and watch the youngsters while tucking in to some sugary funnel cake – a fairground specialty.

The Great Barrier Reef, Australia

In the crystal-clear waters of the Great Barrier Reef, there are more than 400 different types of coral in beautiful colours. Samson is in heaven – his mum says he's always been a water baby and he's having a whale of a time swimming with the fish and sea turtles.

Even though the reef is one of the seven wonders of the natural world, Sofia took a lot of coaxing to join in the diving excursion, as it will mean getting her fur wet, and then it might go 'all massive and frizzy'.
Which would be a disaster, apparently.

Marrakesh, Morocco

No trip to Marrakesh would be complete without a visit to the magical complex of markets, called 'souks'.

There are piles of dates, spices and fruit, bright silks and coloured leather bags, pots, plates, and all manner of other things to be bought and bargained for. Unfortunately, it seems that Matthew hasn't quite understood the concept of haggling, as he keeps offering higher and higher prices for the small carved camel he wants! Thankfully, Miranda is on hand to step in and stop him spending too much.

Kruger National Park, South Africa

There's time for one more stop off before the family head back to their warren. They've decided to go on a safari break, where they can see the bigger animals (who normally scare them all quite a lot) from the safety of the jeeps.

After a drive through the bush, the guides set up camp, and soon it's time for dinner under the stars. Hannah loves watching the flickering flames of the campfire, but she can't help jumping every time a lion roars in the distance.

Answers

Spotter's Checklist

- A man in a green wig ☐
- Sixteen blue balloons ☐
- A tambourine ☐
- A drummer ☐
- A purple baseball cap ☐
- Some tasselled trousers ☐
- A polka dot bikini ☐
- White elbow gloves ☐
- An orange bag ☐
- A dancer with mismatched shoes ☐

RIO DE JANEIRO, BRAZIL

NEW YORK, USA

Spotter's Checklist

- Four taxis ☐
- A clock ☐
- A woman jogging ☐
- A boy reading a map ☐
- A man taking a photo ☐
- A brown baseball cap ☐
- A red sports car ☐
- A police officer ☐
- Some dropped litter ☐
- A girl in a bobble hat ☐

Spotter's Checklist

Cups of coffee being spilt ☐

A man eating a bag of doughnuts ☐

Two alpine rescue doctors ☐

A red and yellow snowboard ☐

A man with a red bow tie ☐

Someone relaxing on the ski lift ☐

Some dangerous driving ☐

A child learning to ski ☐

A snowboarder with a goatee ☐

A man getting his hat knocked off ☐

Spotter's Checklist

A birthday cake ☐

A cat among the pigeons ☐

A man with a walking stick ☐

A man on a laptop ☐

A saxophone player ☐

A woman eating crisps ☐

A man with a purple briefcase ☐

A lost boy with a map ☐

An umbrella ☐

A man sweeping ☐

Spotter's Checklist

A boy in a Jewish cap ☐

A man reading the paper ☐

A group of mobsters ☐

A purse thief ☐

A man in a bow tie ☐

A woman with pink hair ☐

A man waving ☐

A group of nuns ☐

A man holding a child ☐

A man in ski goggles ☐

THE GREAT WALL, CHINA

Spotter's Checklist

- Three men photographing the sunset ☐
- A young skateboarder ☐
- A man with a beard and moustache ☐
- Two girls with fans ☐
- A guard in pale grey ☐
- A performance of sword Tai Chi ☐
- Friends linking arms ☐
- Someone wearing a purple beret ☐
- A water bottle ☐
- A man scratching his ear ☐

Spotter's Checklist

- A romantic picnic for two ☐
- An angry mother ☐
- A stingray ☐
- A pair of treasure hunters ☐
- A game of cards ☐
- A boy sucking his thumb ☐
- An artist ☐
- Men discussing the size of fish ☐
- Someone who fell in a hole ☐
- A man reading ☐

EASTER ISLAND, SOUTH PACIFIC

SYDNEY, AUSTRALIA

Spotter's Checklist

- A baby in a sling ☐
- Two space hoppers ☐
- A bowler hat ☐
- A red umbrella ☐
- Two didgeridoos ☐
- A barefoot person ☐
- A man wearing shades at night ☐
- Two ladies wearing the same dress ☐
- A break dancer ☐
- A pink headscarf ☐

LONDON, UK

Spotter's Checklist

- A news reporter ☐
- A blue trumpet ☐
- A lost camera ☐
- A guard in the wrong trousers ☐
- A man hugging his daughter ☐
- A girl sucking her thumb ☐
- Three Union Jack flags ☐
- A sunburnt man ☐
- Some stripy trousers ☐
- A broken lamppost ☐

Spotter's Checklist

- A monk ☐
- A man with mismatched shoes ☐
- A pink and red umbrella ☐
- A violinist ☐
- A polka dot tie ☐
- One yellow sleeve ☐
- Four couples holding hands ☐
- Two gold masks ☐
- A girl in purple waiting for her date ☐
- A waitress on her way home ☐

VENICE, ITALY

GIZA, EGYPT

Spotter's Checklist

- A boy with a finger trap ☐
- A modern-day pharoah ☐
- A man toppling over backwards ☐
- A boy with a tray of basboosa cakes ☐
- A man on his mobile phone ☐
- A girl putting her hair up ☐
- A man with a large cardboard box ☐
- A tiny mummy ☐
- A child on her mother's shoulders ☐
- A man in an orange cowboy hat ☐

Spotter's Checklist

BANGKOK, THAILAND

A pink hat ☐
A boat in trouble ☐
A woman with a red rucksack ☐
A man in a tie ☐
A seller wearing glasses ☐
A basket of fish ☐
A pink parasol ☐
Two Thai flags ☐
Bongo drums ☐
A man in midair ☐

Spotter's Checklist

A teddy bear ☐
A sumo wrestler signing autographs ☐
A man with green hair ☐
A stag ☐
A man with a video camera ☐
A couple checking their photos ☐
Schoolchildren with a samurai ☐
A woman searching in her bag ☐
A girl with a touch-screen phone ☐
A T-shirt with a target symbol on it ☐

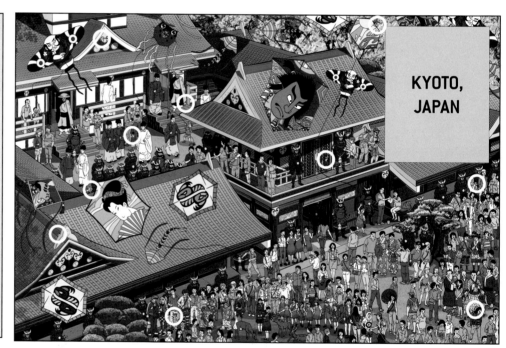

KYOTO, JAPAN

SANTA CRUZ, USA

Spotter's Checklist

A yellow kite ☐
A bodybuilder ☐
A human pyramid ☐
A stray dog ☐
A man with a Frisbee ☐
A boy with turtle armbands ☐
A football ☐
Someone who can't swim ☐
A guitar jamming session ☐
A man carrying green shoes ☐

GREAT BARRIER REEF, AUSTRALIA

Spotter's Checklist

A pink lobster ☐

Two fish with big pink lips ☐

An ugly eel ☐

A jellyfish ☐

A swordfish ☐

A dawdling clown fish ☐

A red crab ☐

Seven fish with a diamond pattern ☐

A diver with a knife ☐

A pair of yellow flippers ☐

Spotter's Checklist

A girl on a pogo stick ☐

A woman with a blue suitcase ☐

A green flag ☐

A large, grey camel ☐

A couple arguing about a plate ☐

A girl stealing an orange ☐

A bookworm ☐

A snake charmer ☐

A pair of yellow slippers ☐

A man picking his nose ☐

MARRAKESH, MOROCCO

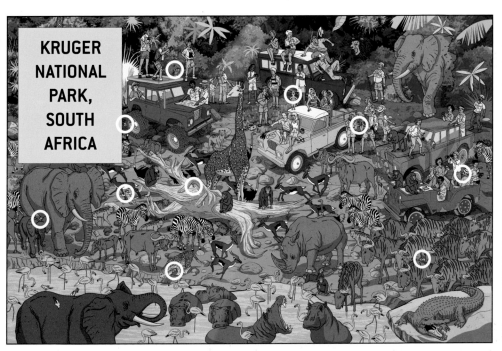

KRUGER NATIONAL PARK, SOUTH AFRICA

Spotter's Checklist

A baby elephant ☐

A shy buffalo ☐

A monkey tempted by sandwiches ☐

A leopard-print hat ☐

A lion terrifying tourists ☐

A woman in a stripy top ☐

Three warthogs ☐

A chimpanzee relaxing ☐

A flamingo with a white tail ☐

A thirsty predator ☐

Published in Great Britain in 2011 by Michael O'Mara Books Limited,
9 Lion Yard, Tremadoc Road, London SW4 7NQ

www.mombooks.com

A CIP catalogue record for this book is available from the British Library.

Hardback ISBN: 978–1–84317–710–4
Paperback ISBN: 978–1–84317–711–1

1 3 5 7 9 10 8 6 4 2

This book was printed in July 2011 by
Shenzhen Wing King Tong Paper Products Co., Ltd., Shenzhen, Guangdong, China

Papers used by Michael O'Mara Books are natural, recyclable products made from
wood grown in sustainable forests. The manufacturing processes conform to the
environmental regulations of the country of origin.

DUCK in the TRUCK

For Gail

First published in hardback in Great Britain by HarperCollins Publishers Ltd in 1999
First published in paperback by Picture Lions in 2000

10 9 8 7 6 5 4 3
ISBN: 0978-0-00-773585-3

Picture Lions is an imprint of the Children's Division, part of HarperCollins Publishers Ltd.
Text and illustrations copyright © Jez Alborough 1999
The author/illustrator asserts the moral right to be identified as the author/illustrator of the work.
A CIP catalogue record for this title is available from the British Library.

Visit our website at: www.harpercollinschildrensbooks.co.uk
Printed and bound in Italy

HarperCollins Children's Books supports Bookstart.

DUCK in the TRUCK

Jez Alborough

HarperCollins *Children's Books*

This is the Duck driving home in a truck.

This is the track which is taking him back.

This is the rock struck by the truck   and this is

the muck   where the truck becomes stuck.

These are the feet which
jump the Duck down

into the muck
all yucky and brown.

This is the frog who
spies from the bush

and croaks, "I'll help you
give it a push!"

This is the push of a Frog   and a Duck…

And this is the truck still stuck.

This is a sheep
driving home in a jeep.

"Get out of the way,"
he yells with a beep.

This is the quack of an angry Duck.
"I can't," he snaps, "my truck is stuck."

This is the
quiet…

…as they think
what to do.

"Got it!" croaks Frog,
"Sheep can push too."

This is the slurp   and squelch   and suck

as the Sheep steps slowly through the muck.

This is the push of a Sheep, a Frog and a Duck

and this is the truck… still stuck.

This is the happy sleepy Goat
relaxing on his motorboat.

This is the ear that
hears the shout,

"My truck's in the muck
and it won't come out!"

This is the rope
and here's the Goat's plan,

to tie a knot
as tight as they can.

This is the push at the rear once again

This is the pull as the boat takes the strain.

These are
the wheels

finally
gripping.

This is   suddenly
the knot   slipping.

This is the truck with the engine on fast

back on the track…   UNSTUCK AT LAST!

This is the Duck driving home in the truck

leaving the Frog, the Sheep and the Goat…

STUCK IN THE MUCK!

New Public Sector Marketing

DAVID CHAPMAN

Manager of International Business Development, Sheffield Business School
Visiting Professor, Masaryk Institute of Advanced Studies, Prague
Chairman, Chartered Institute of Marketing

THEO COWDELL

Principal Lecturer, School of Cultural Studies, Sheffield Hallam University

Prentice Hall
FINANCIAL TIMES

An imprint of **Pearson Education**

Harlow, England • London • New York • Boston • San Francisco • Toronto • Sydney • Singapore • Hong Kong
Tokyo • Seoul • Taipei • New Delhi • Cape Town • Madrid • Mexico City • Amsterdam • Munich • Paris • Milan

Pearson Education Limited
Edinburgh Gate
Harlow
Essex CM20 2JE
England

and Associated Companies throughout the world

Visit us on the World Wide Web at:
http://www.pearsoned.co.uk

First published in Great Britain in 1998

© Financial Times Professional Limited 1998

The rights of David Chapman and Theo Cowdell to be identified as
Authors of this Work have been asserted by them in accordance
with the Copyright, Designs and Patents Act 1998.

ISBN 0 273 62347 8

British Library Cataloguing in Publication Data
A CIP catalogue record for this book can be obtained from the British Library

10 9 8 7 6 5
07 06 05 04

Typeset by Pantek Arts, Maidstone, Kent
Printed and bound in Great Britain by 4Edge Ltd, Hockley, Essex.

CONTENTS

FOREWORD

As our society moves towards a more customer-oriented culture, this book brings a new approach to the understanding and the importance of marketing in the public sector. Although most of the large public utilities have now been returned to private ownership there is still a significant segment of the UK economy that is dependent on Government and local government contracts and spending (currently in excess of 40 per cent GNP). Market forces, the introduction of competition and the demand for efficiency and cost-effectiveness have all highlighted the importance of marketing in this sector. Therefore, with the public sector now more 'transparent' than ever in reflecting contemporary trends, plus Government policies and European legislation requiring compulsory competitive tendering, this book will be welcomed for its development of the subject and its application in an environment unique with its constraints and mores.

The layout of this book provides a comprehensive summary plus a range of discussion issues and a bibliography for each chapter, and therefore it is highly recommended both to those who have executive responsibility in the public sector and those who are studying marketing at diploma and degree level. Furthermore, its particular focus also makes it eminently suitable for those committed to the CIM's Continuing Professional Development programme.

Norman Waite
Director of Education
CIM.

PREFACE

Over the last twenty years, more and more public sector organisations have had to address the issues arising from competition, privatisation and an increasing emphasis upon good management practice. It is therefore surprising to find that there has been relatively little attention paid to the specific nature of marketing in a public sector environment. It has become increasingly evident to us that those working in 'The New Public Sector' have rather different perceptions of, needs for, and attitudes towards marketing compared with those working in the private sector.

This book is unlikely to gain immediate favour with those who believe that marketing as a discipline is a subject which can be understood and applied as a set of procedures to any organisational activity, regardless of differences in culture, attitudes and environment. A body of literature exists, predominantly developed for and applied to a world of commercial business, which considers marketing as a competitive activity, even as an aggressive or 'offensive' one – an approach alien to the cultures of a large number of organisations in the public sector. The cultures of such organisations originated in times of monopoly or near-monopoly provision; they were founded on the principle of providing services in the spirit of social altruism and in the interests of equal opportunity and fairness. However, as the nature of public sector provision has changed, the sector has been faced with the need to adapt to varying conditions, the introduction of competition and a more professional business management focus.

This book is based on the premise that marketing is about identifying user needs and finding the 'best' ways of meeting these needs to the mutual benefit of both user and provider – an essential adaptation of the profit-making philosophy which informs marketing in the commercial sector. Important distinctions remain between profit-making and non-profit-making industries and organisations. Many public sector organisations continue to operate on a non-for-profit basis. However, in the present climate they are increasingly engaging in activities which can provide additional sources of income. Income from government sources is often insufficient to fund the levels of activity which are considered socially desirable. Moreover, many public sector organisations are now obliged to operate systems of internal competition and competitive tendering policies in attempts to reduce costs and improve efficiency. These developments have resulted in major changes in the UK public sector, and can justify the use of the term 'The New Public Sector' in the 1990s. Many other countries are adopting similar strategies.

Many privatised organisations continue to serve traditional public sector needs. The need for regulation in these industries highlights the complex nature of public sector markets, which are usually subject to a number of constraints and controls which differ from those affecting purely commercial ones.

We offer a number of frameworks within which public sector activities can be understood, and the distinctions between the public and the private sectors can be drawn. In addition, we stress that, in the final analysis, the application and implementation of relevant marketing principles is industry specific. In the successful management of public sector organisations, managers will always have to make judgements and decisions in relation to their own specific industry and organisational requirements.

This book is designed to help both the student of public sector management and anyone working in public sector organisations to understand the role and implications of marketing in the new public sector environment. Each chapter discusses an important topic or dimension of marketing, defines it in a public sector context, and provides a framework for considering its implications. A number of tables and figures have been included for this purpose. The text is also punctuated by a number of minicases which draw on relevant events which have received public attention. The 'Implications for management' sections give an indication of the ways in which the topics have practical relevance for those engaged in public sector management. A number of issues for further discussion have been identified as a means of ensuring that any student (in the sense that learning is a continuous process for everyone) can consider the most important issues addressed. Finally, a collection of case studies – mostly fictional in form, but modelled on actual research and analysis – have been provided to serve as a basis for further discussion and consideration.

Although this text takes the form of a relatively 'academic' work, we hope that you will be able to use the discussion constructively. References to a number of relevant published sources provide opportunities for further reading. We are reluctant to suggest that this book should be used as a 'recipe' for efficient or effective marketing management in public sector industries. We hope that it will stimulate thought, discussion and development. We believe that marketing is not merely a method or a function of business or organisations. It is a means of facilitating the processes of exchange and, as such, contributes much to the forms of social relationships on which our concepts of society depend in the modern world.

Acknowledgements

The illustrative material in this book, and the case studies, have been prepared by the authors on the basis of their experience in consultancy, research and teaching. The material is intended to be used as a basis for class discussion rather than to illustrate either effective or ineffective handling of a management situation. The cases are based on composites of real life situations and, as such, are essentially works of fiction which are based on fact. Any resemblance to particular organisations is coincidental.

The authors would like to acknowledge the help and specialist input of numerous individuals, with particular thanks to: Tony Clayton, Geoffrey Cox, Gill Guest, John McKinney (now retired), and Uri Rennie.

David Chapman
Theo Cowdell
January 1998

CHAPTER 1

The public sector – origins and environment

CHAPTER OVERVIEW

During the 18 years of Conservative government in the United Kingdom preceding 1997, the public sector was increasingly exposed to what is often described as a 'competitive environment'. Similar developments took place in other countries. At the same time, public sector organisations were subjected to regulatory control and restrictions which made competitive operation difficult to achieve. Nevertheless, during that period, the concept of marketing within a public sector context attracted considerable interest from both practitioners and academics.

It became clear that the history of the public sector had contributed to a number of specific operational characteristics, cultural attitudes and public expectations which have had a considerable influence on the difficulties encountered in introducing marketing, both as a function and as a philosophy, to public sector organisations. This chapter of this book is, therefore, concerned with the historical development of the public sector. The chapter discusses the ways in which initial success, resulting from the satisfaction of identified social demands, contributed to a considerable and continuous growth, accelerated by nationalisation in the 1940s and 1950s. The public sector is massive and diverse, even after a major programme of privatisation.

The chapter also discusses the ways in which the growth of the sector created a sense of complacency, a burgeoning bureaucracy and a legislative framework which still tends to inhibit the development of marketing within the public sector.

KEY LEARNING OUTCOMES

By the end of this chapter, you should be able to:

- define the public sector;
- understand the historical context within which the public sector is evolving;
- examine the factors influencing the role of the state; and
- explore the concept of 'social equity' and its relationship to public sector provision.

Introduction

The so-called 'public sector' has grown enormously in most countries in the twentieth century. It consumes a very large percentage of the UK's Gross Domestic Product (GDP). Lord Skidelsky (1996), Chairman of the Social Marketing Foundation, has estimated that in 1995 Britain's public spending accounted for some 42.5 per cent of GDP. According to the Adam Smith Institute (Fildes, 1996), in

1996 those in work in the UK would spend 142 days working for the State before they started working for themselves. The size of the public sector is a frequent subject of political debate and, even at its present size, many would like the public sector to do more. The public sector shapes and influences the lives of every man, woman and child in all developed and developing countries.

So what is the public sector?

The term 'public sector' is usually used as a way of referring collectively to those institutions which a society considers necessary for the basic well-being of its members. Adam Smith, the famous eighteenth-century economist, defined the public sector as:

> ... those public institutions and those public works, which though they may be in the highest degree advantageous to a great society, are, however, of such a nature, that the profit could never repay the expense to any individual, or small number of individuals; and which it, therefore, cannot be expected that any individual, or small number of individuals, should erect or maintain.
>
> *from* Adam Smith (1776) *The Wealth of Nations*. Book V, Chapter 1, Part III.

These institutions are founded and funded by the State, in the interests of the State and, through the State, in the interests of its citizens. Their aims are politically determined by the State. Their budgets are sourced from taxation, both nationally and locally. Funding is determined by allocation, rather than by use, and they are controlled, or at least regulated, by the State. The State is responsible for the legal obligations given to such institutions and for the legal controls over what they do. Indeed it is one of the characteristics of public sector organisations that they are bounded by and operate within extensive legislation which creates an often creaking bureaucracy, much of which is concerned with the 'proper' use of public money.

Its origins

Beginning early in the nineteenth century, public sector institutions grew and developed at an unprecedented rate in many countries. The demands of the State, usually expressed in the forms of taxation and military service, were once generally frowned upon. However, in the wake of the Industrial Revolution, as cultural values and attitudes changed, the concept of social philanthropy developed. Despite increasing national wealth, the effects of industrialisation and the growth of cities created many new social problems, and debates about the quality of life exercised some of the most influential thinkers. The State took an increasingly active role in response to social problems.

In so doing, the State assumed more and more responsibility for seeking to redress the most unpleasant results of a free-market economy. William H. Beveridge (1944, p. 27 and Appendix A) maintained that since the Industrial Revolution of the eighteenth century fluctuations in supply and demand had brought insecurity to all developed countries 'with an unplanned market economy'. Unemployment, perhaps the most visible sign of economic problems, was an obvious consequence of an imbalance between the demand for labour and its supply. The remedy for such problems was state spending or 'outlay', not just in terms of consumption expenditure and business investment, but in terms of communal investment and public spending.

Once such a philosophy had been accepted, the State needed to develop the mechanisms required to implement its policies. Inevitably, as the activities of the State expanded, the number of its institutions grew, both at national and local authority level. The public sector is now almost as big as the private sector, and is equally complex. As a result, marketing in the public sector needs to address a wide range of situations.

Its institutions

An 'institution' is something formed and established for the promotion of some object – a definition that fits easily with the idea of an organisation. 'Institution' is a word which can be used in two distinct senses. Used in one way, it refers to specific organisations, especially those that are seen as belonging to the 'establishment'; hence, the various government ministries and local authorities can be termed 'institutions'. Used in another, sociological sense, 'institutions' can also refer to social conventions, customs and ways of doing things – for example, the institution of marriage, or democracy as a social or cultural institution.

Public sector institutions are usually understood in the sense of the first category. They are generally organisations, the purpose of which is to benefit society in some way. They are concerned with satisfying social wants and needs – that is, with meeting demands for services or support which benefit society as a whole. They may therefore be said to be 'altruistic', with concern for others as a guiding principle. As a result, they are generally non-profit-making organisations.

Its culture

In the public sector, the marketing exchange takes place between the provider – in the form of the organisation – and those in need of the service or benefit – in the form of members of society. Public sector marketing has a number of characteristics which are distinctive and different from commercial marketing (*see* Chapter 2). The fact that public sector organisations operate on a non-profit basis has very fundamental implications. Since they are essentially altruistic, both the profit motive and the existence of a competitive market are traditionally foreign to such organisations. Historically, they have not been able to increase their revenue by increasing the level of their activities, as is normally the case in a business organisation. They depend upon public, that is state, funding, which usually takes the form of annual budget allocations. In the past, their nature and origins have usually protected them from competition and this has had an important effect on traditions of organisational culture in the public sector. Anyone who has worked in a public sector organisation will appreciate that its culture – the sum of its values and belief systems – is usually very different from that in any commercial organisation.

In order to understand an organisation, its people – especially its managers – need some knowledge of its culture. They need to know something of its history and the reasons why the organisation has evolved into its existing form. This can also be very useful in the management of change, as historical factors are often the key to understanding why people resist proposed changes. After all, organisations themselves are made up of people and to change the organisation it is usually necessary to change the attitudes of its people.

Over the last 20 years, most public sector organisations in the UK have been subject to considerable, externally imposed pressure for change. To illustrate some of the most important ways in which changes have affected the public sector, and especially its relationships with its markets, we shall consider the example of the Welfare State in the UK, from its origins *circa* 1942. This provides some insight into the ways in which public sector provision developed on a large scale, and allows consideration of some of the major problems which the public sector has been experiencing in a changing political and economic climate since the mid-1970s. Indeed, Isaac-Henry *et al.* (1993) noted that a modified term, 'The New Public Sector', has emerged as a way of recognising the radical nature of changes to the structure and culture of the public sector since the 1970s.

The development of the UK public sector

Modern Western societies at the end of the twentieth century are generally accustomed to the idea that the State takes responsibility for providing a minimum level of social care and subsistence. It may be easy, therefore, to forget the length of time it took people to accept the State in this philanthropic role. For centuries the State had been regarded all too often as the source of forced tribute. Conscription into the armed forces and taxation were traditionally the most feared and disliked forms of state authority. The transition from one situation, in which the State was detested as making unwelcome demands on its citizens 'in the common interest' (for example, defence and administration), to another in which the State became the accepted provider of those benefits, quickly and commonly understood as the 'rights' of the individual in society, was a gradual one. Only in the period after the Second World War was the State expected to provide the range of social and economic benefits that many societies now take for granted – for example, health care, housing, and social security.

Twentieth-century social reforms began in 1908 with the introduction of old-age pensions; national health insurance followed in 1911. However, the Second World War (1939–45) proved an important catalyst in increasing the pace of change. Clarke *et al.* (1987) identify a number of factors which came together and effected major changes in the British social system. During the new form of 'total' war, the Government had had to become involved in most aspects of people's lives. Although continuation of a wartime level of central control would have been unacceptable after hostilities ceased, the war had accustomed the nation to a high level of state supervision and intervention. The State had deliberately encouraged a sense of unified purpose. The return to peace created the conditions under which radical changes became possible.

Pressures for a better, more equitable society had been increasing during the war itself, and were reflected in the desire for a 'New Britain' expressed well before the war ended – for example, in popular magazines like *Picture Post*. Wartime consensus government had helped planning develop in an atmosphere temporarily free of rival-party politics. Moreover, there was a general agreement that solutions had to be found to pre-war social problems. Lowe (1993, p. 12) points out that wartime efficiency had stood in stark contrast with the inefficiencies and waste of the pre-war free market, and had given the population an understanding of the advantages of state intervention. It was apparent that the free market could not guarantee the elimination of poverty, and so there was some general agreement that citizens should have defined social rights in a more equitable post-war society.

The Welfare State

The 1942 *Beveridge Report* (*The Report on Social Insurance and Allied Services*) – published on 20 November 1942 – was an important redefinition of social policy. Sir William Beveridge was a former Director of the London School of Economics who had Civil Service experience. He was originally given the job of rationalising social insurance provision by Arthur Greenwood, a Labour member of the UK Cabinet.

Beveridge started from the premise that society needs full employment as a means of achieving more consumption, more leisure and a higher standard of living. Beveridge was clear that 'full employment' did not mean no unemployment at all. A small level of unemployment was necessary, he believed, because 'some margin for change and movement is needed' (Beveridge, 1944, p. 126). Beveridge observed that a figure of 5 per cent unemployment is sometimes seen as the minimum reserve of labour. To achieve full employment, Beveridge believed the country needed adequate investment, the controlled location of industry and an organised mobility of labour. Full employment could not be obtained, therefore, without a significant extension of state powers. Beveridge set out by identifying 'Want, Disease, Ignorance, Squalor and Idleness' as the main obstacles to social reconstruction. He proposed to start attacking want by providing income security as the first step in a more comprehensive policy of social progress and improvement.

He identified eight primary causes of need and suggested appropriate provision for each, as shown in Table 1.1.

The popular press, responding to these proposals, coined the term 'from the cradle to the grave' – an expression often attributed to Harold Wilson – recognising the importance of the *Beveridge Report* as a recipe for a new, more egalitarian society that looked after the basic needs of its members throughout their lives. Beveridge himself became something of a national hero, despite the fact that he received scant initial political support. His ideas did stimulate a lot of public debate, however. Some welfare legislation was backed by a coalition of all three major political parties, but it was only in the aftermath of the 1945 election, which returned a Labour government, that the policies of a Welfare State were first implemented.

Table 1.1 Beveridge's identification of needs and the appropriate provision for them

Need as a result of:	Answered by providing:
Childhood	Children's allowance
Illness	Medical treatment
Disability	Disability or industrial pension
Unemployment	Unemployment benefit
Woman's marriage	Marriage grant
	Maternity grant
Employment loss	Training funding
Retirement	Pension
Death	Funeral grant
	Widow's benefit

Like so many other historical labels, the term 'Welfare State' seems to have origi-nated as a derogatory one. It was first used to criticise the social provisions of the German Weimar Republic after the First World War. However, it came to be used in Britain (*see* Lowe, 1993, p. 10) as a deliberate alternative or antonym to the 'warfare state' of some other European governments. At the same time, some fears were expressed that the powers the State needed to implement a welfare state – albeit one conceived in the interests of its citizens – could produce a totalitarian regime. By the end of the 1940s, however, politicians, academics and the media were using the term 'Welfare State' much as we do today. Lowe (1993, pp. 13–14) cites Asa Briggs' definition in 1961 of the Welfare State:

> an attempt to modify the way in which market forces work by guaranteeing minimum incomes irrespective of the market value of work, reducing uncertainty by helping indi-viduals meet the costs of sickness, old age, etc., and providing a range of social services to all citizens.

It has been pointed out by many (for example, Clarke *et al.*, 1987) that Beveridge's work was based on an assumption of citizenship and a belief that those citizens in need were entitled to benefits as a right, instead of as charitable provision. In marketing terms, the citizens of the State are its primary market. Their approval of the exchange involved – payment through taxation in return for the provisions of a welfare state – was given through their political support of gov-ernments which maintained and sought to improve it. However, the providing services have usually operated on the assumption that 'the State knows best'. Tom Harrisson and Charles Madge (1986, p. 11) noted in 1939 that social reforms are usually 'imposed from above', and that 'the few' in government presume that they know more about what 'the many' citizens want than the citizens do themselves.

Beveridge was keen to point out (Beveridge, 1944, p. 36) that he was not propos-ing any weakening of local government in advocating more state involvement in certain areas, nor was he proposing any extension of the activities of government that were not in the interests of the people. However, Beveridge's assumption that full employment was essential to maintain a welfare state is one of the main reasons why it has proved so difficult to maintain faith in the concept in the later years of the twentieth century.

Nationalisation

In the event, not all public sector provision took the form of services. The nationalisation of industries considered socially essential (but not necessarily profitable) also formed part of the post-war programme. Industries nationalised by Acts of Parliament between 1945 and 1951 are listed in Table 1.2.

Table 1.2 The nationalisation of UK industries

Industry	Act given Royal assent	With effect from
Bank of England	Feb 1946	Mar 1946
Civil aviation	Aug 1946	Aug 1946
Coal	July 1946	Jan 1947
Cable and Wireless	Nov 1946	Jan 1947
Transport	Aug 1947	Jan 1948
Electricity	Aug 1947	Apr 1948
Gas	July 1948	Apr 1949
Iron and steel	Nov 1949	Feb 1951

Despite the initial post-war consensus about the logic of nationalisation and the general acceptance of an increasing state intervention in the economy, the nationalised industries soon attracted economic and political controversy. Dunkerley and Hare (in Crafts and Woodward, 1991, pp. 381–416) have argued that the deficits in industry before 1979 were caused partly by the failure of the industries themselves to adjust to changing economic conditions, and partly to the priority given to addressing social needs over economic considerations. Although nationalisation was originally seen as a solution to real problems, and the public corporation as the appropriate means, there were a number of drawbacks to nationalisation which soon emerged.

1 Changes in ownership often altered very little in the industries themselves; it became apparent that management, not ownership, was often the real issue.

2 The nationalised industries quickly started to demand more resources, so making political intervention inevitable.

3 Co-ordinated policies frequently failed to materialise. For example, despite the post-war assumption that a co-ordinated transport policy could be achieved through a unified approach, there was in fact little co-ordinated planning in transport, as was also the case in the energy industries. As a result an opportunity was missed, and the maximum benefit was never realised. It could be argued that this was a consequence of taking a production-focused, instead of a market-focused, approach.

4 The 'Civil Service corporation' became a kind of bureaucratic organisational formula, an 'establishment'. In time, many people came to believe that public sector institutions benefited their own employees rather than their users, and that the rationale for such organisations was employee led.

The formation of the Welfare State

The origins of the Welfare State were laid down in seven important Acts of Parliament, enacted between 1944 and 1949, and another in 1959. A useful, more comprehensive review of the provisions of these Acts is given in Jones (1991). A brief summary follows.

Education

As early as 1941, a memorandum entitled *Education after the War* was circulated to many organisations for discussion. R.A. Butler became President of the Board of Education in that year, and encouraged development of education policy, despite Churchill's belief that social issues were of less immediate importance than the war effort itself. Many believed that equality of opportunity did not necessarily mean giving everyone the same type of education. Different groups of individuals could benefit from different kinds of opportunity (an early form of market segmentation). The Council for Educational Advance was established in 1942. In a climate beginning to feel more confident of an Allied victory, many suggestions for reforming the existing system were made.

The 1943 White Paper, *Educational Reconstruction*, and the *Norwood Report* were followed by the 1944 Education Act. R.A. Butler, who steered the Bill through Parliament, believed that education was the key to creating a better society. Education was to be provided free of charge from the age of five. Education's aims were defined as:

● preparing the young for work;
● inculcating a sense of citizenship; and
● enabling the individual to realise his/her potential.

It was assumed (somewhat arbitrarily, and with little scientific basis) that aptitudes could broadly be characterised as practical, technological and academic. In theory, these enjoyed equal esteem, and the 11+ test was meant to identify which aptitudes students possessed. Three kinds of secondary school – secondary modern, technical and grammar – were intended to meet their needs. People could still choose to send their children to private schools if they wished and could afford to do so (we would now call this 'opting out' of the state system), but the reform of the State's educational provision was intended to provide a sound foundation to create active members of society.

The belief that education was a foundation for future prosperity and was a panacea for many social ills was initially very powerful and continues to be – as exemplified by the 'stakeholder' concept, used by Mitroff (1983) and subsequently adopted in the UK political arena by Tony Blair in 1996. However, ideological and political divisions soon resurfaced. Grammar, technical and secondary modern schools were not, in fact, perceived as 'different but equal'. Traditional class values still affected (and continue to affect) the perceptions of schools and the values they were seen to represent.

Family allowances

Policy on child poverty and low pay were influenced by the economic theories of Maynard Keynes, who had published his *How to Pay for the War* in 1940. Keynes was in favour of a national minimum level of income, exempt from taxation. He also proposed family allowances as a means of ensuring that all families, including large ones, could avoid poverty. Unfortunately, some unions initially opposed allowances on the grounds that allowances were merely a cheap way of avoiding the 'real' issue of raising wages. However, in the summer of 1941, an all-party group of Members of Parliament asked the Chancellor of the Exchequer to explore a family allowances scheme. A 1942 White Paper was supportive of the principle. Even with the backing of the *Beveridge Report*, progress was relatively slow. The Government's intention to introduce allowances was published early in 1943. The 1945 Family Allowances Act provided families with a weekly income for every child, except the first one, until the age of 16. Unfortunately, the Act did not recognise the fact that first children demand relatively greater expenditure than subsequent brothers and sisters. It was not until 1977 that first children became eligible for allowances. In the 1990s, both main political parties in the UK reconsidered their commitment to such allowances.

Health

The 1946 National Health Service Act (which became operational in 1948) set out to provide a service which would improve the physical and mental health of the people, and the prevention, diagnosis and treatment of illness. Its final form was negotiated by Aneurin Bevan, but not before protracted negotiations had taken place with hospitals, local authorities (which had interests in the old Poor Law infirmaries), and the medical profession. Training and research became the responsibility of teaching hospitals, administered by boards of governors and responsible to the Minister of Health. Other hospitals were administered by management committees. Thirteen regional hospital boards were created, based upon the wartime civil defence areas. Doctors were still permitted to take on private patients, however, and during the implementation of the Act, it was evident that the medical profession exercised a powerful influence in defending its members.

The new National Health Service (NHS) was intended to be free at the point of delivery, except where the Act made provision for certain charges. Local authorities became responsible for many services and, under section 28, were even given a preventative role in combating disease. They were also given responsibility for helping the disabled and long-term infirm.

National Insurance

The 1946 National Insurance Act also became operational in 1948. In many respects, this was the culmination of Beveridge's recommendations. It made financial provision for unemployment, maternity, sickness, retirement, widowhood and death. Only a marriage grant was missing from Beveridge's original list (*see* Table 1.1). The Ministry of Pensions and National Insurance was the original authority in charge of implementing these provisions. Standard rates of benefits were established. Inevitably, the financial implications for the State were heavy.

Planning

The 1947 Town and Country Planning Act was also the culmination of earlier reports, and made planning permission compulsory for the first time. The 1940 *Barlow Report* had drawn attention to the redistribution of the industrial population. Planning was obviously the means by which a better balanced distribution of population could be achieved. The report advocated a more centralised, controlled planning of housing, jobs and transport. The 1942 *Uthwatt Report* recommended that local authorities be given powers of compulsory purchase in order to help them plan and redevelop systematically. In consequence, the Town and Country Planning Act (an interim bill was introduced in June 1944) empowered local authorities to develop their own plans. The creation of new towns was on the agenda. Nature conservation and National Parks also featured in government planning.

National Assistance

The 1948 National Assistance Act finally killed off the existing Poor Law. The State now intended to help all those who did not possess enough resources of their own. This process was conceived not only as the provision of a minimum level of subsistence, but as a means by which those affected could seek to improve their welfare. Local authorities were also made responsible for providing accommodation for the old and ill, and for those in urgent need. Recreational and workshop facilities were also to be provided. It will be noted that this Act was intended to devolve a substantial share of responsibilities to local authorities.

Housing

The 1949 Housing Act sought to address one of the most urgent post-war needs. Due to the complete absence of building during the previous six years, nearly half a million homes had been damaged or destroyed in the war. At the same time, the birth rate was rising rapidly. Accommodation was becoming a serious problem for many people. The 1949 Housing Act established the principle that need was more important than social class.

Social work

Somewhat belatedly, and partly in response to the 1959 *Young–Husband Report*, the 1962 Health Visitors' and Social Workers' Training Act was a formal recognition of the fact that those who were incapable of helping themselves needed help from the State. Post-graduate social workers' courses had started at the London School of Economics in 1954. The 1962 Act recognised the urgent need for growth in the profession of social work and for new structures to regulate it.

Culture

There was also an extension of state involvement in areas less concerned with material benefits than with leisure and intellectual ones. During the Second World War a vast range of activities had been undertaken by CEMA (the Council for the Encouragement of Music and the Arts) and ENSA (the Entertainments National Service Association). These two organisations are acredited with highlighting the existence of huge audiences for the arts. As a result of their activities, state support for the arts was not so controversial as it had once been. The formation of the Arts Council was announced in June 1945. The Council started to provide public sector funds for the contemporary arts at a time when the level of private patronage was seen to be falling. However, many people, including the economist Maynard Keynes, were keen to avoid nineteenth-century assumptions that the purpose of the arts was to act as a panacea for social problems and as propaganda for middle-class values (Minihan, 1977, p. 119). This belief in the arts' power to civilise was now translated into a more modern faith in the appreciation of the arts as an indication of culture and 'cultivated' tastes, although, as Borzello (1987) has pointed out, the paternalistic belief that 'art is good for you' was retained.

As a result of these developments, six main welfare services emerged:

- Education
- National Health
- National Insurance
- National Assistance
- Housing
- Social work

The state also increased its involvement in culture.

Implications of the Welfare State

The concept of a more egalitarian society remained an important principle during the period when the Acts were passed. A number of consequences soon became apparent. Initially, the demands of reconstruction after the war and the nationalisation of public sector industries kept government spending high. It also ensured that the level of unemployment after demobilisation was limited. The 1945–75 period is often represented as a period of 'social democratic consensus', or as 'the post-war settlement' (MacInnes, 1987). In the 1950s and 1960s, as the world economy grew, the policy of direct government intervention was fairly successful.

However, after the 1960s, increasing international competition, a growing demand for public services and claims for increased wages all contributed to growing inflation and balance of payment deficits. Unemployment grew.

The following consequences of the development of the Welfare State became evident.

A growing administration

When the new legislation became effective, it did much to maintain the numbers and responsibilities of 'public servants' which had been increased during the war. Many thousands were needed to staff the new organisations, despite the belief of many – for example Lewis and Maude (1950, pp. 111–29) – that a gradual reduction in 'detailed government controls' after the war would eventually reduce the number of 'public servants'. The legislative framework and the need to manage public funding responsibly created their own demands. This resulted in a 'systems approach', stressing the importance of procedures. Unfortunately, this growth in bureaucracy also contributed to a popular perception of public sector institutions and of the Civil Service as impersonal, unfriendly and mechanistic in their adherence to 'the rules' and a 'systems rule' approach. Lewis and Maude (1950, p. 116) noted that the public, confronted with inefficiency and slowness, had already developed a sense of hostility towards public officials, and attempts to ignore or 'short-circuit' bureaucratic controls were having deplorable effects upon public morality. A tension between political democracy and bureaucracy had been recognised by the earliest advocates of bureaucracy, who thought it the most efficient form of social organisation (*see* Minicase 1.1). In the Civil Service, differences between its permanent 'mandarins' and their political masters have often been explained in terms of 'departmental views', signalling the political power and influence of top officials. This difference of opinion was parodied in the immensely popular UK television programme, *Yes Minister*.

The 'we know best' approach to supply

Although both individual people and society as a whole could benefit from the Welfare State, the individual had little direct influence on the nature of the benefit or the service he or she obtained. The 'we know best' attitude of the providers usually prevailed. Political elections provided some indirect influence at local and national levels, but the benefits of the Welfare State were initially determined by the provider. This was the equivalent of a 'product-driven' approach to the market. The State determined the 'products' – in this case the provisions of the Welfare State – which were then made available to the consumers – in this case those in need. This was a traditional and paternalist strategy with two important consequences.

- The final user of the benefits or services provided had relatively little market influence over the form of that provision.
- The State effectively assumed a monopoly position, in which there was usually no alternative supply of these benefits and services and therefore no real choice for the user.

MINICASE 1.1

Administrative bureaucracy and complaints

Few areas of the public sector attract so much concern as the National Health Service. As one of the initiatives designed to raise the standards of public sector activities signalled by the 1991 *Citizen's Charter*, the *Patient's Charter* made an attempt to set targets for improvements in the NHS. However, *The Daily Telegraph* (8 July 1994) noted that the Health Service Ombudsman, William Reid, in his annual report was scathing about the apparent inability of NHS management to deal satisfactorily with a record number of complaints. Eighty per cent of the grievances he was able to investigate had been upheld. 'An abdication of responsibility and neglect of management' were common failings.

The Ombudsman's report provided the substance for editorial comment from *The Daily Telegraph*. The situation gave real cause for concern to the Health Secretary, Virginia Bottomley, not least because many of the complaints that came to the Ombudsman's attention could be traced back to the results of NHS reforms. The new NHS emphasis on internal marketing and on profit and loss had apparently failed to take proper notice of the needs of patients. Mr Reid believed that many problems resulted from poor communications within the administrative bureaucracy.

In fairness, the actual number of complaints made (1384) is extremely small compared with the number of in-patients treated (approximately 7 million), and the majority of NHS users are satisfied with the service provided. However, the episode does illustrate how politically difficult it is to run the NHS successfully. Personal tragedies are emotive issues, easily exploited by the media and by opposition politicians alike.

Blaming administration and procedures for perceived shortcomings is common in many public sector industries. It may well be necessary to standardise procedures and systems in the interests of both user equity and efficiency, but many complaints concern the apparent insensitivity with which those procedures are sometimes applied. The *Daily Telegraph* article cited the case of a woman whose baby had died and who had waited eight months for an explanation of the causes, and was then presented with a bill for medical notes. The hospital eventually apologised, but only after the Ombudsman had intervened.

Rising costs to the State

The financial implications were huge. By the early 1950s the Professor of Economics at Oxford University, John Jewkes, was already convinced that the problem of how to pay for the new services would be a permanent one. Jewkes thought that services should be paid for directly in a free-market economy (*see* Chapter 8). Opponents were of the opinion that, if financial considerations became dominant, conflicts of interest were inevitable. For example, if doctors were constrained by spending limitations (that is, if they were to act in the interests of controlling expenditure) they would not be able to provide the best medical care to their patients. In 1996, the cost of the UK public sector is estimated to be in the order of £900 billion, approximately £18 000 for every man, woman and child in the UK.

The thirty years after 1945 saw respectable economic growth and relatively high levels of employment. However, a number of different factors began to raise serious questions about the country's ability to maintain the Welfare State in its original form. Unemployment grew. Economic events, such as the 1972–4 oil crisis and its fallout, tended to increase inflation and require constraint in public spending. Unfortunately, the demand for public spending cannot be controlled in the same way as the money supply. For example, demographic developments, in particular, affect demand. On the one hand, improved living conditions and better health care raise the average life expectancy, and an increasing number of elderly people needing health and welfare services naturally increase demand. On the other hand, welfare provision competes with other areas of government policy for its resources.

By the 'Winter of Discontent' of 1978–9, labour relations in public industries were poor, and Conservative politicians were arguing that there was too much state regulation and insufficient individual choice.

The return of the free market after 1979

In response to these problems, after 1979 Conservative governments followed a policy of privatisation and sought to reduce the level of state involvement. Privatisation was intended to increase efficiency, keep down the Public Sector Borrowing Requirement (PSBR), raise revenue and encourage greater public participation in share ownership.

When the Conservative government came to power in 1979, it challenged a number of assumptions on which public sector developments after 1945 had been based. It challenged the relevance of traditional trade unionism, long dominated by manual workers, in a society which was becoming increasingly dependent on 'white collar' workers, new practices and new technologies. New lifestyles and patterns of employment were already emerging which were changing traditional patterns of social behaviour and expectations. In an apparent reversal of the ideology and policies which had inspired the creation of the Welfare State, the Government adopted a faith in the power of the free market to produce a beneficial social order. 'Enterprise consciousness' gathered strength.

A 'hands-off' approach was intended to assist the process of 'rolling back the frontiers of the State'. The Government abandoned the commitment, which had long been thought essential, to full employment (in the Beveridge sense), and started to cut public expenditure, taxation and the money supply. It raised interest rates to combat inflation, and reduced controls on incomes and prices. The term 'market forces' became more and more familiar, but the term also became synonymous with cost cutting and the development of internal markets rather than with the real understanding and provision of end-user satisfaction.

It was argued that market forces would 'naturally' provide competition, and therefore increase efficiency and the health of industry. Severely deflationary economic policies between 1979 and 1982 were accompanied by less and less government intervention in industry. Since the power of the labour unions was seen as a threat to the effective working of free-market mechanisms, the 1980 and 1982 Employment Acts limited and controlled industrial relations. In March 1985, after a one-year strike, the miners were beaten – an important symbolic event signalling a curtailment of union power.

The rising unemployment figures were interpreted by many, including one minister in 1981, as evidence of progress. The Government believed (MacInnes, 1987, p. 57) that if it refused to intervene in labour relations, both employers and employees would learn to appreciate the true effects of their agreements with each other. If the Government refused to stimulate demand, employers would have to become more competitive in order to survive, and labour would see the logic of having to accept lower wages. High unemployment levels were seen as a consequence of delays in adjusting to new market conditions. There was, in fact, a fall in manufacturing employment in the years 1980 to 1982. It was claimed at the time that this fall was largely due to a world-wide move towards restructuring industries, especially in the countries of the Organisation for Economics Co-operation and Development (OECD), although there was some evidence of a faster turndown in Britain.

Market forces were presented as the means by which a 'natural' balance would be established between supply and demand. Given freedom from interference, the market would only supply what people needed. Under Margaret Thatcher, it was assumed that price inflation was often caused by problems in the market system due to the activities of the unions or excessive government intervention. If these imbalances were removed, it was argued, the markets would be free. At the same time, the idea that market forces create a 'natural' match between supply and demand appeared to provide a solution to many questions of how to coordinate efforts and results, especially in the public sector.

This policy also makes the assumption that organisations respond to market forces. It is true that the demands and expectations of users have increased dramatically since 1979. In many private sector areas, the lot of the consumer has been improved. In the public sector, however, the user is experiencing a reduction in provision in many cases which contrasts uncomfortably with the increased expectations encouraged by various 'Citizen's Charters'.

Unfortunately, this argument assumes that free markets are perfect, self-regulating mechanisms. In practice, they may not always be so. In the public sector, especially, the very concept of 'the public' can be a problem (*see* Chapter 5). It can be used too often to disguise the fact that society is made up of different interest groups and individuals; there is no automatic harmony of interests between them (McInnes, 1987, p. 164). It is not always easy to identify their needs.

Nevertheless, within the UK public sector, the increasing political faith in market forces was to have a dramatic impact. This new faith, characteristic of UK government policies from 1979 to 1997, was in many ways a rejection, or even an inversion, of the Keynsian economic thinking which had supported the setting up of the Welfare State. Keynes had thought that the State would benefit society by intervening to avoid the limitations and dangers of market economics, and by actively helping develop economic prosperity and social welfare (Self, 1993, p. 56). The new market ideology looked to free markets as a means of avoiding the failures of state intervention policies. Peter Self (1993) called the result 'government by the market'.

Three important developments characterised the government's implementation of these policies in the 1980s and 1990s:

● a reduction in the range of state functions;
● the privatisation of many public sector functions;
● the restructuring of the public sector in terms of management, 'healthy' competition, efficiency and marketing.

<table>
<tr><td>MINICASE
1.2</td><td>

Choice and morality: social work

It is often said that Britain's most unpopular educational quango is the Central Council for Educational and Training in Social Work (CCETSW). In July 1993, a Norfolk couple were denied permission to adopt a mixed-race child because a social worker deemed them 'racially naive' after they had said that they had not encountered racism in their home town. Robert Pinker, Professor of Social Work Studies at the London School of Economics, provided a critique of the problems inherent in social work training in the *Times Higher Educational Supplement* of 10 September 1993.

It appears that social work training has long been dominated by forms of political correctness, developed so far as to encourage social workers to assume responsibility for areas such as the right to decide what is racist or sexist. Social work training seems to have assumed a 'politically correct' orthodoxy which demands conformity. Professor Pinker has been a long-standing critic of the CCETSW, and made it clear that he believed social work training was dominated more by obsessions with ideology than by a desire to meet the needs of adults or children who are in difficulties.

Unfortunately, the legacy of such ideological training is likely to perpetuate professional practices which cast some public sector agencies in controlling and unsympathetic roles, even when the nominal purpose of those agencies is to ensure a basic level of human rights.

</td></tr>
</table>

Reducing the range of state functions

When Margaret Thatcher became Conservative Party Leader in 1975, it was clear that she did not approve of the extent of existing state involvement in managing the economy. During the Heath administration in the 1970s, she achieved notoriety as the Education Minister who 'cut the children's milk allowance', hitherto provided as a free, daily, one third of a pint for all children at school. In particular, she associated the Welfare State with a 'dependency culture', with the worst aspects of official bureaucracy (including inefficiency), and with the absence of any real individual choice. She believed that the operation of a free market would ensure a better utilisation of resources. Since public expenditure was regarded as a major contribution to inflation, she was keen to encourage competition within the public sector and the denationalisation of public industries. Commercial practices would reduce inefficiencies. Naturally, there was resistance to this from those working within the public services themselves, who saw these moves as inevitably leading to redundancies. In any case, many employees were not willing or able to take the 'philosophical leap' from a public sector culture to a commercial culture.

Privatisation

Privatisation contributed to this 'slimming' of the State (Self, 1993, pp. 59–60). It was a way of increasing efficiency; the aim was to drive down costs by introducing competition in the public sector. After 1979, the Government made strenuous efforts to reduce state involvement and give free rein to market forces – for example, by the deregulation of services such as regional road transport. A large percentage of publicly owned industries, corporations and utilities were sold to private investment during the 1980s. In others – for example, the Health Service – internal markets were introduced to develop competition and promote efficiency. Government also sought to develop the same philosophy and practices in its own operations and the Civil Service (*see* Self, 1993, p. 59 ff.).

In spite of all these developments, public sector spending remains stubbornly in excess of 40 per cent of Gross National Product (GNP). Within that spending there has been a shift of resources towards benefits paid to the unemployed and pension provision for those taking early retirement.

Public sector reorganisation

The use of market forces to restructure the public sector has involved a number of initiatives. The most obvious one was the introduction of a more commercial concept of management in public sector organisations, which generally involved demanding a more 'professional' attitude towards efficiency and cost-effectiveness. In view of the fact that civil service organisations were often perceived as secretive (that is, in modern jargon, failing to be adequately 'transparent') and sometimes wasteful of public resources, they were encouraged to take a more business-like approach to their operations. Competition was also advocated as a means of achieving lower costs and 'value for money'. It was also hoped that bureaucracy would be made more efficient by subjecting its established hierarchies to pressures of the kind experienced in the private sector – for example, performance-related reward systems. In the final analysis, it was intended that the public sector should move as close as possible to a free-market situation of supply and demand. Users were to take a direct and active role in shaping demand and supplying the resources to fulfil it.

These ideas found public expression in John Major's *Citizen's Charter* (1991). According to its foreword, the Charter involved giving more power to the individual citizen. The main themes were:

- a desire to improve the quality of public services;
- a commitment to user choice by encouraging competition, wherever possible;
- a belief that the citizen (that is, the user of public sector services) should understand and influence the standards of provision;
- the principle that the public services should give value for money within an affordable national tax bill.

The Citizen's Charter stated that these aims were to be met by nine objectives:

1 more privatisation;
2 wider competition;
3 further 'contracting out' (that is, allowing commercial competition for certain work);
4 more performance-related pay;
5 published performance targets;

6 information on standards achieved (for example, 'league tables');

7 more effective complaints procedures;

8 more effective and independent regulation;

9 better redress for the user when things go wrong.

An analysis of *The Citizen's Charter* suggests, however, that these objectives are mainly concerned with the quality of the service process, a 'responsible' attitude towards costs, and issues of promotion, information and distribution. There is actually little attention paid to the *nature* of the market for state services, other than continual references to the 'citizen' as customer and consumer.

This might appear surprising, since *The Citizen's Charter* was a description of political aspirations for the public services, and can be seen as an example of 'societal marketing'. Societal marketing is normally understood as aiming to create long-term customer satisfaction and welfare as a key business strategy. In a political context, this means that the Government sought to satisfy the users of the services it provides. As a White Paper, however, *The Citizen's Charter* had to try and appeal to as wide an audience as possible, and there was no political advantage in opening up a debate about the nature of social needs and welfare. As a result, social needs were implicitly understood as 'given', in a way which was typical of 'top-down' political initiatives.

Key features of the UK public sector

The origins and history of the public sector give marketing in this sector an added dimension.

The perceptions of users are critical to anyone engaged in the process of managing and negotiating exchanges between demand and supply. They have an impact on people's understanding of needs and the nature and quality of provision. For this reason the perceptions of the users of public services must be taken seriously.

There are a number of key features of the UK public sector which must be kept in mind when marketing a public sector organisation.

Political conflict between local authorities and central government

The original post-war Acts of Parliament concerning the Welfare State gave a great deal of responsibility to local authorities. These duties included the provision of help and residential accommodation for the homeless, the old and infirm, district nursing, midwifery and health centres. Local authorities had to prepare their own planning and redevelopment strategies. They also had to provide housing. In view of the levels of spending involved, it is hardly surprising that the economic relationships between central government and local authorities became strained; this became particularly obvious in the period of Conservative power after 1979. Inevitably, conflict involving power and the ownership of services highlights the political dimension of public sector operations. They also further complicate the diverse nature of public sector markets (a problem addressed in Chapter 2).

The 'free' provision of services

The ideal of providing services 'free at the point of delivery' was, in fact, compromised early on. This is particularly evident in the National Health Service. Of course, national taxation and insurance actually paid for the service, but it had been intended that users would not pay directly for the various services they might require (which differ vastly in nature and in costs). However, it proved difficult to resist setting fixed charges for certain services – for example prescriptions. Costs soared by some 70 per cent between 1948 and 1956. Charges for spectacles and dentures were introduced in 1952. It took a very long time for many to realise that health services had an insatiable demand for growth. Not only did improving technology create new demands for treatments which would not have been obtainable before, but the ability to help people live longer added to the population of the elderly, who needed more and more health and support services. Technology also added significantly to costs. The resultant popularity of the NHS created problems of a very political kind for government. Any government will naturally try to limit and control costs. Issues of price, value and exchange are discussed in Chapter 8.

Limited user choice

The concept of user choice has been one of the major principles adopted by those who have advocated a market-led approach to the public sector. It was prominent in the Institute of Economic Affairs (IEA) publications of the 1970s, and has since been given a high profile in the various Charters of John Major's government. It is usually argued that the market – as a mechanism of exchange by which the goods and services we need and want are organised and distributed – enables the individual to express choice and exercise personal responsibility.

Most of the public sector services, however, are designed to answer needs. These needs are very basic ones, such as health, accommodation, subsistence income, etc. Again, taking the case of health, it is unlikely that most people choose to be ill. Unless they have psychological problems, they are unlikely to choose to fall sick just because they want the doctor's services. The health service available thus becomes a 'distress purchase' – that is, something patients need even if they might wish they did not. The same argument can apply to many other kinds of human conditions. As a result, it can be argued that it is virtually impossible to create the proper conditions for free choice when external constraints play such important roles.

It has also been argued by those supporting a market-based approach to all public sector provision, that, in order to make a 'free' choice, an individual must have proper control over the funds by which he or she can purchase the goods/service needed or required.

Allocated levels of revenue

Most public services are funded predominantly through taxation. Historically, the user has had relatively little direct influence over the goods/services needed. As a result, it has been claimed that a better system (for example, the use of vouchers) would ensure that users could have some direct control over the ways their taxation payments are spent in the event of need.

However, vouchers would not remove one critical difference between the public and the private sectors. The 'free at the point of delivery' concept means that increased use does not increase revenue for the provider, it merely increases the demand for resources. As a result, the increased use of a public service invariably means that the organisation concerned is likely to move into deficit rather than into profit, as in the private sector. This is one of the fundamental differences between many public sector organisations and those in the commercial sector (*see* Fig. 1.1). The public sector organisation with a fixed budget is a non-profit-making organisation. Once its level of activity exceeds the level of funding available, it overspends and is technically in deficit. The commercial company, on the other hand, is in profit once its sales revenue exceeds its total costs.

The question of morality

'Open' markets are usually thought to be based upon the self-interest of individuals, even if they are regulated by instruments such as contracts, statutory rights, etc.

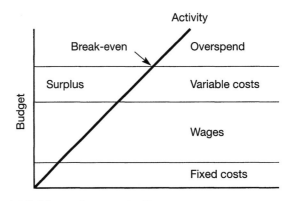

(a) Public sector organisation

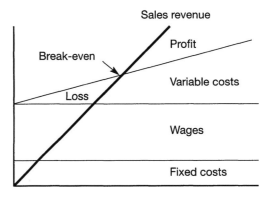

(b) Commercial company

Fig. 1.1 A comparison between non-profit and profit-making organisations

However, most markets move, whenever possible, from dealing with subsistence needs towards satisfying hedonistic wants. In doing so, the idea of altruism and the principle of equity may be lost. Market competition can create unequal satisfaction for both providers and users. Yet social justice usually demands an equality of opportunity and satisfaction. It is possible to claim that, ideally, social justice and social equity should mean the same thing. Unfortunately, the 'free' market generally operates with little collective, community interest. Conversely, it is possible to argue that the Welfare State takes away the individual's responsibility for many central and very personal aspects of life – for example, health, security and provision for old-age. Bureaucracies, especially public sector bureaucracies, are still too experienced as impersonal and unfriendly, despite the fact that they are concerned in many cases with social rights and basic human needs.

Absence of economic rigour

From an economist's point of view (for example, David Heald in Tims (1980)), public services may well be inevitably wasteful. They encourage a greater level of activity than users/consumers would otherwise be prepared to pay for. In the private sector, managers reduce inefficiency in their own interests and in those of their shareholders. Savings in costs can be seen to benefit the organisation and its owners. Historically, public sector organisations have not seen themselves as accountable in the same way. They have lacked a culture to do so. The work of the National Audit Commission is now attempting to help many public sector organisations improve their efficiency. In so doing, however, it runs the risk of representing the private sector somewhat uncritically as the ideal, competitive market (*see* Chapters 2 and 3). It can be argued that efficiency may sometimes be achieved at the expense of effectiveness.

Competition for resources

Many of the problems associated with the public sector involve competition for resources. We have already noted that the Welfare State is costly to the nation. So too has been the cost of investment and subsidy in the nationalised industries. Since the 1960s, many of the problems encountered by the public sector have been related to national economic difficulties. The impact of public sector demand upon the national budget is enormous, and has therefore become a priority target of government budget decisions. It is inevitably an important political question (*see* Chapter 7). One solution, privatisation – the transfer of public sector assets and activities to private companies – has been compared to 'selling the family silver'.

Cultural and social considerations

We live in a society in which social stigma still attaches itself to some benefits. Once an individual is identified as a claimant of, for example, supplementary benefit, his or her self-esteem may well be damaged. Moreover, the nature of the public sector as it developed produced a combination of bureaucratic controls and practitioner expertise which produced an inward-looking focus, often interpreted as 'unfriendly' to the user.

Conclusions

The history and nature of the public sector mean that its marketing has to be understood in terms of a framework which is both different and more complex than that for commercial marketing.

1 The *legislative context* often involves statutory responsibilities to provide minimum levels of support to the users of services.

2 *Resources* are usually limited, and the user is very often not the person who provides revenue directly in exchange for the service.

3 *User choice* is often severely constrained by the nature of supply.

4 There is a tendency to focus on *basic needs*, rather than on non-essential wants.

5 The public sector markets remain intimately connected to *changes in society*, social, political and economic.

In the final analysis, most of the questions which have been raised about the philosophy and propriety of marketing in the public sector are political in nature. Unfortunately, political argument can only too easily polarise opinion into black and white. The issues raised above indicate some of the problems involved.

The pace of change affecting public sector organisations increased during the 1980s and 1990s. This has placed new demands and emphasis upon management as a means of creating greater efficiency and, increasingly, of reducing costs. However, it must be borne in mind, whatever the means adopted to supply public services, public sector organisations are designed to benefit 'society' – a collective term for the sum of its individual members. In that public sector organisations seek to identify and satisfy some of society's more basic needs, marketing has an important management role to play in the sector. Marketing has, by definition, a user-focused approach – matching the needs of the user with provision.

Summary

1 **Definition.** The term 'public sector' is usually used to refer to institutions that are wholly or partly funded by the State and local government, and whose activities are also in most cases state controlled. These institutions are those which contribute to the general well-being of the public.

2 **Opportunities provided by the war.** The return to peace after the Second World War provided an opportunity to create a blueprint for a better society. The concept of the Welfare State emerged.

3 **Social justice.** A desire to create a more socially just society initiated legislation to ensure more adequate satisfaction of basic needs in the areas of education, health, insurance, assurance, housing and social work.

4 **Implications.** There was a growth in administration requirements to work the system. The economic costs to the State proved considerable.

5 **After 1979**, a new Conservative government began to reduce the level of state involvement that had been central to the original post-war consensus developments in the public sector. The government adopted a policy of 'rolling back the frontiers of the State'. Market forces were expected to create a 'natural' balance between supply and demand.

6 As a results of these developments, there are a number of key considerations for marketing in the public sector: political implications in the relationship between local authorities and central government; the difficulties of providing a National Health Service 'free at the point of delivery'; the inevitable nature of resource constraints which make it difficult to create the conditions for real freedom of user choice; the moral problems implicit in attempting to apply marketing principles to the public sector.

7 The public sector is subject to political concerns in a very direct way. Marketing in the public sector is perhaps a somewhat more complex activity than marketing in the private sector.

Implications for management

Any organisation carries in it some sense of its own history. Its history is part of its identity, its 'roots'. An organisation consists of its people, and as a result its history is very important in a number of ways. Long-serving members inevitably identify with their experiences of the organisation's function and operation over a period of time. Even an organisation with a relatively high staff turnover uses – consciously or unconsciously – its sense of historical purpose in order to 'socialise' its new members. Any new organisation has to establish some sense of purpose, culture and habits ('the way we do things here') for its members in order to achieve its goals.

As public sector organisations have increasingly looked to management techniques as ways of increasing efficiency, great emphasis has been placed on tools such as 'mission statements'. Unfortunately, many of these have shown a tendency to become bland, since they are often written as much with an eye on 'pleasing the public' and meeting the organisation's political requirements as they are for the practical benefit of their members. However, they do represent one, admittedly rather crude, attempt at establishing some sense of purpose.

The history of an organisation is a central part of its culture – the body of beliefs, assumptions, ideas which inform the behaviours of its members. An organisation's culture can be mapped using a number of dimensions. Of these, the historical dimension is often a useful starting point. It should certainly be added to any map of organisational culture, such as that used to describe 'the recipe' – used effectively as another term for culture in Johnson and Scholes' book on corporate strategy (1993). The manager will develop a better understanding of an organisation if a systematic attempt is made to understand the ways in which the organisation has evolved. An initial audit will try and define:

1 *The original aims and objectives of the organisation* or, within a large, divisionalised structure, that part of it in which the manager operates. All public sector organi-

sations were incorporated with a set of aims with which to express their intended functions.

2 *The historical changes which have modified those original aims,* resulting from responses to political, social and economic factors over time. Even a new agency or privatised service is likely to have historical roots in its predecessor's culture and practices. This has particular relevance to the ways in which the organisation is understood by its users, as well as by its members, many of whom will continue to think in terms of the original forms in which the service was provided.

3 *The reasons why changes have occurred and are considered necessary.* Since all organisations are constantly adapting themselves to a changing environment, it is important for all managers to understand the forces which create those changes.

More detailed ways of mapping organisational culture are discussed in Chapter 11, but it is worth noting at this point that only by understanding a specific organisation's culture and history can the manager begin to grasp the (often unstated) assumptions that underpin the activities of its members.

A simple way of beginning to map these changes is suggested in Table 1.3.

Table 1.3 Mapping historical changes

	Name of service or industry	Mission statement or equivalent	Sources of funding Treasury grant, local authority, etc.	Type of organisation department, agency, etc.
Then				
Now				
Changes				
Reasons for changes				

ISSUES FOR DISCUSSION

The following issues for discussion are presented in the form of questions. Examples from specific public sector industries should be incorporated into responses. Case studies can be used to provide some illustrations of the issues raised.

1 What are the arguments for and against the nationalisation and privatisation of 'key' services and industries?

2 What are the arguments for and against state intervention in the range of services provided to the public as 'public services'?

3 How may 'The New Public Sector' be defined?

4 How does the history of the public sector influence people's perceptions of its services?

References

Beveridge, W.H. (1944) *Full Employment in a Free Society.* London: George Allen & Unwin Ltd.

Borzello, F. (1987) *Civilising Caliban. The Misuse of Art 1875–1980.* London & New York: Routledge and Kegan Paul.

Clarke, J., Cochrane, A. and Smart C. (1987) *Ideologies of Welfare.* London: Hutchinson.

Crafts, N.F.R. and Woodward, N.W.C. (eds) (1991) *The British Economy Since 1945.* Oxford: Clarendon Press.

Fildes, C. (1996) 'Settling down to 142 days' hard labour, with not enough to show for it', *The Spectator,* 6 Jan.

Harrisson, T. and Madge, C. (1986) *Britain by Mass-Observation.* London: The Cresset Library. Originally published in 1939.

Her Majesty's Government (1991) *The Citizen's Charter.* London: HMSO.

Isaac-Henry, K., Painter, C. and Barnes, C. (1993) *Management in the Public Sector.* London: Chapman & Hall.

Johnson, G. and Scholes, K. (1997) *Exploring Corporate Strategy* (4th edn). London: Prentice Hall International (UK) Ltd.

Jones K. (1991) *The Making of Social Policy in Britain 1830-1990.* London: Athlone Press Ltd.

Lewis, R. and Maude, A. (1950) *The English Middle Classes.* London: Phoenix House.

Lowe, R. (1993) *The Welfare State in Britain Since 1945.* Basingstoke and London: The Macmillan Press Ltd.

MacInnes, J. (1987) *Thatcherism at Work.* Milton Keynes: Open University Press.

Minihan, J. (1977) *The Nationalization of Culture.* London: Hamish Hamilton.

Mitroff, I.I. (1983) *Stakeholders of the Organizational Mind.* San Francisco, Washington and London: Jossey-Bass.

Self, P. (1993) *Government by the Market?* London: Macmillan.

Skidelsky, R. (1996) 'Cuts to benefit the nation', *The Sunday Times,* 11 Feb.

Smith, A. (1776) *The Wealth of Nations,* Tims, N. (ed.) (1980) *Social Welfare: Why and How.* London: Routledge and Kegan Paul.

CHAPTER 2

Marketing perceptions and realities

CHAPTER OVERVIEW

It can be seen from Chapter 1 that the public sector is almost as large as the private sector, and just as diverse. As a result of political and social change, the public sector is now being 'downsized', and this trend is likely to continue under the new Labour government elected in May 1997. Nevertheless, the priorities of the new government may differ from those of the previous one. The changes to the public sector will mean that marketing, both as a function and a philosophy, is likely to become more, rather than less, important in the future. Wherever the term 'focus' is used, marketing, in whatever guise, will be needed.

Many commentators consider that the victory of the Labour party in the UK elections in May 1997 was a direct consequence of marketing trends. Conservative policies appeared to be in the declining stages of the product life cycle and 'New Labour' was seen to adopt marketing techniques. These techniques relate not just to the effective promotion of policies, but also to the development of a clear understanding of the needs, wants and aspirations of the electorate. However, the fact that a political party which developed from a strong ideological base has used tools which are so clearly derived from the world of capitalist business has attracted considerable adverse comment.

The conflict between the culture of community service and the perceived role of marketing is one which has a considerable influence on the development of marketing in the public sector. This chapter examines the development of marketing in general terms, identifying its core role as an instrument in developing customer satisfaction and its implications for organisational development. It also explores issues related to the development of the marketing philosophy as a prerequisite to the introduction of effective public sector marketing functions. The chapter considers some of the special circumstances, including budgetary constraints and legislative frameworks, which make the application of marketing, in the private sector sense, difficult to achieve. Public sector marketing therefore has had to develop appropriate models of its own.

KEY LEARNING OUTCOMES	By the end of this chapter, you should be able to:

- consider the comparative images of marketing in the public sector;
- understand the role of marketing as a social institution;
- explore the differences between product-led marketing and demand-led marketing;
- examine the constraints of working in public sector industries in terms of political, social and economic constraints upon the nature of provision and upon service choice;
- appreciate the differences between marketing goods and services; and
- consider the nature of provider-user relationships.

Introduction

In today's turbulent social and business environment, marketing has become increasingly important as both a function and a philosophy of business. It has also developed as a new academic subject, advancing knowledge and drawing together aspects of many other disciplines, including economics, psychology and the social sciences. Unfortunately, because profit, or indeed profiteering, is often popularly seen as the main aim of marketing, there is often perceived to be a conflict between the traditionally altruistic values of the public sector and those attributed to the marketing profession. This conflict can be illustrated by a letter, dated 14 May 1990, from the UK Customs and Excise to the Chartered Institute of Marketing. The letter questioned whether marketing could be justifiably described as a 'profession', rather than as merely an 'occupation'. It stated that:

> The Commissioners do not believe that the ordinary, intelligent person would regard marketing/salesmanship as a profession.

The letter cited an argument made in the UK Court of Appeal judgment of du Parcq, LJ in the case of *Carr v Inland Revenue Commissioners*, 11 July 1944:

> Ultimately one has to answer this question: Would the ordinary man, the ordinary reasonable man – the man, if you like to refer to an old friend, on the Clapham omnibus – say now, in the time in which we live, of any particular occupation, that it is properly described as a profession?

Ultimately, the contention that marketing was not a profession was withdrawn, but the example does highlight the ways in which marketing may be commonly misunderstood.

Negative images of marketing

Such perceptions of marketing can be represented by 'the 4 Ms' of marketing: *misinterpreted*, *misused*, *misunderstood* and *miscast*.

Misinterpreted

Marketing is seen as manipulative, brash, and brazen (*see* Fig. 2.1) – the tool of the whore and profiteer. Marketing is sometimes associated with the worst and least popular aspects of manipulation and exploitation, despite the increasing sophistication of modern marketing theory and methods. Nevertheless, there are some good reasons why the term 'market' can evoke such a response, given the activities of some so-called marketing organisations.

It is often assumed by critics of marketing that marketers have some Svengali-style influence, whereby suppliers can induce the consumer to behave exactly as they wish. However, Abraham Lincoln noted astutely that you can fool all of the people some of the time, and some of the people all of the time, but not all of the people all of the time. His observation is a good way of dispelling the myth of manipulation. Some businesses may well try to manipulate consumers but, in effective marketing, customers are more likely to manipulate business. In devising marketing strategy, businesses need to have a vast knowledge of the behavioural characteristics of those markets to which their products are being channelled. This point will be developed further in Chapter 3.

However, good marketing companies are not passive in the marketplace. For example, organisations such as Marks and Spencer and Cadbury's (voted the most admired company in 1996) are very active in the search for new, long-term customer relationships. Few of the negative associations of marketing are usually applied to those companies and others in the same league, although Cadbury's has been criticised for promoting its products indirectly with its educational publications.

Fig. 2.1 One public sector view of marketing

Misused

Marketing is often seen as just advertising, promotion and selling. The misuse of the advertising concept was exemplified by Michael Checkland of the BBC television company. In discussing a proposed joint venture with SKY, he asserted that the BBC would be responsible for editorial policy and content while SKY would be responsible for programme transmission and marketing. In fact, marketing is an integral part of the whole activity. If the content and editorial policy are not satisfactory, no matter how good the technology and promotion are, the whole proposal is likely to fail.

Similarly, 'marketing' is still popularly confused with 'selling'. Selling is still viewed with some suspicion in some cultures because it is associated with aggressive sales tactics and with competition between the seller and the potential purchaser. The seller attempts to take the initiative. The potential customer – for example, the 'victim' of a 'cold calling' double-glazing sales representative – may well regard the attempted sale as an unwarranted intrusion into his or her privacy. In the recent past, 'overselling' of important products, such as pensions, has left both government and the financial services sector seriously compromised because of a basic misunderstanding of marketing concepts.

This cultural mistrust of selling is exemplified by the way in which aggressive selling has often tried to appeal to customers' desire for a good bargain ('a real half-price offer'), their competitive social instinct ('all your friends are having one') and their aspirations to social status ('if you don't have one soon, they'll think you're not one of them'). Such an argument is appealing to three basic, and not very attractive, human instincts: greed, envy and fear.

The very heritage of Christian culture does not really approve of these emotions, particularly greed. Tertullian (122–222 AD), one of the father figures of the early church, described the Virtues as female warriors struggling against the Vices in the arena of life. Greed, having gathered up the riches dropped by Luxury (who had been conquered by Temperance) was finally defeated by Reason and Charity, who distributed the gold to the poor. However laudable the moral of this story, the value system it represents has also produced its share of tragedies. Much persecution of non-Christians during the Middle Ages was caused by the fact that the use of money to make money (a modern business might call it efficient employment of capital) was condemned as 'usury' by the Church. The Church originally adopted a policy which disapproved of activities like money-lending, despite the parable of the talents in St Matthew's Gospel.

Misunderstood

In the past few years the adoption of so-called marketing techniques has led many organisations – for example, British Rail – to attempt to focus on customers. In the process of attempting to establish a generic customer orientation, the organisation frequently failed to recognise the specific needs of particular customers and customer groups. There was a failure to understand the real needs of its user groups.

Miscast

'Market forces' are now often associated with the reasons given for cutbacks and redundancies in organisations. In an increasingly competitive, capitalist environment, and one in which technology provides more and more means to effect greater efficiency, cost savings have been used as a way of achieving competitive advantage in the commercial world, and of reducing expenditure in the public sector (*see* Fig. 2.2). However, good marketing is not about cutting costs, but about adding value to the product or service.

Negative attitudes towards marketing express the reactions and responses of users who are, or have become, disillusioned with certain aspects of it. In particular, they illustrate the dangers of the mistaken assumption that marketing is concerned with selling a product rather than negotiating an exchange and establishing a constructive relationship between supply and demand, between the supplier and the user. Few purchasers or users like to feel that they are being dictated to or are being told what is best for them. Most people want to feel that they are 'in control' of, or at least have some real influence on, the transaction or process of exchange.

The implications for marketing in the public sector are considerable. The cultural mistrust of marketing within the public sector may be related to the fact that many public sector industries and services have established reputations for being rela-

Fig. 2.2 Cost-cutting?

tively unresponsive and even unsympathetic to their users' needs. Many of them have grown into large bureaucracies (*see* Chapter 7) characterised by their adherence to 'the rules' and by a reputation for impersonal relationships with their users. It is therefore appropriate to examine the development of marketing in all its dimensions within industrially developed nations, and to evaluate the opportunities for, and the impediments to, the effective adoption of marketing within the public sector.

The development of marketing

In many ways, the words 'market' and 'marketing' have rarely been used so commonly as they are today. Yet, historically, markets were among the earliest features of organised societies (*see* Fig. 2.3). The word 'market' means *a meeting of people for the process of exchange*. 'Market' still refers to the event when, and the place where, people come together to buy and sell. Originally, in the vast majority of societies, most villages and towns set aside a specific location for the marketplace, often situated in a central position and serving as the hub of social, as well as commercial, exchanges. The modern tourist industry often represents markets as places of local 'colour', where local produce, customs and traditions may be seen. Physically, markets remain places of exchange, where commodities are bought and sold, and where the prices of those commodities are decided. In this respect, the Stock Exchange in a city is as much a market as a livestock market in a rural town, even if the commodities are different.

For a long time the word 'market' has also been used as a way of referring to a concept, to *the process of exchange controlled by supply and demand*, and to the prices involved. Used in this way, references to 'the market' have been mainly associated with the world of profit-making business. Indeed, the bulk of available literature on marketing has been written from the business, profit-making perspective. However, the market defines the relationships between supply and demand in any sector of the economy, and is therefore a key social institution. Society only endorses those institutions which serve its needs, and the process of exchange is a central one.

The history of marketing has been a history of the relationships between supply and demand. Before the Industrial Revolution of the eighteenth century, goods

Fig. 2.3 'Now we need to discover marketing.'

were produced, mostly by craft skills, to satisfy demand. Demand was itself largely responsible for encouraging the development of machinery and automation which, with economies of scale, could satisfy demand for more and cheaper products. Essentially, the early pioneers of the Industrial Revolution had identified a demand and set out to satisfy it. Thus there was considerable demand pull and with increasing levels of income, particularly among the burgeoning middle classes, demand continued to increase and the effective management of production became of paramount importance. The development of the industrial society also created new social problems of its own. Attempts to find solutions to them led to the origins of the public sector as we know it today.

F. W. Taylor's theory of 'scientific management' and the production lines of Henry Ford prioritised efficiencies of production, parodied by Charlie Chaplin's shopfloor experiences in the film, *Modern Times* (1936). (It is suggested by many writers that this cost managing, production focus is so strongly ingrained in the Anglo–Saxon industrial psyche that it is leading to defeat in the Third World (economic) War.)

In a situation where demand exceeded supply, marketing was easily identified with selling or even order-taking with the adoption of a strong 'take it or leave it' approach. In the 1920s and 1930s the depression led to a strong 'hard-sell' approach to the market because buyers were relatively lacking in sophistication. The Second World War was followed by a period of acute shortages in Europe (a situation still unresolved in many of the former Soviet Union countries) which led to a redevelopment of the 'take it or leave it' approach.

However, with the development of new industrial economies, particularly since the early 1960s, the business environment has changed dramatically. Consumers have become increasingly demanding as a result of improved communications and levels of education. The development of global supply networks and high-volume

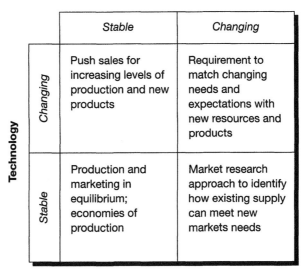

		Market	
		Stable	Changing
Technology	*Changing*	Push sales for increasing levels of production and new products	Requirement to match changing needs and expectations with new resources and products
	Stable	Production and marketing in equilibrium; economies of production	Market research approach to identify how existing supply can meet new markets needs

Fig. 2.4 The relationship between market stability and technological change

technology has led to a wide range of cheap, quality products. To survive in this climate, industry has increasingly benefited from a modern marketing philosophy which sees its function as identifying and meeting the needs of customers in order to gain competitive advantage. The relationship between supply and demand now favours demand and consumer choice. Henry Ford's automobile black has given way to a large range of colours. Changes in technology are bringing about the development of customised, mass-produced products. A recent (1996) promotion by Volvo enables potential purchasers to work with interactive technology to design their own version of a standard model range. (*See* Fig. 2.4.)

Relationships between providers and users

It is important in both the private and public sectors to consider the nature of the relationship between supply and demand. The (commercial) relationship between the seller and the customer has been modelled (for example, by Avi Mesulach, as quoted in a Manchester Business School Seminar) using a 'proactive' to 'reactive' dimension. This is a way of indicating the different likely outcomes of a situation. In Fig. 2.5, both seller and customer are seen either as 'proactive' – that is, taking the initiative – or 'reactive' – that is, responding to the other's request or offer.

In attempting to describe the typical outcomes of a customer–seller relationship, therefore, the model assumes that the customer can either actively seek a product or a service, or simply react to the opportunity to obtain one when presented with it. Similarly, the seller is either actively searching for a way to make a sale, or is passively waiting for the demand to become apparent.

Clearly, the relationships between supplier and customer are often more complex than this, but the matrix does identify some of the key situations arising in different circumstances.

- *Passive buyer, passive seller.* In this relationship there is virtually no prospect of doing business. The seller – for example, a corner grocery shop in an area where the local population buy their provisions from the supermarket – is unlikely to

Seller

		Proactive	*Reactive*
Customer	*Proactive*	**Marketing** Seller works to identify and satisfy the customer's needs	**Accommodation** Seller's business is based on providing service
	Reactive	**Foot in the door** Aggressive selling	**No business** No transaction

Fig. 2.5 Seller–customer relationships

do good business because the shopkeeper is waiting for customers and the potential buyers already have most of their needs satisfied, especially when supermarkets extend their opening hours.

- *Active buyer, passive seller*. If, however, the customer, who may have run short of something, takes the initiative to look for the product or service she or he requires, while the seller merely offers a 'point of sale', the seller is merely accommodating the customer with the product or service available. This is often described as 'accommodation selling' and can result in obsequious service and attendant high prices.

- *Active seller, passive buyer*. A seller who seeks aggressively to interest a customer who is not actively looking to fulfil a need or want is usually guilty of those tactics which often alienate potential buyers. They resent the 'hard sell' or even a 'cold-calling' approach, because it can easily appear as an unwanted intrusion into their lives. It is this activity which often gives marketing a poor reputation, particularly when the organisations describe themselves as 'marketing companies'.

- *Active buyer, active seller*. In practice, of course, effective marketing organisations are endeavouring to convert passive customers to active ones, through a whole range of activities. These start with the identification of potential and actual customers and their needs and wants. If both the seller and the customer are looking for a market exchange, both can be satisfied. The result is a successful marketing relationship. The seller identifies and satisfies the customer's requirements.

The corner shop analogy can be taken a stage further. The successful shop will be located in an area where there is a population of transient shoppers. It will open at times relevant to the population, legislation permitting, and will seek to offer a range of goods relevant to the needs of the shopping population. The shop is active in a marketing sense in that it has identified an appropriate location and takes action to open at appropriate times. The buyers are active because of their shopping habits.

The marketing mix

Active marketing companies are therefore concerned with:

- identifying the nature of customers' needs and wants, and how these needs can be satisfied by the provision of goods and services;
- identifying how the needs of different groups of the population differ;
- deciding how the supplier organisation can structure itself to enable it to differentiate itself from its competitors or, in the case of monopolies, avoid the dangers of operating as a monopoly supplier.

This mix of activities relating to active marketing is described as the *marketing mix* or '*the 4 Ps' of marketing*. These are *Product, Place, Price* and *Promotion*. Wilson and Gilligan (1992, p. 3) identify a number of activities under each aspect of the marketing mix. These can be interpreted as follows:

- **Product**
  - Managing the products or services
  - Developing new products or services
  - Ensuring the clear identity of specific products and services (branding)
  - Designing appropriate ways in which the finished product or service is packaged and labelled or presented to customers and users

- **Place**
  - Managing the ways in which products and services are organised and given added value
  - Providing good customer/user care and service
  - Organising the delivery of products and services to customers and users

- **Price**
  - Determining the prices of the products and services
  - Offering incentives to purchasers
  - Providing appropriate contracts

- **Promotion**
  - Advertising and promotion of products and services
  - Public relations and communications
  - 'Relationship marketing'.

The '4 Ps' of the marketing mix are well established in the marketing disciplines but, over time, a number of writers have suggested a number of other 'Ps' which are associated with the development of good marketing practice. The authors' experience indicates that three additional important 'Ps' are *Profit, People* and *Planning*.

Profit

The definition of marketing of the Chartered Institute of Marketing is:

> **Marketing is the management process responsible for identifying, anticipating and satisfying customer requirements profitably.**

In general terms, the objective of marketing is to have satisfied customers. However, the other side of the satisfaction equation demands that the organisation should be profitable in order to sustain it in the long term. Much debate in the mid-1990s concerned the level of profits being made by public sector organisations which had been privatised and were popularly perceived as profiteering. As nationalised organisations, such businesses were rarely seen as profit-making. As self-standing organisations, such companies had to generate profits in order to fund capital expenditure. It is often thought, mistakenly, that capital expenditure derives from revenue, rather than from profits.

However, effective marketing has a very significant impact upon the profitability of an organisation. Chapman and Hill (1993) show that relatively small changes in volume of sales and levels of price can have considerable leverage upon the absolute profit and profitability (rate of profit). Effective marketing is about managing value added. As with all high leverage activities, however, careful management is essential. Mismanaged profits can go down as well as up.

People

The '4 Ps' are concerned with the mechanics and functions of marketing. However, modern marketing is not just about the provision of products and services. It is about people and how people react to the provision of products and services created by people in supplier organisations. Furthermore, it is about the exercise of consumer choice. For the organisation, this means identifying and satisfying customer needs and wants. Customer satisfaction becomes an important measure of quality performance (*see* Chapter 6).

Planning

Wilson and Gilligan (1992) propose that one view of management holds it responsible for defining organisational objectives and selecting the appropriate means by which to achieve them. Essentially, marketing is a future-based activity for the reason that it is about the continuance of customer satisfaction.

This is perhaps summarised best by considering definitions of strategy (*see also* Chapter 12) and success. Success can be defined as the ability to achieve high, sustained and acceptable profitability, while also, ideally, maintaining market position. Strategy is concerned with much more than simply determining what to sell to a customer. It is about predicting what the customer might (or could) require in the future – and why. The organisation needs the managerial and financial resources to ensure that it gets the available business consistently and profitably. Successful strategy is about having the right resources in place to survive and prosper.

This approach is taking marketing away from a rigid, formalised planning approach towards one which has been successfully adopted by the Japanese and others in global markets. David Mercer (1996) cites the Japanese approach as a good example. There is no real need for strategy without competition, because strategic planning is only needed to gain and maintain competitive advantage as efficiently as possible. Mercer (1996) is convinced that the strategy of Japanese business is not based on the discovery of fresh marketing principles, but on a better understanding and application of established marketing principles. However, as Western society has again become concerned with ethics, other considerations are also becoming important – for example the impact of an organisation's activities on society and on the environment in general.

Effective marketing is therefore concerned with a number of issues.

- The aim of effective marketing is the long-term survival of the organisation through profitable exchanges with satisfied customers.
- Organisational competitive advantage is obtained by a continual review of the environment within which the organisation is working at a number of levels. These include a thorough understanding of the needs, wants and expectations of its target customer groups. This involves not just market research or control systems for planning purposes, but information reflecting the whole of the organisation's relations with its various constituencies. This requires a greater understanding by marketers of qualitative as well as quantitative information.

- The organisation's response to those identified needs works within the 'marketing mix' framework and is flexible and adaptable to take account of changes in the markets. Above all, this means taking risks. It moves into uncharted territory. The development of new marketing frameworks is needed in response to changing working environments.

- Business structures need to be designed organically to meet the changing needs of the business environment. This is a process of radical change, taken over time, with the focus upon the customer. Marketing has to work closely with, or be integrated within, other management disciplines to enable the changing requirements of different parts of the market to be satisfied. The market becomes the 'engine' driving organisational change.

Let us therefore consider the application and relevance of various marketing concepts to the public sector.

The changing role of marketing in the public sector

A market has been defined as all those who share a particular need or want and who may make an exchange in order to satisfy it (Kotler, 1994). In a commercial market, goods or services are usually exchanged directly with the purchaser in return for money. In the public sector market, however, the exchange is of a different kind. Many public services are, in fact, in the business of distributing benefits on behalf of society in return for revenues provided by taxation.

In a *commercial exchange*, the purchaser exchanges money with the seller in exchange for the goods or services the purchaser wants and actively seeks. Competition ensures that producers and suppliers compete for sales, and seek to establish advantages over one another by pricing or quality strategies. In a *public sector exchange*, the State often purchases the services needed by the client *on behalf of* society.

Fig. 2.6 Hunting for a living

For example, those who pay taxes from the proceeds of their work provide the money to pay benefits to those who are out of work or who cannot work. Taxpayers exchange some of their incomes in return for a basic level of social infrastructure.

Essentially, the practice of contemporary marketing can be related to Darwinism and the theory of the survival of the fittest. This metaphor can be used to explore some of the differences between organisations in the public sector and those in the commercial one. Any animal that has to hunt for a living (*see* Fig. 2.6) is necessarily inquisitive, adventurous and adaptable. This is as true for organisations as it is for animals. For *commercial organisations*:

- *Inquisitiveness* means understanding the environment. Managers have to develop effective information systems for monitoring and anticipating the rapidly changing environment within which businesses work.
- *Adventurousness* means taking advantage of market opportunities.
- *Adaptability* means changing the organisation to meet the demands of the market-place.

However, many *public sector organisations* do not have to hunt for a living. They are more akin to animals in a zoo. They do not have to find their own food, they are fed by their owners, and often lose their ability to survive in the wild. They are constrained by an environment which keeps them carefully controlled (and usually separated from the public by fences, bars or screens!).

Early approaches to marketing in the public sector

There was once little or no competition between providers in what were effectively monopoly industries. When the Welfare State was set up after the Second World War, government and local authority departments were given responsibility for providing the basic services society agreed that it required. As might be expected, there was, at first, no real competition to provide them.

Many of the services W. H. Beveridge defined in 1944 (*see* Table 1.1) as the answers to basic social needs were once provided by charities. The relationship between supply and demand had traditionally favoured the power of the supplier. As more and more social institutions were developed by the State and local government to provide for basic physiological needs, this relationship changed little.

The indirect nature of many of the exchange processes in the public sector and the absence of competition meant that marketing was scarcely considered relevant to most parts of the public sector before the 1970s. This situation resulted, in marketing terms, in an emphasis on what has been called the *production concept* approach to the market (Kotler, 1994, pp. 12–13). Availability and low cost were considered to be most important. The fact that the users of many public services had relatively little influence over the exchange process led many of the services themselves to develop a *provider culture*, in which the supplier effectively determined the nature of the product or service available. This seems far removed from the *marketing concept* identified in earlier paragraphs which believes that it is the supplier's job to understand the nature of demand and find effective and efficient ways of fulfilling it.

The perception of marketing as irrelevant

It can be argued, therefore, that organisations in the public sector have been, and in many cases continue to be, less sensitive to market needs, and by their very nature less autonomous and flexible than those in the private sector. They are usually subject to a much higher level of statutory responsibility and regulatory control. For a long time they were actually protected from competition and market forces by their very constitutions. They have traditionally relied on government funding (central Treasury and/or local-authority allocations) for most, if not all, of their revenue and capital. They are intended to serve and benefit the community as a whole. They are largely non-profit organisations and so in the past did not have to generate their own income by their levels of activity; they had less reason or incentive to reduce their costs and improve their levels of performance. However, they are subject to political influence and control to a far greater extent than any purely commercial, profit-making organisation.

Those in need most often have no direct influence over the exchange process, which is controlled and regulated by the organisations and government departments which have responsibility for satisfying social needs. Government, nationally and locally, actually decides on the level of need that it can afford to meet from the public purse. Even those industries which were nationalised after the Second World War and generated income from their levels of activity – the railways, for example – also relied on some levels of public subsidy, investment or 'outlay', and were similarly subject to state controls.

Given these very considerable operational constraints, the concept of marketing, especially in those public sector industries which provide basic benefits to those in need, remains strange and foreign-sounding, both to those who work in them and to those who receive the benefits. 'Marketing' has been a term which seemed to belong properly to the commercial world. For most people, the word is associated with trade, with buying and selling, with competition between supply and demand, and with profit making. Public sector industries, like the charities which many of them replaced, are largely non-profit organisations, and until recently few have seen the potential relevance of marketing. Public perceptions of marketing have often been dismissive.

This situation produces a number of problems for public sector organisations. Their relatively protected environment has encouraged a marketing short-sightedness, or myopia – one of the principal causes of business failure in the commercial sector. A clear understanding of the business in which an organisation operates is vital if it is to be effective.

Furthermore, there is still much cultural dislike of the very concept of profit as a driving force. Indeed, the difficulties of measuring profit or any other form of commercial outcome gave the introduction of marketing to the public sector a very faltering start.

Marketing in 'The New Public Sector'

Since 1979, the environment within which the UK public sector operates has undergone profound change. Public sector organisations are being subjected to legislative and competitive pressures – for example, through compulsory competitive tendering – which have led them to recognise the need to reconsider their relationships with their users and customers.

Organisations are being privatised or given agency or trust status. In large organisations, such as the National Health Service, internal markets are being developed. Furthermore, the expectations of users are changing dramatically as a consequence of Citizen's Charters, more active consumer groups and the activities of customer-focused private sector organisations.

Given the costs constraints associated with the public sector, however, much of the application of market forces has been associated with cost cutting and restructuring apparently as a response to 'market forces'. This has led to much 'business process engineering' or 'business process re-design', although this has often failed to raise the levels of user satisfaction. The phrase 'process re-engineering' was used by the UK Secretary of State for Social Security on 8 February 1996 in announcing plans to reduce his department's running costs by some 25 per cent over two or three years. The implications of this desire to 'slim the State' include the use of market forces, the privatisation of services, major staffing reductions and a demand for greater efficiency all at the same time. This is unfortunate. As Oscar Wilde once implied, we seem to know the cost of everything and the value of nothing.

However, the zoo animals are being let out of their cages. In some cases new wild animals have been introduced into the enclosures. It is therefore vital that public sector organisations adopt marketing strategies for both their own survival and for the satisfaction of their clients.

The nature of public sector markets

The demand for public sector provision is huge and the market is actually just as complex as that of the private sector, in terms of the primary markets it serves. The public sector is active in:

- industrial markets
- governmental markets
- consumer markets
- societal markets.

In addition, the public sector is characterised by high levels of internal marketing. Relationships between supply and demand are complex.

Public sector organisations, nevertheless, still need to face three fundamental issues for management:

- Who are their clients?
- How can they best respond to them?
- How can they resource their activities?

In the past, it was the State that took the initiative in defining the needs for public services, even if it did so in a rather paternalistic manner. There gradually emerged a belief that 'the State knew best', that government was best qualified to determine what was good for the people. Yet there have always been some, like Tom Harrisson and Charles Madge (1986), who highlighted the way that most social reforms were effectively imposed on people, and represented 'what's good for them', rather than 'what they want'.

Providing services, rather than products

Most public sector industries are actually concerned with the provision of services rather than the marketing and manufacture of products. Of the recently privatised industries, only coal was concerned with the provision of tangible goods (products), although there is an increasing tendency to use the word 'product' for both goods and services. This means that much public sector provision has to be seen in the context of a service market rather than a product market, and that relationship marketing issues will also be important. (The difficulties encountered in trying to distinguish between 'products' and 'services' in the public sector are addressed in Chapter 4.)

Moreover, public sector services often take the form of *intangible benefits* – benefits which cannot be stored or even easily quantified (Cowell, 1984). The quality of nursing care cannot be measured in terms of weight (although the quantity of care can be measured in terms of working hours, staff–patient ratios, etc.). The quality of such services, and thereby their perceived value, are often inseparable from the attitudes and qualities of the people who provide them. They usually serve a social need.

Meeting a social need

In the public sector, the social role is central. The State buys the services which it considers that the country's infrastructure demands. Again, the market acts as a broker between supply and demand. In the private sector, most forms of social provision have developed in exchange for payment by the individual, but in the public sector most of these payments are made indirectly. They are made in the form of income tax, rating or community charges, national insurance payments, etc., which are exchanged for the provision of a social infrastructure. This gives the individual a degree of personal security, health services, pension rights, etc.

Offering a limited degree of choice

It is important to consider the extent to which the purchaser is free to make a decision to buy or not to buy in public sector markets. Many public sector exchanges are necessarily 'distress purchases'. Individuals may need a benefit or a service because they have no other alternative. For example, injured pedestrians may well have little or no choice how or where they receive emergency medical treatment once they have been knocked down, especially if they are unconscious.

It thus becomes obvious that public sector exchanges do not normally provide the same, or even a similar degree of choice as that usually offered in the private sector. Only certain services offer the customer a chance to change the nature or increase the standard of service provided, and then the only available alternative may well be to pay more by 'going private' – by opting out of the public sector domain altogether.

It is therefore appropriate to modify the seller/customer model in Fig. 2.5 in order to take into account the fact that many public sector users may also be in some way constrained in their demand. They may be constrained by a number of factors, which range from a personal sense of independence which rejects any help perceived as 'charity', to conditions of poor health which limit their ability, for example, to travel long distances for medical out-patient treatment. Moreover, the providers themselves are likely to be limited in their ability to respond to demand. Most public sector supplier/providers are constrained in their ability to supply services by legal restriction, and by limited financial budgets. For this reason David Chapman's model adds a 'reluctant/restricted' dimension. When this is applied specifically to the public sector provider–user relationship, the result obtained is more complex (*see* Fig. 2.7).

This model introduces another category of attitude into the equation. The addition of a 'reluctant/restricted' dimension highlights the fact that, especially in the public sector, provider–user relationships are extremely complicated.

The difficulty of identifying a marketing situation, as one would be understood in the commercial sector, and which is represented in Fig. 2.5, emphasises the differences between the two sectors. In the Chapman model of the public sector (Fig. 2.7), it may actually be necessary to 'opt out' in order to find a proper marketing relationship between a provider and a user. Many of those seeking what they regard as high quality education for their children do just that. However, such an option is often simply just not possible, especially in a situation constrained by economic realities.

		Provider		
		Active	*Inactive*	*Reluctant/ Restricted*
User	*Active*	**Private sector** Opt out of public sector	**Political demand** Lobby groups Social pressure	**Rights** As provider's duty; as user's privilege
	Inactive	**Societal marketing** 'It's good for you'	**No transaction**	**Resignation** User must accept, provider cuts costs
	Reluctant/ Restricted	**'We know best'** Legislation makes it work	**Distress purchase** Dire necessity	**Hostility** Mutual distrust

Fig. 2.7 Public sector provider–user relationship
Chapman's model

Complex and changing user–provider relationships

Many public sector organisations may also find themselves working in a series of different relationships – for example, in the police service. In the UK at Christmas time the police have, for some years, mounted anti drink-drive campaigns. In this case, the police force is an *active provider* and the motorist who is stopped, guilty or not (the primary user in this instance), is a *reluctant user*. However, if the same motorist arrives home and finds the house has been burgled, then the motorist becomes immediately an *active seeker* of police services and any delay in response caused by a limitation of service due to budgetary pressures will lead to pressure for a diversion of resources.

MINICASE 2.1

Active provider and reluctant/restricted user

Sandra Barwick (*The Independent*, 10 October 1992) questioned the effectiveness of *The Patient's Charter*. Her dismal experience of an outpatients' clinic is an apt illustration of the resignation engendered by the combination of a reluctant/restricted provider and an inactive user. As the aged and infirm were ordered curtly about by an (unidentified) member of staff, Ms Barwick decided that they were called patients simply because their function was to exercise patience passively.

MINICASE 2.2

Active provider, reluctant user

The Daily Telegraph of 25 June 1994 carried an article by Robert Hardman on the case of Mr John Panvert from Kent, UK. Having bought an old oast house, damaged by the 1987 storms, at Underhill, near Sevenoaks, Mr Panvert spent hundreds of hours restoring it, convinced it was an agricultural building. Unfortunately, Sevenoaks District Council maintained that the building had been derelict, and could not be classed as agricultural. Since 1991, Mr Panvert has been fighting an order to restore the property to a ruin, an argument in which Mr Panvert estimates the Council has spent perhaps £100 000 trying to prove that the oast house isn't an agricultural building. The chief enforcement officer for the council's planning department argued that restoration would merely encourage unwanted Green Belt development. He seemed proud of the fact that Sevenoaks is the 'strictest authority for enforcement in the whole of the South East'.

Many public services owe their origins to a desire for social equity and improvement. If the services provided to meet these intentions are to be administered fairly, some system of rules and controls is necessary. This need was the main reason why the Welfare State created a huge demand for new civil service administrative jobs in the late 1940s. However, although this element of control, usually taking the forms of government bureaucracy, was developed for the benefit of those in need, in certain cases it is also needed to police the system it created, to lay down minimum acceptable standards for areas such as health, safety and hygiene. Yet in taking responsibility for providing mandatory levels of provision, government also runs the risk of imposing controls and requirements upon people when they may not be really needed. There has always been a danger that state provision of welfare could interfere with the individual's civil rights and self-responsibility. However, there are many examples of bureaucratic rules and regulations which seem to have been applied more for the sake of observing the existing rules than for any desire to benefit either the individual or the community. The 'it's more than my job's worth' syndrome is still alive.

In David Chapman's model, the combination of an active provider and a reluctant/restricted user produces a 'we know best' situation, enforced by the rules and regulations. Examples of its application abound.

A situation can emerge where the provider resents the demands being made, and the user resents having to make them – a mutual distrust. Providers who take the initiative run the risk of being seen to want to impose a service on their users ('it's good for you' or 'we know best what you need'), while active users may be seen as political lobbyists, claiming 'their rights' from providers who are restricted in their ability to meet those demands in full.

The complexity of public sector user–provider relationships can be illustrated by the problems of societal marketing. Some societal marketing is concerned with promoting a message designed to discourage, rather than encourage, consumption. The provider may be actively seeking to communicate a beneficial message to a target market, but the target market may express no real interest in it. As an example, we can cite the experience of anti-drug campaigns. Victoria Macdonald (*Sunday Times*, 15 November 1992) reported some of the difficulties encountered by European Drug Prevention Week in 1992. After the 1988 'Heroin Screws You Up' campaign was deemed to have failed, the UK Government, as part of a drugs prevention initiative which was later extended to March 1995, then backed a new campaign fronted by 'nice' celebrities warning younger people about the dangers of drug abuse. Such campaigns, many argue, are likely to be ineffective, or even counter-productive when most young people want to decide for themselves about the risks involved. The campaign might have been more successful if it used people who had experienced drugs themselves and had some real credibility with their target sector.

The importance of this 'reluctant/restrictive' third dimension for the provider cannot be over-emphasised. In the private sector, such stringent financial inhibitions are rare, even though UK industry has the reputation of being in the hands of cost accountants. Good marketing in the private sector will increase revenue or, for a properly managed organisation, increase profits. In the public sector, the reverse is almost the case. With fixed budgetary allocations, increases in use will generally cause an organisation to move from surplus into deficit. Thus the management of cost becomes the prime focus for a public sector organisation whereas, in the private sector, the management of revenue, or more importantly of value added, becomes the major driving force. These issues will be dealt with in more detail in Chapter 8.

Multiple markets

Many such problems are undoubtedly the result of the fact that the public sector is more constrained and restricted than the private sector because it serves many different markets at the same time. Four markets can be identified, each of which influences the service provided (Theodossin, 1986).

1 *The primary market* consists of the actual users or direct beneficiaries of the service – for example, doctors' patients and university students. They are the 'end-users' of the service, the 'customers' of the public sector. Many public sector organisations since the 1980s have attempted to adopt the language of the commercial market by referring to their primary markets in terms of 'customers' or 'clients' instead of 'passengers' or 'claimants'.

2 *The secondary market* consists of those who are in positions to influence the choice of transaction – for example, the patient's partner, the student's family, teachers and friends.

3 *The legitimiser market* consists of those individuals and bodies who/which exist to ensure that the service is provided in the approved manner, subject to quality standards etc. – for example, the British Medical Association, the Universities' Quality Audit systems and authorities.

4 *The resourcer market* involves those who are responsible for allocating the resources which are necessary to provide the service which is needed – for example, the Department of Health, the University Funding Council and the Department of Education and Employment. Public interest and accountability, in the form of agencies like the National Audit Office, the job of which is to ensure public value for money, have also to be satisfied.

Examination of these four markets can cause considerable debate among public sector managers. Given the existence of at least four public markets, all of which have to be satisfied at the same time, public sector marketing at once begins to appear intrinsically more complex than commercial marketing. The point has already been made that, in the public sector, the primary user is rarely the one who pays money directly for the service needed. In reality, many resources are directed at satisfying the other three markets identified. This can produce apparently ludicrous situations.

The driving forces of public sector marketing

There are three major forces that play important roles in deciding what services are considered essential to community interests, and the forms which those services should take (*see* Fig. 2.8):

● social considerations and aspirations;

● economic realities and necessities;

● political guidance.

'More than my job's worth'

A householder supplied with a domestic waste 'wheelie bin' in Sheffield was told that she could be fined for leaving it out on the pavement overnight, despite the fact that she hadn't wanted a 'wheelie bin' in the first place and was rarely up in time to put it out for a 7.30 a.m. collection. A Council cleansing department spokesperson was reported by a local paper as claiming that the householder might be held responsible if the bin caused an obstruction, injury or damage, because 'the law is not clear'. This is a good example of a 'we know best' situation. The householder had little or no influence over the nature of her refuse collection service.

The law seemed to be only too clear in another reported case when Joanna Coles (working for *The Guardian* in 1992) was ordered to move from her pre-booked rail seat by a British Rail conductor because British Rail had confused reservations. The conductor and BR police insisted that Ms Coles provide her private address in order that BR could invoice her for a full first-class fare, despite the fact that the fault was clearly BR's, and despite a fellow traveller's offer to give her a first-class seat for which he had a spare ticket (because 'it's an offence to transfer tickets!'). A strict adherence to rules and procedures appeared nonsensical, and it appeared that Ms Coles had to accept the situation.

Social considerations

Many of these have already been discussed. The nature of choice is limited. The payment for many services provided by the state is mandatory – for example, income tax on earnings over given thresholds, and national insurance contributions for those in work. The users of public services find it easy to develop a particular kind of attitude towards them and towards the people that represent

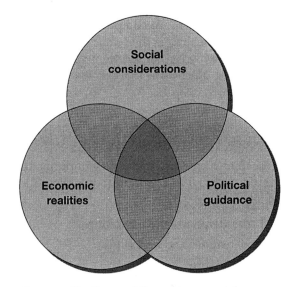

Fig. 2.8 The three forces affecting public sector provision

those services. Most people will claim the right to criticise the shortcomings of public services because they are, as taxpayers, etc., already 'stakeholders' in those services – they perceive themselves as having a vested interest in the service. The 'stakeholder' concept appeared in a business context when Mitroff (1983) argued that the behaviour of an organisation can be understood in terms of those forces which have vested interests, 'stakes', or claims in it. The idea was developed as a political strategy by Tony Blair's 'New Labour' in 1995. However, a sense of social ownership can foster criticism as well as involvement. As an expression of social ownership, the response to proposed admission charges for a public museum, for example, can be the statement: 'I'm not paying an admission charge; I've already paid for this museum by paying my taxes.'

This is a problem which may often occur in public sector marketing. In response to a simple desire to express a buyer's normal measure of influence in the process of exchange, the user who is restrained from making a free choice, and thus who feels pretty powerless, is likely to feel resentful of the offer which cannot be refused, resentful of the process which attempts to provide or impose a service, even if that service is seen as in the interests of society as a whole.

Public sector industries have themselves contributed to such resentments. In the past, most have been guilty of adopting the classic selling proposition 'we have the product', instead of devoting necessary time to good marketing practice and finding out what their users and customers actually needed or wanted. The existence of consumer councils, which many regarded as ineffective sops to public indignation, can be seen as one example of the way in which the customers themselves may often feel relatively unimportant. Brian Cathcart (1996) noted the way in which Yorkshire Water's handling of water supplies during the 1995–6 English drought created 'the perfect case study in needlessly alienating the customer'. The privatised public utility was accused of putting the interests of its shareholders before those of its customers, making large profits and inadequate investment. The Chair of OFWAT's Customer Service Committee in the region between 1989 and 1993 was quoted as saying that the level of complaints had always been high, but the company's response was to maintain that it knew best and that its 'customers should be grateful for what they were getting'.

The traditional scale of public sector industries has itself contributed to this situation. 'Big', in public perception, is often associated with the impersonal. The individual loses significance amid the crush of numbers. Large scale also seems to make it difficult to establish accountability. An impersonal, 'faceless' bureaucracy can add frustration to resentment.

Some public sector services may make things even worse by the way in which they are seen as agencies of government control, as well as of support. A large number of popular 'sitcoms' have poked fun at forms of public sector bureaucracy and the cultures they have produced. The popularity of *Yes Minister* (BBC), was largely due to the way in which audiences could recognise the storylines used from a simple familiarity with British political events and the UK civil service system.

Modern marketing in the public sector is gradually coming to understand the necessity of making more efforts to learn from private sector marketing, understanding and satisfying the customers' or clients' needs, wants and preferences. If public sector operations are to serve their social functions successfully, they need to demonstrate their ability to satisfy what people need and want. Criticism of public services has long centred upon those services' apparent insensitivity to user needs.

Political guidance

A dictionary definition of the word 'political' associates it with the State, its government and policies. In some ways, the State is itself a public sector organisation. It is more autonomous than most, because it can set its own level of resources by deciding on issues such as the rate of taxation by which it raises funding. However, most modern societies claim to be democratic, and those rates must first be agreed by an elected body of representatives of the public, and ultimately by the electorate itself.

Politics – 'the science and art of government' – sets the agenda for responses to social need. Whenever members of society seek to effect changes and developments they need to create the political will to do so. Government possesses the power to implement change, and the political dimension is an unavoidable influence on the nature and activities of public sector provision. There are two factors, in addition to the historical and ideological ones discussed in Chapter 1, which have contributed in recent years to an increased political emphasis upon marketing principles in public sector industries.

- *There is obvious political capital to be made out of any initiative which pays at least lip-service to increasing the power of the individual, and the individual's influence upon the exchange process.* Hence, most politicians are eager to be seen to make public services more responsive to the wishes of their users, 'the people'. As a rallying cry, 'the people' – full of emotional resonance despite its vague, catch-all nature – is a very useful term for politicians trying to unite their followers, blur differences, and attract as many votes as possible. The term has, therefore, overtones of populism (Canovan, 1981) and the political potential for representing the interests of 'the ordinary people' as a unifying appeal. As a marketing term, however, 'the people' has only a limited usefulness (*see* Chapter 5). It fails to distinguish between the wide range of different interest groups and 'market segments' which together constitute society.

- *During the last ten years it has become increasingly plain that marketing has a great deal to offer the non-profit public sector.* Changes in cultural attitudes in society, economic developments and changes in government-spending policies have all encouraged public sector organisations to use marketing. Of course, many public sector organisations provide services which are seen as social rights to which people should be entitled. The idea of competition in the provision of those services is still regarded by many as strange and somewhat out of place in the public sector context. Yet, increasingly, competition is seen as a good way of reducing state involvement and public costs. It can also be seen as a way of increasing real choice, improving quality and giving the individual more power in the exchange process.

Such arguments were put forward in the British Government's *The Citizen's Charter* in 1991, although that document actually pays little attention to the marketing element other than in its continual references to the 'citizen' as customer and consumer. However, as a description of political aspirations for the public services, it can be seen as a good example of 'societal marketing'. 'Societal marketing' is a term now often used to describe marketing techniques which aim to create consumer benefit and long-term public welfare as a way of attaining an organisation's (in this case the Government's) social goals and meeting its responsibilities. In practical terms, such aims are typical of a desire to improve the quality of public services by increasing efficiency, choice and competition. The principle of 'making things better' obviously requires a degree of change, justified on the grounds of political desires and beliefs. All political parties usually claim that their policies are going to create improvements in society.

In the final analysis, politics are associated with power – the authority and control that determine the nature and policies of public sector provision. The political dimension is an unavoidable influence. However, if political needs are going to be met satisfactorily, they have to be funded at an adequate level. The economic influences upon the public sector have to be understood.

Economic realities

Since the Industrial Revolution it has been virtually impossible to imagine a truly self-supporting individual or community. Everyone has become dependent upon other people. For most, this means that they rely upon their ability to sell their labour to an employer or an organisation. In exchange for their labour, they receive money (and perhaps other benefits). Their ability to earn, therefore, depends upon a market for their services. They spend much of the money they earn on buying goods and services for their own use. As a result, what they spend in turn helps make the demand which creates and maintains jobs and work for others. 'The market' is again the link between supply and demand. Nevertheless, there are a number of important distinctions to be made between the ways in which the private and the public sectors operate in economic terms.

In the private enterprise economy, the business person aims to maximise profits, and hopes to achieve the biggest difference possible between the costs of production and the value of sales in order to do so. Profitability is the main incentive and measure of success. Business expresses its results using profit and loss accounts. In the public sector, however, many organisations are non-profit ones. They may have charitable status. Their results are expressed in terms of income and expenditure. They also tend to pursue a number of objectives at the same time, many of which are qualitative and non-financial. They rarely depend solely on financial results as their main measures of performance.

This gives the public sector a distinct set of problems. For most of their revenues they generally rely upon income derived from state taxation rather than from any trade or commercial exchange. The non-profit sector believes in the concept of 'service', and thus understands revenue or income as the *means* of meeting users' needs. Conversely, the private, commercial sector understands revenue as the *result* of meeting users' needs. The commercial marketing world sees the customer or user as the focus of marketing activities because the goals of commercial organisations are generally met by satisfying the needs of the customer. Resources are used to satisfy customer needs and thereby to make profits. The public sector non-profit organisation, on the other hand, usually aims to satisfy wants or needs that the user cannot, or does not, want to pay for directly. Instead of offering only those services which a public will pay for, the non-profit organisation will offer those services which it believes, or which are politically determined as, appropriate for the benefit of society.

As a result, most public sector organisations have a very specific set of financial and economic considerations, which differ from those affecting private industry.

- *Measurement of performance* is rarely based on profit or solely on financial criteria. Public sector organisations usually have aims and objectives which express social needs. Although these are inevitably linked to, and are constrained by, economic forces, most public sector organisations are non-profit.
- *Income is usually derived from allocated revenues*, rather than deriving directly from levels of activity. Indeed, an increased level of activity in a public sector organisation could well result in a financial deficit, whereas in the private sector it can often increase profit.

Economically, most public sector industries contribute to the social and economic infrastructure. However, their contribution to a country's economic well-being is difficult to measure directly. For example, it is extremely difficult to *measure* the amount of financial benefit generated for private industry by the National Health Service, or by the education system.

Nevertheless, it is precisely because the public services aim to satisfy a level of social need that is considered economically necessary for a country's infrastructure, that they are funded from the public purse. This also implies that they have, or should have, a high level of public accountability. In turn, this means that public expenditure is subject directly to political influences and control.

Marketing and needs

Three forces – social, economic and political – represent the main influences upon public sector organisations. Together, they form a major part of the environment that all organisations exist within, and over which they have only very limited control. The environment is such an important source of uncertainty. Social, political and economic perceptions of need are constantly changing. Public sector organisations, like any other sort of organisations, need to understand their environment and monitor it as well as they can, if they are going to be successful. Legislation, for example, can have a profound effect upon a public sector activity. If society only sanctions those institutions which meet its needs, it is necessary to ask what kinds of needs the public sector tries to fulfil. If public sector organisations are mainly involved in meeting the need to provide a social, economic and political infrastructure, it follows that most of the needs served by the public sector are related to society's perceptions of what it thinks is necessary to achieve minimal and acceptable standards. How buyers respond to public sector provision will be dealt with in Chapter 3.

Public sector organisations mostly seek to benefit the public. As such, they often have charitable status. Based upon Lord MacNaghten's 1891 definition of charitable purposes, a charity has now to satisfy the Charity Commissioners that its activities fall entirely within one of four categories:

- the relief of poverty;
- the advancement of education;
- the advancement of religion;
- other purposes beneficial to the community.

A charity must therefore provide a public benefit. In doing so, the organisation is obviously on the side of Tertullian's virtues. If it is looked at in this way, the identification of the public sector's market needs could even be interpreted as a moral imperative.

Summary

1 **Negative images of marketing.** Marketing has become an essential function and philosophy of modern business. Unfortunately, it still has a number of negative associations.

2 **The development of marketing.** Although 'marketing' and 'the market' have assumed a prominence in the 1980s and 1990s, markets are one of the earliest forms of social institutions. The relationships between supply and demand are constantly changing, but now favour demand and customer choice.

3 **Relationships between providers and users.** All businesses need detailed knowledge of their markets, their needs and wants, and need to structure themselves to use that knowledge effectively.

4 **The marketing mix.** Marketing activities can be described using 'the 4Ps' of marketing: Product, Place, Price and Promotion. Profit, people and planning are also important.

5 **The changing role of marketing in the public sector.** Public sector organisations have traditionally behaved more like animals in the zoo, and many have lost the ability to survive in the wild. They now need to be taught those skills. Many have now been forced to reconsider their relationships with users and customers as more and more services are privatised, or given agency or trust status.

6 **The nature of public sector markets.** These include industrial, governmental, consumer and societal markets. Most public sector organisations serve multiple markets (primary, secondary, legitimiser and resourcer markets) simultaneously.

7 **The driving forces of public sector marketing.** Social, political and economic forces are all important. Public sector revenue is seen as the means, not the result of, meeting users' needs. Public sector performance cannot be measured solely using financial criteria. Income is usually allocated to, not generated by, activity.

8 **Marketing is about needs.** Social, political and economic perceptions of need constantly change. Public sector organisations need to understand and respond to these changes. The identification of market needs often has a moral dimension.

Implications for management

The environment is obviously a major influence on the manager's job. The 'classical' school of management (developed during the period around 1910 to 1935) sought to identify the functional elements of management – for example, planning, organising, staffing, directing, coordinating, reporting and budgeting. Subsequently, other approaches to management have included emphases on decision-making, leadership and work activity. Increasingly, understanding the environment has been seen as a key management task. Mintzberg (1980) saw informational roles as a major category of management activity. These include monitoring the organisational environment in order to detect changes.

Stakeholder analysis

Earlier this century it was customary to concentrate upon the internal efficiency of organisations as a means of achieving success. Organisations were often seen as 'closed systems', and much attention was devoted to designing efficient structures and processes which maximised their efficiency in producing products. Management theory only developed a real concern with issues external to the organisation after the Second World War. Peters and Waterman (1982) refer to the ways in which management theory developed from a 'closed rational' to an 'open social' approach, exploring ways in which organisations relate to their environment – the broader context in which they operate. This is also central to a modern concept of marketing. No matter how efficient the product or the service, to be effective an organisation has to interact with its environment successfully. The environment needs to be understood because it is the source of uncertainties, of threats and opportunities.

It is thus important to identify and map the 'driving forces' that affect each individual organisation. It has become customary to start with a PEST analysis (an acronym for **P**olitical, **E**conomic, **S**ocio-Cultural and **T**echnological factors) of the organisation's environment. This is, however, a highly simplified method and can only be regarded as a relatively crude tool. The available literature on organisational environment is extensive, as are the methodologies which have been developed. All, however, seek to map the identities of the environmental forces which affect the organisation, and the nature of the relationships involved. The following models and references may help managers consider the most appropriate ways to describe their organisations' environments.

Mitroff's (1983) concept of stakeholders can be a useful first step in understanding how an organisation relates to its environment. A stakeholder is anyone or any group of people (for example, another organisation) which influences, or is influenced by, the organisation and its activities. Mitroff argues that, as a result, an organisation can be understood as a set of relationships – relationships which are both within the organisation and outside it. Moreover, since relationships change, the organisation itself changes over time.

Managers have to look at the environment from the point of view of their organisation. They need to understand its complexities and monitor its changing nature. So who or what has a 'stake' in your organisation? There are likely to be a number of categories of stakeholder, ranging from those within the organisation to those outside it, in the local, the national, and even the international environment. R. H. Miles (1980) suggested that an organisation's external environment can be seen on at least three levels:

1 those elements which have direct contact with the organisation;

2 those elements which have indirect and potential contact; and

3 those elements in the wider socio-economic and cultural environments.

On whatever level the stakeholder exists, it is important to consider what the stakeholder expects from the organisation, and what the organisation may expect from the stakeholder. Stakeholders may be identified using the matrix in Fig. 2.9, which combines Miles' (1980) three levels of environment with the political, social and economic dimensions discussed in this chapter.

Identifying the public sector multiple markets

Markets are critical parts of an organisation's environment. Table 2.1 can be used to identify the four main categories of public sector markets (*see* p. 54) which exist for a specific organisation. The organisation will be trying to satisfy the demands of all these markets.

It is relatively easy to begin the process by using both stakeholder and multiple market analyses as ways of identifying an organisation's environment. However, the initial result is likely to be a picture of the environment as perceived in the present. It is important to realise that the environment is constantly changing. In many respects, change is now one certainty in an ever increasingly uncertain environment. Williams *et al.* (1989) maintain that an organisation which focuses on its external environment is better able to change its culture and, implicitly, remain successful than one which is internally focused. This is largely because the environment has become increasingly subject to change and turbulence. This trend has been recognised by management literature for a long time, certainly since the 1960s when some original work on environmental modelling began to address the issue of increasing 'disturbance' and 'turbulence' in the environment. This has

	Political	Social	Economic
Direct contact			
Indirect and potential contract			
Wider environment			

Fig. 2.9 A stakeholder matrix

Table 2.1 Multiple-market analysis

Markets	Identity
Primary Who are the primary users or beneficiaries of your service? Who are its 'end-users'? What kind of benefits are desired by this market?	
Secondary Who or what influences the primary market in deciding the service provided? What kind of benefits are desired by this market?	
Legitimiser Who regulates or controls the nature, standards and quality of the service provided? What kind of benefits are desired by this market?	
Resourcer Who or what provides the funding for the service provided? What kind of benefits are desired by this market?	

since become an important issue in the work of, for example, Gareth Morgan (1989). The implications of change for the public sector, however, have only really become a major issue since the late 1970s. The introduction of market forces, competition and an emphasis on management into non-profit public services has meant that the public sector has had to develop a greater awareness of, and sensitivity to, the environment. The environment is rapidly changing its character and complexity. The manager needs to be constantly vigilant, and to understand the implications of changes which are likely to influence the organisation.

This chapter has stressed the importance of social, economic and political influences which influence the public sector in specific ways. The technological environment is also important. The ever-increasing use of information technology continues to have a major impact on management, particularly in public sector organisations, where management information systems are critical. Michael Earl (1989, p. 5) has pointed out that many government strategies – for example, in health and social security and income tax – are dependent upon computer systems, and policy changes cannot be implemented without the necessary systems.

ISSUES FOR DISCUSSION

The following issues for discussion are in the form of questions. Examples from specific public sector industries should be incorporated into responses. Case studies can be used to provide some illustrations of the issues raised.

1 What are the factors most likely to affect users' and suppliers' attitudes towards the public sector services provided?

2 What are the most common results of technological changes on public sector demand and supply?

3 What role do moral and ethical considerations play in public sector provision today?

4 What are the most compelling reasons for the political desire to 'slim the State'?

References

Canovan, M. (1981) *Populism*. London: Junction Books.

Cathcart, B. (1996) 'Fat Cataclysm', *Independent on Sunday*, 18 February.

Chapman, D.J. and Hill, B. (1993) *The Power of Value Added*. Cirencester: Eagle Head.

Cowell, D. (1984) *The Marketing of Services*. London: Heinemann.

Earl, M.J. (1989) *Management Strategies for Information Technology*. Hemel Hempstead: Prentice Hall International (UK) Ltd.

Harrisson, T. and Madge, C. (1986) *Britain by Mass Observation*. London: The Cresset Library. Originally published in 1939.

Kotler, P. (1994) *Marketing Management. Analysis, Planning, Implementation and Control*. Englewood Cliffs, New Jersey: Prentice-Hall International.

Mercer, D. (1996) *Marketing* (2nd edn). Oxford: Blackwell Publishers Ltd.

Miles, R.H. (1980) *Macro Organizational Behaviour*. Illinois: Goodyear: Scott Foresman.

Mintzberg, H. (1980) *The Nature of Managerial Work*. London: Prentice Hall.

Mitroff, I.I. (1983) *Stakeholders of the Organizational Mind*. San Francisco, Washington and London: Jossey-Bass.

Morgan, G. (1989) *Riding the Waves of Change*. San Francisco and Oxford: Jossey-Bass.

Peters, T.J. and Waterman, R.H. (1982) *In Search of Excellence: Lessons from America's Best-Run Companies*. New York: Harper and Row.

Theodossin, E. (1986) *In Search of the Responsive College*. Bristol: Further Education Staff College.

Williams, A., Dobson, P. and Walters, M. (1989) *Changing Culture*. London: Institute of Personnel Management.

Wilson, R.M.S., Gilligan, C.T. and Pearson, D.J. (1997) *Strategic Marketing Management: planning and control, analysis and decision* (2nd edn). Oxford: Butterworth-Heinemann.

CHAPTER 3

Understanding behaviour in markets

It has been established that the origins of the public sector, its culture of public service and the frameworks within which it functions, can lead to a strong production orientation which can be encapsulated in the expression 'public sector provision'. In other words, the managerial focus in public sector organisations tends to be on effective administration and an understanding of the process, rather than on an understanding of the users.

From the mid-1980s onwards, the marketing profession has moved away from the mass marketing of volume-produced goods towards 'new marketing' which enables buyers to exercise greater choice over both goods and services which more closely 'match' their particular requirements. Modern technology has made mass-produced, custom-made products a reality. This change in marketing focus has been brought about by changes in behaviour of consumers. Those organisations which failed to recognise those changes often went out of business. Thus the study of the behaviour of consumers, buyers and customers has become a fundamental part of effective marketing.

This chapter discusses how behaviour in public sector markets is affected by the ways in which they are more complex than private sector ones and by the fact that they have many constituencies, some with conflicting interests. Additionally, the nature of the relationship between user and provider is affected by the type of the transaction involved.

The chapter investigates why an understanding of the behaviour of buyers and users is so important; the nature of the influences acting on buyers and users; how such influences affect the perceptions and behaviour of individuals and groups; and how managers in the public sector can measure and use such information as the basis for developing marketing strategies and plans.

**KEY LEARNING
OUTCOMES**

By the end of this chapter, you should be able to:

- **understand how marketing policy derives from an understanding of user behaviour;**
- **appreciate the public sector constraints upon user choice;**
- **explore the nature of public sector multiple markets; and**
- **examine the nature of, and influences upon, user behaviour.**

Introduction

Since the mid-1970s the environment within which the public sector has been working has been very turbulent. Much of this turbulence has been brought about by political change, but it has also been affected by major changes in people's behaviour, attitudes and lifestyles. These have occurred not just in the UK, but throughout both the developed and developing world. As a result of the speed of change, it has become increasingly difficult to match supply and demand in the public sector. There is often a perceptible difference between what the markets actually require or desire and what the public sector understands as the appropriate provision.

For too long marketing has been seen as a manipulative management activity, focusing on persuading reluctant buyers to purchase the goods and services they do not really want. At one time there may have been an element of truth in this view. However, the concepts and practices of marketing have evolved and developed considerably over the years, and it is demonstrable that only those goods and services which meet the expectations of buyers and users survive in the long term. A principle noted in Chapter 2 is worth repeating here:

> *Modern marketing is not just about the provision of products and services. It is about people and how people react to the provision of products and services.*

Furthermore, marketing is about the exercise of consumer choice. For the successful organisation, this means identifying, and then satisfying customer needs and wants. As a result, customer satisfaction becomes an important measure of quality performance.

Customers, consumers, buyers and users

Within marketing terminology, the terms 'customers', 'consumers', 'buyers', 'clients' and 'purchasers' are used extensively and sometimes synonymously. For example, Mercer (1996, p. 126) states that a market is, of course, a term used for a group of customers. The customers effectively determine what needs to be supplied and who wants it. In the final analysis, the customers decide *who* a market *is*.

The terms 'user' or 'end-user' have already been introduced. The terms 'user' and 'consumer' actually have very different connotations. For example, Partridge (1964, p. 85) defines the term 'consume' as to *use up*. In real life consumption usually destroys, or at least transforms one resource into something else. Food is both used and consumed.

The terms 'user' and 'consumer' are still sometimes used synonymously. In private sector marketing such terms usually carry with them the implication that the user is involved in a transaction where money is exchanged to purchase goods or services. Furthermore, the processes of mass production often mean that the end-user or consumer of the product may be 'unseen' by the producer, who could be at some distance along the demand chain, separated from the consumer by distribution, wholesale and retail mechanisms (*see* Fig. 3.1). The producer's initial 'customer' – that is, the organisation which is first in the demand chain – will be a

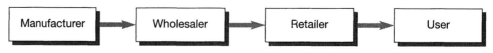

Fig. 3.1 A simple demand chain

very different entity from the individual or organisation who consumes the product. For example, the cornflakes which are consumed for breakfast by the child will have been bought by the parent from the supermarket, which will in turn have bought them from the manufacturers. In fact, the needs and behaviour patterns of each constituent of the demand chain are different.

In public sector markets, often because of the service element involved in these industries, the demand chain can often be relatively short. The payment for goods and services may actually take place 'outside' the demand chain. For example, those students who are still eligible, receive their fees for attending a university in the UK from their Local Education Authority (LEA), which is not a formal part of the demand chain but provides some of the essential funding to put the student through the university. The complexity of this kind of market may also mean that the end-user or consumer may actually incur additional costs – for example, living expenses incurred while living away from home – the price of which may be attributed to another party – for example, the student's parents. This issue will be further developed later in the chapter.

Within the context of this book, the term 'consumer' will now be used generically to describe different constituents of the demand chain. The term will not necessarily imply the existence of a transaction in which there is an exchange of money for goods and services. This is particularly the case in respect of public sector markets, where the actual consumer or user of a service may not pay for the service directly and the concept of 'purchase' may be problematic.

Over the past 20 years, there has been a growing recognition that the consumer, not the supplier, is the centre of the economic universe. This development has led to a more general acceptance of the modern marketing concept, and its emphasis on the achievement of long-term, sustained profitability by developing a close relationship between consumer demands and the organisation's products, services and resources. For the business company, 'consumer orientation' requires a solid body of information about the consumers that it seeks to satisfy. Analysis of consumer behaviour and demand has assumed a vital importance in marketing and marketing research, and involves an examination of how and why people behave in certain ways.

In the private sector, an understanding of consumer behaviour makes a key contribution to the design of innovative marketing plans and strategies which take account of changes in customers' tastes and expectations. In public sector organisations, consumer satisfaction can also be increased if the provider organisation has a much better understanding of end-user perceptions and requirements.

However, as has been noted in Chapter 2, the markets for public sector provision are generally complex. This complexity and the inevitable financial constraints upon public sector activity mean that that there is always the possibility that at least one market constituent is likely to be dissatisfied. Even the most careful marketing strategy may well make unrealistic assumptions about consumer satisfaction. There is, therefore, as vital a need for a good understanding of consumer behaviour in the public sector as there is in the private sector.

Howard (1989, p. 2), in a report to the New York City government, argued that changes in customer behaviour had contributed to an 'imperfect link' between New York's municipal services and its spending. New York's officials found that, by using a mixture of educational campaigns, pricing policies and regulations, they could effectively modify the behaviour of residents. A decline in the number of false alarms and the amount of refuse to be collected were among the results of campaigns designed to change consumer behaviour. Howard concluded that public policy should be targeted at changing behaviour in order to produce the desired results.

In the UK, the concept of understanding consumer behaviour is less well established in public sector industries. Market forces, which are essentially concerned with how people behave, are usually interpreted primarily from an economic viewpoint. Competitiveness is most frequently seen in terms of price competition rather than in terms of consumer satisfaction. Before examining the concept of consumer behaviour and its importance for the public sector, some issues of competition and choice need to be discussed.

Competition

It is important at this point to consider how the concept of competition operates in the private sector. Bateson (1995, p. 41) makes an analogy between marketing and warfare. The 'enemy' is the competition, often the suppliers of the same goods or services or, alternatively, the suppliers of goods and services offering the same benefit. Bateson identifies the 'weapons' with which the war is fought as the elements of the marketing mix. Some more jaundiced views of marketing suggest that the main enemy of suppliers is the customer! In more production-oriented companies, the expression 'educate the customer (to our way of thinking)' is frequently used.

In marketing-oriented companies, the consumer is not the enemy, but the source of sustenance for the organisation, which depends upon the consumer for its survival. As a result, consumer behaviour patterns need to be understood properly before an organisation can make satisfactory transactions with its consumers. In other words, marketing is about creating an appropriate climate which encourages potential purchasers to buy products. It is not about 'hard selling' products. However, it may involve the introduction of new, attractive products or services and the use of techniques designed to reinforce existing customer habits.

The animal analogy of Chapter 2 can be developed further. It will reveal that commercial organisations are essentially competing for the resources of the marketplace with other organisations who are seeking to 'feed' from the same sources (customers). The eagle is in competition with a number of other wild animals which feed on the same prey. In fact, there is a chain of demand in which all parties are competing with each other in the same environment.

Even with a limited number of manufacturers, suppliers and end-users, there are a very large number of potential competitive situations (*see* Fig. 3.2).

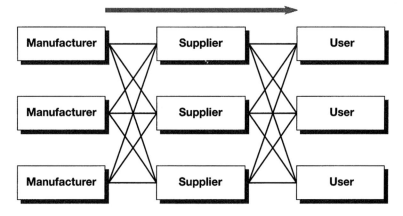

Fig. 3.2 A competitive user relationship model

In private sector marketing, consumer behaviour and choice, as will be demonstrated later, is often conditioned by the available sources of information obtained by the consumer, often as a consequence of competition within the working environment. Within public sector markets the concept of 'equality of opportunity' can mean that the choice of the end-user is strictly limited because choices may well be determined by other elements of the multiple market. While marketing assumes the existence of competition, the concept of competition itself assumes that the potential end-user can exercise choice.

Choice

Choice may be described as the ability to prefer or select from alternatives. *The Oxford English Dictionary* also includes a Middle English reference to the power, right or faculty of choosing. Power is an important consideration in this context, because it draws attention to the importance modern marketing attaches to user/consumer choice. Modern marketing is essentially concerned with identifying and satisfying consumer needs and wants. As a result, consumer, or user choice assumes a particular significance. User/consumer satisfaction is often used as an indicator of quality performance.

In Tims (1980), Alf Davey analysed the concept of choice in a public sector context. At the time, Davey argued that the Institute of Economic Affairs (IEA) saw the market as the most obvious and efficient method of marrying supply with demand. The principle of choice would ensure an efficient allocation of resources. Choice is therefore seen as an economic (and thus political) good. However, Davey pointed out (in Tims, 1980, pp. 94–102) that the conditions for real choice require:

- the existence of a number of possible results;
- the chooser's awareness of the range of alternatives and their implications;
- the absence of any external restraints and (coercive) influences.

Although it may appear that a free market provides these conditions of choice, in the public sector it is very difficult, if not impossible, to meet the last requirement, let alone the first two. Davey made the point that, without legal regulation, the relationship between provider and user can be a competitive one. If need is the condition that is being addressed, in order to protect the individual, some regulatory distribution mechanism is required. Ability to pay will not, by itself, satisfy social demands to protect the interests of all those in need.

The Citizen's Charter (1991) was presented as concerning itself with 'the people's right to be informed and to choose for themselves'. In many ways, it is unfortunate that competition, with its associations of winning/losing and risk-taking, is so often perceived as alien to the public services. Public services are often understood as 'rights' rather than as benefits. *The Citizen's Charter* sought to address such problems by arguing that competition stimulates choice. It was to act as a spur to improve quality and the level of individual involvement in the exchange process. In reality, however, *The Citizen's Charter*, and the subsequent, industry-specific charters, had more to do with the provision of peripheral activities and 'intangible benefits' (*see* Chapter 4) than with the provision of 'core' benefits.

Whilst most provider/user relationships in the private sector are voluntary (though not always welcome), many transactions in the public sector take place as a consequence of legislation. They are therefore coercive, thus eliminating one of the elements of choice. In other situations, monopoly conditions may prevail, again reducing choice. These factors will have an important impact on consumer behaviour.

Unfortunately, despite all the attention paid to the principles of extending choice and user awareness in the public sector, economic restraints alone impose a level of constraint which will necessarily limit the levels of choice severely. Furthermore, the choice of supplier is often exercised *on the end-user's behalf* and thus effective choice is unavailable to the end-user.

Providers and users in the public sector

In the public sector, provider–user relationships are affected by social, political and economic forces, as discussed in Chapter 2. Although we represented these in Chapter 2 as the 'driving forces' of public sector marketing, they may also be represented as constraints – constraints which limit the provision of services in very powerful ways. It is therefore appropriate to examine the Chapman model (Fig. 2.7) again. We can consider the 'driving forces' as constraints influencing the nature of both the inactive and the reluctant/restricted dimensions of the model.

- *Social considerations.* Social (including cultural) considerations determine the ways in which public services are seen as necessary social benefits. Society defines the minimum levels of social support provision it thinks is acceptable. It may also define the maximum levels acceptable. Social structures and cultural value systems are likely to define the extent to which the nature of provision is deemed viable by the political dimension.

- *Political guidance.* Political ideology always tempers what is possible with the need to retain voters' support. However, *The Citizen's Charter*'s desire to increase the power of individual choice in relation to public services, which have traditionally often been seen as impersonal, patronising and bureaucratic, is itself constrained by economic realities.

- *Economic realities.* For example, the need to control and/or reduce the Public Sector Borrowing Requirement finds expression in a need to keep a tight control over costs. The pressure to cut costs appears inevitably to compromise the desire to expand choice.

All of these factors are likely to inhibit rather than improve customer satisfaction.

We also need to consider the structures, information systems and technologies which also characterise the operations of any organisation. Although these are conceived and designed as enabling mechanisms, the organisational forms and technologies used will also impose certain limitations and restrictions on the way in which public sector operations work. This is particularly noticeable in bureaucracies.

We maintain, therefore, that it is important to recognise the nature of the reluctant/resistant dimension in public sector marketing. If the reasons for reluctance and resistance can be identified, the market will be understood more completely, and strategic decisions will be of better quality.

However, resistance and reluctance may not be the exclusive result of the kinds of constraints we have been discussing. Some may derive simply from a dislike of change and a suspicion of any introduction of new practices. Any political agenda will include an obvious commitment to improvement and (by implication) to change. However, public sector organisations traditionally take the form of bureaucracies which pose their own cultural problems in accepting and managing change. Bureaucracies are perhaps essential mechanisms for allocating public resources (*see* Lane, 1987, p. 2). Bureaucracies (which are discussed further in Chapter 7) have long been represented as the most relatively efficient forms of organisation: they are rational, hierarchical, centralised and systematic. However, since the 1940s, bureaucracies have been criticised for a number of reasons. In particular, they are frequently seen as organisations with an excessive adherence to routine, rule books and red tape. They become rigid, with less innovative capacity – essentially conservative. Much research seems to suggest that modern bureaucracy can be a major influence on political power. The Civil Service seems quite adept at resisting some of the implications of introducing the principles of private sector style competition for top jobs, despite the government's demand for cutbacks in civil service jobs (Inglis, 1993).

At this stage, it is possible to conclude that user/provider relationships in the public services are very different from those in the private sector. The constraints affecting both supply and demand are very powerful. Supply is necessarily both limited and controlled. Need and necessity provide very different kinds and levels of motivation for exchange decisions. Some decisions are actually unlikely to be made using the principle of choice at all, and would, in a commercial context, be labelled 'distress purchases'.

The multiple-market model

In Chapter 2, we argued that public sector markets were generally as complex, if not more complex, than private ones. Before we can use the market segmentation methods discussed in Chapter 5, we need to understand the diverse nature of public sector markets and their implications. Public sector organisations need to serve a number of markets simultaneously. A commercial organisation is likely to try and satisfy only two generic types of market: that of its shareholders and that of its customers. In a seminal article, Charles W. Lamb Jr. (1987) called attention to the fact that whereas private sector organisations usually pursue measurable financial objectives, those in the public sector have multiple, non-financial, qualitative objectives as well. Public sector organisations are expected to respond to the simultaneous demands of a number of different constituents – users, funders, politicians, public officials among them. Public sector markets involve an understanding and categorisation of those forces which directly influence the provision and use of a service in some way.

This can be exemplified in the health sector. McNulty *et al.* (1994) proposed that, in the context of the NHS internal market, the customers are the purchasers – that is, the people who fund and resource the process – rather than the patients or end-users. However, many hospital staff are uncomfortable about subordinating the needs of patients to those of the purchasers. As a result, according to Sheaff (1991), hospitals adopt a hybrid marketing philosophy which attempts to reconcile the needs of the payer and the user. Consequently, the customer is perceived as the payer and the patient as the consumer, whose needs and wants may need to be rationed as a result of limited resources. Although a health service example has been cited here, similar situations exist in most organisational contexts in the public sector, particularly where the service is free at the point of delivery. An illustration of these relationships, developed by a senior manager within the NHS, is shown in Fig. 3.3.

The concept of a multiple market has been successfully applied to public sector industries by researchers such as Theodossin (1986) in his work on further and higher education. The multiple-market model used can accommodate an 'internal markets' dimension – an important feature which has become an essential part of public sector marketing since the 1970s. The description of the multiple markets in Chapter 2 (*see* p. 45) can be developed further.

1 The primary market

This refers to the direct users and/or beneficiaries of a service. These are the ultimate end-users or consumers. These users of the service are those who benefit personally, or who are intended as direct beneficiaries. There is, admittedly, some danger of confusing the provider with the user in certain instances. In some situations both the direct provider (e.g., a clinician) and the user (e.g., a patient) can be seen as the recipients and users of the resources provided. However, it is usually possible to identify an 'end-user' – someone who is targeted as the primary market.

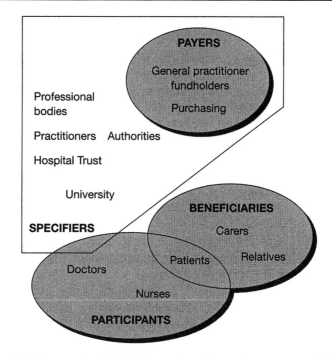

Fig. 3.3 A model of perceived provider and customer/consumer relationships in the NHS

The individual who is suffering pain in his big toe joint, and who goes to see his general practitioner for diagnosis and treatment, may be considered a primary market. His need is for relief from pain and cure. The degree of choice open to him is, however, limited. He may have chosen his particular doctor for a number of reasons: the distance of the surgery or medical centre from his home, the friendliness of the receptionist and staff, the reputation of the practice, etc. It is likely, however, that there are relatively few practices within a reasonable distance, and perhaps no other which is so easily accessible. Furthermore, choice may be limited by geographical constraints. In the case of an accident or emergency requiring immediate treatment, the individual has effectively no choice of treatment at all, since the quickest available treatment will be provided by the emergency services once they are alerted. In the public sector, therefore, the primary market may have only a limited opportunity to exercise choice. The individual's relationship with and degree of control over the exchange process is limited by a number of factors.

2 The secondary market

This could be described as the 'facilitator' market. It involves all those who can influence what choice is made by the primary market. Influences can be particularly powerful. They may include the person or persons who can persuade the patient to seek medical help in the first place. The partner who is persuaded that the patient's bad-temper is the result of the problem with his big toe may be a very important secondary market. Should the condition need referral to a specific clinic and consultant, the general practitioner may fulfil the role of the secondary market by advocating a specific consultant or treatment. Secondary markets are often social or cultural: they represent a way of doing things and a specific value system. This is usually rooted in a specific location and environment – the one where the exchange takes place. For example, the term 'alternative medicine' is used as a label to describe therapeutic practices which are alien to accepted Western medical ones, and highlights the fact that Western medical practices are still regarded as the norm in our own health service. Such cultural attitudes can form important constraints.

3 The legitimiser market

This denotes the system and the agencies by which standards are controlled and which define the obligations of the providers. Many, if not most, of these are legal obligations. For example, doctors can be sued for professional negligence if they do not provide an acceptable service. The British Medical Association, as the profession's regulatory body, can 'strike off' doctors for misconduct. Medical School qualifications try to ensure that doctors' skills are developed to an appropriate level. The individual (primary) market usually exercises no choice in the legitimiser market, which rather acts to ensure a minimum level and standard of provision.

4 The resourcer market

This provides funding for any public service. In the public sector, this usually takes the form of a level of resources determined by budget allocations. The logic of fundholder medical practices, for example, gives a large element of resource control to the doctor. Critics of the system are keen to point out that such doctors can be expected to experience some conflict of interests. Their roles as providers of a good quality service (doing their best to meet their patients' needs) and as managers of resources (finding the most cost-effective means of providing the service) may not be fully compatible. There is also a very basic distinction to be made between private and public sectors. A 'private' doctor will generate more income, the more patients he sees and treats. His patients pay him directly for his services. A National Health doctor is constrained by the level of funding he or she receives. The doctor will only receive the money the budget system allows. If too much is spent too quickly, there are no funds left to last to the end of the financial year. Financial constraints are usually regarded as imperatives.

The components of this model are also parts of the demand chain. It is also important to note the existence of internal markets.

5 Internal markets

An internal market can be defined as one which involves a contractual relationship between a consumer and a supplier within the same organisation. Some of these may be termed 'captive markets' in that they restrict choice. The concept of *internal transfer* is also a product of an internal market. During the 1980s, increasing emphasis was put on developing internal markets within the public sector. This was intended to foster competition, thereby increasing efficiency, reducing costs and notionally increasing consumer/client choice. Competition is an essential aspect of the free market which has served to differentiate products and, it is argued, improve quality in the interests of the consumer/user. However, the most obvious benefits of internal markets in the public sector are the savings represented by cost reductions. Cost reductions are likely to benefit efficiency – that is, how well specific tasks are carried out – but may well compromise effectiveness – that is, how well the result is applied to the demands of particular situations.

Market complexity in the public sector

The existence of multiple markets and of internal markets adds to the complexity of the 'marketing mix' in the public sector. The marketing mix was introduced in Chapter 2 (*see* p. 34). It is the most commonly used method of mapping the individual elements which make up the marketing process – a framework to identify the most important elements which, together, form any organisation's marketing programme. If they are identified incorrectly, the marketing project will not work. The marketing mix for the public sector can be described as consisting of five parts: the market, followed by the '4 Ps' of marketing.

- *The market.* This may be thought of as the identification of customer/user needs and wants. The public sector interpretation of these has been discussed earlier in the chapter. The private sector's understanding of 'the customer' needs to be modified in order to represent the various individual components of the public sector market which all demand to be satisfied at the same time. This involves finding out what each constituent needs and wants, and finding out the best ways of meeting all those, sometimes conflicting, requirements.

- *The Product.* This is usually conceived as the right article or service to fulfil these requirements. As has already been pointed out, the majority of public sector requirements take the form of services, where the 'product' is inseparable from its mode of delivery. Unlike tangible hardware articles, most services cannot be stored, and are evaluated on the evidence provided by the way in which they are delivered.

- *The Place.* This refers to the channels by which the product and services can reach their users. For the public services, information and locations are obviously very important ways of making people aware of the services provided and helping them use them to their best advantage. 'Place' can also be related to the sequence in which the markets are served and the ways in which it influences distribution.

- *The Price.* The price of the product/service is dependent upon what the user is prepared to pay. In the public sector, multiple-market situation, there are obviously strong pressures to reduce the price to as close as possible to the level of 'cost', in whatever way that is calculated. On the basis that the 'public', as principal stakeholder, is entitled to the best value for money, the main justification for profit-making comes from a desire to produce sufficient income for reinvestment and an improvement in efficiency/effectiveness.

- *Promotion*. This denotes the way in which the product/service is represented in such a way as to encourage its use. In the public sector this may well depend largely on public information campaigns, even 'social marketing' initiatives, which try to influence people's habits and actively encourage them to use certain services or facilities.

These elements of the marketing mix are all interrelated. Such is their relationship that any adjustment of one is likely to have some impact upon some or all of the others. Wilmshurst (1984, p. 16) gives a good illustration of how these principles can be applied to marketing in the private sector, but public sector needs may include additional considerations. In Rice and Aitkin (1989, p. 91), Douglas S. Solomon calls attention to the way in which social planners may need to add another 'P' – namely, positioning.

- *Positioning* is about creating a user perception of the product or service as having certain kinds of benefits and characteristics, especially when compared with others. For example, a 'positioning map' may attempt to identify the main criteria users employ to evaluate a service, and plot the relative positions of alternatives (*see* p. 166).

The market audit

The market audit is a way of modelling and understanding the key factors in the marketing environment which influence marketing policy. These need to be analysed systematically. A marketing audit is an essential tool for the periodic reassessment of any organisation's marketing effectiveness. It is a way of examining an organisation's environment, objectives, strategies and activities critically, and with the intention of improving them. It will seek to review:

- the environment,
- the nature of the markets,
- the nature of the organisation and its systems, and
- what Kotler (1991) calls 'the marketing function'.

Chapters 1 and 2 of this book provided a framework for considering the environment. This chapter is concerned with ways of approaching the nature of the markets and the marketing function and, within that, a more detailed analysis of the complexities of understanding consumer behaviour. The complexity of public sector markets means that all four market groups need to be considered in an analysis of its 'consumers'.

Buyer behaviour or user behaviour?

Howard (1989) defines customer behaviour as 'how consumers think and act in buying and consuming products and services from both profit and non-profit organisations'. In public sector provision, a high proportion of transactions are free at the point of delivery (FAPD), and some of these issues will be discussed in Chapter 8. This market complexity has important implications for how we understand the market and the behaviour of all participants in the market. Furthermore, different sections of the market may exhibit segmentation characteristics (*see* Chapter 5), and each part of the market will be influenced by the user/provider matrix discussed in Chapter 2 (*see* Fig. 3.4).

Before developing these issues, it is worth examining some of those concerned with changing needs and wants within the demand chain. Whereas public sector and private sector markets are often seen as separate and independent, there is actually an important level of interdependence between them at the level of 'industrial marketing'. However, private sector marketing is unlikely to increase demand from the end-user through the public sector (*see* Fig. 3.5).

With the private sector, total demand is determined by the level of activity of the end-users or consumers. The example of a child and the cornflakes has been used to illustrate the process. In private sector markets, much marketing activity, product development, advertising, promotion and pricing is aimed at end-user/consumer markets. The level of demand at the intermediate points of the demand

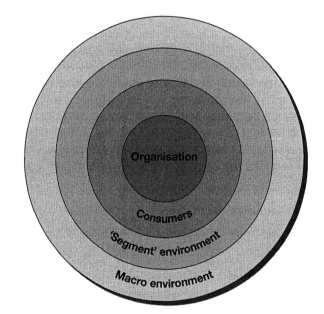

Constituency of market	Components of market	User/Provider relationships	Segmentation
Primary Secondary Facilitator Legitimiser	Need to consider the 'players' in each part of market	What is the state of the relationship between each market competitor or supplier?	Is this relationship influenced by segment variable? (See Chapter 5.)

Fig. 3.4 An initial approach to market constituencies

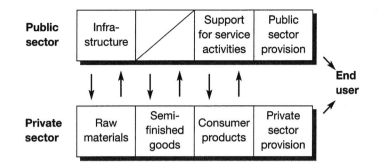

Fig. 3.5 Demand-chain relationships between the public sector and the private sector

chain is derived from the level of end-user demand. Where the product or service is used by the individual as a consumer, the marketing activity is described as 'consumer marketing'.

However, a high proportion of business activity is not concerned directly with producing goods and services for consumers. Instead, it is aimed at providing goods and services to organisations who provide infrastructures, raw materials, semi-finished goods, etc. to consumer goods manufacturers. This is known as *business-to-business marketing* or *industrial marketing*. For example, the printer providing cartons to a cornflakes manufacturer is not selling the main product used by the consumer of cornflakes. Thus the *demand* for the carton is derived from the pattern of demand for cornflakes. In business-to-business markets, demand is described as *derived demand*. In consumer markets, marketing activity – for example the introduction of a new product – can increase market size, whereas marketing activity in industrial or business-to-business markets generally increases market share rather than market size. There are, however, some notable exceptions to this – for example, in the microcomputer industry.

There is also another kind of market where organisations, in both public and private sectors, respond to demand from national, local and international governmental markets. Demand in these markets is determined by a series of complex factors which are significantly 'de-coupled' from end-user consumer demand, and are directly subject to political direction. These are described as *governmental markets*.

In general, however, the requirement for goods and services by consumer markets will be determined by the needs and wants of those markets. Since the exchange relationships are voluntary in general terms, the success and failure of products and services are determined by the perception and behaviour of the buyer. In public sector markets, the point has been made that the provider/user relationship is more complex (*see* Chapter 2). Furthermore, the public sector includes internal, essentially business-to-business markets, and increasingly has established relationship with parts of the private sector as well.

The complexity of public sector provision means that the public sector, in its many different forms, is subject to demand from all three market areas. For example, a local authority cleansing services department will have demand from private householders as well as from business and commercial enterprises and from governmental offices. A local authority swimming pool may have demand from individual swimmers and from a corporate sports club. A highways department may experience demand from the governmental highways agency. Consequently, public sector organisations, in general, need to have an understanding of the behaviour of consumers and buyers in all three market areas. The precise nature of behaviour will, however, be determined by the nature of the markets within which the organisation works – that is, by the consumer or organisational markets. The public sector is seen to work primarily in consumer markets, and so consumer behaviour will be examined first.

Behaviour in consumer markets

Understanding the behaviour of the individual as a participant in a consumer market requires insights into human behaviour and an understanding of the fundamental processes of perception and motivation, as well as of sociological factors such as social class, social mobility, leadership, reference group theory, etc. Economic analyses supply the framework of buyers' needs; behavioural data adds value to the understanding of market behaviour.

In devising marketing strategy for public sector organisations, a vast knowledge of the behavioural background of all those markets to which their products and services are being channelled is required. Kotler and Andreasan (1987) define a customer-centred organisation as one that does its utmost to satisfy the needs and wants of its markets within the resources available to it.

The acquisition of comprehensive knowledge about every aspect of consumer behaviour involving goods and services and organisational needs should take into account not only economic factors, but also the many other, and complex, motivations which may arise from psychological, cultural and social influences. Changes in behaviour are not always easy to identify; this does not mean that they should be ignored. The growing complexity and the greater experience of consumers, and the dynamic nature of the environment, point to the necessity for managers to develop a relatively comprehensive knowledge of their consumers' complex and changing needs.

Understanding human needs

Perhaps the most influential and popular model of human needs commonly in use today is that devised by A.H. Maslow (1954). Maslow's hierarchy was not devised as a descriptor for marketing strategies but for an understanding of individual behaviour in a management context. His model has been extensively used by buyer behaviour theorists to examine the nature of consumer needs and wants.

Maslow stated that the human being is a wanting animal, rarely reaching a state of complete satisfaction, and then only for a short time. As one desire is satisfied, another pops up to take its place. When this is satisfied, yet another comes into play – a process which is usually continuous. It is characteristic of human beings throughout their whole lives that they are practically always desiring something.

Maslow argued that human beings experience several different kinds of needs which motivate them to achieve satisfaction in life. Moreover, these needs can be prioritised in an order of urgency and attainment. It was a pyramidal diagram in which needs are layered in a hierarchy, starting at the bottom with basic survival requirements. Maslow's categories of needs are organised in at least five levels, in ascending order. The conventional representation of these needs has been modified in Fig. 3.6, based on the ripples created by a stone thrown into a pool of still water.

- *Physiological needs* refer to needs such as food, water, air and sex – that is, the fundamentals for survival and reproduction.
- *Safety needs* involve needs such as shelter and security.
- *Belonging needs* include needs such as group identification and love.
- *Esteem needs* are exemplified by self-respect.
- *Self-actualisation needs* refer to needs such as the desire for self-fulfilment.

Maslow (1954) argued that this model presents human needs in the order that they develop and demand to be satisfied. Once one level of need has been met the individual will seek to satisfy the next. If lower-level needs are threatened, the individual's attention will immediately return to them. If this model is used in the context of most public sector industries, it is evident that the majority of public services serve the first two levels: physiological and safety needs.

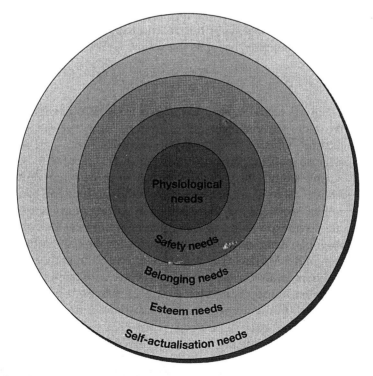

Fig. 3.6 A re-interpretation of Maslow's hierarchy of needs
(*Source*: Adapted from Maslow, 1954)

Understanding physiological needs

The importance of providing for physiological needs is demonstrated historically by the fact that many of the original charities were concerned with public health, provision of clean water, etc.

Legislation and culture encourage the procreation of children within marriage, but even changes in patterns of social behaviour are recognised by the provision of an economic safety net for single-parent families. Welfare legislation gives provision for food and clothing for those who have low incomes or no income at all. However, as the provision of basic needs become threatened, there is an immediate focus on restoring them. In the UK, the Clean Air Act of 1953 is a classic example of a response to urban pollution. The debate in the 1990s about the water companies, who are seen as profiteering from the provision of a *non-substitutable* essential for the maintenance of life, is also concerned with society's perceptions of basic, physiological needs. The situation in the UK Health Service has given rise to a similar level of concern. The current extended debate on the Health Service is concerned with sustaining human life. The provision of water and health care are seen as basic social needs, which should not be compromised. Politicians and public sector managers who fail to understand the consequences of threatening or withdrawing provision do so at their peril.

However, many governments are now seeing that an open-ended commitment to a basic needs safety net cannot be sustained by the State alone. They are making considerable effort to convince people to make contingency plans. In these circumstances, the user–supplier relationship is one of an active user confronting a reluctant supplier, as far as the State is concerned.

Safety needs

There are considerable areas of public sector provision involving security and shelter under two main categories: societal infrastructure and consumer infrastructure. *Societal infrastructure* provision includes roads and highways, public building, defence, policing, etc. – services which are essential to the operation and security of a community. The extent to which poor provision of these services impact upon the individual may not be immediate although they can cause considerable public irritation. Reactions may be confined to writing angry letters to appropriate bodies but are often expressed in general terms at political elections. Some writers argue, for example, that one of the main reasons for the Labour Party's defeat in the 1983 election under Michael Foot was its failure to address the issues of defence realistically.

There is also *consumer infrastructure* provision where the individual makes a decision to use the service – for example, housing, special kinds of refuse collection, etc. In the immediate post-war period, there was considerable activity in the provision of council housing. Since 1979, there has been a move towards transferring council housing to the private sector through council house sales to both individuals and housing associations.

There are also additional areas of provision which it could be argued fall into this security category. They include such provisions as basic education, communications, electricity and gas. Some of these have recently been privatised, and the political 'fall-out' from this process is an indication of their perceived importance to individuals.

Belonging needs

These psychological needs include needs such as group identification and love. In general terms this area is influenced largely by community groups. However, the provision of such services as social care is also motivated by the need to provide care and affection over and above basic physiological provision.

Esteem needs

An understanding of this drive for self-respect and a self-image is important for all marketers. However, it is sufficient at this stage to draw attention to the fact that the issue of personal status can be a vital element in some public sector marketing, not least because of the poor perceptions of public sector organisations and provision. Changes in perceptions which have occurred since the 1950s can mean that living in a council house may be seen as possessing inadequate social status. People are increasingly not just seeking somewhere to live, but are also seeking other factors related to psychological rather than physiological needs.

Some sectors of public sector marketing are actively concerned with issues of status – for example, higher education. Research indicates that academic awards confer status and esteem. This is an indication of the fact that the better the provision for the 'core' needs, the more a focus develops on the psychological needs.

It is interesting to observe how some products and services change roles. For example, consumers may complain about the high costs of provision of basic water supplies, but are prepared to pay an inflated price for bottled water because of its status connotations. Such behaviour is often rationalised as a concern for security – for example arguing that bottled water is 'healthier' – whereas there is some evidence to the contrary.

Self-actualisation needs

In developed societies where all lower needs have been met, self-actualisation is a major motivating force. It is also concerned with issues of self-esteem, and it could be argued that self-actualisation is concerned with feeding the mind rather than the body – a demand which is met by, for example, the rapid growth in entertainment of all forms. Satisfaction of this need is not a major part of public sector provision, although the public sector supports extensive arts activities. *Living with lifestyle*, a Channel 4 documentary, suggests that owning possessions is also seen by marketers as 'self-actualisation'.

For marketers in both the public sector and the private sector an understanding of these levels of motivation is an important first step in understanding individual consumer behaviour. However, other issues of consumer behaviour need to be addressed. The Maslow model provides some broad indicators of consumer behaviour motivation processes, but we need a more sophisticated understanding of them if they are to be used practically.

Models of behaviour

The whole issue of consumer behaviour has been a subject of study for many years and numerous models attempting to describe and predict behaviour have been developed. Howard (1989, p. 110) believes that the Engel, Kollat and Blackwell model developed in 1968 was the pioneering model which helped crystallise many previously unrelated ideas. It was relatively crude, however, and in more recent years behavioural studies have recognised the complexities involved in trying to model behaviour. Howard (1989) refers to the Zaltman and Walendorf (1983, p. 623) definition of the desirable qualities of a consumer behaviour model, which should be:

- capable of explaining behaviour as well as predicting it
- general
- high in heuristic power (heuristic meaning serving to find out or discover)
- high in unifying power
- internally consistent
- original
- plausible
- simple
- supported by facts
- testable and verifiable.

Bateson's three-stage model

In general, consumer behaviour models use a series of stages. For example, Bateson (1995, p. 24) proposes a three-stage model. (Note that in the public sector, purchase may mean adoption or use without the exchange of money, as we discussed earlier.)

- *The pre-purchase stage.* This relates to all activities before the purchase of the good or service.
- *The consumption (purchase) stage.* This also incorporates a set of assumptions about the expected performance of the service or product.
- *The post-purchase evaluation stage.* Essentially the 'feedback loop' where customer satisfaction will be established and the reality compared to the expectation, this stage determines any level of post-purchase dissonance, leading to complaint or satisfaction, leading to re-purchase and indeed recommendation to other potential users.

The ERRPDR Model

As can be seen, this three-stage process incorporates many activities which can be usefully analysed in more detail, and some writers (e.g. Mercer, 1996) consider models such as the *'ERRPDR' model* as one which is more successfully integrated with the steps in the marketing/promotional process, although the approach used tends towards being product driven rather than user led. This model involves the stages of existence, relevance, reinforcement, perception, decision and repetition (hence its title), and the process can be represented as in Fig. 3.7.

Existence involves making the consumer aware that a product or service exists. Relevance is about persuading the potential customer that a product or service is relevant to his or her needs. Reinforcement is about emphasising the message. Perception means developing a positive attitude towards the product or service and encouraging trial use. Decision takes place where there is positive intent to buy. Repetition occurs where the consumer has no post-purchase dissonance and decides to repeat the use/purchase.

More advanced models

The ERRPDR model has a particular starting point, that of the supplier influencing the buying process. However, while the supplier does have a part to play in influencing buyers, there are many other influences on the buyer, some of which will be described later. Mercer (1996) therefore developed the *an enhanced adoption model* (*see* Fig. 3.8), taking into consideration:

● the growing involvement of the consumer with the product or service;

● the changing participation of the supplier from influencing to involvement;

● the involvement of the consumer with peer groups in the buying or adoption process.

In today's climate this involvement of peer groups is important and complex and the process is considerably influenced by others who are described collectively by Wilkie (1990) as 'influences' and in the public sector context 'influence groups'.

Existence	Is the potential user aware that the product/service exists?
Relevance	Is the product/service relevant to the needs?
Reinforcement	Creating a better knowledge/understanding of the product/service.
Perception	Encouraging a positive attitude towards, and trial of the product/service.
Decision	Making the decision to use or buy.
Repetition	Deciding to repeat the use/purchase.

Fig. 3.7 A model (ERRPDR) of the stages in product/service adoption

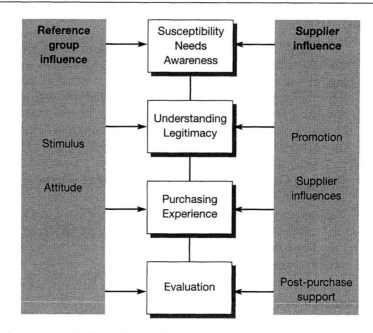

Fig. 3.8 A more sophisticated adoption model

Wilkie maintains that consumers *adapt* to situations. They respond and react to their environments, and their decision processes are influenced by these 'outside' forces. Some of these may be judged good, others bad.

In more developed models, the consumer process is much longer and more complex. The effect of external influences at each stage can be seen in Fig. 3.8. However, there are a number of additional, important components to be considered – namely, susceptibility, legitamacy and experience – before consumer behaviour can be properly understood.

Developing susceptibilities

Before a consumer becomes aware of a product or service, the consumer needs to be susceptible – that is, to be in a state of mind which will be receptive to the opportunity to satisfy a need or want. A well-known commercial product can be taken as an example. In marketing *the Walkman*, Sony identified user susceptibility by observing the numbers of people carrying around large radios. Technological substitution in the form of a miniature tape player using new technological developments was a logical development. In the public sector context, there is likely to be a continuum of susceptibility, varying from the very strong – for example, an unemployed person's susceptibility to the offer of help in finding work via a job centre – to strong negative susceptibility – for example, to mechanical checks on a vehicle that is being driven in an unroadworthy condition because its owner is unable to pay for repairs. In the Chapman model described in Chapter 2 (*see* Fig. 2.7), 'negative susceptibility' may be equated with the 'reluctant user'.

The right-hand side of the model in Fig. 3.8 shows vendor or supplier influence. Much of this support in the early stages is identified as promotion but, unless consumers are already susceptible, this promotion will have little effect and legislation may be needed – for example, to enforce the wearing of safety belts in cars.

Legitimacy

A second additional concept is that of legitimacy. It generally occurs after trial or first use. This legitimacy is influenced by both supplier promotion and by reference to influencer groups. For example, on the basis of a series of objective factors, an individual may decide to purchase a SKODA car. Key influence groups may deride the decision which brings into play subjective dissatisfiers which have little to do with the actual physical performance of the vehicle.

Public sector provision can suffer in similar ways. There is, for example, a widely held view that, in general, public sector organisations are less efficient at provision than private sector companies. Public sector organisations may therefore not be perceived as 'legitimate' in the sense of the model. The issue of legitimacy is a key factor in developing public sector marketing.

Experience

The role of experience is also related to this concept of legitimacy. If an individual has a good experience of the product or service, then its legitimacy will be reinforced. A poor experience will reduce the consumer's sense of its legitimacy. Regrettably, bad news travels fast and influences may give negative messages rather than positive ones.

In today's marketing climate, *brands* have also become an important marketing issue, and even in the public sector, the development of a 'brand' can become an important part of marketing strategy, since brands, or brand names, are easily associated with the consumer's prior experience.

A number of alternative consumer decision models exist, but most include the concepts and sequence represented in Fig. 3.7, *see* p. 75.

Models of influence

There are numerous models available which attempt to describe and predict the unpredictability of human behaviour. They can provide useful starting points and systematic frameworks for making an analysis of consumer behaviour.

Mercer (1996) identifies a number of key influences. They are summarised in Fig. 3.9. This model provides the first link between buyer behaviour and market segmentation, an issue which will be more thoroughly discussed in Chapter 5.

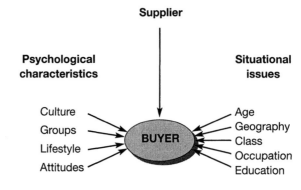

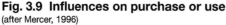

Fig. 3.9 Influences on purchase or use
(after Mercer, 1996)

Sources of influence on consumers

Wilkie (1990, p. 21) suggests a method of 'mapping' the influences on consumers, considering the breadth of the influence, the duration of the influence and the number of sources of the influence. A table with which to identify these is shown in Table 3.1. Sources of influence might include specific reference groups, cultural factors, the economic status of consumers, *etc.*

Many of these influences will be discussed elsewhere, but there are two factors which need to be addressed here specifically: culture and peer pressure. These are particularly important influences experienced by consumers in the decision-making process.

Table 3.1 The nature of influences
(after Wilkie, 1990)

Source of influence	Breadth of influence	Duration	Number of sources

The role of reference groups

John Donne (1573–1631), the English poet, proposed that 'no man is an island, entire of itself, every man is a piece of the continent, a part of the main.' Essentially, the role of reference groups is an extension of this concept, proposing that an individual's behaviour is not just conditioned by self-will, but is substantially conditioned by a series of external factors, not least by the groups to which the individual belongs.

A reference group is defined by Engel, Blackwell and Miniard (1990, p. 13) as 'a person or group of people that significantly influences an individual's behaviour and attitudes'. Most readers will be aware of the impact of external influences on behaviour patterns, exemplified in the expression 'keeping up with the Jones's', and numerous studies have been made which identify how an individual's behaviour is conditioned, in both the short and long term, by pressure from influencer groups or reference groups.

Reference groups function in numerous ways to affect consumer behaviour. They play important roles in the process of socialisation. They are used by the individual in the development and maintenance of self-image and identity, providing 'benchmarks' by which individuals continuously evaluate and modify their concepts of 'self'. This evaluation is closely related to the perceptions of whether other people in a reference group will approve or disapprove of the 'self' that is presented to the group by the individual. Reference groups also achieve individual compliance with group norms.

The public sector marketing interest in reference groups derives from the ways in which group standards can be associated with certain patterns of behaviour or use. If an organisation is able to establish a positive association with a particular reference group, and that group can exert compliance from members and aspirants, then this can be a method of obtaining competitive advantage, or improved perceptions of the organisation. The extent to which this concept has significance in public sector marketing is determined by how conspicuously the product is consumed or used. The more conspicuous its use, the more relevant is the reference group to the marketing process.

Existing literature on the subject identifies a number of different types of reference groups and group influences. The types of groups can be classified in terms of *level of association* and *group structure*, and the nature of the influence can be categorised by *level of pressure*. These complex relationships are modelled in Fig. 3.10.

Associative groups

The groups considered to have the greatest impact are the *associative groups* – that is, groups with whom an individual clearly associates – and these associative groups can be divided into primary groups and secondary groups.

A *primary group* is one which Engel, Blackwell and Miniard (1990, p. 147) describe as being cohesive and well motivated. Its members will share many beliefs and behave in similar ways. In modern society, an individual will probably belong to a number of associations or groups – for example, social groups, sports and/or interest groups, work groups, family groups, etc.

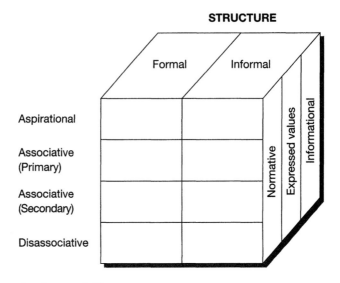

Fig. 3.10 Levels of association

- In the *family group*, both the immediate and extended family can exert considerable influence. Family influences form the experience base that affects individual evaluative criteria and beliefs, and such beliefs can be lifelong. The family influences the decision-making process involved in the purchase of products and services. The differences among families that affect their consumer behaviours lie not in whether they are organised but rather in how they are organised. This will be discussed further in Chapter 5.
- The *work group* is one in which patterns of behaviour reflecting the culture of the organisation are often expected. This can have an important effect on organisational buying.
- In the *social group*, group norms are developed, and these may be at variance with family and cultural norms. Individuals often belong to a number of different social groups, resulting in the possibility of conflict between the norms of different groups.
- *Interest groups* are related to special interest activities, and the behaviour of individuals in such groups can often be extreme. For example, this is frequently clear from the behaviour of football supporters.

A *secondary group* is one where the individual experiences face-to-face interaction with other members, but the influence is less strong than with primary groups. Examples cited in the literature of secondary groups are trades unions, political parties and professional organisations. Nevertheless, such groups can have a considerable influence on an individual's behaviour, depending upon the nature of the product or service and its perception within the group.

Aspirational groups

The influence of *aspirational groups* can be very important in conditioning an individual's behaviour. Under such circumstances, individuals adopt the perceived norms and values of groups to which they would like to belong and they anticipate moving into those groups. Some writers suggest that adopting aspirational group norms is often done unconsciously rather than consciously, in the same way that individuals progress through the hierarchy of needs. In private sector marketing, getting potential buyers to adopt aspirational norms through purchasing habits is a well-known technique, often promoted through the use of high-profile individuals to endorse products.

Disassociative groups

At the opposite pole to the aspirational group is the *disassociative group*. This influence has a negative connotation and individuals take action to avoid being associated with such groups. For example, a government minister of transport once made a political gaffe by posing the question 'Who would want to mix with the sort of people who use public transport?'

Group structures

The structure of groups can be important in the form of influence on members and two types of structure have been identified: informal and formal structures.

- *Informal structures* are often associated with primary, socially based groups where the patterns of behaviour are not formalised and structured, even though they may be strict.
- *Formal structures*, identified as those with 'written constitutions and structures' often relate to those groups earlier identified as secondary groups. The influence on consumer behaviour varies, depending upon the individuals' involvement with the group and their acceptance of group norms.

Influence types

The literature identifies three major types of reference group influence: the normative influence, expressed value influence and informational influence.

- The *normative influence* is where group norms are expressed clearly, formally or informally, and where there is considerable pressure to conform. Often the need to conform is determined by an individual's concern about what the group will think of him or her – that is, about perceptions of self.

- *Expressed value influence* takes this concept of self a little further and is often associated with aspirational reference groups.
- *Informational influence* is identified where the point of reference is seen as knowledgeable.

The impact of reference group influence

The level of impact of reference group influence varies, depending upon the utility and necessity of the product or service purchased and how it is consumed. Thus a product, such as a wrist watch, which in today's society could be considered an essential, is worn by members of the public, but there is little reference group pressure to wear a watch because it is an essential. However, the brand of watch could be influenced considerably by reference group influence, as it would make an external statement about the user and the group to which he or she belongs. This external expression of associative or indeed aspirational groupings is illustrated by the extensive adoption of branded items for use by individuals, from clothes to cars.

In the public sector, the model developed by Beardon and Etzel (1982) can be adapted, as shown in Fig. 3.11.

Product/ Service	*Satisfying needs*	*Satisfying wants*
Public use	Weak product, strong brand RG influence	Strong product, strong brand RG influence
Private use	Weak product, weak brand RG influence

Refuse collection Aid and support | Strong product, weak brand RG influence

Interests |

Fig. 3.11 The influence of reference groups (RG)

Organisational buyer behaviour

Public sector marketing activity is not restricted to dealing with individuals. There is a good deal of marketing between public sector organisations and other organisations both in the public and private sector. Similarly, the terms 'purchasing' or 'buying' in the public sector marketing context are subject to the same provisos as those discussed earlier in the context of the private sector. The nature of the transactions between organisations is subject to many of the same influences as those affecting 'consumer' transactions. For example, organisations may be 'reluctant users' of public sector provision as in the case of a health and safety inspection of a factory. The nature of organisational buyer behaviour does have particular characteristics which need to be identified.

Organisations themselves are inanimate objects and the term 'organisational buyer behaviour' may be a misnomer. However, the extended model of the marketing mix identifies people as a major constituent, and it is the behaviour of people acting as a group within organisations which determines the nature of organisational buyer behaviour. Furthermore, it is the nature and stage of the transaction which determines the role of different players in the group.

Over the years there have been many different models developed for organisational buyer behaviour. However, inter-organisational marketing remains a somewhat neglected topic

Ford (1990) suggests that, in business markets, buyers develop an idea of their requirements, and then seek out and evaluate a chosen supplier. Individual buying companies have pronounced differences in size, power and requirements. In fact, organisational needs are usually unique and are determined by the nature of the business they are in. The relationship between buyer and supplier is one of interdependence and interaction. Nevertheless, most organisations do have some needs in common, often relating to infrastructure. It is in these areas where public sector marketing in an organisational context comes into play. However, there are many areas where the organisational uniqueness does need to be considered and where a bureaucratic approach can fail to recognise the particular needs of the organisation concerned and can be inconsistent with the development of long-term relationships and interactions.

Organisational drives for demand

In consumer behaviour, the Maslow model was cited when identifying the drives for demand. In an organisational context the drives for demand are essentially created by the organisation's customers and users. In organisational markets demand is identified as being *derived* from the next stage in the demand chain, which is itself ultimately derived from the activities of end-users and consumers. Chisnall (1989) emphasises the fact that organisations' purchasing decisions are the product of organisational objectives, which determine their behaviour. Thus, in organisational markets, marketing has greater influence on market share than on market size. Nevertheless, there are drives for organisational demand which need to be understood if effective marketing is to take place. Organisational demand, therefore, will be related to a series of factors which relate to its *survival, operational security, profitability, obligations* and *reputation*.

In the same way that individuals have *survival needs*, so do organisations. These needs relate to the fundamental requirements of the operation of the business. There are needs for raw materials, components, operating labour and utilities. Prior to privatisation in Britain, the public sector was very active in the provision of some of these basic requirements, but in today's climate, the public sector has much less influence. The main area of public sector involvement is in the areas of *operational security* – for example in infrastructure provision, policing, military, education, training and waste disposal – and *obligations*, such as social, welfare and safety provision for the workforce, obligations to health and safety to the community. However, since the nature of the relationship between the public sector and the organisation may be significantly influenced by the statutory frameworks surrounding the provision, the relationship may not always be a comfortable one.

The decision-making unit (DMU)

We have already indicated that organisational buyer behaviour is concerned with groups rather than individuals. The group is often called the *decision-making unit* or *DMU*, or it may even be referred to as 'the buying centre'. Oliver (1990) suggests that defining the composition of a DMU is problematical. Its composition changes, depending upon the nature of the circumstances and on the nature of the transaction. A DMU consists of *all* those people who are in a position to influence the buying process, even if they do not recognise their roles in it.

Suppliers who fail to recognise the importance of some individuals in the buying process may find problems in the buying and adoption process.

Summary

The modern public sector environment is a very turbulent one. As a result, there is often a gap between users' perceptions of need and suppliers' perceptions of what is necessary to answer needs.

1 **Customers and consumers.** In public sector marketing, the payment for goods and services is often made indirectly, and each part of the demand chain effectively constitutes a different consumer. Consumer satisfaction can also be increased in public sector provision, if consumer/user requirements are properly understood.

2 **Competition.** The concept of competition assumes that the end-user can exercise choice.

3 **Choice.** Choice is often very limited in public sector markets.

4 **Relationships between providers and users** in the public sector are therefore subject to social, political and economic constraints.

5 **The multiple-market model.** Public sector institutions must respond to a number of simultaneous demands. These can be generally represented as primary, secondary, legitimiser and resourcer markets for their activities.

6 **Internal markets.** It is also important to address the concept of competition in public sector markets, represented by internal markets.

7 **Market complexity.** Complexity is also a characteristic of the 'marketing mix' – the marketing concept of product, place, price and promotion. This also needs to include the idea of market positioning.

8 **The market audit** is a means of systematically modelling and understanding an organisation's marketing environment and marketing effectiveness.

9 **Buyer behaviour or user behaviour?** Public and private sectors have a number of established relationships with each other within the demand chain although, in both sectors, the *level* of demand is derived from end-users.

10 The nature of **behaviour in consumer markets** needs detailed analysis. A successful customer-centred organisation is one that seeks to satisfy the needs and wants of its markets within the limitations of its resources.

11 **Understanding human needs.** Consumer/user motivation has long been an important area of study.

12 **Models of behaviour** have been developed which suggest increasingly sophisticated stages within the process of purchase or use.

13 The **sources of influence on consumers/users** therefore include culture, social class, reference groups, external conditions and market situations.

14 **Organisational buyer behaviour.** Public sector marketing also involves marketing between organisations – business-to-business marketing.

Implications for management

There are a number of issues which the manager needs to address. In particular, the following exercises can prove useful as initial steps towards developing a more comprehensive understanding of market behaviour. More detailed discussions of market segmentation will follow in Chapter 5.

What is the nature of your own experience of public service provision?
Think of five recent events in your own use of public service provision, and consider the following questions:

- What was the need or want to be satisfied, or the benefit sought, which caused you to use the provision?
- Where did the stimulus come from?
- Were you an active, passive or reluctant user of the provision?
- What alternatives, if any, did you consider in your decision process?

- Did you use the service on impulse, or did you give it some thought?
- Was there a conflict or 'gap' between your expectations and what was delivered?
- If there was, was this 'gap' created by any constraints imposed by the provider – for example, financial, legal or political obligations?
- Would you prefer not to have used this service? Was there an element of coercion?

Influences

Consider the answers you provided to the above questions. How may they have been influenced by:

- the nature of the information available to you;
- the amount of perceived risk in purchasing/using the product/service;
- the credibility of the reference group/s that may have affected you?

Reference groups critically affect levels of aspiration and types of consumer behaviour. Marketing managers need to assess the extent to which consumers identify with the behavioural patterns of certain sections of society. Managers have several types of specific interest in knowing about social groups.

- They need to identify why people join certain groups.
- They need to understand the inner organisation/operation of groups.
- They need to be aware of opinion leaders within various groups.
- They need to know the effect on consumers of belonging to several groups at the same time.
- They have to know the effect of consumer status or position in the group.
- They need to know how consumers that are new to a community utilise groups.

ISSUES FOR DISCUSSION

The following issues for discussion are presented in the form of questions. Examples from specific public sector industries should be incorporated into responses. Case studies can be used to provide some illustrations of the issues raised.

1 What are the consequences of the public sector being restricted in its ability to offer choice?

2 Why are user–provider relationships in the public sector likely to be more complex than customer–supplier relationships in the private sector?

3 What particular problems does the 'marketing mix' concept pose for public sector organisations?

4 In what ways can many public sector services be described as 'distress purchases'?

References

Bateson, J.E.G. (ed) (1995) *Managing Services Marketing*. Fort Worth, Texas: Dryden Press.

Bearden, W.O. and Etzel, M.J. (1982) 'Reference Group Influence on Product and Brand Purchasing Decisions', *Journal of Consumer Research*, September.

Chisnall, P. (1989) *Strategic Industrial Marketing*. Hemel Hempstead: Prentice Hall UK Ltd.

Engel, J.F., Blackwell, R.D. and Miniard, P.W. (1990) *Consumer Behavior*. Chicago: Dryden Press.

Ford, D. (ed) (1990) *Understanding Business Markets*. London: Academic Press Ltd.

Her Majesty's Government (1991) *The Citizen's Charter*. London: HMSO.

Howard, J.A. (1989) *Consumer Behaviour in Marketing Strategy*. Englewood Cliffs, NJ: Prentice-Hall Inc.

Inglis, F. (1993) 'So farewell then, citizen servant', *Times Higher*, 6 August.

Kotler, P. (1991) *Marketing Management, Analysis, Planning, Implementation and Control*. Englewood Cliffs, NJ: Prentice-Hall Inc.

Kotler, P. and Andreason, A.R. (1987) *Strategic Marketing for Non-Profit Organizations*. Englewood Cliffs, NJ: Prentice Hall Inc.

Lamb, C. W. (1987) 'Public Sector Marketing Is Different', *Business Horizons*, 30 (4)July–August, 56–60.

Lane, J.-E. (ed) (1987) *Bureaucracy and Public Choice*. London: Sage Publications.

McNulty, T., Whittington, R., Whipp, R. and Kitchener, N. (1994) 'Improving Marketing in NHS Hospitals', *Public Money and Management*, July–September, 51–7.

Maslow, A.H. (1954) *Motivation and Personality*. New York: Harper & Row.

Mercer, D. (1996) *Marketing*. Oxford: Blackwell.

Oliver, G. (1990) *Marketing Today*. Hemel Hempstead: Prentice Hall UK Ltd.

Partridge, E. (1964) *Usage and Abusage*. Harmondsworth: Penguin Books Ltd.

Rice, R.E. and Aitkin, C.K. (eds) (1989) *Public Communication Campaigns*. London: Sage Publications.

Sheaff, R. (1991) *Marketing for Health Services*. Milton Keynes: Open University Press.

Theodossin, E. (1986) *In Search of the Responsive College*. Bristol: Further Education Staff College.

Tims, N. (ed) (1980) *Social Welfare: Why and How?* London: Routledge and Kegan Paul.

Wilkie, W.L. (1990) *Consumer Behavior*. New York: John Wiley & Sons Inc.

Wilmshurst, J. (1984) *The Fundamentals and Practice of Marketing*. Oxford: Butterworth–Heinemann.

Zaltman, G. and Waltendorf, M. (1983) *Consumer Behavior – Basic Findings and Market Implications*. New York: John Wiley & Sons Inc.

CHAPTER 4

Defining demand

CHAPTER OVERVIEW

Marketing is about ensuring an exchange of satisfaction between user and provider, buyer and seller. Previous chapters have noted that the public sector provision is very complex, and that there are numerous constituencies existing within the public sector marketplace which all have to be satisfied simultaneously.

All of these different constituencies will be seeking a variety of goods and services from the public sector, some of which will be in demand while others will be 'pushed' on to a reluctant public. The same product or service will have different meanings to different groups. This necessitates a discussion of the nature of needs, wants and rights, and how managers can evaluate the mix of benefit, tangibility and transaction factors which comprise the product or service offering. This is particularly important in evaluating how products, services and campaigns will be received by the markets, since they will inevitably be assessed in the context of various user groups. Therefore, a knowledge of these groups is important as a basis upon which to determine marketing action.

The chapter goes on to consider a range of issues specific to the delivery of services, where public sector provision is particularly strong. One of the most important factors identified is the difference between the 'core' service being delivered, that is the benefit derived from the product or service, and the support service given to the user during the course of the transaction. Other issues which are of particular importance to the public sector include managing demand, societal marketing and the development of products and services 'in the public interest'.

KEY LEARNING OUTCOMES

By the end of this chapter, you should be able to:

- establish definitions of needs, wants and social rights;
- analyse the nature of user benefits;
- understand the nature of the product life cycle and its application to services;
- explore the comparative issues in the marketing of services as opposed to products; and
- appreciate the need for, and basic methods of, managing demand.

Introduction

Chapter 3 argued that an understanding of user behaviour is essential to the process of identifying the nature of demand. All markets are basically driven by demand – the desires and needs that are responsible for any relationship between producer/supplier and consumer. However, the concept of 'demand' in the public sector is a complicated one. In a free market, it is assumed that consumers or users can exercise demand through choice. They can choose whether to buy or not. They can select which products or services they think will give them the desired benefit. In the public sector, however, most demand is created by need, by necessity.

Individuals and society

Much, although not all, of public sector provision is concerned with meeting people's basic needs – with housing, income support, unemployment benefit, etc. However, there are some exceptions to this principle. Society can be said to have its own needs and community interests. For example, education has long been regarded as of social, as well as of individual, benefit. A basic level of education is seen as a social, and hopefully socialising, need for all young members of the community. Vocational training is often represented as necessary for its contribution to national economic performance, although an opposing view holds that it is of primary benefit to the individual only in competition for jobs. By the mid-1990s, the post-war German training system was being criticised for its excessive regulatory framework, which had proved no real protection against levels of unemployment among trained, qualified and skilled workers. Further and higher education may be seen as both the individual's opportunity for self-realisation and as a means of obtaining qualified graduates to benefit the national economy. This situation is a good illustration of the concepts of the primary and secondary markets.

There are, therefore, distinctions to be made between the needs of society and the needs of the individual. In an ideal world – for example, in the *Republic* of Plato (428–347 BC) – these needs might coincide, governed by the principle of justice, defined as the proper relationship between individuals, and between individuals and the State. The desires of the individual are even today compromised by the demands of society in terms of its cultural norms and political expectations, and by society's economic ability to provide the individual with the desired opportunities. It is unfortunate that the term 'compromise' has attracted a somewhat negative connotation and meaning. Compromise is actually an essential mechanism of negotiation and exchange. It mediates between supply and demand.

Needs and wants

Another very important distinction can be made between needs and wants; this is particularly important for the public sector.

1 *An individual's basic* or *physiological needs* – for example, shelter, food, clothing and health – are the products and services now commonly regarded as minimum social rights or entitlements. They are necessary for survival. Many societies have decided that there is a minimum standard of provision for these human needs, below which none of their members should fall. The development of the UK Welfare State (*see* Chapter 1) as a comprehensive welfare system was designed to provide for these needs, if and when people were not able to provide them for themselves. The individual has little discretion here and without the satisfaction of these fundamental needs, survival is in doubt.

2 *An individual's wants* may be defined as the products and services which people desire, or even aspire to, but which are not defined by society as essential to 'basic' survival. These wants are psychologically motivated. The individual may want them because they achieve and confirm, for example, a sense of self-worth, status or ambition. Such wants correspond to the 'higher' levels of Maslow's hierarchy of human needs (*see* Chapter 3, Fig. 3.6).

We maintained in Chapter 3 that marketing, particularly public sector marketing, is about satisfying user needs. Perhaps the concept of need, as distinct from wants, is indeed useful in distinguishing the functions of many kinds of social services from those of other institutions and organisations. In theory, public sector marketing would be much simpler if it were only possible to define social needs in some clear, objective way which could avoid the complexities of social, political and economic values (*see* Plant, Lesser and Taylor-Gooby, 1980, pp. 20–21). Criteria for evaluating the efficiency of public sector services would then be easy to identify and apply.

Unfortunately, there are social and political difficulties in defining needs, some of which are discussed in Chapter 5). People's perceptions of needs, even those which may be considered 'basic' ones, often differ widely. 'The public' is not a homogeneous mass, but is composed of many different individuals, interest groups and market segments.

Modern social services, for example, are only too well aware that different users will exhibit different attitudes towards the providers of those services. Some older recipients may remember a time when it was thought undignified and shameful to accept help from anyone other than family and friends. There are still even some people who disdain to accept what they see as charity – rather than benefits to which they have a clear entitlement – and feel that any such help demeans their sense of self-respect. Others have no such inhibitions and regard such benefits as social rights.

If different people can interpret benefits in such different ways, it is obviously necessary to re-examine the definitions of needs and wants and the distinctions between them. A number of writers (reviewed in Plant, Lesser and Taylor-Gooby, 1980, pp. 29–30) have argued that 'needs' can be understood as being in the 'best' interests of the individual. However, such an argument carries with it implications of a 'we-know-best' approach, so often associated with public sector provision. The provision available may not even match the individual's own perception of his or her need. In such cases, the interests of the community may take precedence over those of the individual. As examples, we may cite the workaholic's potential need for personal stress management and the alcoholic's actual need for help and therapy to counter his or her addiction and the problems that it may cause.

On the other hand, 'wants' may well be desires for things or experiences which are not strictly 'needed' in the interests of society. Tibor Scitovsky's distinction (1976, pp. 106–31) between necessities and luxuries was made from an economist's viewpoint. Scitovsky drew a parallel between the difference between necessities and luxuries and the psychologist's distinction between biological needs and all others. It should be noted also that definitions of needs and wants have been modified throughout history. A socially acceptable standard of living in the 1990s is unlikely to conform to a definition of the same thing made in 1890, and will almost certainly differ from a definition to be made in 2090. Moreover, perceptions of social need will vary from culture to culture, as many international charity appeals illustrate all too clearly with comparisons between standards of living in Western countries and those in the Third World. As societies develop, people's levels of need move up the Maslow hierarchy (*see* Chapter 3).

Unfortunately, the task of drawing distinctions between needs and wants – however logical they may appear to be – is made more difficult by two important factors:

1 *Needs and wants are likely to mean different things to different people.* Although democratic societies try to ensure that there is some political consensus regarding the definitions of social needs, and the minimum levels of public sector provision required to meet them, social realities will always ensure that there are some individuals and groups within these societies whose definitions of needs and wants are different. For example, minority groups such as Romanies and travellers may well have lifestyle expectations which do not conform to the norms of 'society'.

2 *The State may be seen as imposing a value system on its members.* If 'standard' definitions of need are adopted, the State runs the risk of taking away some of the individual's responsibility for him- or herself. The State may be perceived as imposing its own interpretation of need upon the individual.

It is safer to conclude that the distinction between needs and wants usually needs to be examined carefully in the context of each specific example and case.

This then raises the issue of *who* decides distinctions between essentials and non-essentials. On a practical level, decisions are made by the State, using social, political and economic considerations. Marjorie Reeves (1988) has highlighted the way in which the State usually holds that the wants of the individual should be moulded into conformity with the needs of the community by a process of socialisation. For example, higher education should serve both the needs of the country – by providing it with skilled and useful personnel – at the same time as it meets the wants of the individual – by providing an opportunity for self-fulfilment. In practice, there is often some tension between these needs and wants.

Services and rights

Many services provided by the public sector are commonly perceived as social rights – just and fair treatment by the State. Claims on state provision are made on the grounds of legal entitlement. In many ways the Welfare State was set up precisely to provide a more egalitarian social order by ensuring minimum levels of entitlement and provision for those in need (*see*, for example, Kathleen Jones' analysis of the Welfare State (1991, pp. 134–48). The services which contribute to social welfare exist to facilitate a humanitarian and political ideal of equality and equal opportunities. Just as consumer rights are intended for the good of those who possess them, social justice seeks to help people obtain the services and benefits to which they have rights.

The idea that all members of society possess the same basic rights suggests that the principle of equality is all important (Downie, 1980). The satisfaction of one individual's needs should be as important as any other's. However, situations can arise when there is some tension between the State's desire to make equal provision for all those in need and the individual's desire for self-determination and responsibility. For example, there is a difference between ensuring that the individual has the right to what society defines as a minimum level of social security, and imposing that definition upon the individual, possibly even against his or her will. It has sometimes been argued that welfare legislation has effectively removed the individual's responsibility for his or her own health, future retirement etc. In the ideal welfare state that seeks to satisfy a minimum level of need for all its members, the individual's ability to choose may even be restricted to 'non-essentials' – to *wants* rather than *needs*.

If most public sector services are understood as 'rights', it is only too easy to see them as services which *must* be provided, rather than as services which *can* or *may be* provided. As a result, the provider may easily be understood as 'reluctant' (*see* Chapter 2) because the provider is *obliged* to make the service available. In fact, both the provider and the user are restricted in their freedom of action. The provider is restricted by the nature and extent of the resources available and by the obligations, both social and legal, to provide the service. The user is restricted by the lack of alternative provision to satisfy his or her needs.

In order to address the problems generated by this approach to public sector markets, we need to explore the meaning of 'value'.

Values and costs

The concept of value is central to any understanding of people's attitudes towards products and services. Value is defined as the *worth* or *cost* of something – that is, the amount of something considered equivalent to something else. Value is, therefore, an attribute given to something by people. Value is not an intrinsic property of any object, product, service or experience. It is a property conferred on, or given to, that object, product, service or experience by people, markets or society.

Moreover, values change. Before the Second World War, the price of chickens in the shops was relatively high in the UK. Unless you lived on a farm, or kept hens,

MINICASE 4.1

Reconciling individual wants and community interests in the education system

Education is frequently represented as a remedy for most social and economic problems. Education represents investment in the future. A well educated and suitably trained workforce will, it is argued, provide the skills and know-how the country needs for future prosperity. The education 'industry' is, after all, one of the largest public sector services.

On completion of compulsory education, school leavers are faced with a confusing range of choices. Further and higher education do their best to attract them as students. A *Times Higher Education Supplement* 'Synthesis' report (18 March 1994) contained the results of a survey of 1000 16-year-olds, designed to find out how young people decided what to do next. The survey found that the majority of 16-year-olds (83 per cent) planned to stay in education or training, and nearly a third wanted to take a first degree. There was a strong belief that the qualification gained was more important than the place of study. Further education was generally seen as being focused on vocational qualifications, usually held in lower esteem than academic ones. The most important factors influencing the choice of courses were academic standards, relevance to future employment, the presence of well qualified teaching staff, a wide choice of subjects and the chance to extend academic knowledge.

In the present environment, institutions of further and higher education must compete for students. Failure to recruit to targets inevitably means budget cuts for some. Funding follows students. Marketing becomes more of a necessity as a result. In the same issue of the *Times Higher*, Jeanne Coburn made the point that colleges need to understand that their marketing must be consumer-led in just the same way as marketing for commercial or industrial organisations. Needs and consumer research need to be turned into practical curriculum development.

This can only be achieved, however, with the genuine commitment of senior managers and the willing involvement of academic staff. This is often easier said than done, although there are signs that this lesson is being learned. It is sadly true, however, that old attitudes die hard. Too often, students are still seen as the products of the system, rather than as its customers. The university system, with its crude attempt to use, for example, research as the major performance indicator, appears to have been guilty of undervaluing the importance of its primary market – the students themselves. Student wants and community/social needs also have to be reconciled. The argument between those who see post-school education as self-actualisation and those who see it as vocational preparation may well be a false one. It should be possible to achieve and reconcile both ambitions. Lord Bullock (*The Guardian*, 26 July 1994) has argued that we have allowed the idea of education for its own sake to become too powerful.

chicken was once something to be eaten rarely, on special occasions. As a meat, it was not eaten so often as it is now, simply because it was relatively expensive. Production methods were not then supplying the quantity which modern chicken farming methods make possible. Beef and mutton were regarded as staple meats. By 1996 beef was sometimes regarded with suspicion by the market, due to worries about the association between Bovine Spongiform Encephalopathy (BSE) in cattle and Creutzfeldt-Jacob Disease (CJD) in humans. Beef's younger form, veal, had also encountered some market opposition thanks to the objections to crate rearing and public objections to live calf export. Mutton has now effectively been replaced by its younger form, lamb, which the consumer market generally considers superior. Today, chicken is one of the most plentiful and cheapest meats available. As a white meat, it is also frequently considered more 'healthy' than red meats, such as lamb and beef.

Most modern societies express 'worth' or cost in terms of *monetary value* – that is, how much money a product or an experience or a service is worth. Money is easy to quantify. It is the most common, standardised form of expressing worth. However, value is not something which can only be measured by money or financial price (economic value is covered in greater detail in Chapter 8). Something may have a cost in terms of *effort and energy, time* or *emotions*. 'Was it worth the effort?' is a common question. 'How much time is it going to cost me?' is another. In both these questions, benefit is being compared with, or measured against, a scale of value which is not a financial one.

The understanding of such values will vary from person to person, just as ideas of need will vary. One person may consider satellite television a priority need; another will be far more likely to prioritise healthy food. Since exchange is the basis of a transaction (*see*, for example, Kotler, 1991, p. 4) and is a key concept in marketing, it follows that concepts of value are central to any understanding of worth or cost, and therefore to the evaluation of any real or potential exchange process.

Another aspect of value is *added value*. 'Value added' is a term familiar through its use as a category of tax in many countries, usually in the form of a revenue raising surcharge imposed on certain categories of products. However, the term 'added value' is important from a marketing perspective.

In the commercial sector, value added is an element of worth which increases the perceived value of a product, at a cost consistent with customer satisfaction – for example, by converting raw materials into completed products, processing products in some way, or by making them more easily and conveniently available to the customer (Wilmshurst, 1991, p. 8). (The management of value added is increasingly seen as a key issue in marketing and the topic will be pursued further in Chapter 8, related to the issue of pricing.)

The concept of value added is as relevant to services as it is to products. Value added is not just related to the 'tangible' dimensions of a service. In service marketing, value added is usually related to the helpfulness and attitudes of those providing the service. Mark Franchetti, reporting from Berlin for *The Sunday Times* (7 April 1996), noted that a German psychologist had spent twelve months teaching public transport workers in Berlin to smile. The act of smiling while providing a service may be interpreted as *psychological* value added. Value added, as expressed by public transport drivers' and conductors' friendliness, enhances the customers' perception of a service, and hence their valuation of that service. The Berlin initiative was part of an attempt to prepare public transport services to face competition from the private sector by improving market perceptions of the service. Politeness and friendliness can certainly provide a psychological added value for a service.

Tangibles and intangibles

The concepts of 'product' and 'service' are not as easily separated as we might think. The word 'product' is sometimes used as a generic term to refer to any goods or services which are exchanged in the marketing process. Increasingly, many organisations which are offering services define their output as a product. However, we usually find that people associate *products* with goods, with tangible items, things which are physical and 'real', and *services* with the activities and attitudes of those who provide them. In the area of services, however, some problems of definition remain (*see* Table 4.1).

A conventional distinction is too often made between *tangible products* – items which have a physical identity – and *intangible services* – which most often depend upon the activities of the people who provide them.

Although, in Table 4.1, the distinction between 'people', and 'things' may appear relatively straightforward, distinctions between 'tangible' and 'intangible' are not always so easy to make. Table 4.1 could also be interpreted as defining *where* services are carried out *on* people or things. For example, surgery involves quite a lot of human body 'plumbing' and 'engineering' activities, which use, and operate on, tangible things. At the same time, successful surgery may provide 'intangible' benefits to the patient's self-confidence. House maintenance involves builders and technicians, whose performance and attitudes are as likely to affect the householder's perception of benefits (intangible) as do the standards of workmanship and satisfactory quality of the physical repairs (tangible). Repairs to a building may also be making 'intangible' repairs to the tenant's peace of mind.

It is therefore appropriate to consider the difficulties arising when we try to apply the table to situations where services are being offered to people – for example, the hire of tangible goods, vehicles, surgical aids, housing and so forth – as well as situations where facilities are being marketed – for example, leisure premises, libraries, etc. In these examples, the customer is not purchasing ownership, but there is a significant level of tangibility involved.

Attempts to make a mutually exclusive distinction between goods and services are not altogether useful. Shams and Hales (1989) attack the ways in which this approach tends to be misleading. They point out that commodities have to be pre-

Table 4.1 Examples of the provision of services

	Services to people	*Services to things*
Tangible	Surgery Transport Physiotherapy Hairdressing	House maintenance Electricity and gas Transport Road repairs Water installations
Intangible	Education Citizen's Advice Psychotherapy	Ministry of Transport vehicle testing Building Regulations approval

sented in some form that can be experienced. The presentation of the commodities usually involves an element of service. In this way, both services and products involve both tangible and intangible aspects. Restaurants are conventionally classified as services. A diner in a restaurant may order a meal, for example, roast lamb with garlic, wine and rosemary sauce, peas and potatoes. The cooked food on the plate is a tangible product, but the diner is purchasing not only the ingredients of the dish, but also the value-added services that transform them into a meal, serve them at the table, provide the atmosphere of the restaurant and include, perhaps, its relentless piped music and the too frequent enquiries as to whether everything is all right, sir/madam. The restaurant critic will probably include value for money in his or her list of criteria for evaluating the worth of the meal, but is also likely to award points for ambience, quality of service, quality of cooking, presentation of food, etc. Many of these considerations will relate to both the tangible and the intangible aspects of the experience of eating out in the restaurant. Moreover, the customer is part of the process.

Customers and measures of output

Another important issue in the provision of services to people is that because many services are seen as 'performed on the individual', the individual becomes part of the process and can be considered as *a measure of output*, rather than as the primary customer whose needs are being satisfied. For example, British Rail may claim to have moved 1 billion tonnes of coal and London Transport to have carried 1 billion passengers.

To try to change attitudes, organisations now tend to use the generic term 'customer', rather than specific titles such as 'patient' which identify customers as people with specific needs in a particular context. However, patients have specific needs from the health service which are different from those travellers have as passengers, that is as the customers of transport organisations.

So-called 'customer orientation' can also be affected adversely by the development of service organisations into a series of internal markets. The privatisation of the UK railway system may be cited as an example. Each individual process is now often seen as a distinct 'product', leading to the development of a fragmented rather than a holistic approach to delivery. In these circumstances, each part of the delivery system will see the next stage in the process as its primary customer. This can obscure the importance of the real primary customer – the end-user. In fact this so-called 'customer-focused' approach often results in the passenger being seen as part of the process rather than as the customer proper. Organisations providing similar benefits will become competitive, rather than complementary.

In practice, these circumstances arise where the providers are very product or production oriented and fail to understand the real reasons customers use their products and services. In the late 1990s, behaviour-led market forces were still seeking to bring together the various elements of the railway system to recover an integrated whole. There was also serious criticism of some organisations, such as the Health Service, where internal markets were seen as detrimental to the end-user's, the patient's, interests.

MINICASE 4.2

Introduction customer orientation

According to the *Businessman's Encyclopaedia* (1996), in the 1990s, as in the 1980s, recognition has grown that the customer, not the supplier, is the centre of the economic universe. More enlightened 1990s' companies recognise that *customer orientation* requires an understanding of customer behaviour which makes a key contribution to the design of innovative marketing plans and strategies. As a result, customer satisfaction becomes an important measure of quality performance.

There have been some singular successes where customer orientation within a coherent marketing strategy has dramatically improved company performance: British Airways, Marks and Spencer, Cadbury and Rentokil are just a few notable examples, and there are many other unsung heroes.

Unfortunately, one result of this has been the development of 'customer orientation' as a current management fashion. As with many fashions, the term can be used without adequate consideration of customer identity. The real needs of the actual customers are sometimes not identified and met.

In the dash for privatisation, the railway companies became 'customer oriented'. This found expression in the way in which all those who used the railways were addressed as 'customers'. Announcements took the form of, for example, 'we apologise to customers for the late arrival of their train.' Interestingly, calling passengers customers caused some real resentment. There was considerable comment from the media and the travelling public alike. A hundred years before, railway customers were referred to as passengers – that is, customers with particular needs which are met by the benefit derived from using transport. All passengers are customers, but not all customers are passengers. As it happens, British Airways continues to call its non-freight customers 'passengers' and organises its activities to provide maximum passenger satisfaction.

So-called 'customer orientation' can also lead to the wrong group being identified as the primary customer, particularly in complex markets. A recent profile of a head teacher said that she 'called the parents customers'. Implicit in the identification of parents as primary customers is the view that the pupils are not customers, but are merely the raw material for processing – a process measured by school league tables. Parents facilitate, and in some cases pay, for the education of the child, but the levels of satisfaction of the real primary customer – that is, the pupil – will also be measured by many other indicators such as truancy levels. All pupils are customers, but not all customers are pupils.

In the context of the National Health Service's internal markets, many writers propose that the customers are the purchasers – that is, the people who fund and resource the process, for example, the fundholding general practitioners – rather than the patients. Consequently, the customer is perceived as the payer and the patient as the consumer, or part of the process. This can lead to real patient dissatisfaction. In the public sector, similar situations prevail in most organisations, particularly in those where the service is free at the point of delivery.

In reality, the widespread use of the generic term 'customer' is not indicative of customer or indeed marketing orientation. What it does demonstrate is an unthinking application of a current management fad which actually reduces customer satisfaction, and can lead to the birth of organisations such as the 'Campaign for Real Service'.

The real success of customer orientation is demonstrated in those companies which distinguish and differentiate their customer groups and, where appropriate, identify that customer group with a name which encapsulates its specific needs. My core needs as a passenger, as a patient, as a student and as a hotel guest are all different. Don't diminish my needs by just saying that I am a customer.

We may conclude, therefore, that the benefit of any product or service will include a mixture of both tangible and intangible elements. The triangular-shaped model used in Figs 4.1 and 4.2 suggests that any analysis of user benefit always contains both elements. Figure 4.2. illustrates a further point: perceptions of tangible and intangible benefits are unlikely to be evenly distributed. Intangible benefits may well prove much more important than the tangible ones, especially in the case of services.

CAR OWNERSHIP

Benefit
Physical and psychological benefits of the core product or service
The drive for purchase in the first place

Personal transport
Convenience
Flexible, door-to-door mobility

Tangible factors in the transaction		**Psychological factors in the transaction** ('the halo effect')
Engineering quality		Brand image
Physical comfort		Reputation
Shape, form, colour		Supplier's attitude
Engine size		After-sales service
Warranty		

Fig. 4.1 Relative benefits of car ownership

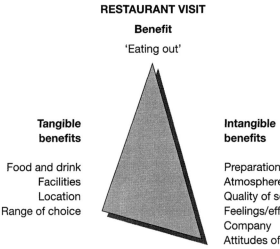

RESTAURANT VISIT

Benefit

'Eating out'

Tangible benefits		**Intangible benefits**
Food and drink		Preparation by others
Facilities		Atmosphere
Location		Quality of service
Range of choice		Feelings/effect
		Company
		Attitudes of staff

Fig. 4.2 Relative benefits of eating in a restaurant

Table 4.2 Perceptions of importance relating to rail travel

Perceptions of importance relating to the benefit of the service

Punctuality	88%
Journey time	83%

Perceptions of importance relating to the tangible quality of the transport

Cleanliness of vehicle interiors	87%
Ease of finding a seat	86%
Seat comfort	84%
Catering facilities	69%

Perceptions of importance relating to the experience of the transaction

Helpfulness of staff	81%
Ease of purchasing a ticket	79%
Station facilities	64%

Source: Chartered Institute of Marketing

How the individual perceives the relative importance of these factors can be indicated by a summary of market research produced for regional railway services (*see* Table 4.2).

The product life cycle

We have already noted in this chapter that people's concepts and perceptions of wants and need change over time; this means that people's attitudes towards benefits also change. In commercial marketing, it has long been realised that this factor influences the ways in which new products are adopted.

The *product life cycle* (PLC) is one of the core concepts of marketing. It takes the idea of the biological life cycle – birth, growth, life, decay and death – and applies it to the inanimate world of consumer products. As with live organisms, different products have different life cycles. However, while each product can have a finite life cycle, the 'core' benefit sought from the product may have an infinite life. There may be a constant demand for *some* product to meet a specific need or want.

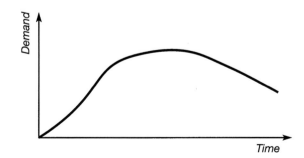

Fig. 4.3 A product life cycle

The product life cycle can be described as having five stages: development, growth, maturity, saturation and decline. The curve illustrated in Fig. 4.3 represents levels of demand for a product plotted against time.

Oliver (1990) refers to some of the ways in which ideas about life cycles have changed. In the 1960s, most studies were concerned with life cycles in general. In the 1970s and 1980s they were concerned more with product class and brand. In the 1990s they have evolved into separate, more specialised areas of study. These may broadly be categorised under the following headings:

- industry life cycles
- product class life cycles
- product form life cycles
- brand life cycles.

For the marketer in the public sector, these classifications may seem, at first, to have little relevance. Many public sector industries are mainly concerned with the provision of services, not products. Most, as non-profit organisations, do not have a commercial focus. Public sector 'products' usually satisfy needs, not wants, and most public sector industry life cycles are very long. However, an example – housing – can be used to suggest that these life cycle categories can indeed be relevant to the public sector.

The requirement for housing in the UK is continually growing, even with a relatively stable population. In the mid-1990s, there was a 'dip' in demand, caused by economic environmental factors, but the underlying demand patterns continued. The environmental factors affecting the underlying demand include demographic changes, changing lifestyles, the increasing number of single families, the divorce rate. These factors have influenced *the industry life cycle*, which can appropriately be described as revealing 'slow growth'.

The overall pattern can be analysed in more detail by considering a number of distinct areas or categories of housing within the industry.

- *Product class life cycles*. These distinguish between private sector and public sector provision;
- *Product form life cycles*. These distinguish different types of housing – for example, bungalows, flats and apartments, semi-detached houses, detached houses.
- *Product brand life cycles*. These distinguish different kinds of demand, which are usually satisfied by different kinds of suppliers – for example housing associations, local authorities, the Ministry of Defence, and private sector house-building companies. The concept of 'brand' for housing will also involve psychological associations: for example, location often carries associations of social status.

Using these classifications with the appropriate data, life cycle curves for differing kinds of housing can be constructed. The concept can also be related to the demand curves of different buyer groups (*see* Chapter 5). The underlying life cycle for housing is created by the core benefit of housing – that is, shelter, security, etc. However, the product form life cycle – for example, relating to house size and type – will be determined by the buyers' (or renters') demographic and psychographic characteristics.

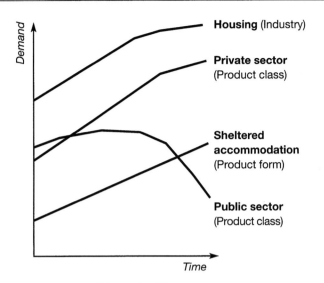

Fig. 4.4 Some categories of life cycles/demand curves

Factors affecting the product life cycle

Related to the concept of the product life cycle is that of 'diffusion of innovation'. For example, if a new product or service is introduced to the market, then its success will be determined by the people who buy or use the product – referred to as the *adopters*. Everett Rogers' (1962) classic analysis of the process of product adoption represented it as a distribution curve, in which five categories of adopters progressively came to use the product over time:

'Innovators'	2.5%
'Early adopters'	13.5%
'Early majority'	34.0%
'Late majority'	34.0%
'Laggards'	16.0%

The scale and pace of adoption is inevitably influenced by the users' perceptions of that product, which effectively means their perceptions of the product's *benefits*. The product, as Kotler (1991, p. 348) has pointed out, only exists as one solution to a need or a want. It is necessary, therefore, to understand how the product life cycle is determined by perceptions of benefit.

These perceptions inevitably change over time, as people's needs and wants change. The environment is constantly changing. The concept of 'progress' has been particularly important to the last three centuries. Leslie Sklair (1970) defined progress as 'the result of any action leading towards a more satisfactory solution to people's problems in society'. Innovation progress produces new things, ideas and processes which have a maximum impact on society. Sklair also made the point that progress is also a *moral* concept, because the decision whether something represents progress or not is effectively a *moral judgement*. The idea of progress is often linked to that of amelioration – becoming better and improving the human condition.

Wimshurst (1991, pp. 36–8) lists a number of factors which influence changes in customer needs. Broadly, these can be categorised under the following headings:

- *Economic* – changes in levels of income and related expectations
- *Cultural* – increasing levels of education and sophistication
- *Social* – changes in social habits, fashions and customs
- *Technological* – ever increasing technological development
- *Business* – the effects of increasing business competition.

These considerations are just as relevant to the nature and marketing of public sector services as they are to commercial products. For example, perceptions of such services are inevitably influenced by changes in social expectations and in technology.

Social expectations

Perceptions of benefit vary and change considerably. For example, in the public sector housing market, the very standards by which such housing has been built and equipped have been revised extensively since the 1940s. Priorities have progressively included central heating, energy insulation and community facilities. However, perceptions of local council housing provision can also be affected by considerations of personal image and associated social status. In a country where home ownership is significantly higher than in many other countries, and a house is often perceived as an important form of personal investment, the necessity to use 'public' housing may even be associated with admissions of economic or social failure.

Technological substitution

As the pace of technological change continues, so perceptions of needs and wants change. Furthermore, technological substitution can provide the same benefit in an enhanced form – for example, by reducing drudgery and adding convenience. Nevertheless, the growth of technology will be determined by the willingness of users to use it and by how well it satisfies their needs, not by the cleverness of suppliers in supplying it. Technological substitution continues apace and the development of transportation methods provides a good example of how things change (*see* Table 4.3).

The interesting point about substitution is that the older technology often becomes a leisure pursuit for subsequent users. In rail transport, for example, steam has been superseded by diesel, and by electrically propelled engines. Steam

Table 4.3 The development of transportation methods

Legs	Walking, carrying
Horses	Faster, easier, more powerful
Wheeled carriages	More comfort, greater protection, more capacity
Canals	Smoother, greater capacity for goods
Railways	Faster, large capacity, good reliability
Cars	Convenient, door-to-door personal transport

is now a leisure pursuit or interest. Canals and horses are also mostly used for leisure purposes.

Historically, many organisations have failed to recognise where and when technological substitution is overtaking existing products and services – the same benefit is being offered in completely different ways, described by Kotler as 'beneficial competition'. The competition for the product or service will not be something similar – as in product form competition.

An example of this technological substitution is the development of mail services. In the mid-1970s telex was advertised as having the speed of the telephone and the accuracy of the written word. In 1975, telex was already being used, in a limited form, by early adopters. By the mid-1990s, the telex had been superseded by the facsimile (fax) and electronic mail systems. These will be used increasingly at home and the whole mail network will take a declining share of the market.

New technologies often increase market size. For example, the relatively slow decline of passenger rail services over time (measured in passenger miles) hides the fact that its share of the market has declined substantially, because the demand for transport in general has grown very quickly.

Technological substitution can appear in the most obscure areas. For example, the use of sink-installed waste disposal units will impact upon the need for refuse collection.

The marketing of services

We have emphasised that most, although not all, public sector 'products' are understood as services. Levitt (1986), Shostack (1984) and others have made the point that, although the principles of marketing goods (products) and services may be the same, their application may differ profoundly. The history of marketing literature has been dominated by a product orientation. However, as Shostack has shown (1984, p. 41), it is possible to represent all market entities along a continuum, ranging from 'tangible dominant' at one extreme to 'intangible dominant' at the other. Levitt himself, one of the best-known writers on marketing, preferred to talk of 'tangibles' and 'intangibles' rather than of goods and services. A more developed model of the concept, as represented in Fig. 4.5, uses three axes.

The apparent shape of any product or service plotted using this model will reveal the extent to which it is dependent on tangible and intangible components. Perceptions of all these components can be identified and even scaled, using the results of consumer research (*see* Chapter 10).

In service marketing, benefit is defined mainly in terms of intangibles. Cowell (1984) listed five ways in which services may be distinguished from tangible goods.

1 The intangibility of services

It is usually impossible to experience a service before it is actually bought. Strictly speaking, a service is not a physical, material article. Something tangible may be given to represent the service – for example, an appointment card, a prescription or a certificate – but the service to which is related remains intangible. Thus a medical prescription may be the tangible result of a consultation with a doctor, but the con-

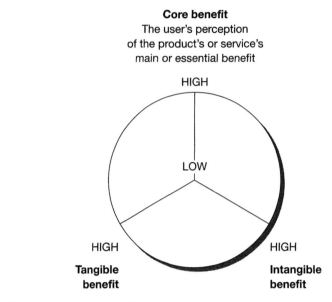

Core benefit
The user's perception
of the product's or service's
main or essential benefit

HIGH

LOW

HIGH

HIGH

**Tangible
benefit**

**Intangible
benefit**

Fig. 4.5 The value component model

sultation itself normally takes the form of diagnosis and advice. In such a case the real benefit or worth of the service remains intangible. The benefit may be measured and even priced on the basis of doctor's time, but its value may also be expressed in terms of emotional relief, removal of uncertainty, etc.

2 The inseparability of the service from its delivery

It is rarely possible to separate the service provided from the person or people who are providing it. The delivery of the service takes place through the agency of an individual or individuals. A doctor's 'bedside manner' or level of interpersonal skills was once thought almost incidental to the provision of health care. It is now more commonly recognised as a necessary and integral part of medical training. A patient is unlikely to separate a doctor's manner from the general experience of a consultation. This leads on to the next point.

3 Heterogeneity, or lack of uniformity

It is virtually impossible to achieve a standardised level of service provision. As each individual is different, so each provider of a (that is, the same) service is different. The quality of the service is usually measured as a degree of customer/user satisfaction with that service. However, just as individuals will differ in their personal manners and delivery, so different customers/users will inevitably have differing levels of expectation and satisfaction. Despite attempts at standardising service provision – as exemplified by Mcdonald's fast food restaurant staff training in customer relations (some UK customers rapidly became disillusioned with the standard exhortations to 'enjoy your meal') – it is difficult, if not impossible, to standardise most service provisions involving people, even if a computer screen that attempts to mimic a human quality by introducing itself with a banal 'hello' can be safely ignored.

4 Perishability

A service cannot readily be stored 'on the shelf' in the same way as some goods can. For example, Berry (1984) highlighted one crucial difference between goods marketing and service marketing when he discussed the difficulties of synchronising supply and demand in service provision: it is usually more difficult, if not impossible, for a service to meet peaks of demand by taking more goods 'off the shelf'. Although there are examples of services being kept in readiness to answer emergencies (for example, the sailing Colin Archer lifeboats which were kept on station at sea off Norway at the end of the nineteenth century), such provision is made usually only if there is a cultural demand for it or a proven cost-effectiveness. This is quite rare. The effective provision of some services – for example, medical accident and emergency services – properly requires spare capacity as well as effective human resource management to meet unforeseeable fluctuations in demand. Recent drives for efficiency within the UK National Health Service have reduced spare capacity in the interests of controlling costs, but in such situations there will remain some doubt about the ability of a service to respond effectively, if a major emergency arises.

5 Ownership

The idea of ownership is much more difficult to apply to a service than to a product. If service is inseparable from the people that provide it, it might seem more logical to talk of 'hiring' rather than 'owning' a service. The user of a service is unlikely to 'own' that service in the same sense that the direct purchaser of a product feels that he or she has paid for it, and therefore 'owns' it. Ownership makes a product the *property* of the owner. It is morally and socially unacceptable to own a person in the same way. Users of a service, therefore, cannot claim ownership.

However, they may claim the right to a certain quality of service as part of the expected benefit of a transaction. This is one of the reasons that value-added elements are so important in services marketing. Even a 'free' public service provision, such as a museum which does not charge for entrance, may encourage certain expectations in the user because 'I've paid for this out of my taxes'. The user expects a certain level of provision because a certain percentage of national or local taxation has been used to provide this public service. This situation is changing, for example, as shareholding in privatised public services increases, but services can never be treated as possessions in the same way as products. However, there are also some public services which involve no direct exchange transaction between the users and the providers, and the users of a public service such as housing benefit may well expect good service as a social *right*.

For these reasons, a growing body of marketing literature has been spelling out the message that services marketing has its own distinct characteristics and problems. Moreover, different service industries have their own, 'industry-specific' issues.

Managing the demand for public sector services

In Chapter 2, we discussed some of the problems experienced when reconciling supply with demand in the provision of services, especially in the public sector which is usually constrained by limited funding and demands for efficiency.

Simply because the public sector is largely budget-driven, and cannot use inventories of stored goods to provide some flexible response to fluctuations in demand (it is, after all, largely concerned with the provision of services, not goods), most of its organisations seek to manage *both* capacity and demand.

Many factors will continue to interact to produce continual changes in demand. Demographic changes, technological developments and changes in social expectations all contribute to this process, and are among the reasons why market intelligence is as important to the public sector as it is to the private sector. These changes will affect users' perceptions of needs and wants and, since the beginning of the 1980s, there has been an obvious shift in power from the providers of public services to the users of them.

Public sector provision is constrained by the amount of material and human resources available. This is usually dictated by the level of public funding allocated. Unlike private, commercial organisations, most public ones can rarely generate more income or revenue by increasing their levels of activity, although this can be achieved by some. Some public sector services are also constrained by the fact that their relationship with their customers may be one of control or dependency. The organisation's ability to meet the demand for its services depends upon its ability to manage capacity by tailoring it to meet variations in demand. 'Performance management' is a term often used to describe the process of improving services to achieve a more efficient match between supply and demand in the interests of value for money (Rouse, 1993). Managing resources, scheduling staff, finding alternative uses for plant at appropriate times, are all familiar techniques. However, a marketing strategy needs to understand demand and the variables that affect it. Since any service organisation, at any one time, is likely to have a fixed capacity and a fluctuating nature and level of demand, such organisations need to have a number of strategies available.

Lovelock (1984) suggests a number of ways in which capacity can be related to demand. Broadly speaking, an organisation is likely to find itself in one of three situations:

- It may not have enough capacity to meet the demand for its products or services.
- Its capacity may match demand.
- It may have more capacity than it has demand.

Each of these situations requires a strategic answer, and managers have a number of strategic alternatives.

1 It is always possible simply to take no action but, unless capacity already matches demand, this is unlikely to improve matters.

2 Demand can often be increased, but many public sector industries constrained by allocated funding may be unable to do so, and are more likely to favour a reduction in capacity in order to save costs (*see* Chapter 8 for a more detailed discussion of the implications which may be involved).

3 Demand may be reduced – for example, by promotional and educational campaigns, or even by legislation such as hosepipe bans in times of water shortages.

4 Demand may be controlled by prioritisation methods: queueing or rationing.

Pricing (*see* Chapter 8) can also be used to respond to and control situations of excess demand. Pricing can work as a means of rationing supply, but only in cases where financial exchange is involved in the provision of the service. In situations where no such transactions take place, as in many public sector services, it can be argued that rationing systems are the most logical and obvious ways of controlling demand.

In the public sector, we have already noted that there are difficulties in making inventories of services (although this is obviously done in terms of resources, for example, when there is a need to allocate patients to the clinic of a hospital consultant, or to operating theatre capacity and funding). Sasser (1984) pointed out that whereas goods can be stored after being bought, services are usually consumed at once. As a result, there are only a limited number of strategies available to those managing services. It may be possible to vary staffing levels to accommodate varying volumes of demand. However, responding to demand in this way may prove extremely difficult unless the organisation has a high staff turnover, or is normally working in a field where demand itself is normally variable – for example, in the emergency services. Alternatively, it may be economically possible to maintain a high enough level of capacity to meet all fluctuations in demand. Unfortunately, drives to reduce costs, especially in public service industries, can make the second alternative appear very unattractive.

As a result, Sasser (1984) believes that the *'chase demand'* alternative is most commonly used by service organisations which tend to employ fairly low-skilled workers who have little individual discretion in the ways in which they work and are relatively poorly paid. Organisations with workers who are highly skilled and paid, and who have more discretion, are more likely to maintain a high level of capacity. It can also be argued that in reality such organisations may prove less costly than those 'chasing' demand, because the latter incur more staff training costs, have higher error rates, and therefore need more staffing to control and maintain quality.

In addition to these basic strategies, the manager of a service can also seek to control the demand itself. This might involve the use of differential pricing, the development of off-peak demand, complementary services and reservation systems. It should be noted that most of these techniques (for example, the way in which reservation systems have been used successfully in doctors' surgeries) are applicable to both commercial and public services.

Social marketing

At this point, it is appropriate to consider the fact that the principles of 'community interest' and social responsibility can sometimes involve an active control of demand, even the suppression of demand. Kotler and Roberto (1989) pointed out that countries throughout the world are trying to solve social problems by changing the ways people live their lives. People need to be persuaded that such changes really benefit them. This is the aim of *social marketing*. In many ways, it is the antithesis of conventional marketing in that it assumes that, in certain situations, the suppression of needs is a social good. For example, public campaigns directed at encouraging people to give up smoking or to avoid drug abuse fall into this category. The State assumes, usually as a result of a political consensus, that community interests take precedence over those of the individual. It is argued, for example, that the individual will benefit by improved health, and the State will save on the cost of medical care.

However, smokers, for example, continue to argue that bad publicity, increasing taxes on tobacco and restrictions on the places where people may smoke all erode the freedom of the individual to choose his/her own lifestyle, although it may be considered acceptable to legislate against some practices on perfectly reasonable grounds. A ban on smoking in underground transport systems is perfectly comprehensible in view of the fire hazards involved. However, most democratic governments will prefer to use persuasion, rather than legislation, to market the other advantages of giving up a habit which can have so many serious health consequences for the addict.

Implications for marketing in the public sector

There are some fundamental distinctions to be made between marketing in the public sector and marketing in the private sector.

1 The aims of most commercial organisations can be expressed in quantitative, financial terms. One obvious criterion of success is profit. The public sector involves many more qualitative aims and objectives. It is much more difficult to use economic criteria as the main measurements of performance. Performance criteria tend to be complex in their nature and interrelationships. Cost–benefit analysis is less precise and objective as a result. Lamb (1987) holds that public agencies, in seeking value-for-money performance criteria, typically use *effectiveness* (success in meeting goals), *efficiency* (ratio of inputs to outputs) and *equity* (fairness). Rouse (1993) also lists another 'e' – *economy* (the purchasing of resources and inputs at the lowest possible price) – and notes that *excellence* and *enterprise* have also been suggested as criteria. Most of these are more difficult to define and measure than financial profit and loss or income and expenditure accounting. Public sector organisations need a broader definition of accountability, and a wider range of performance indicators.

2 Whereas the marketing of goods often needs to emphasise the benefits of the 'extended product', stressing the value of the 'intangibles' associated with it, service marketing often feels the need to represent the service by some 'tangible' with which the service is associated. Nowhere is this more obvious than in advertising and promotion campaigns.

3 Public sector organisations have less autonomy and flexibility than private ones simply because of the complexity of their markets.

The public sector has a diverse range of services and objectives, both social and economic. Since 1980, there has been a major change of emphasis away from the traditional preoccupations with policy making and planning, towards the operational concerns of management, distribution and marketing. Users have been given much more power in their relationships with providers. As a result, perceptions of public services have assumed a new importance. After all, it is users' rights, needs and wants which largely define the demands of the public sector market.

In the past, public services have been largely provided by monopoly markets where demand has often exceeded the organisations' ability to supply services. 'Demarketing', allocation and rationing techniques have often prevailed as a result. Many public sector organisations still have dual roles as both providers and controllers. There is, therefore, something of a marketing conflict of interests in many public sector organisations. On the one hand, it can be argued that if public sector organisations are going to respond more effectively to the needs of members of society, they must market their services for the benefit of their users, taking advantage of the marketing concept and applying it to strategy. On the other hand, public sector organisations have a duty to provide the State with value for money. Many are also responsible for rationing their services, and even 'policing' their provision in order to prevent fraud and abuse.

The increasing level of privatisation of public sector organisations attempts to use competition as an incentive to increase efficiency and thereby give better value for money. As a result, however, there is a risk of creating apparent conflicts of interest between the wants of shareholders and the wants and needs of users. Any audit of product or service benefit to an organisation's customers or users should include as comprehensive an analysis as possible of the product's or service's value and benefits, both tangible and intangible. Only then can the manager assess the nature of the markets.

Summary

The concept of 'demand' in the public sector is complicated. Providers are restricted by both funding limitations and legal obligations. Users are restricted in their relative freedom of choice.

1 **Needs and wants.** It is not always easy to make distinctions between needs and wants. Moreover, needs and wants are likely to mean different things to different people, and they are also subject to changing perceptions.

2 **Services and rights.** Many public sector services are provided and understood as social rights. Public sector provision usually, but not exclusively, caters for basic needs.

3 **Values and costs.** A product or service has not only a monetary value and cost, but also a value in terms of emotions, time, effort, etc.

4 **Tangibles and intangibles.** Perceptions of value and benefit can be modelled using 'core benefit', 'tangible benefit' and 'intangible benefit' components.

5 **Customers and measures of output.** The adoption of a customer orientation can have serious consequences, if not applied with care.

6 **The product life cycle.** People's attitudes to benefits change over time. The product life cycle (PLC) uses a biological metaphor to describe histories of demand.

7 **The marketing of services.** Cowell (1984) identified services as intangible, difficult to separate from their mode of delivery, lacking in total uniformity, perishable, and difficult to 'own'. Services marketing has its own characteristics and problems.

8 **Managing the demand for public sector services.** There are also obvious problems in matching supply with demand in the public sector. Services pose their own problems of supply and demand management.

7 **Social marketing.** Social responsibility sometimes involves the taking of active steps to suppress demand.

8 **Implications for marketing in the public sector.** There are a number of distinctions to be drawn between public and private sector market orientations. Public sector organisations usually have less autonomy than private ones. The public sector needs to market its services for the benefit of its users, if it wishes to respond more effectively to society's needs.

Implications for management

Any organisation needs a proper understanding of its products' or services' benefits to its markets. These are likely to be a mix of both tangible and intangible benefits. Different markets (*see* Chapters 3 and 5) may well have different perceptions of the same product or service. As a first step, the following questions can be addressed.

How do you define your 'total product'?

What mixture of tangible and intangible benefits does it involve? How do your users perceive the nature of the benefits they obtain from you? To answer these questions, a simple table can be used (*see* Table 4.4).

Table 4.4 Sample table for definition of 'total product'

Core benefit	
Tangible benefits	*Intangible benefits*

It is important to identify your *users' perceptions* of benefit. There is often a temptation to make assumptions about perceptions of benefit that may not be correct. Whenever possible, these should be checked against available evidence, and market research provides useful information (*see* Chapter 10). Perceptions of benefit depend upon people's values. Different groups of people may have different values. Remember, too, that perceptions of benefit can and do change, just as perceptions of value change.

What supply and demand strategies are currently in use in your organisation?
Again, it is important to consider both the suppliers' and the users' perceptions of the service provided. Generally, such an analysis can be made under two headings:

1 *Supply systems.* How does your organisation deliver its services? How is it organised to respond to demand? What mechanisms does it employ to ensure as fair a method of delivery as possible? These may include:
   - location and place
   - availability (e.g. opening hours)
   - appointment systems
   - professional attitudes of staff
   - speed of service.

2 *User demand.* What do your users require? What influences their perceptions of the service? What do they require that influences their level of satisfaction with the service? These may include:
   - ease of access
   - convenience
   - fair treatment
   - friendliness and helpfulness
   - speed of service.

ISSUES FOR DISCUSSION

The following issues for discussion are presented in the form of questions. Examples from specific public sector industries should be incorporated into responses. Case studies can be used to provide some illustrations of the issues raised.

1 What are the principal issues in services marketing as opposed to product marketing?

2 What tensions are likely to exist between the principles of state provision for those in need (in the sense of altruism) and individual self-determination (individual responsibility)?

3 What difficulties are involved in defining individual rights in the context of benefits provided by the State?

4 What are the distinctions between 'needs' and 'wants'?

References

Berry, L. (1984) in Lovelock, C.H. (ed.) (1984) *Services Marketing. Text, Cases and Readings.* Englewood Cliffs, New Jersey: Prentice-Hall, Inc., pp. 29–37.

Cowell, D.W. (1984) *The Marketing of Services.* Oxford: Heinemann.

Downie, R.S. (1980) 'The market and welfare services: remedial values' in Tims, N. (ed) *Social Welfare, Why and How.* London: Routledge and Kegan Paul, pp. 42–54.

Franchetti, M. (1996) 'Germans learn to grin and bear it', *The Sunday Times*, 7 April.

Jones, K. (1991) *The Making of Social Policy in Britain 1830–1990.* London and Atlantic Highlands, New Jersey: Athlone.

Kotler, P. (1991) *Marketing Management. Analysis, Planning, Implementation and Control.* Englewood Cliffs, New Jersey: Prentice-Hall, Inc.

Kotler, P. and Roberto, E.L. (1989) *Social Marketing.* New York: The Free Press (Macmillan, Inc.).

Lamb, C. W. Jr. (1987) 'Public Sector Marketing is Different', *Business Horizons* 30 (4), July–Aug, 56–60.

Levitt, T. (1986) *The Marketing Imagination.* London: Collier-Macmillan.

Lovelock, C.H. (1984) *Services Marketing. Text, Cases and Readings.* Englewood Cliffs, New Jersey: Prentice-Hall, Inc.

Oliver, G. (1990) *Marketing Today.* Hemel Hempstead: Prentice Hall UK Ltd.

Plant, R., Lesser, H. and Taylor-Gooby, P. (1980) *Political philosophy and social welfare.* London: Routledge and Kegan Paul.

Reeves, M. (1988) *The Crisis in Higher Education.* Milton Keynes: SRHE and OU Press.

Rogers, E.M. (1962) *Diffusion of Innovations.* New York: Free Press. A commentary on Rogers' categorisation of adopters is provided by Kotler, P. (1991) *Marketing Management. Analysis, Planning, Implementation and Control* (7th edn). Englewood Cliffs, New Jersey: Prentice-Hall International, Inc., pp. 342–3.

Rouse, J. (1993) 'Resource and performance management in public service organisations' in Kester, I.-H., Painter, C. and Barnes, C. (eds) (1993) *Management in the Public Sector.* London: Chapman & Hall.

Sasser, W. E. (1984) 'Match Supply and Demand in Service Industries' in Lovelock, C.H. (ed) (1984) *Services Marketing. Text, Cases and Readings.* Englewood Cliffs, New Jersey: Prentice-Hall, Inc., pp. 330–38.

Scitovsky, T. (1976) *The Joyless Economy.* London: Oxford University Press.

Shams, H. and Hales, C. (1989) 'Once More on "Goods" and "Services": A Way Out of the Conceptual Jungle', *The Quarterly Review of Marketing*, Spring, 1–5.

Shostack, G.L. (1984) 'Breaking Free from Product Marketing' in Lovelock, C. H. (ed) (1984) *Services Marketing. Text, Cases and Readings.* Englewood Cliffs, New Jersey: Prentice-Hall, Inc., pp. 37–47.

Sklair, L. (1970) *The Sociology of Progress.* London: Routledge and Kegan Paul.

Wilmshurst, J. (1991) *The Fundamentals and Practice of Marketing* (2nd edn). Oxford: Butterworth-Heinemann.

CHAPTER 5

Customers and the fallacy of equality

CHAPTER OVERVIEW

One of the major tenets of public sector provision is that of equality of opportunity. The principle that all users should be considered 'equal' implies that all people are the same and should be treated equally. This assertion needs to be examined carefully in situations where demand has to be managed. One of the most important principles of marketing teaches that all people are different and have different needs. Success in satisfying customers will be determined by dividing up a homogeneous mass of people into smaller groups with similar needs. This technique is called segmentation and it is in the application of this concept that resistance to marketing in public sector industries frequently occurs. However, effective targeting can only be achieved by effective segmentation.

This chapter demonstrates that, in reality, the public sector applies both segmentation and targeting formally and informally. Moves to provide particular help to under- privileged groups represents a move towards a policy of targeting but, until there is formal acceptance of the need for this policy, its necessary implementation will not be properly achieved. The chapter then discusses concepts and methods of segmentation and targeting, and their strengths and weaknesses for public sector applications.

KEY LEARNING OUTCOMES

By the end of this chapter, you should be able to:

- appreciate the fact that markets are not homogeneous;
- understand the ways in which the principles of equity and equality have particular meanings for the public sector;
- consider the necessity for market segmentation and the conflicts this may generate; and
- examine some segmentation techniques and consider how they can be applied.

Introduction

In Chapter 4 important issues were raised about buyer/consumer/user perceptions. Of course, different groups of people have different characteristics and patterns of perceptions and behaviour. In this chapter, we shall examine this concept further and explore ways in which the identification and analysis of different characteristics and forms of behaviour contribute to the process of market segmentation.

Market segmentation

Within the public sector, market segmentation is difficult to implement due to the prevalence of two powerful cultural norms: the concept of 'the public' on the one hand, and 'equality' and 'equity' on the other. The pursuit of equity led the former UK Prime Minister, John Major, to express a desire to introduce a 'classless' society. However, each individual is, physiologically and psychologically, different and yet it is human nature to be attracted to groups with similar interests and value systems. Society is therefore composed of different groups. A 'classless' society would, therefore, seem to be a contradiction in terms. If individuals and groups possess differences, they are clearly not 'equal', and can certainly be classified (sic!) into a number of different groupings.

In spite of these considerations, the terms 'society', 'the people' and 'the public' continue to have a populist appeal, used in a way which assumes the existence of a population as a homogenous mass.

'The public' as a single entity

We talk about 'the public', or even the 'general public', without thinking very much about it. One dictionary definition of the public calls it 'the community as an aggregate', with 'community' meaning a body of people living in the same locality, and an 'aggregate' meaning a collection of units, in this case people, into one mass. 'The public' is also useful shorthand for purchasers or users in general. There is even a popular stereotype associated with it – called 'the man in the street' – who is usually understood to represent some sort of average person whom we think of as in some way representative of the public – a sort of human mean.

The terms 'the public' and 'the people', are often used with effect in the political arena, especially by those who claim to speak on behalf of all the people rather than for any specific group or groups of them. The term 'the people' is sometimes attractive precisely because it is so vague and general. Some political programmes have actually been founded on such a belief in 'the people', and have opposed systems of party politics on the grounds that they are divisive and unrepresentative. One such political programme was proposed in 1926 by the Distributionist League in London, and advocated by the writers, G. K. Chesterton and Hilaire Belloc. The League sought, unsuccessfully, to restore property to 'ordinary people' by challenging big business and large-scale property ownership. It encouraged self-employment, craftsmanship and smallholdings. Its members believed in the equal rights of the 'common man'. Malcolm Muggeridge (1989), however, scathingly denied that 'the average man' could ever be identified. 'Everyman', he argued, 'is an abstraction, who cannot really exist, although he may be used as a symbol.'

In the twentieth century, the idea of a mass society and a mass culture has often been associated with the idea of a homogenised, egalitarian and capitalist consumer society. Swingewood (1977) noted the way in which the Frankfurt School of social theorists (the Frankfurt Institute of Social Research, founded in 1923, later re-established at Columbia, USA, where its leading figures fled from the Nazis) believed that modern society, in a rationalised and totally managed world, was destroying the independence of individuals. Everything was being reduced to mass-produced commodities. Herbert Marcuse (1964) argued that mankind in a capitalist society had become powerless within a system of false consumer needs, within a 'mass culture'.

These ideas were deeply pessimistic, and ignored most of the benefits of capitalism and mass consumption, including their ability to generate different groups of audiences and consumers within societies. Swingewood (1977) was highly critical of the myth which represents 'the masses' as a majority demanding uniform products and popular culture, simply because some people believe that they have homogenous patterns of consumption and low standards. Nevertheless, much of modern marketing has been concerned with mass marketing, and many popular brands are aimed at as wide an audience as possible. In these circumstances, marketing is concerned with the marketing of products – or 'product push' – and such an approach was at one time a dominant marketing philosophy.

The idea of trying to satisfy all the needs of a population may be very attractive to public sector industries. Frequently, representatives of those industries state that their missions are to provide services which satisfy as many people as possible. Even organisations which experience a 'natural' match between provision and demand try to broaden their scope of provision in order to attract more users. In 1996, there was considerable debate about the character of the BBC's Radio 3 and Radio 4, where schedules were being modified in order to attract different audiences. One obvious effect was to dissatisfy members of existing audiences for those services. Similarly, a cost-driven culture was moving production for BBC World Service programmes towards an emphasis on domestic products, which ran the risk of ignoring the special needs of existing World Service audiences.

'The public' as a collection of individuals

However effective the words may be on the political soapbox, it is difficult to believe in 'the public' or 'the people' as a single entity. Statisticians highlight the dangers, as well as the uses, of using such aggregated figures and 'summary measures'. Most of the dangers involve the ways in which summary measures inevitably lose some accuracy. Aggregated figures can be very misleading. It is often said that statistics can be used to prove anything.

In reality, the generic terms 'people', 'public' and 'the masses' are not really much use to the manager who is trying to identify the needs of particular groups for products or services. Needs are first generated by individuals. Each individual is actually a separate entity, with his or her own tastes, desires, preferences and wants. Individuals are all psychologically different from one another. For these reasons, it becomes dangerous to assume the existence of an 'ordinary person in the street'. 'Ordinary' can take on a huge range of meanings, dependent on the culture and circumstances of the user.

For similar reasons, 'the market' is rarely a homogeneous concept. The human components of a market are never going to be uniform, consistent or exactly the same as each other. It has long been recognised that the process of exchange is really like a long sorting process, through which individual products or services find their ways to individual purchasers or users.

'The public' as a collection of groups

Although each buyer of a product or user of a service is potentially a separate, individual market, there are at least two important reasons why buyers and users are normally considered in terms of groups.

1 *Within any community certain people behave in similar ways when they expect the same things.* The psychologist George Kelly (1955) pointed out that the expectations of a group are often used by the individuals within it to confirm their own feelings of identity. Groups have their own cultures, ways of life, shared patterns of behaviour, common ideas and beliefs. In marketing, such groups are usually referred to as 'reference groups'. Culture, in this sense, is an extremely important influence on human behaviour. The word 'culture' is usually used as a way of defining a specific, social way of life, in which certain meanings and values are expressed. Culture is not always easy to identify, however, even though cultures often express themselves in forms of rituals, using signs and symbols to establish or communicate group identity. Uniforms and specific codes of dress are obvious examples. The vast majority of all individuals are members of groups, even if we do not all wear uniforms. Moreover, most of us are members of more than one group at a time. For example, we may belong to one group at work, to another for a particular sport, and to a third for other social activities. Each group may well have its own, different culture. In each group we may well have unique wants and needs.

2 *Serving the needs of groups is more cost-effective.* Profit-making organisations rarely find it profitable to customise their products for individual buyers. If they do so, they need to be assured that their buyers can afford the consequent prices. Certain manufacturers, like Rolls-Royce cars, can usually rely on a small niche market for their products, and will often customise the product to the individual requirements of the purchaser. However, most manufacturers and most service providers find that the market for personalised products is extremely small, and certainly too small to provide economies of scale.

Economies of scale are important to private industry if costs are to be kept low or reduced and profit margins maintained or increased. They are important to public sector services if costs are to be reduced and activity maximised. Indeed, they are usually a very important element in determining whether the minimum resources are being used in the best ways possible.

The triple 'E' test is used as an assessment of performance in some public service industries and is based on the categories of *economy*, *efficiency* and *efficacy* (*see* Chapter 6, p. 160). As a result, public sector organisations are unlikely to find it cost effective to treat every individual as a unique market. Admittedly, there may be exceptions. Some services such as health, may require a personal service by their very nature. An artificial limb or a false eye will require individual fitting, and usually design and manufacture. Yet in general, such kinds of demand are relatively rare. The market can usually be divided up into groups of clients with similar needs or wants.

In marketing terms, these groups are called *segments*. The process of *market segmentation* can be described as dividing an apparently homogenous group into different groups of individuals with similar needs, and which are sufficiently different from other groups with different needs. We need to understand the market as a collection of groupings, each with its own lifestyle, set of values, attitudes and beliefs, needs and wants. Analysing the market in terms of segments can provide a great deal of information about clients, users and consumers which can be used in the development of marketing strategy.

Consumer, organisational and governmental markets

Before examining the details of market segmentation, we can divide total demand into three distinct markets:

- consumer markets;
- industrial or organisational markets, in which demand is derived from consumer markets;
- governmental markets, where demand is complex and is derived both from consumer demand and governmental policies.

In reality, the public sector operates in all three markets, sometimes simultaneously, as determined by the multiple-markets model (*see* Chapter 3). For example, an educational organisation may be providing training to an individual whose needs are driven by the need to improve competency (a consumer market). The success of the training will be determined by the training establishment's need to place the trainee. That placement will be determined by the firm's current level of business (an industrial market). Funding for the training may be provided by a government agency (a governmental market) (*see* Fig 5.1).

There is, however, one major distinction to be made between commercial consumer markets and public sector markets. As Kotler (1991) observes, a consumer

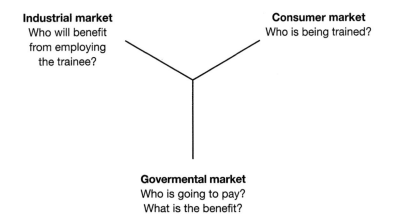

Fig. 5.1 The potential complexity of public sector markets, as illustrated by the market for training

market consists of all those who buy or acquire goods and services for personal use. In practice, there is a distinction to be made between those who have the power to buy these goods and services directly and those who do not. This distinction is an important one for the public sector: on the one hand, there are services which provide for the wants of those who can afford to use them; on the other, there are services for which the demand is so obvious that limited resources must be managed, and some form of rationing is required. This latter category will include provision for those who use public sector services because they cannot afford to do otherwise. However, they can still be defined and understood as market segments.

Introducing market segmentation to public sector industries

There are a number of reasons why it is sometimes difficult to persuade members of public service organisations to recognise the importance of marketing in the public sector market.

1 Many public sector services struggle not to encourage demand, but to ration supply in the face of limited resources. A consequence of this is the fact that the cultures of many public sector organisations do not possess a user orientation.

2 The primary market (the end-user) is often seen as part of a process, rather than as the end-user or customer with specific needs. Unless the primary market is clearly identified as the end-user, then segmentation will be impossible. This sort of confusion is particularly prevalent in health industries. A radio news report about an accident to a cable car in October 1996 contained the observation that 'the 15 injured were processed ...'

3 Public sector organisations are often hemmed in by extensive legislation which aims to protect the public's and taxpayers' interests, but which actually inhibits the development of marketing techniques which might enhance user satisfaction.

4 Initially, the principle of equality may appear to conflict with the real need for market segmentation. In assuming that, in the interests of equity and fairness, all users should be treated as equals, there is a danger that individual needs and priorities are not considered adequately. Thus patients represent a *category for market segmentation.*

As providers, many public services were in the past simply unaccustomed to thinking in marketing terms, even though, from the late 1960s, there was a growing dissatisfaction with the bureaucratic, impersonal and paternalistic attitude of many public services. Moreover, functional divisions and lack of collaboration, especially between departments at local government level, often highlighted the need for more co-ordinated responses to individual user needs. Elcock (1994), in a historical survey of developments in local government management, noted the way in which public service management has moved from a dual relationship between service providers and politicians to a tripartite one involving politicians, providers and users. Since the mid-1980s, and especially since the 1991 *Citizen's Charter* initiative, there has been a steady shift towards recognising that the users of public sector services are also 'customers' and 'clients'. Stewart (1986) reinforces the point that 'the customer is the citizen'. The citizen is, in reality, more than a passive recipient of, for example, a local government service; he or she has the right to expect an acceptable level of customer care. In fact, most of the UK *Citizen's Charter* initiatives appear more concerned with the manner in which transactions are conducted than with the 'core benefits' involved.

King and Pierre (1990) recognised the way in which public service management is responding to the growing importance of market segmentation and the need to satisfy different customer groups and their demands. The significance of these techniques and objectives was already well established in the private sector. The Audit Commission (1988) was convinced that local government should learn lessons from the way in which customers had become much more demanding, and had developed a greater confidence and ability to articulate their wants and needs. Since no customers had identical needs, it was important to understand customers better, rather than making assumptions about what those needs might be. This represented a very significant change from a traditional 'command-led' towards a 'demand-led' approach to local government.

Equality and the public sector market

The *Declaration of the Rights of Man and of the Citizen* was passed by the French National Assembly on 20 August 1789. It contained a famous first clause stating that 'men are born and remain free and equal in rights' – a position reinforced by the assertion, in another part of the document, that 'all men must be equal in the eyes of the law'. The principles which were embodied in the *Declaration* still seem valid in most democratic societies today. In many Western countries they have inspired a number of developments which have tried to ensure that all members of society are entitled to equal treatment and certain basic 'rights'.

Some of these 'rights' have long been interpreted as public institutions and services. Adam Smith's *The Wealth of Nations* was originally published in 1776. In it, Smith argued that the State, which he then identified as the 'sovereign' or the 'commonwealth', had an important duty to provide three main public services: defence, justice and 'public works and public institutions'. These works and institutions were, he thought, highly beneficial to a great society, but cost too much for any individual or group of individuals to maintain. It was therefore the State's responsibility to provide, for example, a transport infrastructure of roads, bridges and waterways, and a system of public education.

In practice, however, the State took a long time to assume responsibility for the full range of services most countries provide today. The creation of the Welfare State in the UK (*see* Chapter 1) marked the point at which the UK government was still accepted full responsibility for a wide range of public services, and in 1991 the UK government continued to emphasise that 'essential services – such as education and health – must be available to all, irrespective of means'. The scope of the public services was defined as including government departments and agencies, nationalised industries, the local authorities, the National Health Service, the courts, and the police and emergency services. *The Citizen's Charter* (1991) also covered the key utilities.

As noted in Chapter 1, it was not until after the Second World War that the National Health Service Act was passed in the UK; it became operative in 1948. Originally this was intended to be a service offering health care to all, available to everyone on the basis of need and free at the point of delivery. Although the last principle was compromised at an early stage, when charges for spectacles and dental treatment were introduced in 1951, the National Health Service still survives in principle. However, it has failed to live up to original expectations of a cheaper service for a healthier nation. The demand for health care is actually insatiable, and continues to grow. Expectations have changed. More people expect to live longer. The UK population over the age of 75 increased dramatically between 1976 and 1996. Medical technology has advanced. Despite the continual development and improvement in care, medical science and management, however, there is still ample evidence of disparities in the population's state of health, revealed by analysing health data for the population by, for example, location, socio-economic class, levels of deprivation, etc.

Minicase 5.1 illustrates an important fact: the egalitarian principles upon which the National Health Service was founded do not appear to have been wholly successful in practice. An important factor in this lack of success is the fact that needs themselves differ; they have different meanings for different groups of people at different times.

Maslow's (1954) hierarchy of human needs (discussed in Chapter 3) can be used to explore this point. The three lower levels of needs are concerned with the basic necessities of life and social organisation: air, food, water, safety and security, social identification. Together, the satisfaction of these needs provides a basic level of subsistence and social comfort. The majority of public sector services contribute to these levels of need. However, it is possible to find instances where, for example, a fourth-level, esteem or status need for one individual may be a second-level, security and safety need for another person. For example, a married person who does not work may employ a home help as a convenience and confirmation of social status, whereas a disabled individual living alone may need home-help provision in order to survive with any dignity and in any comfort at all.

We can therefore conclude that the same products or services can have different meanings for different groups of people. Consider, for example, the ways in which rail travel can represent different activities to different constituencies. Although many transport systems which were once taken into state ownership 'in the public interest' are now being privatised, they still exist to provide a service *to* the public. Their users fall into a large number of different categories. Travellers on a railway train in the UK, for example, may well include the following categories:

- *The student*, who may use the train to see family and/or friends. The student may not possess a car. If the price is affordable (for example, at a student concessionary price) and the train provides certain benefits (for example, relative speed of journey and comfort), the train can be an attractive alternative to the service provided by competitors (for example, coach companies). To the student, rail travel can represent a good way of taking mountains of dirty washing back to the family home and washing machine, or to visit a friend for a weekend's leisure activities. Moreover, it is even possible to do some work or reading on a train.

MINICASE 5.1

A problem of equity in the NHS internal market

The UK's National Health Service (*see* Chapter 1) has continued to maintain that it is committed to the principle of equity. In an interview with *The Independent* on 17 March 1994, NHS chief executive elect, Alan Langlands, stated that equity was one of the most important principles driving the internal market in the Health Service. He reportedly defined equity both as providing health care on the basis of need, and as allocating resources to populations (that is, giving purchasing power to users), rather than to institutions (that is, giving funding directly to the providers). We may presume that these institutions include hospital trusts.

In practice, establishing the internal NHS market has been far from smooth. The decision to enable general practitioner fundholders to buy the services they require from hospitals appeared to make matters much worse for some patients who had GPs that were not fundholders. A British Medical Association survey of 173 acute hospitals, published in December 1993, showed that 42 per cent of them were offering fundholders services which were not available to other patients. These services included faster admissions into hospital for the patients of fundholders. The Minister of Health denied that a 'two-tier system' of health care was developing, but many claims have since been made that the system has created inequalities. Had all GPs been required to become fundholders at the same time, the 'equal rights' of patients might not have been compromised in this way. It seems, however, that the principle of equal choice – in this case the general practitioners' right to choose whether or not to become fundholders – conflicts with the principle of patients' equity.

The British Medical Association Council's chairman, Dr Sandy Macara, referred to the NHS reforms as an 'uncontrolled monster'. (*The Daily Telegraph*, 10 April 1994) Patients of GPs who had not become fundholders – the majority – were losing out badly, and he claimed that the percentage of NHS funds devoted to administration had risen from 4 per cent in the mid-1980s to 11 per cent in 1993.

- *The commuter*, who uses the train as a daily means of transport to and from work. The train merely represents the most efficient and economical way in and out of the city, when traffic congestion and the price of parking deter the commuter from attempting to use a car. For these reasons the commuter appears to tolerate overcrowded trains and an element of poor time-keeping rather than considering living closer to his or her place of work. Poor travelling conditions may be accepted as a necessary trade-off against the advantages of living 'in the country' outside the city. The commuter may even be on friendly terms with a number of fellow travellers who share his or her routine. It might even be possible to talk of a 'commuters' culture'.

- *The business person* who uses the train for meetings and for the opportunity to travel and work at the same time. Portable computers and telephones can be used while travelling. Travel expenses may be borne by the business, and the benefits of first-class travel, where available, can include the privileges of a higher standard of comfort and better facilities. The train 'takes the strain', especially on long distance and intercity routes.

- *The day-shopper* who, without a car, wants a day out, with or without family, to shop in some city, town or commercial centre and for whom the train provides the most convenient means of getting there and back.

- *The holiday maker*, who is a leisure user, enjoying travel for its own sake and as a means of taking a break at a leisurely pace. Families may use the train for visiting tourist attractions, especially if price incentives, such as family railcards, make it economically viable.

- *The 'distress purchaser'*, who bought a ticket because it was the only way he or she could find to get to a particular destination conveniently and at the right time. Unable to find another form of affordable transport to the destination, the passenger decided that the train was the only option. Railway stations are, after all, readily identifiable sources of public transport.

Differential fare structures often benefit some of these individual market segments. Young persons, senior citizens and family railcards, commuter season tickets, and other pricing incentives are used to attract different segments of the market. All these travellers use rail travel as a service, but they use it in different ways for different reasons.

The mere existence of differing user groups probably makes it impossible to talk usefully of a homogeneous market, even for those services our society likes to think of as 'rights'. All users of public services may, in theory, have equal rights to those services as they are needed. The nature of the needs, however, will vary from individual to individual, and from group to group.

The significance of market segmentation to the public sector

The most sophisticated models of market segmentation seem to have been developed for the commercial world. In discussing commercial markets, Kotler (1991) distinguished broad differences between buyers' wants, purchasing power, geographical locations, buying attitudes and practices. Although the bulk of available literature on segmentation examines approaches to buyer characteristics and behaviours in the commercial marketplace, most of the variables involved are just as useful in segmenting public sector markets, including those that provide for needs rather than wants. A growing body of literature addresses the segmentation requirements of specific public sector industries.

In searching for ways in which to identify market segments, marketing has borrowed extensively from the work of anthropologists, sociologists and social psychologists. Williams (1992) highlights the ways in which 'marketing behaviour' uses ideas and methods which were originally developed for other disciplines, and warns that consumer behaviour has its own, distinct requirements in a marketing context. The aim of any marketing process is to satisfy as many consumers as it can, whether to increase the profitability of a commercial organisation or to meet those needs which society, in the form of the State, has decided to support.

Market segmentation is essentially a means of developing a better understanding of user needs and improving the nature of the delivery of services to the user or to the customer. In the commercial, private sector, or in the case of public services which may seek to compete with private sector ones, it can also be a very important source of competitive advantage. Segmentation aims to divide the market into groups of similar customers/users so that an organisation can identify and satisfy their differing needs. In the public sector, such segmentation may lead to forms of 'positive discrimination' in order to ensure that some groups are rationed or persuaded to use private sector provision, while scarce resources are directed towards other groups which have greater needs.

While modern marketing is usually seen as concerned with the identification and satisfaction of demand for products and services, a significant problem for many public services is the paucity, even inadequacy, of services to meet demand. Stewart (1986) makes the point that methods of limiting demand can play a major part in reconciling demand with scarce resources. Constrained by limited funding, many services are often engaged in trying to limit demand to the level of 'essential' provision, rather than trying to stimulate consumption, as is usually the case in private sector business. They may actually want to focus on inhibiting demand in some market segments. This concept (using the term *'demarketing'*) is discussed by Kotler and Roberto (1989) as an answer to the problems caused by the level of demand exceeding the capacity of a social programme. Although pricing can be a very effective means of doing this when financial exchanges are involved, pricing may be irrelevant to some public services which are provided on the basis of need. Kotler and Roberto list abandoning promotion and reducing accessibility as other 'demarketing' techniques, although they recognise the risks of appearing immoral or 'hard-hearted' which this process involves.

There is, nevertheless, a growing awareness that marketing can have an important part to play in services such as local government provision. This was recognised by the UK's Audit Commission (1984), when it stated that there was a need for a greater understanding of marketing in local government. The Commission commented on the way in which marketing appeared significantly under-developed in areas of local government – including further education, school meals and leisure centres – despite the fact that these were areas where marketing might easily provide benefits. The public sector presented new challenges for marketing. Both services which all citizens use and those for which there is discretionary demand need to know who uses the services, who might use them, and how the service is related to demand. To answer these questions it is necessary to understand the nature of the markets, the identity or identities of the customers, their needs and behaviours.

Public sector provision, therefore, needs to approach market segmentation in two contexts.

- *Non-discretionary demands*. Some public services satisfy community demands that everyone needs – for example, refuse collection and disposal and basic health care.
- *Discretionary demands*. Others satisfy discretionary demand – for example, leisure services and some forms of educational provision.

Market segmentation techniques developed for commercial industries can usefully be applied to both, on the basis that it is important to understand the needs of the users and purchasers. Not only will these differ from individual to individual and from group to group, but they will change over time. Kerley (1994) highlights the way in which local government has often failed to understand the ways in which users and customers change their requirements and demands. Patterns of social behaviour alter. Marketing has to be understood as being much more than promotion; it is, after all, about establishing satisfactory relationships between providers and users, customers, and beneficiaries. To do so successfully requires a fairly detailed understanding of these users. Market segmentation is an obvious method of doing this.

Croft (1994) sees the process of dividing up the market into distinct segments as central to modern marketing theory. Despite the fact that his book, *Market Segmentation*, is written for the private sector manager, many of the arguments made are relevant, or can be adapted to public sector marketing. However, the distinction between discretionary purchasers and non-discretionary users must be borne in mind when seeking to apply segmentation techniques to public sector operations. This status difference has a profound effect on the nature of power within the supplier–user relationship – power that can be abused. Word-of-mouth stories about abusive claimants and arrogant or rude service staff abound.

To be successful, this marketing-focus approach must be accompanied by two key elements:

1 *A commitment to marketing from the senior management of the organisation.*
    Without support from the top, marketing can easily become relegated to the position of one among many discrete functional departments. The appointment of a 'marketing officer' may be a gesture towards recognising marketing's importance, but it runs the risk of remaining a token one unless the marketing function is integrated into, and owned by, the whole organisation. In fact the term 'marketing officer' may even seem to be an oxymoron – a contradiction in terms – since the word 'officer' might be understood to imply a hierarchy of responsibilities, and marketing and rigid hierarchies do not easily mix. For marketing to achieve an effective integration into an organisation, support from the top is essential. All members of the organisation need to understand the importance of identifying their users and their users' needs. This should be a key focus of all the organisation's members, and should be integrated well into the culture of the organisation.

2 *Good quality market information.*
    One of the biggest dangers is complacency – an organisation's *assumptions* that it already 'knows' its market or markets, and their requirements. Hill *et al.* (1995, p.56) point out that such organisations often resist the use of tools such as marketing research, because they are confident that they already know what their users need or want. The 'we know best' syndrome sometimes takes a long time to die. Since many public sector organisations, unlike commercial organisations, may not depend directly on their markets to generate their income, but instead rely on grants and sponsorship, some non-profit organisations have not been as sensitive as they might have been to the importance of their users' perceptions and opinions. It has already been pointed out that these change. They are subject to a large number of variables, and constantly need to be updated. Any attempts to improve services rely heavily on getting to know markets *better*. Good quality information becomes essential.

Although information technology has become a familiar tool for comm-unication and control in many public service industries since the 1970s, the development of microcomputers and networks has enabled more staff to access more information directly for decision-making purposes. Market information is a prime candidate for computerised data collection, and current developments are increasingly sophisticated in their techniques – for example, in the use of post-code analysis. However, even if the analysis of business data can be achieved effectively by the use of new technology, human skill and expertise is still required to interpret that data, and that skill requires good marketers.

The reference to postcodes as a means of using locations to provide information highlights the role of *situations* in market segmentation. Different situations generate different needs. Oliver (1990, p.109) notes the ways in which both the benefit sought and the perception of the product (or service) can vary according to situation. He cites the way in which segment conflict may even occur when different market segments may be using the same service – for example, hotel facilities – at the same time for different reasons. The implications of conflict (for example, between conference and tourist guests) could be serious for the organisation concerned.

The segmentation process

The segmentation process can be divided into a number of discrete steps.

1 Defining the market

The first step in this process is to define the market for a service as a whole. To do so, Croft (1994) points out that it is essential to think in terms of user needs, not in terms of products or services. Managers need to start by identifying the benefits users are seeking. (*See* the discussion of 'core benefit', 'tangibles' and 'intangibles' in Chapter 4.) It may be tempting, for example, to think that the users of a cleansing department service would define their needs in terms of a dustbin, but the benefit sought is really a convenient means of disposing of household waste. Black and Decker argue that people don't buy drills, they buy holes.

The perceived benefit of both a product and a service is usually a collection of different attributes. A good understanding of how the user or customer sees these benefits is necessary, if managers are to avoid making inaccurate assumptions.

Croft (1994) thinks that the concept of 'customer' may actually be misleading in this context, and prefers to concentrate on the end-user. This is because, for example, the industrial market may have a number of different customers within the value chain, who are marketing to each other before the end-user is reached. The fabricator provides a market to the material supplier. The assembler provides a market for the fabricator. The wholesaler provides a market for the assembler, and the retailer will provide a market for the wholesaler before the end-user provides a market for the retailer.

Services also use comparable value chains, albeit in different ways. For example, the market for a surgeon will be a hospital trust. The hospital trust may see its market as fundholding general practitioners. The general practitioner will recommend the service to his or her patient – the end-user. The final, and most important perception of benefit is therefore the end-user's. The importance of this primary market (*see* Chapter 3) should never be forgotten.

Dividing the market into segments and selecting those that are relevant

The concept of market segmentation can be described with some confidence, but putting it into practice is often more difficult. A good starting point is to describe the total market (as shown in Fig. 5.2), establishing a clear definition of a specific market, its users and its suppliers. Such a description is referred to as a *value system*. It should also include any relevant services that may influence the market. In the public sector, these would include not only competitors – for example, in the area of public transport services – but also those organisations and services which may have an interest in the user's benefit. For example, in the provision of mental health care, there have been many instances where calls have been made for better co-ordination between the social services, the police, hospitals and psychiatric units, all of which may be concerned with the same 'customers'. A marketing map should identify the relationships between these.

The total market for a particular product or service can be described using a three-dimensional box. In the example in Fig. 5.3, the three sides of the box represent buyer groups, products purchased and buyer locations. If, for example, the demand for university education were to be described using this method, buyer groups could be defined by age and gender characteristics – for example, school-leavers, post work experience candidates, retired persons, male and female. The vertical axis of product purchase could describe the range and type of courses available – for example, undergraduate courses in various disciplines, post-graduate degrees, part-time non-vocational courses, etc. The third dimension could identify

Fig. 5.2 The value system

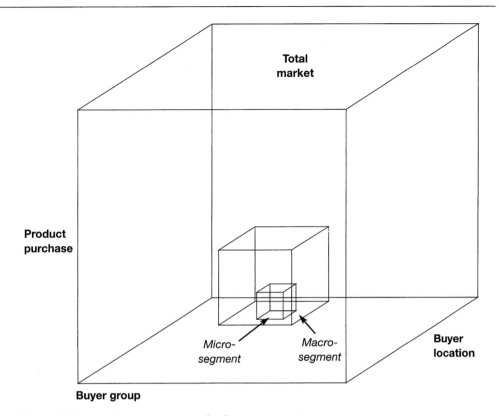

Fig. 5.3 The market: macro- and micro-segments

the locations of the buyer groups. These three dimensions would relate to a range of segmentation variables. The total size of the cube would represent the potential market size. An individual *macro-segment* within it could represent an all-female, 18-year-old, school-leavers group of candidates who are seeking undergraduate courses in the East Midlands. A *micro-segment* could represent 18-year-old female school-leavers wanting undergraduate degrees in leisure management living in Leicester (*see* Fig. 5.3).

Once the market is considered in these terms, the manager needs to use the concept as a means of identifying market segments – the roughly coherent groups of primary users within it.

Methods of segmentation have become increasingly sophisticated. In the early days of mass marketing, when individuals were often more concerned with survival needs, segmentation was based on the physical characteristics of the individual, on demographic data, defining populations by quantifiable size, location, etc. In the recent past, with a growing understanding of buyer behaviour, more sophisticated forms of segmentation have been developed which further categorise the behaviour patterns of customers/users.

Broadly speaking, the constitution of groups, or market segments, can be considered under two headings: user characteristics and user behaviour.

User characteristics

This form of market segmentation addresses the question 'who are the users?' Three forms of data are particularly useful in this context:

1 *Geographic data.* Such data analyse populations by their locations and densities and representation.

2 *Demographic data.* Forms of organising population census data have also long used information on age, gender, occupation, racial origin and family size. (The development of technological methods of recording such data made a significant historical contribution towards the development of the computer.)

3 *Socio-economic data.* This includes information on factors such as income levels and social class. In spite of the pride taken by the USA in its image as a 'classless' society, early segmentation models there used socio-economic classifications which are still in use today and which have become widely used throughout the world (*see* Table 5.1).

Each of the categories – geographic, demographic and socio-economic – will, of course, be subject to variables, which can be scaled in certain ways. Thus, age could be divided into pre-school, 5–16, 16–21, 21–30, etc., depending on the relevance of the variables to the specific market which is being analysed.

In practical terms, managers need to know which characteristics and which variables are relevant and particularly significant (that is, big enough and important enough) for analysing the particular needs of the market with which they are concerned. Segmentation, as a marketing technique, is industry specific, and must be interpreted and applied to the context in which it functions. For example, a marketing segmentation for local bus services will certainly be very different from that used for refuse collection, or the one used for art gallery visitors.

The use of demographic variables – for example, age, gender, ethnicity, culture – and socio-economic classifications can lead to user perceptions of bias and discrimination. Nevertheless, such factors are important to the manager who wishes to ensure that the offer made by an organisation matches the expectations of the user. For example, the feminist movement has objected to some forms of categorisation on the grounds that it is discriminatory. Marketers should guard against stereotyping segments as simple segmentation variables can create more, not less, confusion. However, some writers have argued that, as women's roles have changed, there is a need for increased levels of segmentation to take account of them.

Table 5.1 Socio-economic groupings

Classification	Description
A, B	Managerial and professional
C1	Supervisory and clerical
C2	Skilled manual
D, E	Unskilled manual and unemployed

One method of doing so is the use of the *product market matrix*, as shown in Fig. 5.4. The matrix enables managers to identify specific characteristics of buyers' needs within a particular product/market combination. The matrix in Fig. 5.4 uses some of the factors involved. If a particular product/market combination is selected, full details of the expectations and behaviours of the users can be developed and described. This process is time-consuming, and requires a thorough understanding of the segment. However, it does enable the manager to identify needs more exactly and to differentiate the characteristics of provision for different groups.

	Commuters	Holiday makers	Business people
High speed trains		Facilities for luggage	Fast, peak demand
Express trains		Integrate with high speed trains	Intergrate with high speed trains
Trams	Regular, frequent, fast, local travel		Integrate with buses
Buses	Reliable integrated service		Integrate with trams
Coaches		Facilities for luggage	

Fig. 5.4 A product market matrix

The process also raises serious questions about the extent to which the principle of equality is always relevant. On the other hand, it could be argued that 'equality' is concerned with enabling everyone to obtain the level and type of provision sought and required, rather than one which is only an approximate 'fit' designed to meet the needs of 'everyman'.

User behaviour

This addresses the questions 'what services do users need?' and 'why do they need them?' An enormous amount of attention has been paid to analysing the *individual* differences between one user and another. Much research in this area has been undertaken with the intention of finding out if there are enough similarities between the wants, needs and attitudes of individuals to identify viable groups or market segments. This is particularly true of attempts to construct psychological profiles of the members of different market segments.

Within any group, the individual plays a *role*, which may vary according to the situation, and is understood in terms of the system of behavioural expectations operating in that group. Many roles are associated with certain symbols, especially in a society of 'conspicuous consumption'. Therefore, the ways in which individuals assume roles can provide useful methods of segmenting a market.

Any large market – for example, a national one – consists of a number of *social* groupings, each a potential market segment. Most individuals are subject to considerable pressure to conform socially – to identify with, and behave according to, the culture of a social group. Certain behaviour patterns are both the distinguishing characteristics of, and the entry qualifications to, the memberships and cultures of social groups.

Peer groups, for example, can be important and formative influences on, and reference groups for, the individual, and are often strong enough to challenge or counteract the influences of other social groups, such as families. Children at school often appear particularly vulnerable to peer group pressure. The amount of power an individual may exercise is also largely determined by his or her *status* within a group. However, social classes are usually perceived as having their own order of status, or hierarchy.

Most societies possess some form of *class* structure, although the forms taken may depend upon the extent to which members of classes are conscious of their class identity, the existence of obvious differences between class groups and the presence of strong elements of uniformity within them.

Elements of uniformity within groups are often reinforced by an existing *culture*. It is common to use the term 'culture' to refer to activities like art, music and literature. However, anyone studying a society will use the word 'culture' to talk about the whole way of life of a group of people. Used in this sense, 'culture' refers to the group's shared patterns of behaviour, its members' commonly held ideas and beliefs, their technology, art, science and history. It provides a system of norms for a particular group.

Cultures usually contain a number of *sub-cultures*, each with its own patterns of life and behaviour, and which may well be related to user characteristics. Thus, within the general culture of a society, it is possible to identify groups of other national origins, different religions and religious sects, groups which also 'belong' to particular geographical areas and locations, and groups which share similar age profiles. Some of the more extreme forms of sub-cultures – for example, punk culture – have emerged in deliberate opposition to the overall social norms.

The example of a sub-culture can be used to illustrate the idea of *lifestyle*. Social and cultural factors influence the ways people live, and lifestyles are expressed by peoples' activities, interests and opinions. Market research has developed a number of systems to classify the 'psychographic' character of individuals. A *psychograph* is a chart which plots a profile of an individual's personality by using the results of various tests. J. T. Plummer, in a well-known article published in 1974, identified the major elements as:

- Activities
- Interests
- Opinions
- Demographics

The *AIO Test* (Activities, Interests and Opinions) is frequently combined with demographic information to provide individual personality profiles. Each heading can be broken down into a number of factors (*see* Table 5.2).

This kind of approach has been used successfully by some organisations which supply published (that is, 'secondary') data on marketing for the use of public sector organisations. Hill *et al.* (1995) comment on the way in which both CACI Information Services and BMRB International provide marketing research data used by the Arts Council in the UK.

- CACI Information Services designed the *ACORN consumer classification system* which classifies consumers into 'types' (the system is described as '*Geodemographics*') who are likely to share similar characteristics and behaviours. Each ACORN primary category is broken down into a number of lifestyle groups, and each group is identified with a number of residential area types. ACORN housing groups are described by Oliver (1990, p.103), and range from Group A, in which modern family housing occupied by manual workers account for 9.6 per cent of housing, to Group J – traditional, high status suburban housing (19.1 per cent) – and Group K – areas of elderly people (6.4 per cent). These can be related to databases of postcodes within specified geographic areas, and used by organisations such as art galleries and theatres to obtain information about their potential attendance markets.

- BMBR International produces the *TGI survey*, based on regular survey questionnaires which enable a wide range of behaviour variables, including attendances at different categories of arts events, to be related together.

Methods of distinguishing different sorts of groups, and hence potential market segments, should not tempt us into believing that we can establish a neat, permanent and invariable model of society. As in any life cycle model, lifestyle analysis recognises the dimension of time. As people age, their wants and needs change. Society is constantly evolving and changing, and so we need to consider the ways in which changing circumstances affect users. This is an important point to bear in mind when using any (conceptual or normative) market model as a way of understanding and predicting market needs and behaviour. No market is static, particularly in a culture which has long used an idea of progress which assumes constant growth and change.

Table 5.2 Segmentation variables

Activities	Interests	Opinions	Demographics
Work	Family	Personal	Age
Hobbies	Home	Social Issues	Education
Social Events	Job	Politics	Income
Vacation	Community	Business	Occupation
Entertainment	Recreation	Economics	Family size
Club member	Fashion	Education	Dwelling
Community	Food	Products	Geography
Shopping	Media	Future	City size
Sports	Achievements	Culture	Stage in life cycle

This point can be illustrated by one of the most familiar market segmentation techniques using the life cycle concept. The family is one of the most commonly used reference groups in marketing, not least because *the family life cycle* concept has, historically, proved such a useful way of segmenting consumer markets as they change.

The use of the family as a model persists, despite the fact that society's ideas of the family unit are themselves changing. The social institution of the family unit is increasingly being challenged by changes in social customs. An increasing number of couples simply live together for varying lengths of time. The divorce rate continues to grow, as does the number of single-parent families. The concept of 'serial monogamy' is becoming more familiar in some societies. Reforms to the taxation system sometimes provide less financial incentive to get married. However, the family has long been regarded as the most important decision-making social unit in consumer terms. Today, in Western culture, the idea of the 'nuclear' family, consisting of parents and children sharing a home, is still often used as a model social institution. The family establishes norms of behaviour, and is thus an important reference group.

The needs and wants of a family unit change and vary according to circumstances. A (normative) model of the family's changing lifestyle identifies a number of typical stages in the family's development (*see* Fig. 5.5).

- *Bachelor stage*. Single, young people not living at home. Their outgoings are fairly small, if they are employed, and they are likely to be able to spend a relatively high proportion of their income on leisure, equipment, socialising etc.

- *Newly married/cohabiting couples*. Without children, both often work, they can afford to spend on durable goods and home-building.

- *Full nest one*. Young couples with children under the age of six (that is, established in school). As one partner will often need to give up work, the family may be faced with increased expenditure at the same time as the income decreases. The family's needs are therefore growing at the same time as constraints upon its ability to spend increase.

- *Full nest two*. Couples with children over six. In this situation both parents may once again decide to work, thus improving the family's financial situation, albeit with children influencing the family's expenditure heavily.

- *Full nest three*. Older couples with dependent children. Incomes generally have risen, although the demands of the children may also have increased. However, the amount of disposable income is likely to have increased.

- *Empty nest one*. Without children at home, increased parental earnings coincide with decreased expenditure requirements. Discretionary spending power thus increases. Travel, recreation and leisure expenditure is now at its highest.

- *Empty nest two*. Retirement of one partner reduces income levels and realigns expenditure towards health, comfort and convenience.

- *Solitary survivor one*. An employed widow/widower still enjoys a good income, but may move house and spend more on leisure and health.

- *Solitary survivor two*. A retired person, with a reduced income and particular needs for security and health care.

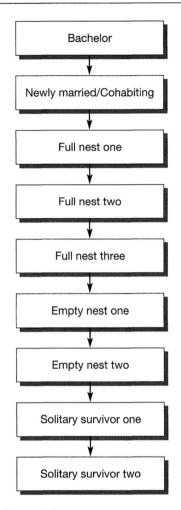

Fig. 5.5 The family life cycle model

The family life cycle concept can be useful in both private and public sector marketing. It is a clear illustration of the principle that the nature of human needs change over time. It also demonstrates again that markets, therefore, are certainly not homogeneous. They need to be segmented if they are to be understood and served. This does not necessarily deny the principle that everyone may be entitled to the provisions of a specific public service, but it does underline the point that different groups of users have different needs at different times.

Whichever segmentation techniques are selected as appropriate ways of identifying, selecting and scaling the characteristics and behaviours of the relevant segments, it is advisable to evaluate them against the organisation's main objectives. Are the chosen segments sufficiently distinct and different from each other? Are they big enough to be useful?

Using market segmentation

The first three steps of the segmentation process can therefore be listed as:

1 identifying the market;
2 defining the segments;
3 selecting the relevant ones.

By the last step, it will have become obvious that there are significant differences between a commercial approach to a discretionary market and public services' requirements for non-discretionary markets. In a commercial market, by now managers have arrived at the point of 'picking the winners' (Croft, 1994). They are interested in determining which market segments are most attractive by virtue of their potential for market penetration, growth of market share, market exploitation and profitability. Non-profit organisations will have very different priorities. The needs of their market segments may well be already defined by necessity, not by choice. Nevertheless, managers still need to address the problem of how best to match resources with demand.

Users' perceptions of benefit are very important in this context (*see* Chapter 11), and at this stage it is important to recognise that there may well be differences between users' views and those of the service supplier. These can only be compared by obtaining comparative information from both the supplier and from each user segment. Their priorities may turn out to be ordered in very different ways. For example, the supplier of a service may well think that the most important priority is a good supplier–user relationship, whereas the user may put service availability at the top of the list.

Different market segments may well have different perceptions of priorities in this way. To understand user requirements better the manager needs to ask the users. As already discussed, good quality market information is of crucial importance.

Methodologies and the use of models

Having looked at some of the principal ways in which markets are segmented, analysed and used, we shall now consider the methodologies used in the context of public sector marketing.

The ways of segmenting markets described in the preceding section – largely derived from private sector marketing and the social sciences – were initially devised as means of segmenting primary markets.

We have already noted (*see* Chapter 2) that public sector markets are multiple markets. The primary market is not the only one that the public sector organisation seeks to satisfy. Secondary, legitimiser and resourcer markets make their own demands, adding yet more variables to a situation which is already complex, and this is why it is important to be aware of the nature and limitations of the systems which we use to try and understand it.

The ways in which information is used are usually structured and embedded in the concepts associated with a particular system or model. However, any model can only provide an approximate guide to reality, based as much upon the designer's own conceptions as upon 'facts' and data. Data does not become information until it is *interpreted* in some way. For example, designers of information systems software have sometimes made extraordinary assumptions about the kind of information needed, and thus modelled, by their systems. This has been recognised by writers on the uses of information technology (e.g. Land, 1987). In fact most situations in the real world are so complex that it is simply not possible to observe, measure and quantify them comprehensively, or even to know what variables may actually be most important or relevant to a particular situation. Managers need to make judgements on the basis of their own industry's experience and their understanding of its environment.

Interpretations of situations are therefore usually constructed around a set of *typical* concepts – assumptions that allow us to make the simplifications and generalisations necessary in a normative model. Social scientists observe certain facts and events which they then use to construct typical behaviour patterns. The family life cycle model (*see* Fig. 5.5) is an example of this process. The models of behaviour that result remain *normative* models of typical behaviour only. Such is the complexity of the world that we need such models to find our way around it and understand it. We also need such models as part of our learning strategy, to help us extend our knowledge of the world (and our markets).

Kolb (1979) suggests that the formation of abstract concepts and generalisations – much in the sense in which we have been talking about 'models' here – is an integral part of a learning cycle. We then proceed to test the implications of the concepts or models in new situations, apply them to concrete experiences, observe and reflect on the results, and finally return to modify our models as necessary before continuing with the cycle.

A model is, therefore, a simplified representation of a phenomenon. Since it can select only those aspects which are of interest to a user, there can be many different models of the same phenomenon, according to the purposes and functions for which they are needed. In marketing, most models serve as useful tools which help predict patterns of demand. As such, they are as essential to understanding the public sector market as they are to the private sector. However, it is important to remember that models are essentially limited by their normative nature. Even with the aid of powerful modern computing, it is most unlikely that it will ever be possible to provide a comprehensive model of a market and all the variables which affect it. Moreover, models are inevitably based on the assumption that human behaviour is rational. Much of it is not. Good management will always require good intuition as well as good practice.

Summary

1 **The market is not homogeneous.** The word 'public' is often used to describe a general body of people or users. The market, like the public, is never homogeneous. Both society and the market are composed of groups, each with its own value systems and cultures. We refer to these as market segments.

2 **Equality and the public sector market.** Unfortunately, needs are rarely egalitarian. The same services can have different meanings, and even uses, for different people.

3 **The significance of market segmentation.** There is a range of techniques available for segmenting markets, mostly based on sociological and psychological methods. The nature of demand needs to be understood, and market segmentation methods offer structured ways of doing so.

4 **The segmentation process.** Once the market and its position in the value chain has been defined, the manager has a number of segmentation techniques available.

5 **Using market segmentation.** Having identified the market, defined its segments, and decided which ones are most relevant, managers need to consider how best to match resources with demand.

6 **Methodologies and the use of models.** In using any of these methods and techniques it is important to think about ways in which models structure and limit our understanding of the world.

Implications for management

The market audit

At this stage, a market audit is needed to evaluate the market and your own organisation's place in it. A market audit is an essential step in market planning and strategy. It requires a great deal of information, but is central to any real understanding of the relationship between the organisation, its environment and its users.

Kotler (1991) recommends six major components of the marketing audit.

- *The macro-environment audit.* This identifies the major external factors which provide the context for an organisation's operations. These include the three main influences on public sector marketing discussed in Chapter 2 – social (cultural), political and economic – but also include the demographic, ecological and economic dimensions. Ecological constraints are increasingly important in an environment where we are becoming increasingly conscious of the importance of 'green' issues, and the need to sustain natural resources. Certain countries – the Czech Republic, for example – already operate public sector incentive schemes, which include measures such as a pricing policy on the use of electric trams and trains, designed to encourage public use of transport systems which do not use the internal combustion engine with its attendant pollution problems.

- *Strategy.* This take the form of an analysis and description of the organisation's aims and objectives and the extent to which they are adapted to the environment. It involves an understanding and definition of the organisation's mission and its relationship to the market and its segments, which must include an understanding of competition and the nature of the value chain. These elements have been discussed in this chapter, and we have suggested that they are central to any useful understanding of user demands and requirements. It is also important to identify the resource constraints within which the organisation operates, and the channels by which its services are promoted (*see* Chapter 9).

- *Organisation.* A consideration of the organisation's marketing structure and its efficiency is necessary. How well is the marketing function integrated into the organisation? How successfully does the organisation 'own' marketing as a focus essential to its successful operations?

- *Systems.* How, and how well, does the organisation collect and analyse data, and use the information in terms of planning and control? This must include an assessment of the ways in which the individual organisation's management actually uses and acts upon marketing information. It also involves an examination of the ways in which the organisation organises, collects and distributes information about its markets, and the (ongoing) changes that affect them. Does this information provide sufficient and appropriate material for decision making? Does it 'feed into' the market planning process in the most effective way? Is there adequate research being carried out?

- *Productivity.* This involves an assessment of the extent to which marketing analysis and information contribute to the real effectiveness of the organisation. How does it contribute to satisfactory performance? What benefits does it provide for the organisation in measurable terms?

- *Functions.* There should be an audit of the organisation's marketing functions. What are the objectives of its services? How sensitive is the organisation to the demands and capabilities of its users? How, and how well are its services delivered? How effectively are its services promoted?

Croft (1994) offers a simpler and rather more pragmatic approach to the marketing audit. Its components are grouped under four headings: the environment; the market; the organisation and the competition. As has already been pointed out, competition is increasingly of concern to public sector organisations, many of which need to consider the nature of, and the threats posed by, competitors.

The *environmental analysis* may well use the familiar PEST (Political, Economic, Socio-cultural and Technological) checklist for identifying the environmental constraints (and opportunities) within which the organisation operates, but it also needs to identify and monitor the regulatory and legal environment. Each of these headings can be used to develop a list of considerations appropriate to the individual industry or service.

The *market analysis* will need to include many of the dimensions discussed in preceding chapters, but should focus on the *needs* generated by the relevant markets, their trends, their user characteristics and behaviours, and the effects of the methods used for their supply.

The *organisation analysis* needs to identify the organisation's aims and objectives, its capacity and its performance, its resources and strategy. Insofar as any competition also derives from other organisations, the same checklist can be used to *analyse competitors.*

Public sector complexity

The manager also needs a clear understanding of market focus in the context of the public sector multiple market. The matrix in Fig. 5.6 can be used to identify the degree to which an organisation pays attention to these markets.

	Primary	Facilitator	Legitimiser	Resourcer
Very attentive				
Attentive				
Adequate				
Inadequate				
None				

Fig. 5.6 The public sector market attentiveness grid

Market and market segmentation definition

Once the manager has defined the market for the specific organisation or the task involved, it is important to bring together as much data and information about it as possible. A vast amount of data is already published in social statistical form, without the need to engage in market research immediately. Using the categories of user characteristics and behaviours mentioned earlier in the chapter, the questions 'who uses the service?' and 'why do they use the service?' should be used to generate a list of ideas that will provide the broad basis of segmentation. This process can be 'brainstormed', but should involve personnel from as many different functional areas in the organisation as possible. Care should also be taken to retain a focus on user needs, rather than current practice.

This exercise should produce a list of user categories, each containing a number of characteristics and behaviours which are common to the users in that segment. The results should be assessed critically to ensure that the bases for segmentation are sufficiently relevant to the organisation's service, and large enough to constitute

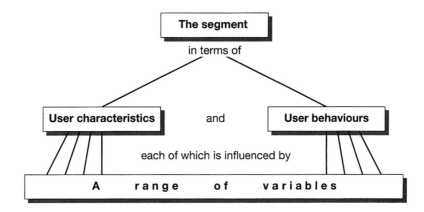

Fig. 5.7 Segmentation as a process

worthwhile market segments. Each characteristic or behaviour will usually involve a variable or condition which, in conjunction with the other features of the segment, help define it. Thus, the manager needs to define the segment as shown in Fig. 5.7.

The results of the process must be carefully evaluated, however, in order to determine *the viability* of each market segment. In public sector industries, as in private sector ones, resource limitations usually mean that managers have to develop and apply criteria to decide which segments are really viable in a given situation.

Once significant/viable segments have been identified, it is also possible to map the relationships between products/services and user groups/market segments. The benefits desired by market segments/user groups can be related to characteristics of the organisation's expertise in a matrix (*see* the sample matrix in Fig. 5.8). The user group can be identified along the top axis and the nature of the provision/expertise on the vertical axis. In each cell the benefit sought in the transaction is recorded, as is an indication of the nature of the transaction from the user group's viewpoint. The competition and the nature of their competitiveness, should also be identified in each cell.

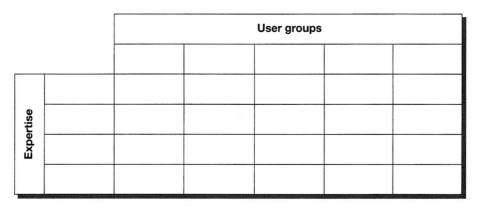

Fig. 5.8 A sample product/market grid

Checklist

In all segmentation processes, the manager needs to remember the following principles.

- In marketing, the product itself can be a variable. This principle is particularly true of service and industrial marketing.
- The same product will have different meanings to different customers/users.
- The most important decisions concern which markets and which market segments to serve.
- The 'product' is the total 'package' of benefits provided.

ISSUES FOR DISCUSSION

The following issues for discussion are presented in the form of questions. Examples from specific public sector industries should be incorporated into responses. Case studies can be used to provide some illustrations of the issues raised.

1 In what ways, and for what reasons, may different individuals have different 'needs'?

2 What does the principle of 'equity' imply for both providers and users of public sector services?

3 What actions can an organisation take to focus provision on those areas of the community which have the greatest need? Does this differ from the concept of 'demarketing'?

4 Why does successful marketing need market segmentation?

References

Audit Commission (1984) *Report and Accounts.* Year ended 31 March 1984. London, HMSO.

Audit Commission (1988) *The Competitive Council.* Management Papers No.1. London, HMSO.

Canovan, M. (1981) *Populism.* London: Junction Books.

Croft, M.J. (1994) *Market Segmentation.* London and New York: Routledge and Kegan Paul.

Elcock, H. (1994) Local Government. London and New York: Routledge and Kegan Paul.

Her Majesty's Government (1991) *The Citizen's Charter.* London: HMSO.

Hill, E., O'Sullivan, C. and O'Sullivan T. (1995) *Creative Arts Marketing.* Oxford: Butterworth–Heinemann.

Johnson, G. and Scholes, K. (1997) *Exploring Corporate Strategy* (4th edn). Hemel Hempstead: Prentice Hall International (UK) Ltd.

Kelly, G. (1955) *The Psychology of Personal Constructs.* New York: W. W. Norton and Co.

Kerley, R. (1994) *Managing in Local Government.* Basingstoke and London: The Macmillan Press Ltd.

King, D.S. and Pierre, J. (eds) (1990) *Challenges to Local Government.* London: Sage Publications.

Kolb, D. (1979) *Organisational Psychology. An Experiential Approach.* New York and London: Prentice-Hall.

Kotler, P. (1991) *Marketing Management. Analysis, Planning, Implementation and Control.* Englewood Cliffs, New Jersey: Prentice-Hall, Inc.

Kotler, P. and Roberto, E.L. (1989) *Social Marketing. Strategies for Changing Public Behavior.* New York: The Free Press, Macmillan, Inc.

Land, F. (1987) 'Social Aspects of Information Systems' in Piercy, N. (ed) *Management Information Systems: The Technology Challenge.* London: Croom Helm.

Marcuse, M. (1964) *One Dimensional Man.* London: Routledge and Kegan Paul.

Maslow, A.H. (1954) *Motivation and Personality.* New York: Harper and Row.

Muggeridge, M. (1989) *The Thirties. 1930-1940 in Great Britain.* London: Weidenfeld and Nicolson. Originally published 1940.

Oliver, G. (1990) *Marketing Today* (3rd edn). Hemel Hempstead: Prentice-Hall International (UK) Ltd.

Plummer, J.T. (1974) 'The Concept and Application of Life Style Segmentation', *Journal of Marketing*, January.

Stewart, J. (1986) *The New Management of Local Government*. London: Allen & Unwin for the Institute of Local Government Studies, University of Birmingham.

Swingewood, A. (1977) *The Myth of Mass Culture*. London: Macmillan Press.

Williams, K.C. (1992) *Behavioural Aspects of Marketing*. Oxford: Butterworth-Heinemann.

CHAPTER 6

Service, control and quality

CHAPTER OVERVIEW

'I have to say I didn't like their attitude' is a comment frequently heard when users have come into contact with public sector and other bureaucratic organisations. The quality of the transaction is an issue which has already been alluded to, and is one which is of considerable concern to public sector managers. The plethora of Total Quality Management programmes is evidence of this. The performance of the public sector is subject to greater scrutiny, and performance indicators are increasingly related to user satisfaction levels.

Earlier chapters have shown that the 'satisfaction mix' is made up of a number of variables. We are living in an age where the expectations of clients and users are rising. Managing the satisfaction mix is a key element in the maintenance of good buyer/user relationships. This chapter examines issues in developing client satisfaction and discusses how appropriate measures can be developed and implemented. It looks at some of the strengths and weaknesses of quality programmes and discusses how to differentiate between normal transactional expectations and those factors which can create higher levels of customer satisfaction.

KEY LEARNING OUTCOMES

By the end of this chapter, you should be able to:

- understand the components of good service delivery;
- examine the nature of user expectations;
- explore the 'orientation' of the organisation;
- understand the importance of control and quality; and
- appreciate the nature of performance measurement and methods.

Introduction

Earlier chapters have discussed the nature of products and services offered by the public sector, and their relationships with market segments. To complete the discussion of this theme, it is important to identify and manage issues concerned with organisational responses and resulting resource implications.

Resource management issues will be dealt with in Chapter 12, which focuses on marketing management. In this chapter, issues of managing and measuring the organisation's responses to its markets will be discussed.

The transaction

We discussed earlier the concept of the product or service 'package', which is made up of three elements: the core benefit, tangible elements, and the intangible elements of the 'extended product' (*see* Fig. 6.1).

This model for understanding the product or service now seems firmly established (*see*, for example, Humble, 1989). Users/customers generally rate the benefits of fitness for use, committed effort to understanding their needs, reliability and after-sales service much more highly than price considerations. The benefits of a product or service, as perceived by the user, are also likely to be far more important to him or her than the inherent characteristics of the thing or the process *per se*. Christopher (1991) recommends that we think of the 'offer' made by the product or service, rather than of the product or service itself. The totality of the 'offer' is the sum of all tangible and intangible elements, the core, expected, augmented and potential benefits, which can be represented together as 'targets' for marketing purposes.

The concept of the 'offer' and the significance of the 'extended product' – or the 'halo effect' – are very important in private sector marketing as they are often key factors in determining market share – for example, in the purchasing of consumer durables, such as televisions, washing machines and kitchen appliances.

A family may decide to purchase a dishwasher in order to reduce the daily task of washing cooking vessels, cutlery and tableware – essential to the maintenance of good health, tidiness, etc., all of which are perceived as benefits. The *pre-purchase process* involves the consideration of issues of product quality, style and design, colour, dimensions, capacity, etc. – all tangible features of a dishwasher. A particular brand may also be preferred, the perception of which has psychological as well as physical characteristics. At this stage of the purchase, the elements of service are not yet predominating, but will be starting to influence the transaction. *At the time of purchase*, however, the buyers will certainly take into consideration the manner in which they have been treated during the pre-purchase stage and particularly at the purchase stage. However, there are significant differences between the expectations of different segments of the market – expectations which will colour their perceptions of the product itself. The purchasers will then choose the outlet which deals with

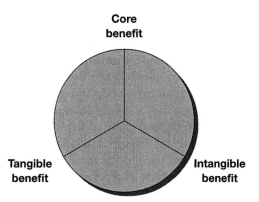

Fig. 6.1 The elements of benefit

them best, according to their expectations. Research indicates that such an outlet may not be the most convenient in terms of location for the user, but other factors involved in the transaction may be perceived as more important than the inconvenience of travel to a retail outlet which is not 'on the customer's doorstep'. Market share for a particular outlet may well depend upon the nature and character of the transaction process it provides for the customer. It is for this reason that so many organisations are developing so-called 'relationship marketing' schemes, although some of these are based upon 'free gift' and loyalty schemes which are a poor substitute for appropriate levels of customer attention.

This concept may be further illustrated by the mature student taking a part-time degree course to enhance his or her qualifications. A Board of Examiners may expect its external examiners to restrict their comments to an evaluation of academic concerns: standards of achievement, design of syllabuses, quality of teaching performance, etc. However, external examiners who actually talk to students about their perceptions of the course will normally be aware that the students see other factors, such as the availability of car parking, helpfulness of administrative staff and efficiency of course organisation, as integral aspects of the course. These elements, perceived simply as parts of the whole student experience, can also act as performance indicators. A low standard of support facilities will usually affect students' perception of the course as a whole. One of the most important 'levers' with which to improve student retention rates in universities is the quality of student support.

When discussing marketing, particularly service marketing, it is therefore important to distinguish between the benefits being sought – the 'core' service – and the issues related to the transaction, which is similarly often described as 'service'.

Customer service has been defined as a system designed to provide a continuing link between provider and user in order to satisfy the user on a long-term basis. Unfortunately, the public sector has a major difficulty in managing this relationship with its primary market. The existence and power of the other, multiple markets (*see* Chapter 3), each with its own priorities, often produce areas of conflicting priorities. It is often far from easy, for example, to reconcile a desire for increased effectiveness with a need to reduce costs.

Nevertheless, in all areas of marketing, it is often issues concerned with the nature of the transaction which cause the greatest problems for users, and they are invariably related to the psychological aspects of the transaction. When people talk about 'getting good service' they are, more often than not, speaking about the manner in which they were dealt with rather than about the quality of the benefit received. Some writers, for example, propose that the measure of an organisation's effectiveness is not how its staff treat customers under normal circumstances, but how they treat customers when things go wrong. Indeed, such are the vagaries of human behaviour that a strong customer-focused transaction can overcome many shortcomings in the provision of the core benefit, particularly where the benefit is being provided by an 'expert'. For example, a doctor with a good 'bedside manner' may have a longer patient list than a doctor who is expert in his or her field, but who has relatively poor interpersonal skills and has a reputation for being brusque with patients. Consequently, for the purposes of this chapter, the discussion of 'service' will be concerned with the nature of the transaction process.

The importance of customers

Since the 1980s, standards of service have become important criteria of quality in the private sector. This may be seen as part of a longer-term trend which has increasingly moved power away from the supplier towards the consumer. A well-known car promotion slogan once claimed that the consumer 'drives' everything the company does. Some sources (for example, NEDO, 1981) indicate that, in the United Kingdom, 90 per cent of companies identify service as the principal factor which differentiates them from their competitors. Often, this service competence is not properly developed. This is why additional services are important in developing and sustaining buyer/seller transactions.

Unless there is a real understanding of the nature of the customer requirement in terms of the manner in which the supplier deals with its customers, the concept of good service will remain on the level of 'telling the customer beforehand that the company will be late with delivery'. Many organisations in both the private and public sectors have made some progress towards a better understanding of the importance of the transaction process. Many have introduced 'customer care' programmes, although these can raise expectations which are not met in reality.

Consequently, Christopher (1991) and others have pointed out that, although much lip service is paid to the importance of customers, few strategies have actually been built around the concept of consumer satisfaction and marketing. Much of the stated concern with customers and users has proved to be cosmetic. Many industries still find it hard to change from a dominant concern with product and with resources to a prioritised interest in marketing. This is all the more surprising since customers and users, not products or services, create profits and determine the effectiveness of any organisation – a point made by Drucker (1989). In the world of commerce, it is increasingly obvious that weaknesses in quality and service drive business away. It is a marketing paradox that good marketing makes life easier or better for the customer, but can make it more difficult for the supplier.

There are areas, however, where the development of relationships in consumer markets is a key issue. This is certainly the case in the area of service markets (and many public sector industries are in service markets). Service markets are very similar to industrial markets because the nature of the transaction is different in each individual case. In service markets it is particularly important to identify:

- *the marketing 'hygiene factors'*, normal client expectations, the absence of which causes dissatisfaction,

  and

- *the marketing 'halos'* – those additional factors in the transaction process which dramatically increase customer/user satisfaction.

In public sector services, it can be quite difficult to understand the importance of these factors, particularly in a situation where an organisation is effectively a monopoly provider, or where scarcity of resources imposes limits on supply. For example, if a householder has an appointment with an official who is visiting for the purposes of assessing the householder's needs, and that official is late for the appointment, the delay is likely to cause dissatisfaction, since timeliness is a normal expectation. It will take a good deal of attention to the householder to over-come the lack of that simple courtesy. If the official is on time, but is brusque, his or her manner is also likely to cause dissatisfaction. If the official is punctual, helpful and explains the situation in relation to benefit clearly and politely, even if the core need and expectation may not wholly be met, there will be a much greater proba-bility of satisfaction than in the first two instances.

It is only when we start to examine organisations from a marketing standpoint that the elements of service can be properly understood. Old habits die hard. The dictionary definitions of 'service' usually contain references to 'public service' – a body of public servants concerned with some particular work done to meet some general need. It follows that public services are accountable to 'the public' (*see* Chapter 5). However, the idea of public accountability, in the sense of being responsible to 'the public', has a number of different dimensions for public ser-vices. We may categorise these responsibilities broadly in terms of the demands made on the public service organisation by:

- *users', clients', and customers' needs and wants* (the core service or benefit);
- *regulatory and legal requirements*, which often place constraints on many aspects of the transaction;
- *political decisions and policies*, which may also influence most aspects;
- *financial obligations to its funding bodies* (and/or shareholders, in the case of priva-tised services and utilities) which put resource constraints on the transaction;
- *public culture and opinion* – an 'intangible' but important dimension of account-ability affecting the perceptions of users.

Public sector organisations always face a complex problem. They have a respon-sibility to ensure that they are economically effective and perform efficiently, which could be mutually exclusive, while they are under close scrutiny from a number of different directions. Cannon (1991) proposes that successful organisations focus on effectiveness rather than efficiency if they really wish to achieve client satisfaction. In their operations, such organisations prioritise the more effective procedures rather than the more efficient ones, as illustrated in Fig. 6.2. *See* Cannon (1991) for an alternative comparison between the goals of efficiency and effectiveness.

It can be seen from Fig. 6.2 that the efficiency column is the one that tends to dominate operations in public sector industries. In order to achieve new levels of efficiency and effectiveness, public sector organisations are increasingly required to disclose information about their operations. They are subject to a wide range of demands from their multiple markets. They must demonstrate that they are responsible to their stakeholders. The UK Government's *The Citizen's Charter* (1991) committed public services to the principle of openness, stating that there should be no secrecy about how they are run, who is in charge, how much they cost and whether or not they are meeting their standards.

Historically, managers in the public sector have concentrated on the allocation of resources and on building internal systems and structures, often formal and bureau-cratic in form, in order to measure internal efficiency. This approach produced many restrictive practices and rigid demarcation lines between areas of responsibility. Any

To be EFFECTIVE	is not always	To be EFFICIENT
• Obtaining best results		• Using the 'correct' processes
• Maximising benefits		• Carefully controlling and reducing costs
• Using resources optimally		• Protecting the resource base as a priority

Fig. 6.2 Effectiveness and efficiency: a comparison

focus on relationships once tended to be internal, within the organisation – for example, between officers and elected members in local government – instead of paying enough attention to relationships with the external environment.

It is still depressingly common to find organisations attempting to devise fresh strategies with no apparent consideration of the needs of their primary markets. In such organisational cultures, managers tend to concentrate on their organisation's 'product', rather than on their users' and customers' needs. This creates a *product orientation*, and can also lead to a dominance of what Levitt (1986) called *system rule*.

A case in point is the UK's Driving Standards Agency. With the introduction in 1996 of written as well as practical tests for driving, the candidate for a driving test now has to write to four different addresses.

1 The candidate writes enclosing a form to one address in order to purchase a provisional licence.

2 The candidate applies to another address, with payment, to obtain an appointment for the written test using another form.

3 He or she applies to a third address, again making a payment and completing a form, in order to obtain an appointment for the practical driving test.

4 The candidate must send yet another form and payment to a fourth address to obtain a 'full' driving licence, once the test has been passed.

Having filled in all the various forms the candidate has to attend two different locations at different times for the written and practical tests (what price 'one stop shopping'?). This is a classic case of systems rule (a concept which will be examined in more detail later) and, because of the active-supplier, reluctant-user relationship, the candidate has no option but to comply. It seems little wonder that there are high levels of candidate dissatisfaction.

Such systems prevail throughout the public sector. Managers would do well to identify the processes that the customer has to follow in order to complete a task. Another example is provided by out-patient hospital treatment for a simple condition. The patient may well have to:

- report to reception;
- see the consultant;
- go to the X-ray department;
- go to Haematology;
- visit the consultant again;
- go to the pharmacy; and
- visit reception again to make another appointment.

While some of these visits to resources which have fixed locations – for example, X-ray – may be unavoidable, an organisation which was more client-focused would enable blood tests, dispensing and appointments to be undertaken at a single point. A production orientation means that this usually does not happen.

In developing an appropriate response to user needs, the various elements of the marketing mix – the 'four Ps', product, price, place and promotion – have much to commend them. They offer a structured approach to the analysis of strategic marketing options. In consumer, or discretionary, marketing they have a lot to offer the marketing manager. In service marketing, however, especially in non-discretionary markets, and also in industrial and organisational marketing, rather than being strategic tools in the marketing armoury, the 'four Ps' are, in fact, tactical options. Their use depends upon the nature of the relationship between user and supplier, between customer and provider.

Of course, may parts of the public sector are providing services for relatively captive markets, in which users continue to be very restricted in their ability to exercise choice (*see* Chapter 3). Historically, much of the public sector has been engaged in distributing resources on behalf of the State. However, since the election of a Conservative UK government in 1979, there has been a growing political belief that market forces contribute to efficiency in managing resources and demand. The term, *consumerism*, has often been used to describe a social phenomenon which privileges the customer. A customer-centred approach, it is argued, encourages access, choice and quality. It helps the organisation to consider how its activities are actually experienced by its users. Kotler (1987) argues that an organisation's customer orientation can be measured by the amount it spends on effective market research. The Audit Commission used the phrase 'value for money' as a means of emphasising the accountability of public sector services, and as a general label for performance measurement.

Customers and expectations

In recent years, trends in both competitive markets and political initiatives have encouraged the development of *commodity markets* – that is, markets in which competing products or services are seen as similar or capable of being substituted one for another. Porter (1985) has written extensively on the subject, and believes that competition is the key factor influencing the success or failure of commercial organisations. He maintains that competition is equally important for dealing with products as it is for services (Porter, 1985, p. 4), and stresses the power of the buyer.

Where the principle of choice has become paramount, either commercially or politically, quality and service have become the most powerful means of differentiating between products or services. There seems to be a trend which has progressively given more power to the user, and by doing so has emphasised the importance of the user's perceptions of quality. However, where there is no competition there may seem to be little obvious need for organisations to develop strategies to develop a competitive 'edge' by recognising this factor.

The Citizen's Charter (1991) and the Charters subsequently published for various public sector industries – for example, general practitioners in the Health Service – have made some attempt to apply these principles and priorities. The Charters may well have had some impact on the process of moving from a product orientation to a market orientation. Politically, it will obviously be expedient to provide 'value for money', to emphasise the principle of public accountability and its relationship with the needs and attitudes of users. It is also claimed that a needs-based focus will enable the direct users of a service to obtain the best resources. Crompton and Lamb Jr. (1986, p. 330) have pointed out that a public commitment to marketing (in the sense of providing people with what they need) is likely to provide more popular and legislative support. *The Citizen's Charter* (1991, p. 2) made a deliberate pledge to make 'the public services more responsible to the wishes of their users'. Competition, it argued, stimulates choice, improves quality and increases the level of individual involvement in the exchange process. The subtitle of *The Citizen's Charter* (repeated as a header on all 49 pages of the text) was 'Raising the Standard'.

Unfortunately, as a marketing document (as distinct from its function as a political statement of intent), *The Citizen's Charter* failed to recognise explicitly the problem addressed in Chapter 5 of this book. Concepts of 'the citizen', 'the market', 'consumers' and 'users', etc. cannot usefully be generalised as a single, undifferentiated entity – 'the public'. It must be recognised that any market is made up of distinct groups of people. The market has to be segmented. Different users have different needs. Moreover, thanks to the nature of the public sector environment (*see* Chapters 1, 2 and 3), absolute choice never exists. It is worth remembering that increased choice is not the same as free choice. User expectations remain relatively restricted, although this should not be used as an excuse for failing to pay them adequate attention. They remain the most direct indicators of demand and important measures of performance.

In practice, the individual's perception of 'good service', related to the quality of the transaction, is intimately linked to the issue of 'clientship' – the client's perceived needs and expected benefits. An organisation therefore has to identify the constituencies it serves.

One of the difficulties in managing 'service' derives from the way in which the components of the 'service mix' will be very much dependent upon the nature of the product–market relationship. Given that service is largely determined by the interaction of human beings as providers and customers, much 'good service' is concerned with issues of etiquette or good manners. There are, however, a number of other dimensions involved. The definition of 'good service' is also conditioned by perceptions of the 'core' service provided. There is clearly a close relationship between the 'core benefit' and the manner in which it is provided.

It is worth taking two examples of provision and identifying the nature of this relationship.

Example 1: the UK Inland Revenue

Historically, the image of the income tax inspector has not been a popular one. Although levels of national tax are determined in the political arena, in the interests of national economy, people are inclined to regard income tax as an imposition, rather than as a source of direct benefit, despite the fact that the revenue funds many of the services and developments provided by the State.

Of course, paying income tax in return for the use of state-subsidised services and infrastructure provision is not a discretionary exchange. The State has the power to enforce payment from anyone legally eligible to pay it. The annual income tax return was traditionally regarded as a statutory nuisance, and the length and language of the forms used contributed to some resentment. The tax inspector's need to enquire into all sources of income, allied to a general distrust of anyone 'snooping' into matters generally and culturally considered as private matters for the individual, helped create a stereotyped image of the inspector as a bureaucratic civil servant obsessed with 'systems rule', and generally unsympathetic to his or her 'victims'. Moreover, the workload for tax inspectors frequently caused relatively long delays in their correspondence with clients, which could easily add to their mythical reputation for unfriendliness.

The *core benefit* most clients are seeking in their contact with tax inspectors is a clear understanding and formal acknowledgement of their tax status and liabilities. The nature of old-style tax return forms, the notes that accompanied them, and the apparently 'arms length' behaviour of inspectors did little to persuade many people that they were receiving good service. Thus the tax inspector who issues dire warnings of retribution for not submitting a tax return on time should also ensure that those completed are dealt with promptly.

Since the *Citizen's Charter* initiative, considerable effort has been devoted to promoting a much more friendly system, easier to understand and with a more personal 'touch'. Although few would yet welcome the presence of a tax inspector under the bed or in the wardrobe (a reference to some promotion campaigns for certain kinds of financial advice), some serious attempts have been made to create a more friendly and helpful image, and new self-assessment tax forms do appear to be easier to understand without the help of an accountant. The response is an indication of the government's and inspectorate's awareness that perceptions of the core benefit are highly dependent on perceptions of good service.

Unfortunately, in this case, the nature of the service itself makes it extremely difficult to change powerful, deeply imprinted popular perceptions very quickly. The active-provider, reluctant-user relationship makes the development of better contact difficult.

Example 2: a museum example

Since 1989, the Czech Republic has made good progress towards becoming a modern, mixed economy. Certain parts of the country, particularly Prague, benefit considerably from tourism. Prague has the reputation of being a romantic city. Heritage is a major attraction in a city with large numbers of historical buildings, museums and art galleries. However, modern concepts of marketing are still relatively new in a country long accustomed to a command-led economy.

St. Agnes' Convent is a complex of buildings near the Vlatava River and is used to house the Prague National Gallery's collection of Czech nineteenth-century art. Although situated in a picturesque area of the city, it is not particularly easy to find without a map. The funding for advertising permanent collections, and even major temporary exhibitions, has been poor. Nevertheless, a determined visitor is likely to seek out St. Agnes' Convent in search of benefits. Hill *et al.* (1995, p. 106) describe the core benefit of an arts experience as 'aesthetic emotion'. Surrounding this core benefit are a number of 'product levels'. These contain elements which could be described as 'psychological value added'. Closest to the visitor's core benefit is a 'central experience' level which contains such elements as atmosphere, staff attitudes, physical environment, venue ambience, 'branding' and ease of access, while the next level of 'extended experience' includes catering, merchandise and ancillary products. These can be represented in diagrammatic form as in Fig. 6.3.

The non-Czech visitor to St. Agnes' Convent in early 1995 was faced with a number of difficulties. The core benefit, in the form of works of art placed in the galleries, was immediately apparent. These were labelled with titles (usually in English as well as Czech), artists' names and dates. However, there was virtually no 'interpretative' material to develop the experience available to a visitor unfamiliar with the history of Czech art or the Czech language. The only relevant publications then available were editions of postcards dating from the Communist

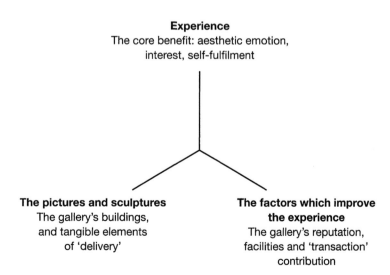

Experience
The core benefit: aesthetic emotion,
interest, self-fulfilment

The pictures and sculptures
The gallery's buildings,
and tangible elements
of 'delivery'

**The factors which improve
the experience**
The gallery's reputation,
facilities and 'transaction'
contribution

Fig. 6.3 Components of a museum experience

era, containing short texts on aspects of nineteenth-century Czech art in Russian, French, German, Czech and English. There were no catalogues of the collection available, and no general histories of nineteenth-century Czech art in the book-shop, although the staff were extremely friendly and polite.

In this case, 'good service' might have been expected to provide more support for the experience, including relevant information which could enhance and/or even modify the visitor's experience of the core benefit. Moreover, these benefits could easily be provided in tangible form – for example, paper publications – although many modern galleries are increasingly using video and interactive video materials in this role.

Issues of response

It is very difficult to evaluate a service experience before experiencing it. Furthermore, because the evaluation will be dependent to some extent upon reactions between personalities, there is a strong element of subjectivity likely to be involved. It is possible, however, to identify several categories of provider attitudes. Given that the market will be made up of people with differing levels of experience and knowledge, the provision of good support for the transaction will be important for everybody involved.

In all industries, a number of different attitudes prevail – sometimes referred to as *business orientations* – and they have been categorised into four major types:

1 customer orientation;

2 product, production or service orientation;

3 system orientation;

4 marketing orientation.

Customer orientation (C)

Customer orientation is identified where:

● 'the customer is always right';

● the organisation can accommodate the problems of individual users or customers;

● those in the organisation who have direct contact with users or customers have a user/customer focus;

Consequences can include disrupted production schedules, high costs and poor matching of needs and resources.

Production or service orientation (P)

Production or service orientation can be found, for example, in manufacturing industries where fundamental business decisions are made solely in the interests of production departments. It is revealed where:

- delivery methods and schedules are set by management without taking user or customer needs into account;

- the design and production of the product or service involves costs which are unjustified in terms of effectiveness;

- the product or service itself is seen as more important than the benefits it provides for its customers or users.

Consequences can include late deliveries and broken promises. Such organisations are in the position of having to sell the available capacity.

System orientation (S)

System orientation is often a feature of nationalised industries and bureaucracies where things have to be done according to the system, sometimes irrespective of production or customer needs. It is revealed where:

- almost all the organisation's activities are governed by standardised procedures;

- its members have virtually no autonomy or opportunity to be flexible in their responses to users or customers;

- a hierarchical system of control and line management is characterised by bureaucratic adherence to 'the rules'.

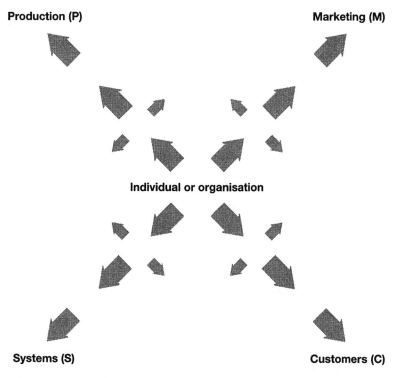

Fig. 6.4 Orientation of an individual/organisation
(after Levitt, 1986)

Consequences can involve dissatisfaction, both internal and external, from suppliers and customers.

The idea of 'system rule' can be related to McGregor's 'Theory X' (1960). 'Theory X' describes a traditional, and now somewhat discredited, view of direction and control, and assumes that human beings have an innate dislike of work. They therefore need to be directed, controlled and, if necessary, threatened with penalties if they do not perform well enough to help achieve their organisation's goals. According to this view, human beings generally have a desire for security, relatively little ambition and a wish to avoid responsibility. This paternalistic approach to management emphasises the role of control and typifies 'classical management' theories. It can also inhibit the organisation's ability to cope with radical change. A bureaucratic organisation will often display signs of a climate of defensiveness when faced with the need to change. As Argyris (1985) has pointed out, most organisations possess defensive routines which inhibit their ability to learn and change.

In a system-orientated organisation, it often seems that nothing matters but the system itself and ensuring that it operates efficiently. Since efficiency is not the same as effectiveness, efficiency can become the inward-looking preoccupation of those within the organisation, which may blind them to the need to respond and relate to the organisation's environment and users. System orientation can produce the unbending official response to apparently reasonable requests, on the grounds that 'it is not the organisation's policy to do this', 'I'm sorry, but the rules don't allow us to do that', or 'Don't ask me, I only work here!'. A system orientation is often dominant in non-profit organisations, particularly public sector ones which are heavily controlled by systems.

Managers cannot afford to concentrate exclusively on the user or customer (point C in Fig. 6.4), nor can they focus on production (or service) or systems, to the detriment of the organisation's other functions. In practice, extremes of orientation do not often occur. The profiles of individual managers will be fairly widely distributed. An average profile will show some care for the company, slightly more care for the customer but no exclusive commitment to one or the other. However, the co-existence of different managerial orientations will lead to conflict. If objectives and attitudes can be developed to ensure an effective management team, the combined organisational effects will be very significant. It is for these reasons that a marketing orientation is extremely important.

Marketing orientation (M)

A marketing orientation is revealed where:

- an organisation's managers identify those areas and activities where its interests are consistent with its customers;
- there is a continual search for better ways of satisfying customers and monitoring effectiveness;
- all the organisation's members 'own' the marketing approach.

This results in more satisfaction for both the organisation and the customer because a marketing orientation, on the other hand, calls for a balance to be struck between the value of things it can do for users or customers and the demands of production and the use of effective systems to achieve long-run company profits, or efficient services. A marketing-orientated company must therefore have marketing-orientated managers, and the marketing attitude must prevail throughout the company. Its people must look onwards and outwards. An organisation which has a team of three marketing-orientated managers will have three times the impact of three managers with customer, production and system orientations respectively. Moreover, a good marketing orientation will help reduce uncertainties and risks.

It is evident that in the P or S situation shown in Fig. 6.4, there is considerable potential conflict between departments because managers tend to prioritise departmental efficiency rather than company effectiveness. In a situation where the marketing concept is accepted, the likelihood of conflict is reduced because the objectives of managers are directed towards the well-being of the organisation as a whole, and decisions reflect the views of the corporate body rather than those of its functional components. As the needs of the organisation and the users or customers become more closely identified, the degree of conflict between departments decreases and organisational and customer satisfaction increases.

A marketing orientation is measured by point M in the diagram and is the most meaningful expression of the marketing concept. A customer orientation is measured by point C; a production or service orientation by point P; and a system orientation by point S.

The managerial choice either to impose rigid systems or to engender a true customer orientation will result in two possible approaches to service delivery: the *managerial approach* (heavy on systems and cost-orientated) which attempts to regiment the service experience and produce control and conformity; and the *customer orientation/enthusiast approach* where everything is dropped in order to serve the customer. The latter leads to a relationship-orientated approach, often involving higher costs but producing higher customer perceptions of service quality.

In practice, an organisation's management rarely exhibits only one particular orientation, although one orientation may dominate. Different departmental managers or directors, because they have different objectives, may display different orientations. In a commercial organisation, for example, the sales manager, prioritising turnover, will tend to be customer oriented. The works manager, concentrating on output, will tend to be production orientated. The office or administration manager, focusing on order and organisation, will tend to be system orientated. In such a situation, fulfilling all three different objectives can lead to conflict and low effectiveness.

An individual's orientation can be tested against an adaptation of Levitt's *orientation grid* (1986) (*see* Fig. 6.4), and some simple questions can be used to identify it.

Concepts of control and quality

Methods of control play a central role in the above process. Control is the means by which any organisation's activities are regulated to ensure that its aims and objectives are met. Gerloff (1985) commented that control would not be such a major organisational issue if it was possible to be confident that all members of an organisation always acted consistently in line with the requirements of the organisation itself. In real life, this consistency is rarely found. Control therefore features prominently in the design of organisations. It is usually represented as one of the basic functions of management. Control systems are designed to assure the manager that performance meets organisational objectives. They provide continuous means of monitoring performance and providing information for decision making.

Control systems

There have been in the past three main forms of control systems:

- *Quality Management* (QM) has become a recurrent phrase in management literature in recent years (*see*, for example, Foster and Whittle, 1990). At one time, quality issues were seen primarily as technological ones, aimed primarily at efficiency.

- *Quality Control* (QC) seeks to maintain standards by continuous inspection. In service industries this takes the form of continuous performance monitoring. A large number of controls are required to produce quantifiable measurements, and bureaucracies tend to do their best to standardise both their inputs and their outputs.

- *Quality Assurance* (QA), as a development, is a term used to describe the use of precise procedures to achieve clearly defined objectives, a process identified easily with the BS 5750 standard and with Statistical Process Control (SPC) in the UK, and is characterised by very detailed manuals on procedures, and a concern with systems.

Unfortunately, although BS 5750 will certainly install prescribed procedures in any organisation, it does not provide any mechanism to diagnose culture and attitudes, although it will certainly influence behaviours (*see* Cooke, 1992, pp. 153–5). There may, in fact, be a danger that BS 5750 can confirm a public sector organisation's existing culture of bureaucracy by the very way it provides clear definitions of roles, responsibilities and work processes. It can establish very rigid procedures in an attempt to 'do things right', rather than ensuring that the organisation 'does the right things'.

Total Quality Management

Total Quality Management (TQM), a phenomenon of the 1990s, tries to address the issue of quality at a more radical level by tackling the issue of culture – that collection of beliefs, assumptions, attitudes and values existing in any organisation (described in Williams *et al.*, 1989, Chapter 1). Total Quality Management tries to achieve a customer orientation by inculcating it at all levels throughout an organisation – by changing the organisation's culture. This becomes an obvious field for professional organisational development, and a long and difficult path for those organisations that attempt it. The rewards for a successful attempt are, however, considerable.

Morgan and Murgatroyd (1994) insist that TQM is more than just 'a management approach'. It is a whole philosophy (as is marketing) and way of thinking which is now attracting many different types of organisations, interested in both increasing quality and reducing costs. In commercial sector organisations it is credited with creating competitive advantage, and for non-profit, public sector industries, it offers a number of useful concepts and techniques. Morgan and Murgatroyd (1994) define its central ideas and practices as a 'paradigm' – a pattern or set of integrated ideas producing a framework for action. TQM requires the involvement and participation of *all* members of an organisation (not just its management), its culture and its systems. It is driven by the needs and wants of its customers, although these are now defined as both the end-users outside the organisation and the 'internal customers' within the organisation – that is, all those who have a 'stake' in the supplier–customer value chain. Feedback from the customers is part of a continuous process of design to improve the quality of product or service.

TQM, and its concern with 'total customer responsiveness' (Foster and Whittle, 1990, p. 18), is primarily about improving ways of satisfying customer needs. In an article published in 1990, Foster *et al.* explored ways of maintaining commitment, motivation and momentum in organisations seeking to apply quality management. This appears to be a particular problem in the public sector industries, where internal requirements have traditionally been seen as more important than customer/user requirements.

TQM encourages those who provide services to adopt a customer perspective. However, providers usually form a number of (sometimes stereotyped) assumptions about their end-users' needs. The customer's or user's experience, from beginning to end, needs to be looked at in detail. It is suggested that this can be modelled using six stages:

- search;
- arrival;
- pre-contact;
- contact;
- withdrawal; and
- follow-up.

The fact that these terms are not unlike the history of a sexual encounter or a visit to the cash dispenser makes the sequence relatively easy to remember! This model can be used to follow the customer's experience of a service from beginning to end, and can prove a useful management tool.

This emphasis on customers' and users' perceptions also challenges traditional notions of organisational control. Conventional models have placed senior management at the peak of the control 'pyramid' *and* at the top of the hierarchy of organisational importance. TQM places the customer/user base in the position of greatest importance. The individuals and teams within the organisation assume more delegated responsibility for improving services to customers and users. They are, after all, much closer to the customers. A key management function thus becomes one of support, helping to identify ways of improving the quality of service and finding ways of implementing them.

Quality has been defined as an object's degree of excellence. In practical terms this means that a product or a service can be evaluated by the extent to which all its features contribute to the satisfaction of its purpose. In manufacturing, this will involve close conformance to specifications. In service provision, this will require the best possible conformance with customer and user demand. The element of human nature, so much less predictable than that of the machine, does, however, figure more strongly in service industries. Morgan and Murgatroyd (1994) identify three elements of service which inform perceptions of service quality:

- interpersonal relationships;

- procedures, process and environment;

- professional and technical aspects.

All three need to be kept in balance, since any undue emphasis on one is likely to obscure the importance of one or both of the others.

Since one of the most important characteristics of service provision (*see* Chapter 4) is the way in which a service is inseparable from its delivery, the nature of processes – the ways in which inputs are translated into outputs – becomes extremely important. If the essence of TQM lies in the need to treat every task as a process, all processes need to be defined, monitored and used to develop and improve performance. TQM therefore relies heavily on control as a means of ensuring that processes provide data which are analysed and used to make decisions. This approach to process explains the importance of performance measurement (*see* the following section). It has also produced a list of TQM concepts, originally derived from manufacturing industries, which are increasingly applied in service and public sector organisations. The most familiar ones include the following concepts.

- *Customer satisfaction.* This involves improving the levels of service satisfaction for both internal (organisational) and external customers.

- *Zero defects.* This means avoiding all mistakes in the process and ensuring that all performance criteria are met. 'Benchmarking' is an important tool for achieving this. Given the variability of service transactions, this can prove impossible to achieve.

- *On-time performance.* Deadlines should be met all the time.

- *Nil defections.* This involves ensuring that customers, clients, etc. stay with the service and do not defect to any alternative ones (*see* Chapter 2 for discussion of the danger posed in an active-provider, active-user situation).

- *Cycle time.* This means reducing the time taken to complete activities.

It becomes obvious that TQM relies heavily on teamwork, especially cross-functional teamwork, and the behavioural characteristics of a 'learning organisation' (*see* Chapter 10) in order to be effective.

Morgan and Murgatroyd (1994) acknowledge the difficulties in applying TQM to public sector organisations. Much resistance to it is inevitably cultural. Attempts to implement TQM in most organisations involve major cultural change, as is recognised, for example, by Cooke (1992) in the context of local government and other public sector organisations. The extent to which public sector organisations are usually highly professionalised, formalised in their structures and carefully regulated, will tend naturally to inhibit the adoption of an organisational philosophy which usually seeks to empower more members of the organisation and reduce the numbers of its decision-making levels in the interests of effectiveness. Public sector organisations are often prime examples of 'role cultures' in which members have clearly defined and differentiated tasks and duties. Collective working skills and shared responsibilities for achieving desired outcomes may well be alien to them. Some members of 'the professions' especially – for example, university lecturers and medical consultants – have seen these as threats to their relative personal autonomy. Some organisations, such as the social services and educational institutions, are, moreover, traditionally sceptical about adopting management practices which were pioneered in business and perceived as intrusions from the world of commercial, profit-making organisations. The role and importance of 'tailoring' the language to fit the relevant industry is an important consideration here (*see* Chapter 11).

The failure to recognise the importance of the end-user – for example, in the way many universities still adopt a product orientation to their work and pay little more than lip service to their students as customers – is still a major reason why so many attempts to introduce quality management techniques encounter difficulties.

Performance measurement

It should not be forgotten that quality, in the sense of 'a standard of excellence', is a relative concept. We talk of good quality and bad quality. The invitation to 'never mind the quality, feel the width' is a revealing one. If we wish to improve and raise the quality of a product or of a service, we need some criteria for evaluating its quality – some standards by which the quality of a product or service can be judged.

There are a number of reasons why performance measurements are necessary.

- At a policy-making level, it can be argued that performance reviews provide essential information for management decisions. Ian Sanderson (1992) recognises that this has an economic basis in the public sector, especially in those organisations which cannot use consumer choice to measure the demand for services which answer needs, not wants.

- Measuring performance is also an important means of demonstrating accountability.

- The definition of performance criteria gives a public sector's multiple markets an element of control over an organisation's activities, a degree of power.

The UK central government's use of the Audit Commission is a good example of how government interest in economy and efficiency may impose the use of certain criteria in areas such as local government housing provision, and emphasises the importance of the political dimension for the public sector (see Chapter 2).

The 'three Es'

Performance criteria are often defined using the headings *Economy*, *Efficiency* and *Effectiveness* – the 'three Es'. Flynn (1990, p. 101) identifies the concepts as follows:

- *Economy* refers to the *costs* of production/service and the resources which are needed.
- *Efficiency* is identified with the *use* of capacity, processes and services.
- *Effectiveness* is concerned with the *results* of operations, including consumer satisfaction.

It is evident that the first two categories can be measured by quantitative methods, using, for example, unit costs and productivity measurements. The third category, effectiveness, uses qualitative measurements, in that it is concerned with perceived values, and will include customer/user perceptions of the product or service. Sanderson (1992, p. 26) adopts the term 'service relationship' to refer to the interaction between provider and user. Effectiveness and efficiency are not necessarily easy to achieve together.

To many, including Rodgers (1990), the 'three Es', adopted by the Audit Commission in the UK, represent 'the new orthodoxy' of the 1990s. The Audit Commission (1989) defined *economy* as the measurement of the cost of acquiring staff, supplies, premises or supplies, *efficiency* as the measurement of the outputs achieved in relation to inputs, and *effectiveness* as the measurement of final outcomes related to input. The whole process can be thought of in terms of the amount of value added created by a service. Performance indicators also provide a degree of 'transparency'. In theory, at least, they enable an organisation to give a public account of its activities, and demonstrate value for money (VFM).

Difficulties in designing performance indicators

Some public sector organisations have produced statistical data on their operations for a long time. For example, statistics of reported crime have been categorised and collated since 1856. However, Kerley (1994) thinks that the Audit Commission (1986) was rather too confident when it asserted that performance review had always been a key element in local authority management. Many authorities only seem to have adopted its systematic use comparatively recently. Local authorities, like many other public sector 'industries', have been under increasing pressure to demonstrate their public accountability and effective use of resources. In fairness, the Audit Commission (1986) did recognise the difficulties of measuring performance in the public sector. In reality, many public sector organisations still appear to believe that performance measurement is much easier in commercial, profit-making organisations, despite the fact that they too face very similar problems. Virtually all organisations need performance measurements as a guide to policy and implementation. The measurements therefore need to be relevant, sufficiently detailed to be useful, and not too few or too many.

The difficulties of designing relevant performance indicators and measurements are largely caused by the very complexity of most organisations' tasks and functions. This feature means that there are large numbers of possible dimensions involved. There is also a vast array of methods available for measuring them.

The control loop cycle

In spite of the difficulties involved in designing performance indicators, most organisations see reviews of performance as important parts of the 'rational planning' management approach, in which an organisation is constantly engaged in a 'control loop cycle', or 'learning cycle'. Briefly, this can be modelled using the following sequence:

1 The organisation defines its objectives.

2 A business plan is devised.

3 An action plan is developed.

4 Action is implemented.

5 Processes and results are monitored.

6 The process is evaluated.

7 The evaluation informs a revision of the organisation's objectives (1).

This approach can also be related to *'management by objectives'* (MBO). First defined by Drucker (1954), it has subsequently become a management norm. Although performance measurements obviously need to be closely related to organisational objectives, however, public sector organisations may encounter difficulties in identifying the most relevant ones simply because they are likely to have many *different* objectives at the same time. Moreover, this systematic approach may fail to recognise the dynamic and changing nature of the environment. If performance indicators are used which focus on one area of work, it is also likely that that area will receive proportionately more attention. Perceptions of its significance will be increased, perhaps to the detriment of other areas (Kerley, 1994, p. 144).

Example: management by objectives in the police service

The authors are indebted to John McKinney of the Sussex Police for an illustration of this problem in the police service. Management by objectives was discussed by the Police Staff College as early as 1969, but it was not until ten years later that Lubans and Edgar (1979) produced a management design 'tailored' to fit the specific nature of policing. They argued that Drucker's MBO system could not be applied in its original, industry-focused form. Policing is a non-profit-making activity. It can have relatively little influence over the nature of demand. The 'intangible' nature of its services make it difficult to relate efforts to results. Moreover, like many other public sector organisations, police service organisations have missions and objectives which are not set or controlled by the police themselves. They operate within a framework of national law. The MBO approach works best in organisations which are structured around specified functions, and much police work is not necessarily categorised in this way, although there are specialised units to combat specific categories of crime.

It was therefore necessary to adapt the Drucker model specifically for policing. By 1983–4, Policing by Objectives was adopted by a number of forces in the UK. The principles of setting goals and objectives, and measuring performance against these 'targets' was supported by the Home Office (Circular 114/83). However, the implementation of Policing by Objectives was not consistent in all forces. Some apparently lacked the top-management commitment to ensuring, for example, that its principles were clearly communicated to, and adopted by, all personnel – an essential requirement if it was to be implemented successfully.

Policing performance reviews have used statistical measurements of reported and detected crime for a long time, both as absolutes and in comparison with the figures produced by other forces. However, crime statistics – however useful they may be to some politicians – provide a good example of the difficulties in using statistical information. It may be easy to equate police effectiveness with stable levels of crime, or with reductions in crime reported (itself an unknown percentage of crime that may actually take place), but crime detection is only one police activity among many. Sir Kenneth Newman (1984) listed police functions under the categories of:

- upholding the rule of law;
- protecting and assisting the citizen;
- co-operating with others;
- maintaining a peaceful community;
- providing freedom from fear of crime.

The list of tasks (and hence objectives) which can be derived from these functions is vast. It also appears to include all those which other organisations do not specifically cover, and many that are but cannot be dealt with in an emergency which requires immediate remedial action. Furthermore, an individual may have a number of contacts with the police which differ in kind, and which involve different kinds of 'transaction relationships'. He or she may be appealing for help as a consequence of a burglary in one situation, and in another may be the recipient of a warning or fine for a speeding offence.

Section 38 of the Police Act 1964 placed a duty on Her Majesty's Inspectors of Constabulary (HMIC) to report on the efficiency of forces. HMIC developed a matrix of performance indicators, although they stressed that these were indicators rather than measurements of direct performance. Mathie (1989) emphasised the point that traditional indicators did not reflect differences in types of crime, seriousness of offences, or the relative efforts required for investigation and detection. In the United States it has been recognised that individual indicators should not be viewed in isolation. They work together as a 'package'. There has always been a tendency to develop measures independently, instead of relating them and integrating them together. This problem still exists, although John McKinney suggests that more recent methods, including 'data envelope analysis', may offer some useful techniques. What is needed is a method of correlating performance measurements, provided by a range of techniques – including attitude surveys, activity sampling, HMIC matrices, Home office statistics and scrutinies – in a more holistic form. This is also necessary to avoid what Rouse (1993) calls 'targetology' – a situation where emphasis on a narrow range of targets or objectives works to the detriment of other necessary tasks.

Evaluating performance indicators

Many UK public sector industries today use the Value for Money (VFM) framework discussed by writers such as Jackson (1994), who highlights the fact that, by themselves, performance indicators are of little value unless they can be compared with the performances of other organisations. However, variations may not necessarily imply poor performance; they may simply indicate the necessity of further investigation.

Jackson (1988) considers a number of criteria with which to evaluate the usefulness of performance indicators.

- *Consistency.* They need to stay the same over time, if meaningful comparisons are to be made between results.

- *Clarity.* They need to be easily understood and therefore relatively uncomplicated. Ratios are sometimes used as performance indicators, but complicated ones can be of little real use unless everyone concerned understands them clearly. A simple ratio between, for example, teaching staff and students in a university is a lot easier to understand than the use of a complicated formula containing more than two variables.

- *Relevance.* Performance indicators should be important to the context in which they take place, both within the organisation and outside it. Perceptions of performance are most often based upon its perceived effectiveness.

Indicators need to express those factors which are important to management decision making and need to be restricted to those which are most likely to be productive.

Conclusions

A number of conclusions may be drawn from this discussion of performance indicators.

- *All organisations need performance indicators as a means of controlling, monitoring and developing their economy, efficiency and effectiveness.* However, a public sector organisation differs from a private sector one, because its accountability and responsibility to provide value for money is usually more complex, and because the definition of its objectives is often controlled from outside the organisation, by politicians and other stakeholders. It has less strategic autonomy. Moreover, most public sector organisations have a responsibility to ensure that their services are provided fairly, in the interests of social justice. The principle of equity is an addition to the 'three Es', although it raises a number of additional questions, not least about market segmentation (*see* Chapter 5).

- *Performance indicators need to be understood in the context of quality* – the quality of the whole transaction. To be used effectively, they need to be culturally integrated within the organisation – to be 'owned' by all those within it. If they are perceived merely as 'bolt-on' additions to management techniques, or as part of cost-cutting exercises, their introduction will, at best, be resented, if not actually resisted. The successful introduction of quality management usually requires cultural change.

- *Performance indicators are industry specific.* Criteria for evaluating quality and performance will vary from task to task, from organisation to organisation. Organisations need to develop effective information systems for their performance indicators. This involves costs, and there is always a temptation to concentrate efforts on the indicators and measurements perceived as most advantageous – for example, unit cost measurement. Doing so, however, is likely to produce an incomplete picture of an organisation's total effectiveness. The range of performance measurements used needs to be broad enough to present a reasonably comprehensive picture of the organisation's activities, but limited enough to be useful to management decision making. This always involves a number of different perspectives.

- *Much public sector activity is difficult to measure quantitatively, because it is concerned with the provision of services.* 'User effectiveness' – measuring performance against user needs and perceptions of benefit – involves research into qualitative levels of customer satisfaction. We return again to the importance of the end-user (*see* Minicase 6.1).

- *The choice and development of performance indicators must always bear in mind the purpose of the exercise, what the measurements are for and who is going to use them.* Sound performance management must possess the necessary technical means and procedures for collating and interpreting relevant data, and the appropriate culture for using the results. Performance indicators have two main functions. They help management plan and control and they provide the information needed to judge an organisation's performance. It must be remembered, however, that they are only a means to an end. They are not substitutes for managerial judgement, only tools to enable those judgements to be made in a more informed way.

Positioning and strategy

'Positioning' is a term used to describe the distinctive place in the market that a particular organisation, product or service is perceived to occupy, although it is probably more familiar to the private sector than it is to the public sector. Positioning has become a useful concept in a competitive market, because it enables comparisons to be made between organisations, products and services. The commercial sector frequently demonstrates its awareness of the importance of positioning in its use of advertising which invites comparisons to be made between one product and another. Promotion can influence positioning by the way it affects user and potential user perceptions of products such as 'brand names'.

According to Lovelock (1984, p. 133 ff.) positioning enables market analysis and competition analysis to be related to an organisation's strategy. It helps the organi-

| MINICASE 6.1 | **Questions of quality in higher education** |

Attempts to measure quality have met more than their fair share of difficulties in higher education. *The Independent* of 21 October 1993 described something of the resentment felt by many institutions and their lecturing staff at the system used as an attempt to measure the quality of degree-level education courses.

The assessment exercise was intended to ensure that courses gave 'value for money' and provided 'accountability'. The results of the exercise (and the one that followed it) were extremely important for the universities, because their central funding allocations were dependent upon the results. Departments were asked to rate their own performances as excellent, satisfactory or poor – judgements which were then reviewed by two 'independent' assessors. Some concern was expressed about the latter's ability to be truly impartial, given their necessary personal involvement in the areas of work they were assessing. Moreover, at first assessors did not actually have to visit a department in order to make a judgement. This was changed, but only as a result of protests about a system that appeared unfair. *The Independent* article pointed to a fundamental flaw in the process. Cari Lodi, of the Centre for Higher Education Studies at London University, maintained that the only effective method for assessing teaching quality was to use the opinions of those being taught.

Unfortunately, universities have a poor track record of responding directly to their primary markets – the students themselves. According to Leeds University's Professor Peter Scott, former editor of the *Times Higher Education Supplement*, academic institutions are showing the strains of widening access and are under such pressure that traditional values of quality and excellence are increasingly being undermined by a standardised and a problem-solving, rather than a knowledge-based, curriculum. Suggestions have been made for some time, however, that students who qualify for higher education should be given vouchers which they could then 'spend' on the course of study of their choice.

On 7 January 1994, Claire Sanders reported on a *Times Higher Education Supplement* questionnaire to academics. More than half of the respondents disliked the existing arrangements for quality audit and assessment, despite the fact that a majority thought that 'external audit' was a useful spur to institutions. Most respondents agreed that the government seemed more concerned with 'a desire for control over higher education' than with genuine concerns for quality. The article gave a very low profile to student opinion. The only reference to it was frankly cynical, to the effect that lecturers would always destroy any evidence of poor feedback from students if their pay was going to be related to their teaching performance. This seems poor comment on the fact that the student remains higher education's primary market.

sation to establish clearly what it is doing, what it would like to do and how to do it. Lovelock (1984, p. 135) describes positioning in marketing management as:

- a way of defining relationships between products and markets;
- a tool for identifying market opportunities; and
- a way of responding to, or anticipating, the competition.

In positioning marketing services, managers need a good understanding of market segments, of all the dimensions of a service and of the ways in which they are valued by customers. Customer perception is a key element in this process, as it is in the development of performance indicators.

Positioning maps have long been used as a means of making visual diagrams of alternative products or services in the marketplace. They are usually drawn using two dimensions (*see* Fig. 6.5). The dimensions are based on performance indicators which represent user perceptions of the service.

Unfortunately, the concept of positioning is only of value in a competitive market. There are still some public sector services which remain effectively within monopoly markets. In these cases, user perceptions are relatively difficult to map in the absence of meaningful comparisons. Nevertheless, they can be extremely useful tools with which to understand user perceptions.

In the context of increased privatisation and internal markets, public sector managers need to be aware of the potential of positioning strategies. Saltman and von Otter (1992) argue that the idea of public sector competition involves a notion of consumer choice which is distinct from the 'free choice' in a commercial market. For example, for the NHS patient, the choice of hospital is likely to be restricted by available facilities, geographical location and other variables. However, having *some* choice may be more important than having none at all. Competition in the public sector is seen as the availability of more than one option, rather than having a large number of equal opportunities.

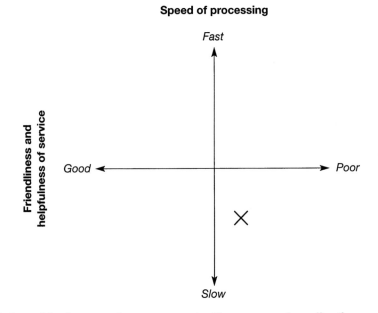

Fig. 6.5 A positioning map for a passport office personal application

Summary

1 **The transaction.** The concept of the 'service package' is now well established. The intangible benefits of a product or service may well be as, or even more, important than tangible aspects of the product or service itself. It is often issues concerned with the nature of the transaction which cause users the greatest problems.

2 **The importance of customers and marketing.** Standards of service have become increasingly important to both the private sector and the public sector. Unfortunately, pressures to increase efficiency are not necessarily the most appropriate means of increasing effectiveness.

3 **Customers and expectations.** Customer satisfaction remains a particularly important measurement of performance.

4 **Issues of response.** In all industries, organisations possess a number of distinct attitudes or orientations towards production, customers and systems.

5 **Issues of resources, control and quality** have become major preoccupations of both the private and the public sectors. Public sector organisations have experienced some difficulties in applying Total Quality Management principles to their work because it normally involves changing the organisation's culture.

6 **Performance measurement.** Public sector organisations are subject to a number of simultaneous demands from users, regulatory bodies, political forces, funding sources and public opinion. Methods of control are central to their operations in order to ensure that they meet their objectives. The choice of performance indicators must be made carefully.

7 **Positioning and strategy.** Positioning describes the place of a product in relation to its competitors. It also gives management a tool for identifying market opportunities and strategies.

Implications for management

The manager needs *a detailed understanding of the organisation's 'total product', its dimensions and characteristics*. The answers to the following questions can act as starting points:

1 What services does the organisation provide?
2 What are the mechanisms by which the customer/user experiences:
   - interpersonal contacts with the organisation?
   - the environment of the organisation?
   - the organisation's procedures?

The manager also needs to identify the *organisation's methods of gathering and interpreting data* into useful information. All organisations already possess systems of recording and controlling their operations, and it is useful to describe them before considering how they might be improved. The following questions should be addressed:

1 What kinds of data are collected?

2 What systems are in place (reporting techniques, computerised records, etc.) to collect it?

3 How is data interpreted?

4 How is the information communicated, and how often?

5 How is the information used in decision making?

Furthermore, the manager also needs to consider *the culture of the organisation and its orientation(s)*. Using Fig. 6.4 (*see* p. 153), it should be possible to identify the organisation's position in the diagram. However, there may also be a number of conflicting orientations co-existing within the organisation. It is important to identify any such conflicts, as these are likely to be the sources of problems which can compromise the organisation's effectiveness. They may also be sources of political conflict within the organisation (*see* Chapter 7).

The importance of the end-user has been stressed at length. The manager should be able to understand *the customer/user experience* (Foster *et al.*, 1990) in some detail. Using the 'search, arrival, pre-contact, contact, withdrawal, follow-up' framework, the manager needs to become familiar with the user's experiences. It is a common fault that managers frequently become 'remote' from the user experience – a feature that can reveal itself in poor public relations performance and accusations of organisational arrogance and insensitivity to user requirements.

The manager also needs to know *what performance indicators and measurements are in use* in the organisation. Some of these will be statutory and regulatory ones, but in each case the manager should be able to identify:

1 what is being measured;

2 what unit of measurement is being used;

3 what is its purpose; and

4 how important it is.

Finally, the manager needs to *map the product's or service's market position* or the user's perception of its quality, using appropriate dimensions. This is best done using one or several two-dimensional maps, using a choice of relevant dimensions (*see* Fig. 6.5). Where an element of user choice is available, the chart can be used to map the relative positions of all competitors.

ISSUES FOR DISCUSSION

The following issues for discussion are presented in the form of questions. Examples from specific public sector industries should be incorporated into responses. Case studies can be used to provide some illustrations of the issues raised.

1 Why are many public sector organisations 'system oriented', and how may this conflict with the concept of 'market orientation'?

2 How may 'quality' be defined in a public sector context?

3 What are the functions of performance indicators in public sector organisations?

4 In what way is 'positioning' a useful tool for public sector organisations?

References

Argyris, C. (1985) *Strategy, Change and Defensive Routines*. London: Pitman Publishing.

Audit Commission (1986) *Performance Review: A Handbook*. London: HMSO.

Audit Commission (1989) *Managing Services Effectively – Performance Review*. London: HMSO.

Cannon, T. (1991) *Enterprise: creation, development and growth*. Oxford: Butterworth–Heinemann.

Christopher, M. (1991) *The Customer Service Planner*. Oxford: Butterworth–Heinemann in conjunction with the CIM.

Cooke, B. (1992) 'Quality, culture and local government' in Sanderson, I. (ed) *Management of Quality in Local Government*. Harlow, Essex: Longman.

Crompton, J. L. and Lamb, C. W. Jr. (1986) *Marketing Government and Social Services*. New York: John Wiley & Sons.

Drucker, P. (1954) *Principles of Management*. London: Heinemann.

Drucker, P. (1989) *The Practice of Management*. Oxford: Heinemann.

Flynn, N. (1990) *Public Sector Management*. Hemel Hempstead: Harvester Wheatsheaf.

Foster, M. and Whittle, S. (1990) 'Quality – It's All In The Mindset', *Total Quality Management*, February, 17–19.

Foster, M., Whittle, S. and Hyde, P. (1990) 'Improving the service quality chain', *Managing Service Quality*, November, 41–6.

Gerloff, E. A. (1985) *Organizational Theory and Design*. Singapore: McGraw-Hill Book Co.

Her Majesty's Government (1991) *The Citizen's Charter*. London: HMSO.

Humble, J. (1989) 'The Competitive Edge', *Management Centre Europe* 1989, quoted in Christopher, M. (1991) *The Customer Service Planner*. Oxford: Butterworth–Heinemann.

Jackson, P.M. (1988) 'The management of performance in the public sector', *Public Money and Management*, 8, 11–16.

Jackson, P.M. (1994) 'Performance indicators: promises and pitfalls' in Moore, K. (ed) *Museum Management*. London and New York: Routledge and Kegan Paul, pp.156–72.

Kerley, R. (1994) *Managing in Local Government*. London: The Macmillan Press Ltd.

Kotler, P. (1987) *Strategic Marketing for Non-Profit Organisations*. Englewood Cliffs, New Jersey: Prentice-Hall, Inc.

Levitt, T. (1986) *The Marketing Imagination*. London: Collier-Macmillan.

Lovelock, C.H. (ed) (1984) *Services Marketing*. Englewood Cliffs, New Jersey: Prentice-Hall, Inc.

Lubans, V.A. and Edgar, J.M. (1979) *Policing by Objectives*. Hartford, Connecticut: Social Development Corporation.

McGregor, D. (1960) 'Theory X and Theory Y' in Pugh, D.S. (ed) *Organizational Theory. Selected Readings* (3rd edn). London: Penguin Books.

Mathie, R.C. (1989) 'Examining Performance', *Policing*, Winter.

Morgan, C. and Murgatroyd, S. (1994) *Total Quality Management in The Public Sector*. Buckingham and Philadelphia: Open University Press.

NEDO (1981) *Make Ready for Success*. London: NEDO Books.

Newman, K. (1984) *The Policing Principles of the Metropolitan Police*. London: Metropolitan Police.

Porter, M. (1985) *Competitive Advantage*. London: Collier Macmillan and New York: The Free Press, Macmillan Inc.

Rogers, S. (1990) *Performance Management in Local Government*. Harlow, Essex: Longman in association with the Local Government Training Board.

Rouse, J. (1993) 'Resource and performance management in public service organizations' in Isaac-Henry, K., Painter, C. and Barnes, C. *Management in the Public Sector*. London: Chapman & Hall.

Saltman, R.B. and von Otter, C. (1992) *Planned Markets and Public Competition*. Buckingham and Philadelphia: Open University Press.

Sanderson, I. (ed) (1992) *Management of Quality in Local Government*. Harlow, Essex: Longman.

Williams, A., Dobson, P. and Walters, M. (1989) *Changing Culture*. London: Institute of Personnel Management.

CHAPTER 7

The political dimension

CHAPTER OVERVIEW

Public sector marketing cannot be separated from politics. The importance of politics as an environmental factor influencing public sector marketing can lead organisations to become too inward looking, with a managerial focus on managing the political dimension rather than on the needs of the primary users.

Even in private sector organisations, marketing has to work within a legislative framework relating to, for example, health and safety regulations and a raft of consumer legislation. This legislation imposes some constraints on organisations designed to regulate unscrupulous (non-marketing oriented) operators.

Directors and managers will have visions and missions to determine the strategies of their companies. Within the public sector, these visions and missions are essentially political and may change an organisation's marketing policy overnight. For example, the decision to change the status of UK polytechnics to that of universities changed the marketing environment and policies of those institutions very quickly. This chapter examines the ways in which managers can deal with the constraints and changes implicit in working within a political environment.

KEY LEARNING OUTCOMES

By the end of this chapter, you should be able to:

- examine the nature of the political influence and the determination of marketing policy;
- understand the definition of social needs as a political issue;
- explore the nature of inter- and intra-organisational politics;
- consider the sources of political power in public sector marketing; and
- appreciate the nature of conflict.

Introduction

All marketing is undertaken within a political framework. The performance and quality issues discussed in Chapter 6 are always subject to political interest, influence, regulation and control, and this dimension is particularly important in public sector industries. Not only does the principle of value for money assume political importance when funding is provided by the public purse, but politics determine the very nature of those services and provision which are deemed to be 'in the public interest'. The public sector environment has both developed and changed significantly in most countries since 1945. Key political changes have affected the nature of government itself, local government and national industries. In the UK, the role of the press, the development of quasi-autonomous national government organisations (QUANGOs) with limited public accountability, the political drive for more freedom of choice, the inherent conflicts between efficiency, effectiveness and funding, the increasing fragmentation of public sector industries and the growth in competitive tendering for public sector services, are all areas of political debate.

Politics as power

'Politics' may be defined as any form of activity which is involved with the acquisition of power or the ability to influence people or events. The adjective 'political' is usually used to refer to the activities of the State or the Government, or to the one-sided, partisan aspects of the process. Elements of conflict are always involved – between opposing ideas or interests, as exemplified by the UK tradition of party politics. In this context, all political parties are interested in marketing. Their desire to communicate and ensure the acceptability of their policies is a familiar feature of the political environment.

Chapter 2 considered briefly the role of politics as one of the driving forces of public sector marketing. It is involved with determining national policies and international relations. The political initiatives of government are likely to have a considerable impact on public sector industries because most of the public sector is, directly or indirectly, in part or in whole, dependent on government for resource allocation, policy directives, legal control and regulation (*see* Minicase 7.1). These are major mechanisms by which power is exercised. The control of information is another, and the government has vast quantities of information resources. Thus central government is a major influence on public sector markets (*see* Chapter 3).

Moreover, some public sector organisations are actually responsible for implementing the policies of government. At this level, politics can be both a driving force, initiating new policies, changes and developments, and a constraint (as discussed in Chapter 3) and may impose controls and limitations in response both to ideological (political) demands and to social and economic realities. This is true of most countries at the present time, as the need to reduce central government expenditure has become increasingly important. This has caused considerable political problems in, for example, the UK, France and Germany.

Local government itself is an important source of political influence and power. Elcock (1994) uses Rhodes' (1987) analysis of the relationships between central and local government. Although about 60 per cent of local authority funding in the UK comes from central government, local councils still have a degree of independence. They control a large number of projects and services, despite the political tensions which can exist between central government and local councils dominated by opposition parties. Both Members of Parliament and local councillors are legally elected people's representatives with constitutional responsibilities. Both can exert political influence on decisions. Like the government, local authorities also possess considerable information resources, in their case related to local services. In Rhodes' (1987) view, the relationship between central and local government is one in which the balance of power is largely determined by the nature of their resources.

MINICASE
7.1

The price of power

Criticisms of UK government policy were expressed very clearly in a 1994 Channel 4 television programme, *False Economy: The Price of Power*, by Will Hutton. The programme argued that the UK had effectively turned its citizens into consumers. It had lost a proper sense of public accountability, which was increasingly obscured as private business took over public contracts. The privatisation process was represented as a political issue: public good against private gain. Hutton's criticism of a political market ideology included the example of the City of Bradford, where compulsory tendering for estates management cost the Housing Department £1 million to prepare a bid which was won by default, simply because no other bids materialised. He was also sceptical about the issue of public accountability concerning £50 billion spent by 64 000 unelected members of QUANGOs. Hutton's criticism was not confined to the ruling political party, and he accused the Opposition of favouring the expediency of 'political acceptability'.

Recent developments in UK politics

The UK political context within which public sector organisations operate has changed a great deal since the 1970s. In many ways these changes have brought the role of marketing 'centre stage'. The general political philosophy which informed these changes was discussed in Chapter 1. In practice, three main developments have had profound effects on the public sector: *privatisation; an increasing attention to managerial professionalism; the introduction of competitive and co-operative activities.* These will be looked at in turn.

Privatisation

The desire to 'roll back the frontiers of the State' in the UK found practical expression in a policy of transferring certain services and industries from the State to the private sector. A similar process is occurring in many other countries pursuing policies designed to reduce direct public sector expenditure.

'Public choice theory' (*see* Self, 1993, pp. 1–20) argues that free markets, consisting of individuals seeking to satisfy their self-interests through voluntary exchanges with others, will 'naturally' achieve equilibrium and will adjust supply to demand in order to maintain it. Transferring state functions and assets to the private sector is an obvious way of 'freeing' industries and services from their reliance upon the State. It also carries the implication that private sector provision is inherently superior and more efficient. As a result, many organisations that once were public corporations and nationalised industries are now private companies. For example, in the UK in 1990, the Central Electricity Generating Board was split into twelve regional companies, the National Grid Company and two generating companies. It should, however, be noted that the government felt obliged to regulate the privatised companies 'in the public interest' by appointing 'watchdog' authorities to try and ensure a balance between their commercial decisions and their public responsibilities.

The benefits to end-users have not always been immediately apparent. Cave (1996) reported that the National Audit Office claimed that it was too early to judge if the sale of UK rail operators to the private sector had helped improve services, but that the Office of Passenger Rail Franchising (OPRAF) had been wrong not to set budgets for advisers' costs when it had begun to privatise the 25 train operating companies. Total fees charged to OPRAF between November 1993 and March 1996 had totalled £39.6 million.

Although Warner (1995) thought that privatisation 'is probably Britain's biggest single intellectual contribution to the evolution of post-war commerce', the appropriate regulatory frameworks were essential if conflicts of interest between customers and company shareholders were to be avoided. By 1992, Eastern Electricity had increased pre-tax profits by 30 per cent, but had made 800 redundancies in two years. Chairmen and chief executives of the new public utility companies were seen to enjoy huge personal financial gains. Shareholders' dividends made any of the price reductions in favour of customers imposed by the regulator appear laughable. By 1995, take-over bids among electricity companies were producing accusations of profiteering at the taxpayers' and the customers' expense. On 14 May 1996, the gas industry regulator was accused of wiping more than 10 per cent off the value of British Gas shares by announcing a cap on distribution charges for five years, reducing charges to British Gas customers, but raising the spectre of up to 10 000 job losses at Transco – British Gas's pipeline business.

Such problems only contribute to an increasing disillusionment with the political vision of a popular, share-owning democracy that was a feature of the 1980s. The idea that common ownership could be realised through the markets has not materialised in many industries. Large numbers of individual shareholders in many of the newly privatised companies sold their shares. Pension fund investments have often performed better. Institutional shareholders gained ground. Effectively, the private sector has increasingly assumed ownership of monopoly industries.

Privatisation has also involved the deregulation of some services in order to expose them to competition. Competition, it is argued, increases efficiency and avoids the pitfalls of monopoly provision. Provincial bus services were deregulated. Local authorities were obliged to put some services out to tender for the same reasons. Schools were given the opportunity of 'opting out' of direct local authority control. Hospitals could choose to become trusts, although they were still to operate within the National Health Service framework. In central government itself, the 'Next Steps' initiative involved some services and functions being passed from the Civil Service to agencies. This development was also motivated by the desire to improve management.

Managerial professionalism

The 1980s also saw an increased emphasis upon the role of managerial skills in public sector industries. This centres around the idea that better management practices will improve efficiency. The desire to reduce public sector costs remains on the agenda of most political parties in the current economic environment. The UK Government itself invested in management information systems at the beginning of the 1980s. Initially the new emphasis on management was alien to the culture of many public sector organisations (*see* Chapter 11), but has slowly been accepted.

Stewart (1986) argued that it was necessary to change management practices in response to a number of developments. Increasing economic and political constraints, changing social, employment and demographic patterns, demanded a more co-ordinated use of resources and provision of services. Above all, the political will to improve economy, efficiency and effectiveness – the 'three Es' – provided a spur to the development of corporate management – for example, in local authorities – despite the fact that efficiency and effectiveness were not always compatible in the public sector context.

The demands of accountability created their own emphasis on professional management. The management of performance has already been discussed in Chapter 6. A desire to improve the relationships between providers and users was generally evident by the early 1980s and was articulated in the form of national policy in *The Citizen's Charter* of 1991. The new 'public service orientation' (Stewart, 1986) stressed the importance of the user and 'consumer responsiveness' (Elcock, 1994).

All these factors have contributed to the growth of professional management practices in the public sector. 'Public service orientation' demands that management knows its users' needs and wants and actively seeks their views and suggestions – a requirement common to both private and public sectors. The marketing function is now central to management practice in both, although the public sector has its own distinctive characteristics.

Competition and co-operation

The political desire to increase efficiency by introducing competition was implemented in the UK by making some public sector organisations 'contract out' some services. Some public organisations found themselves having to bid against competition for the services which they had traditionally provided. This can either be seen as a diminution of the range of public sector functions, or as an opportunity, for example, for local government to free itself from some of the responsibilities of service provision and concentrate upon managing the community. Local authorities were also encouraged to co-operate as necessary with other bodies and agencies, such as housing associations.

The political environment

Politics is a major factor in any consideration of an organisation's environment, and public sector organisations are keenly aware of the potential for change that originates with political policies and decisions. The environment is a major source of uncertainty for any organisation, be it in the public or the private sector. There is an extensive literature devoted to ways of analysing the environment. A typical methodology (*see*, for example, Kast and Rosenweig, 1979) will seek to identify the following dimensions:

- political
- cultural
- technological
- educational
- legal
- demographic
- resource
- social
- economic.

Obviously, the objectives of an organisation must be matched as well as possible to the character and constraints of its environment, which is itself constantly changing. As it changes, the needs and wants of users and consumers will also change. It is part of a manager's job to collect information and to evaluate the importance of environmental factors and events in order to make better decisions. The manager becomes a critical bridge between an organisation and its environment.

Of course, 'facts' and data do not become information until they are interpreted. Understanding the environment is, therefore, a matter of perceptions, of people's interpretations of reality. Managers have to make judgements in deciding which are the most relevant environmental issues affecting their organisations, how they can quantify them and how they can use them or do something about them.

Models of the environment can provide useful tools for this process. Management literature on this subject is extensive (*see*, for example, Gerloff, 1985, pp. 17–47), but much is based on the ideas of Emery and Trist (1965). Emery and Trist developed a method of mapping the environment using at least three kinds of relationships:

- those between elements of the environment outside the organisation;
- those between the organisation and other organisations; and
- those within the organisation itself.

They also believed that environments can be categorised by their relative simplicity/complexity and their placid/turbulent natures (Gerloff, 1985, p. 37).

This methodology suggests three levels of political environment that can be considered (*see* Fig. 7.1):

1 *The general political climate of society*, formed by government policies and influenced by the need for public support, political party ideologies, etc;

2 *Inter-organisational politics*, for example, relationships in the UK between the Treasury and the Ministry of Defence, between Health Authorities and individual hospitals, between one university and another;

3 *Politics within the organisation*, for example, between different departments or managers.

For each level we need to ask where power is located, how it can be recognised, and what implications it has for marketing in the public sector.

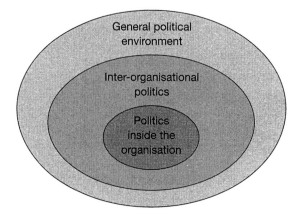

Fig. 7.1 Levels of the political environment

All levels are effectively concerned with power relationships between organisations and/or individuals. Unfortunately, political relationships often involve elements of conflict. Understanding the nature of power and conflict is a very necessary management skill.

The general political climate

We have argued (*see* Chapter 4) that many public sector services are mainly concerned with social welfare, with answering and remedying social needs (Plant *et al.*, 1980, p. 20). The definition of social needs is itself a political question. Public sector services are, therefore, especially vulnerable to political considerations, not just in terms of resource allocation, but in terms of the way in which the social policies and definitions that determine those allocations are decided.

Political power at this level really resides with government – with the ministers and their civil service departments. The influence, or potential influence, of politics on most environmental conditions is considerable. Power at government level can and does affect virtually every aspect of our environment, including the nature of and relative importance given to technological, legal, economic, ecological, demographic and cultural issues throughout the country. Most British government power is centralised in, and implemented through, Whitehall, London – the administrative centre of government.

However, governmental power is never absolute in a democracy. Political policies and initiatives are, of course, subject to parliamentary approval, in that Parliament at Westminster must approve the proposed policies of government. Members of Parliament are themselves dependent on electoral support. Attempts at making changes have to win political approval. Governments need not only a certain level of electorate consent, but some support from the state institutions themselves and specific groups such as the professions. So-called 'white papers' may set out policy and objectives, but government has to follow existing systems and conditions (*see* Hindess, 1987, pp. 163–7).

Once they are legitimised in this way, government and parliamentary decisions in the UK are implemented by Whitehall. Power then takes the form of departmental circulars and directives, legislative statutes, resource allocation and the demand for conformance. Government control of resources is a significant form of power. Some would argue that this is the effective 'bottom line'. Political power also operates at local authority level, where the control of resources is probably the most important demonstration of power.

Since the early 1980s, the general political environment has provided a number of important roles for marketing. 'Public service orientation' and the recognised need to 'get close to your customers' rely heavily on a marketing philosophy which increasingly empowers users.

Inter-organisational politics

Political programmes of governments inevitably involve a wide range of diverse objectives, each one having to compete for resources. This is evident every time ministers apply for Treasury funding. In this respect, government itself is a public sector organisation: it has to perform within the budget allocations agreed. Any level of operation above the set level of funding results in deficit. Increase in activity cannot increase profit levels as it can in a private sector business. Indeed, the major constraint on government may well be the equation between taxation, borrowing and spending (*see* Chapter 8).

Competition has been used as a spur to efficiency in the public sector simply because it acts as an incentive to use resources in the most efficient way. It is frequently argued, however, that *efficiency* in itself cannot guarantee *effectiveness*, and the UK Health Service has provided many illustrations (including occasions when patients have been left on trolleys in hospital corridors) of the ways in which 'efficient' procedures may not be 'effective'.

In the commercial sector, competitive advantage has been seen as the key to successful business strategy. Johnson and Scholes (1997) have pointed out that the traditional state-owned monopoly organisation tended to argue that competition would compromise its public sector commitment to the principle of equity by encouraging the organisation to adopt more selective strategies and concentrate on its most cost-effective operations. In the modern political climate, however, such measures are increasingly necessary, and have led to the transfer of some services to other organisations, such as voluntary bodies, and increasing cooperation with other providers.

Competitive strategies in the private sector are usually based upon cost leadership, differentiation or focus (Johnson and Scholes, 1997). Although these can be adapted to public services, there are a number of fundamental difficulties. Many public services have a remit or even a legal obligation to serve a community as a whole. The principle of equity often seems to compromise potential developments which would otherwise enhance competitive advantage. However, an increasing number of services have been transferred to other organisations.

In this situation, political power is responsible for providing the framework of competition. This power may be exercised through audit and quality control, but it is also evident in the funding systems which reward those organisations which meet agreed targets, and even penalise those which do not. University income, for example, is largely dependent upon maximum aggregated student number targets. Organisations in the UK university sector increasingly see themselves not only as the providers of higher education for all those sufficiently qualified to benefit from it – a principle originally espoused by the 1963 *Robbins Report* – but also in competition with each other for student numbers. A shift away from the block grant system to one more responsive to student demand induced universities to increase student numbers at lower unit costs. In April 1989, the Department of Education and Science argued that a higher income from fees would cover marginal costs and, at the same time, would encourage institutions to exploit spare capacity. This would, it was felt, widen access and 'promote effectiveness in marketing and teaching'. Dahloff *et al.* (1991) argued that existing institutional mechanisms to relate supply to demand were inadequate. The concepts of 'lifelong learning', new labour-market conditions and preferences for higher education were major factors influencing change. Higher education's structures and procedures needed to serve the needs of its customers. Effectiveness, accountability and quality were becoming the dominant issues, and value for money was an important consideration.

In this new environment, marketing has an important role to play. Alan Howarth, MP (1991) maintained that the high profile given to the role of marketing in UK higher education was the product of the Conservative government's faith in the effectiveness of marketing mechanisms. He identified four distinct groups of markets: students; prospective employers; internal markets recruiting staff and allocating resources; the political market controlling funding. Although not identical, this analysis has parallels with the complexity of the public sector markets model (primary, influencer, legitimiser and resourcer markets) already discussed in Chapters 2 and 3. The scope of this definition of the market for higher education may be another reason why marketing can no longer be seen simply as a single function within an organisation such as a university. It has become a central concern for all areas of activity.

Pfeffer (1992) notes that organisations, especially large ones, are also political entities. In order to understand organisations, we need to understand their politics. Organisations are guided by policies and strategies. The acquisition of power and influence is usually part of any competitive strategy, any bid for competitive advantage.

Conflict can arise even within coalitions of organisations. Bolman and Deal (1991) describe the political dimension as an important 'lens' or 'frame' through which we can analyse and understand how organisations function. They use the 1986 NASA *Challenger* space shuttle disaster as an example of a situation in which conflicting political goals within a coalition of organisations – NASA, the contractors for the shuttle's rocket motors, US Congress, the White House, the military, the media and the public – created a tragedy.

Politics as power within the organisation

Although many people would associate the term 'political' primarily with national government, city councils and a party political system, the management of any organisation will involve a political dimension, especially when it comes to defining and agreeing organisational goals (*see* Gerloff, 1985, p. 175 ff.). Chapter 6 considered ways in which managerial conflict can result from the co-existence of differing orientations and priorities. In both government and organisations, the word 'political' can refer to 'taking sides' and being partisan. Politics is often concerned with conflict and argument.

Organisations are frequently represented as cooperative teams of people striving to meet common goals, however, and failure to resolve conflicts of interest is sometimes understood as weakness – the result of poor management, communication, etc. In reality, a valid argument can be made (*see*, for example, Salaman, 1978) to support the view that conflict is a 'natural', even inevitable, feature of all organisations. In their book, Smith and Peterson (1988) entitled a chapter reviewing earlier research into managerial work 'Leadership as Management of Conflicting Demands', and concluded that conflict was a 'crucial element' in most situations.

The goals of an organisation and those of an individual working within it may well differ (*see* Handy, 1985, Chapter 2). Organisations are made up of people, and many of the relationships between them are likely to be concerned with issues of personal power and politics. Of course, power can be used both negatively and positively. As a means of exploitation and personal domination, it is usually regarded as a dangerous attribute. As a positive force, it can be used creatively and responsibly.

Mapping power within the organisation

A number of models exist for categorising organisational structures and cultures. Most of these map ways in which power operates within the organisation. Handy (1985), in his well-known study of organisations, produced a simplified model which consisted of four types of organisational culture, each with its own kind of value system and providing its own political scenario.

1 *Power cultures.* These depend upon a central power source, usually in the form of one central figure who, by virtue of his or her personality and approach, uses a small number of trusted lieutenants to control the organisation directly. These cultures operate best when they are relatively small in size, and depend heavily upon a few skilled individuals who form a 'centre' for the organisation. In large-scale organisations, and many public sector organisations are relatively big, such central control is likely to be resented by some groups of personnel, who may well engage in political activity for a number of different reasons.

2 *Role cultures.* These are often represented by bureaucracies, controlled by set procedures and rules which specify responsibilities for all members of their organisations. Their structures of power are hierarchical, and many of their personnel are specialists in particular roles. However, this focus on specialist roles

can encourage a form of myopia or short-sightedness which, due to an excessive concentration on specific activities, means that employees lose sight of the wider organisational aims and fail to notice important changes in the external environment. Such cultures may also prove very resistant to the needs for change. They are often the breeding ground of personal and inter-departmental rivalries, especially at management level within the organisation. Competition for influence, for example, is often the source of internal political argument.

3 *Task cultures*. These tend to be geared towards project management, using a resource/task matrix structure – that is, ensuring that teams of staff responsible for specific tasks are provided with the appropriate facilities and resources necessary to carry out individual projects. This sort of culture encourages people to work together in teams, and fosters creative, flexible responses to market demands. However, any restraints/restrictions on resources will inevitably produce political competition for them and, in times of difficulty, a tendency to resort to a power culture.

4 *Person cultures*. These favour the individual, and are often referred to as relatively 'flat', that is, non-hierarchical, organisations, in which members share resources and facilities which also benefit them individually. They appear, for example, in very small, highly technical organisations, and their organisational structures are generally minimal. However, they are easily disturbed by interpersonal disagreements.

These 'types' of organisation provide useful *starting points* for analysis, but it is important to remember that, in practice, it is usually difficult, if not impossible to 'fit' any organisation neatly into a single framework or category. Most organisations, unless they are very small or simple ones, are likely to contain elements of more than one type or category. Nevertheless, these types can be useful tools with which to understand and 'map' organisational cultures and the exercise of power within them.

There is, in all these organisational types, ample opportunity for conflict and political activity. Morgan (1986, pp. 141–98) recognises this reality, although he acknowledges the fact that most people continue to pretend that organisations are rational institutions in which members are united by common goals. Unfortunately, this attitude can inhibit people from recognising that political behaviour is a fairly normal sort of activity, only to be expected among groups of people. He discusses organisations as political systems, even as systems of government. His list of 'modes of rule', or types of political systems in organisations, ranges from *Autocracy* ('This is how it will be done'), through *Bureaucracy* ('This is how it should be done'), *Technocracy* ('This is how it is done best'), to *Democracy* ('How do we think we should do it?').

In each of these forms, as in the public political arena, power is exercised in different ways. The point is stressed, however, that most organisations, especially large ones, contain a mixture of different types of 'rule' and the systems associated with them. Handy's (1985) categories of organisational types provides only a very normative model.

Conflict as an unavoidable fact of life

Unfortunately, conflict can present a number of problems for marketing. Morgan (1986, p. 155) cites, as an example of colliding interests, the complaint that 'production people and marketing people never get along.' There are two difficulties with this statement.

1 As Morgan points out, it implies that the organisation would be much more efficient and effective if such conflicts never existed. In real life, conflict is quite normal, and can even be used creatively.

2 The statement also highlights the ways in which some functions of an organisation are habitually departmentalised. It has already been argued that the marketing function is one which needs to be 'owned' by the whole organisation's culture. For that reason alone, it may be counter-productive for an organisation to create the post of 'marketing manager' or 'marketing officer' if that is simply an excuse to delegate marketing responsibilities to a particular person instead of attempting the more difficult, but more rewarding, task of integrating the marketing philosophy into the organisation as a whole.

Bolman and Deal (1991) also argue that politics is unavoidable in organisations. Conflict and power plays are part of ordinary, everyday organisational life, and occur naturally because all organisations contain individuals and interest groups with differing priorities. All organisations have to allocate limited resources, which involves competition for them between individuals and groups – competition in which power plays an important role. Making decisions usually involves bargaining and negotiation, in which individuals and groups vie together for advantage (*see* Minicase 7.2). Power itself is therefore an important resource. Formal authority legitimises power within an organisation. Despite the fact that, since the 1980s, an increasing number of writers on human resource management have focused on the concept of 'empowerment', and suggested that collaboration and participation can reduce the importance of power as a major issue within organisations, it seems likely that conflict over power will always remain a feature in most of them.

A feature of organisational politics familiar to everyone is the conflict between owners/management and the workforce. Increased worker participation in management has often been used as a device to encourage power-sharing (or 'co-determination'), but there will always be those who oppose such systems on the grounds that any system of government, in the sense of Morgan's political metaphor for the organisation, needs some check on its absolute power in the form of a healthy opposition (Morgan, 1986, p. 146).

Any opposing interests produce conflict. Conflict must be regarded as a normal feature of national politics, competitive industry and internal organisational behaviour. It frequently takes the form of coalitions of individuals united against others. These can be used to advance individuals' interests within an organisation. An organisation with multiple goals, and many public sector organisations have multiple goals in the interests of social equity, may often possess a number of such political coalitions in apparent conflict. There may also be an element of conflict within the individual, who may feel tension between simultaneous commitments

Conflicts of power at a UK junior school

A dispute arose at Manton Junior School in Workshop, Nottinghamshire, at the beginning of the 1996–7 school year. The behaviour of 10 year-old Matthew Wilson, accused of assaulting other pupils, had proved so disruptive that the headteacher had twice excluded him from the school. On both occasions, however, the school governors had overruled the headteacher and reinstated the boy. The school's eight teaching staff – members of the National Association of Schoolmasters and the Union of Women Teachers – threatened to strike if Matthew returned to classes with other pupils. They claimed that he was a danger to both teaching staff and to other pupils.

An initial attempt at a compromise – the result of an intervention by the chair of Nottinghamshire's Education Committee – agreed that Matthew could be given individual tuition and more than £3000 was spent on a supply teacher for Matthew over a six-week period. At the end of this time, the governors decided that funding would stop and Matthew should return to normal classes. On 28 October 1996, the headteacher closed the school, informing the parents of some 200 pupils that he was unable to guarantee the safety of the children, if Matthew attended. The teaching staff threatened to strike unless the dispute was resolved.

A number of key 'players' feature in the politics of this situation. Conflict existed between individuals and coalitions of individuals.

- Matthew Wilson's father had died, and his mother had been treated for cancer. She insisted that Matthew should be taught in normal classes at Manton Junior School rather than attending a special school.

- The mother's stance was supported by Eileen Bennett, chair of the school governors, who maintained that Matthew had a legal right to be taught in the school. In her opinion, individual tuition risked 'criminalising' Matthew by isolating him from his peers, and she wished to support the boy and his mother against 'the power of the teaching unions'.

- The General Secretary of the teachers' unions, Nigel de Gruchy, accused the chair of the school governors of being irresponsible, and of acting as a counsellor for one family rather than acting in support of the school as a whole. In his opinion, Mrs Bennett seemed to 'want to play power politics with the youngsters'. He questioned the governors' ability to run the school successfully and publicly urged Mrs Bennett to agree to a request from the chair of the County Council Education Committee to transfer Matthew to another school. He claimed the support of many parents.

- The UK Education Secretary, Gillian Shephard, asserted that the whole business was the responsibility of the County Council, which should intervene in the dispute and provide a solution.

- The chair of the County Council Education Committee, Fred Riddell, denied that it had any powers to intervene since the Government's policy of local management for schools had given school governors responsibility for both school spending and the exclusion of pupils. In his view, the dispute was one between the headteacher and the governing body. The County Council had no legal right to interfere in the situation, and his only possible role was to 'seek to persuade'.

- The headteacher himself, Bill Skelley, was obviously in a very difficult situation. He had a responsibility to pupils, governors, parents, staff and education authorities, but clearly lacked the support of his governors.

- Graham Lane, chair of the Association of Metropolitan Authorities' Education Committee, found the situation 'unbelievable', since 'discipline is a matter for the governing body' and it seemed unclear whether or not a school could be closed without governors' permission. Closure of the school could be interpreted as a threat to the pupils' right to education, as defined by the 1944 Education Act. Mr Lane thought that the action of the Manton teachers was 'outrageous', and an example of 'bully boy tactics' on the part of the teaching unions.

The staff at Manton Junior School went on strike, and talks between teachers and governors failed to resolve the issue quickly. The school remained closed while union leaders tried to persuade the Education Secretary to give the local authority powers to impose a solution. Mrs Bennett and two parent governors resigned. Matthew Wilson's mother was adamant that she wanted Matthew to return to the school and instructed a solicitor to seek a High Court ruling that Nottinghamshire Education Authority should allow him to do so. The headmaster, the teachers, a majority of the remaining governors, the other parents and the local education authority wanted Matthew to be transferred to another school, allowing Manton Junior to return to normal. The other parents were reported (*The Daily Telegraph*, 5 November 1996) as being 'infuriated' by the indiscipline of one pupil and the intransigence of one mother which had effectively closed the school, and rejected a suggested compromise which would have given Matthew a further period of one-to-one teaching until Christmas, while attempts were made to reintegrate him incrementally back into school routine.

After a week during which the school was closed, Matthew's mother finally bowed to pressure after the County Council Education Authority announced that it was prepared to 'act outside its powers' to remove Matthew from the school, if necessary. According to her solicitor, she became weary after two months of dispute and was prepared to take Matthew out of the school and arrange for him to be transferred to another. She felt that no-one else involved appeared to have the interests of the children at heart. The general secretary of the National Union of Teachers said it was 'appalling' that it had taken so long to resolve the matter.

The situation at Manton Junior School arose at a time when school discipline rose high on the political agenda in the UK. The Ridings School in Halifax also found itself in crisis at the same time, when a teachers' union claimed that one in ten pupils should be excluded for violent and disruptive behaviour. A minority of pupils had created real problems for the staff. These and other events, including the killing of a London school headteacher, brought the issue of pupil violence, behavioural problems and school discipline firmly into the public political domain.

The primary market for education may be defined as the pupil or student, who has the legal right to benefit from an experience which should provide him or her with the skills and knowledge-base from which to develop a successful life and career. As is so often the case in public sector industries, however, multiple markets not only create their own demands, but also add to the possibility of political conflict. In the case of Manton Junior School, it is evident that there were conflicting perceptions of what might be considered in Matthew Wilson's 'best interests'.

to his or her job, to personal career aspirations and to individual, lifestyle interests. The relative strengths of these individual elements is likely to change continuously.

Hierarchies of power naturally imply competition for advancement, responsibility, control and influence. Hierarchies actually guarantee an element of conflict in any organisation, because they preserve competition within the system. Role cultures, with their reliance on specialisms and clearly defined areas of work, are particularly prone to internal rivalry and conflict. Competition for resources seems a certain method of preserving this cultural feature, and is common to most public sector organisations.

There are a number of other sources of conflict with political implications. Power is usually contestable, or at least it appears to be human nature to contest power. Power is often associated with the possession and control of information, which can have a major impact on decision-making processes because it influences people's perceptions of reality. This is sometimes associated with the control of technology, both information technology, the importance of which has risen dramatically in the last two decades, particularly important to service industries, and production technology. Gender relations can be another important source of conflict.

Morgan (1986) considers that organisational politics can be analysed systematically by examining the relations between *interests*, *conflict* and *power*. It has already been noted that an individual may experience some tension between his or her job, career aspirations and lifestyle interests – tensions which are common in our society. Different individuals will strike different balances between these. When individuals work together within an organisation, such differences are likely to surface in the form of personal agendas, giving rise to political activity between them. This can produce political coalitions between individuals who co-operate together on specific issues. Conflict between individuals and between groups occurs when their interests oppose each other.

All sources of conflict can be managed in different ways. For example, Morgan (1986, pp. 182–3) lists a number of strategies used in gender relations. Bolman and Deal (1991) consider that a good manager needs a number of political skills:

- *Agenda setting*. They cite Kanter (1983) and other writers who suggest that effective leadership depends greatly on the ability to set an agenda which provides a sense of organisational direction and on determining a strategy to carry it out.

- *Networking and building coalitions*. These are an important step in achieving a political base. The manager can identify those who can help, assess the sources of any opposition, and influence those people who can 'soften' any resistance.

- *Bargaining and negotiation*. These are essential to decision-making processes, and often involve focusing on the interests of, rather than on the positions adopted by, those involved, trying to find possibilities which will bring mutual advantages to both sides (Fisher and Uri, 1981).

A 1980 survey cited by Pfeffer (1992, pp. 36–7) indicates that organisational politics involving the use of power occur most frequently in the functional areas of marketing, boards of directors and sales. At the same time, political conflict can be very complex and very obvious to individual members of an organisation, but may sometimes remain hidden from all but those who are directly involved with it. It may rarely 'surface' or be openly acknowledged in what is supposed to be a collective culture. It would appear to challenge the dominant 'rationality' of organisational behaviour.

It would probably be counter-productive, however, to use Morgan's political metaphor for an organisation in a way which might actively increase an organisation's internal politicisation. The metaphor needs to be used with caution. Nevertheless, the political metaphor does recognise the importance of understanding politics as an unavoidable fact of life in organisations.

Defining social need

The definition of social need is an important political concern because it is central to most public sector services. It has also become important in any discussion of the role of markets. Markets exist to identify and satisfy needs by facilitating the exchange process. However, government purchasing power is constrained by the level of resources it regards as affordable. In any situation where government spending is regarded as excessive, attempts will be made to control costs and to limit expenditure. Historically, failure to do so has resulted in borrowing, and an ever-present need to reduce the Public Sector Borrowing Requirement (PSBR). The problem of affordability will usually persuade politicians in power that the criteria, by which the State decides if and when it must intervene in order to alleviate need, should be applied as rigorously as possible.

During the period of Conservative government in the UK from the 1980s, the government adopted the proposition that free markets and competition can establish an equilibrium between supply and demand. Wherever possible, competition has been encouraged, and the language of the market permeates the reports of, for example, the National Audit Office, the government's watchdog on efficiency.

Example: local authority museums and galleries

The Audit Commission's February 1991 report on managing local authority museums and art galleries, *The Road to Wigan Pier?*, makes it quite clear that debate on the roles of these museums and art galleries has been fuelled by the financial pressures that these institutions face. Public museums and art galleries now have to identify a clear social purpose for their (non-profit) activities. The industry is fully aware of the implications involved, and has responded by developing quite a sophisticated definition of its functions. An International Council of Museums (ICOM) definition can be found in Kavanagh (1994, p. 15). According to this definition, any museum aims to acquire, conserve, research, communicate and exhibit objects for the purposes of study, education and enjoyment. Marketing features prominently in the Audit Commission's (1991) recommended approach towards better management. A marketing analysis of visitor services, based on the 'four Ps' of marketing (*see* Chapter 3) is illustrated. Such an approach gathered political momentum during the later 1980s. It has not gone unchallenged, however, especially in museums' culture. The principal objections are summarised below.

1 *The concentration upon the market and market forces is alien to public sector professions which have, historically, seen themselves as functionally altruistic – that is, providing social service, working to benefit others and committed to the principle of equity.* These attitudes easily provoked a major conflict in museums between collection-related objectives – concerned with collecting, maintenance, research and scholarship – and user-related objectives – concerned with display, interpretation and marketing requirements. This represented an important source of political conflict within many museums. There were many who objected to a new focus on user-related objectives on the grounds that this was 'popularising' museums, despite the fact that, for example, at the Victoria and Albert Museum in London, the development of improved facilities and more 'user-friendly' exhibitions succeeded in increasing the attendance figures and were, in themselves, largely dependent upon good scholarship and curatorial skills.

2 *The relationship between value and price, usually found in the private sector, is foreign to the culture of public services, many of which are designed to help people whose income is inadequate for their needs (see also Chapter 8).* In museums, pressure to generate their own sources of income has led many to reconsider the established policy of 'free entry' and to impose admissions charges. By 1996, the Victoria and Albert Museum had planned to introduce entrance charges, and the British Museum had decided that it was necessary to follow suit.

   Dickenson (1994) had already debated the issue and noted that the origins of the museum as a service seen 'as a public good' for the use of all citizens was based on the desire to provide equity for all. Although, historically, many supported the idea of admissions charges as a 'discouragement to idlers' – including the great Victorian critic, John Ruskin, in 1880 – and despite the fact that in countries such as France, charges have been seen as an incentive to encourage a sense of worth, many still believe that equality of opportunity is a worthwhile endeavour in the public interest.

   Reductions in public spending, however, will inevitably mean that more museums and galleries have to start charging entrance fees. In the UK, in November 1996, it was reported that the British Museum would have to choose between the introduction of an entrance fee of £5 or £6 and the loss of 350 jobs, following a 3 per cent cut in the government grant and the pending loss of contribution from the British Library when the library moves to its new building in 1998. It was projected that, by the year 2000, the museum could face a shortfall of 20 per cent of its level of income in 1996. Many felt aggrieved that the plentiful supply of capital moneys available from the UK National Lottery was in stark contrast with the diminishing levels of revenue funding from central government.

3 *The new belief in the efficacy of the market appears to have become a faith, with a political tendency to override many rational objections.* The contribution from museum entrance fees is variable, and depends a lot on the popularity of the individual institution. Charges undoubtedly affect the level of demand – that is, attendances – although it can be argued that they actually contribute to perceptions of a museum visit's worth. The principle of equity can be used to argue that visitors from abroad, who have not subsidised a museum through taxes in the

UK, should also pay for its use. There is, therefore, some rationale for the belief that public support for social institutions should coincide with the interests of the market.

An increasing disillusionment with, and criticism of, public sector industries have been linked (for example, by Berthoud, 1985, p. 15) to the ever-increasing spread of state influence over aspects of ordinary, everyday life. Historically, governments have taken political and paternalistic decisions about what is good for people. Harrisson and Madge (1986, pp. 11–12) noted, as far back as 1939, that social reforms were often imposed from above by a small majority. This 'what's good for them' approach is, of course, the antithesis of the marketer's question 'what do people need?', and reminds us what happens when an active provider attempts to make a transaction with an inactive user (*see* Chapter 2).

Laissez-faire, free-market ideology and the revival of the belief that markets can provide a 'natural' mechanism for matching products and demand and relating provision to need, have provided a very important rationale for the market (*see* Clarke *et al.*, 1987, p. 131 ff.). Distrust of the scale of the State's 'interference' with everyday life stimulated Rhodes Boyson, MP to argue, in 1971, that the Welfare State was destructive of personal liberty and individual responsibility (quoted by Clarke *et al.*, 1987, pp. 135–8). It actively encouraged the 'dependency culture' so disliked by Margaret Thatcher. In consequence, privatisation was encouraged as a means of opening the door to market forces in the area of welfare provision. It is fair to remind ourselves that the constraints of the public sector markets are very unlikely to provide a level of choice which can compare favourably with that available in the private sector (*see* Chapter 3). Resources are usually far too scarce, and the political will to provide them is diminishing.

Bureaucracy

The way in which many organisations are today re-examining their management structures and eschewing the older forms of monolithic bureaucracies has much to do with the critiques of bureaucracy now available. Unfortunately, a popular image of 'faceless' public sector institutions survives as a social stereotype of the public sector organisation (*see* Chapter 11). It is worth considering briefly how the stereotype was formed in the first place. Max Weber (1864–1920) was an academic, primarily interested in the sociology of past cultures. His study of the structures of authority made an important contribution to the study of organisations. He identified three organisational types, in which authority is legitimised in different ways:

● the *charismatic* domination by the personal qualities of an individual;

● the *traditional* domination by an inherited system;

● the *rational – legal* domination by a structure of rules, regulations and procedures.

This last type is best expressed by the bureaucracy form. The bureaucratic system is designed so that each part performs a clearly defined function in the most efficient way, and as such Weber sees the system as rational. It is also legal by virtue of the way in which authority is exercised through a system of rules and procedures.

Weber considered such a system the most efficient kind of organisation, and used an analogy between an organisation and an efficient machine. The identification of a machine with efficiency became a major part of twentieth-century modernist mythology. For example, the architect Le Corbusier termed the modern house 'a machine for living in' in 1923. Le Corbusier's generation used the metaphor of the machine as the ultimate example of efficiency – a principle adapted by the management theory of F. W. Taylor, the early advocate of 'scientific management' in the USA, in 1912.

As a way of ensuring efficiency in the form of control and standardised output, Weber was convinced that the bureaucracy was a highly efficient system. To him it embodied precision, discipline, reliability. He seems to have seen bureaucratisation as an inevitable process, although he was also aware of the need to limit the bureaucracy's tendency to accumulate power (*see* Albrow, 1974, pp. 45–9).

Unfortunately, Weber's ideal bureaucracy proved hard to realise. The popular image of bureaucracies changed. Bureaucracy, as an organisational form, became synonymous with inefficiency and red tape (*see* Pugh, 1990). Many of the problems were reviewed by Lane (1987). Too often the interests of the organisation itself began to obscure the original, external goals of the bureaucracy. Tendencies towards 'dysfunctions' emerged. Some bureaucracies over-emphasised the importance of expertise, of specialist knowledge, leading to a domination by 'experts'. Conflict between professionals and administrative staff began to emerge. Tensions between personal goals and corporate ones are sometimes difficult to live with. Some research suggests that informal organisational structures are often more important to the individual than the formal, hierarchical structures. The concept of the rational, predictable bureaucratic organisation began to seem less convincing by the early 1960s (*See* Argyris, 1960). (*See* Minicase 7.3.)

It appeared that bureaucracies were likely to under-perform, due to their inherent defects as organisational structures. Most of their characteristics – such as division of labour, hierarchical structure and control systems – do not equate very well with individual needs – for example, the desire of employees to 'own' the process in which they are engaged, and obtain a level of individual autonomy. A number of specific criticisms of bureaucracies can be made.

1 *Bureaucracies tend to become very rigid organisations, run by sets of rules and committed to routines.* They can be very inflexible, full of 'red tape', reluctant to assume direct responsibility, and ponderously slow. They can inhibit innovation and they seem to prioritise administrative functions. As 'rational–legal' organisations, they seem to embody the worst characteristics of public sector organisations which are dominated by written codes of conduct, restrictive practices and an attitude towards customers characterised by a blind adherence to 'the rules'. Rules and regulations are, of course, important sources of power within an organisation.

2 *Bureaucracies tend to develop their own power bases and penetrate political levels of government.* This is nowhere more obvious than in some civil service departments. Public sector industries were traditionally dominated by bureaucratic behaviours, where the need for control led, apparently inexorably, to a bureaucratic system of definitions and procedures. This is still evident in, for example, organ-

MINICASE 7.3

Bureaucracy at work

The *Sunday Express* of 13 February 1994 carried an article by Alastair Law and Steve Haines entitled 'Soaring Civil Servants'. The authors noted that the numbers of civil servants employed by Whitehall had actually grown. Criticisms were made of the 'Next Steps Agencies', established by the government in the late 1980s with the intention of separating policy making from administrative functions. In theory, this should have reduced the number of staff employed by Whitehall departments. According to Law and Haines, the Commons Treasury Select Committee apparently concluded that Next Step Agencies had been subjected to a high level of control by their Whitehall masters, who continued to employ large numbers of civil service staff to monitor the agencies. In real terms, this seemed to have produced an increase in the numbers of civil servants. Unfortunately, control is a central feature of bureaucratic culture, which often has difficulty in sanctioning a significant level of autonomy in divisions for which it is responsible. According to the *Sunday Express*, the Department of Environment had particular difficulty in limiting the numbers of its employees.

Bureaucracy has also proved to be a problem, in a different form, for the BBC. In an attempt to turn the Corporation into a more 'market-led' organisation, it was divided up into some 480 'business units'. The Director-general, John Birt, expressed his intention to reduce that number to less than 200 (as outlined in an article in *The Independent* of 6 November 1993) by April 1994, as the result of discovering 'weaknesses' in the system. Under this system, producers have to buy resources from either the corporation or from external suppliers, whichever is cheapest or gives best value for money. Some producers have called this system a bureaucratic nightmare, and many of the business units initially made losses. On the other hand, it was claimed by Mr Birt that the system saved more than £100 million in 1993–4. The process of rationalisation has also involved the shedding of some 4000 jobs and some two dozen studios.

isations which prioritise efficiency in a literal, inflexible way. Such behaviours, however, are hardly a guarantee of a successful 'public service orientation' which seeks to accommodate the demands of users.

3 *Bureaucracies are not as rational as supposed.* According to some writers (for example, Cohen *et al.*, 1976) bureaucracies are merely dustbins in which problems and solutions are dumped. Such an attitude merely reveals a belief that bureaucracies are not actually as rational as theory would have us believe. Their rationality is restricted to their own definitions of problems and procedures. Examples abound of bureaucratic decisions which seem to defy ordinary logic, but which are the result of applying the only rules available to a bureaucratic system. Such decisions, however, are legitimised by the power such bureaucracies can wield.

4 *Bureaucracies tend to maximise their own size, roles and performance,* even creating a supply in excess of demand (and therefore becoming inefficient). They seem to have a natural tendency to grow and expand. It has even been suggested that they are in some ways uncontrollable. Institutions which have a large bureaucratic component tend to increase the volume of administrative functions. This is

illustrated particularly well by the growth in National Health Service 'management' employees, and by the tendency of administrative departments in some services to grow at the slightest opportunity. 'Empire building' is a typical behaviour inside large organisations, and often involves political coalitions within them.

5 *Bureaucracies are wasteful.* Bureaucratic efficiency may not equate directly with social effectiveness (and many goals of bureaucracies in the public sector are social) and the ability to respond properly to markets. An obvious solution to this problem might be to encourage a greater responsiveness to market forces. The relative inflexibility of bureaucracies can make this difficult.

Organisations in the public sector have long been dominated by bureaucratic forms. Bureaucracy has been the subject of extensive study (for example, by Warwick, 1974). More recently, the historical tradition of professionals disbursing resources via public sector bureaucracies has been challenged. Values have changed. Consumerism has emerged as an important feature of the modern environment. As a result, by the late 1980s, new approaches were being explored. For example, Clode, Parker and Etherington entitled their 1987 edition of essays, *Towards The Sensitive Bureaucracy. Consumers, Welfare and the New Pluralism.* The editors defined three initiatives in modern public sector consumerism: *freedom of choice, more participatory democracy* and *more information.*

However, bureaucracies still appear to monopolise the necessary allocation of public resources. They are under attack from public opinion and political ideology. They are held up as examples of inefficient (how many people are needed to change a hospital light bulb?) management. They are being broken down and their functions allocated to new 'agencies'. Yet the culture of control, the desire for a standardised and regularised activity or output, remains a political priority. As long as this culture of political control continues to dominate, some of the real issues of marketing in the public sector are unlikely to be addressed.

Sources of power

Many public sector organisations are necessarily changing their structures and retreating from bureaucracy, often in response to political initiatives designed to improve and strengthen their structures and management. However, their service roles are unlikely to change dramatically, even as they are transformed into agencies or are privatised. Emphasis on the importance of efficiency often reinforces some of the principal sources of power within the organisation.

Morgan (1986) comments at length on the sources of power inside organisations. His analysis is particularly appropriate to public sector organisations. The more obvious sources of power are described in Fig. 7.2 and include the following:

1 *The power of formal authority.* The ways in which an organisation formally vests power in individuals 'legitimises' that authority; it establishes a social approval for the exercise of power. Most public sector organisations have cultures in which power has been legitimised by a combination of tradition and bureaucratic authority, an adhesion to rules and procedures, a careful definition of roles and responsibilities. This is now changing fast, as many of those organisations

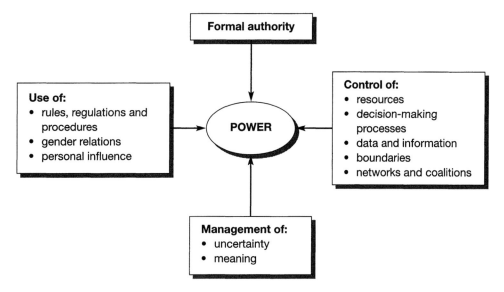

Fig. 7.2 Sources of power
(after Morgan, 1986)

realise the advantages of 'flatter' (that is, less hierarchical and more 'organic') structures and greater flexibility and responsiveness to their markets.

2 *Power as control over resources.* Since most public sector organisations rely upon a fixed and finite supply of resources, the control of these is an important source of power. Budgets and allocations are immensely influential. Dependence (upon resources) is a certain acknowledgement of subordination, and thus of power relationships.

3 *Power through organisational structure and procedures.* Structure is frequently used as an instrument of control. Rules and regulations are obvious visible signs of control, and hence of power. They are particularly obvious in bureaucratic organisations.

4 *Power via control or influence over decisions.* Anyone who can influence organisational decision making exercises a degree of power. Decision making (*see* Cooke and Slack, 1984) is often seen as central to management functions. Good management may depend upon the quality of the decisions made.

5 *Power through the control of information.* By influencing the ways information is collected and interpreted, a member of an organisation can wield significant political power. The increasing reliance on databasing and computerised systems, for example, also highlights the fact that the design of information systems itself, which invariably contain a number of assumptions about why that information is required, influences the way in which information is presented and used. This is obviously of particular importance to marketing.

6 *Power through technology.* Developing the previous point, it becomes evident that most modern organisations are dependent on some form or forms of technology. Changes in technology are likely to change power relationships within or between organisations (*see* Minicase 7.4).

| MINICASE 7.4 | **Power and technology** |

The National Health Service has seen more fundamental changes during the 1980s and 1990s than other public sector industries. One of the most radical has been the result of technological developments.

The insatiable growth in demand for health services (*see* Chapter 1) is itself partly due to advances in technology. The control of costs is an ever-present political concern, and the opportunity to use technology as a means of doing so has recently been realised. *The Daily Telegraph* of 2 July 1994 noted that its specially commissioned Gallup poll placed the then Health Secretary, Virginia Bottomley, as one of the two ministers voters would most like to see sacked. The extent of her unpopularity was some indication of the controversy aroused by proposed changes in one of the most highly valued public services.

In the past, technological advances in medicine have generally added to the costs of the service. We need only look at the number of public appeals trying to raise money for new equipment to illustrate the point. However, increasing demand for capital revenue is not the only result of technological advances. Developments in 'minimally invasive' techniques, often using 'keyhole surgery', have the potential for dramatic reductions in hospitalisation time. *The Sunday Times* of 26 June 1994 carried an article by Lois Rogers praising the benefits to patients. With the exception of joint replacements and organ transplants, many operations can now be done through a 'keyhole', with much less trauma to the patient than that caused by conventional techniques. However, while bed occupancy may be reduced, theatre time and equipment costs increase.

The Health Secretary has expressed hope that some 50 000 hospital beds (40 per cent of the total available) will be able to go. New techniques may enable some 60 per cent of surgery patients to have 'minimally invasive' surgery – often termed 'conveyor-belt' surgery by its critics. A prediction of the cost benefits of using streamlined, high technology surgery forecasts dramatic savings in costs when compared with conventional, open surgery. An appendix removal, for example, is costed at £200 (half a day in hospital) compared with £2000 (four days in hospital).

Criticism of the Health Secretary's proposals comes from those who fear that beds will be closed for the wrong reasons. With very long waiting lists for operations such as hip replacements, there is still plenty of demand for surgery which cannot be done through a keyhole. Nevertheless, the development of the new technology is being used here as a powerful political lever on change.

We can argue, therefore, that a political dimension is present in any organisational structure, and that power can be exercised in a large number of ways – those listed above are not exclusive. Politics will inevitably influence the ways and the extent to which any organisation can successfully develop a marketing culture and a marketing strategy. A political recognition of the need for an integrated approach to marketing is a prerequisite for its successful adoption.

Summary

1 **Politics as power.** Politics are concerned with the acquisition of power and influence.

2 **The general political climate can be very powerful.** The general political activity at government level, although subject to parliamentary and electoral checks, affects all levels of society. The increasing political attention to the importance of the customer has given marketing philosophy a higher profile than ever before.

3 **Inter-organisational politics.** Such politics are evident even at inter-departmental, government level, but have become another important consequence of developing competition.

4 **Politics as power within an organisation.** Any organisation will have its own political dimension, presenting ample opportunity for political activity. Conflict may well be a normal part of their existence. Unfortunately, conflict can also compromise the effectiveness of an organisation's marketing orientation.

5 **The concept of social need is a political issue.** The concept and definition of social need is an important political concern for many public sector organisations. A government is usually under pressure to limit expenditure and control costs. There are, however, some serious questions about the principle of social equity.

6 **Bureaucracy.** Bureaucracy is one form of organisation with a long historical association with the public sector. Bureaucracies today are under attack, for example, from consumerism, a desire for greater public participation, and a need for more information.

7 **Sources of power** can be identified as formal authority, power through organisational structure and procedures, power through control over decisions and power through the control of information and technology. There is a potential political dimension within any organisation.

Implications for management

A model of the political environment

Most managers need some systematic model of the political environment in which they operate. This can be developed using the three levels of political activity identified above: general, inter-organisational and intra-organisational.

Political influences from outside the organisation

At this level, it should also be noted that organisations do not merely respond to influences; they may also *be* influences on other organisations. An organisation can be proactive, by adopting policies and entering into negotiations which deliberately seek to influence political decisions and demands from 'outside' the organisation.

Table 7.1 Identifying political influences from outside the organisation

	Source of authority (e.g. the body making demands)	Form of demand (e.g. legislative requirement, British Standard, etc.)	Nature of response (e.g. *conformance*: financial returns, performance statistics, etc., or *negotiation*: seeking to influence and modify the demands)
1			
2			
3			
4			
5			
6			

Inter-organisational influences

The nature of these can either be *cooperative* or *competitive* (*see* Table 7.2). A local authority housing department may be cooperating with a housing association in property developments. A Next Steps agency may have an information technology department which is involved in competitive tendering for work against bids from private companies.

Table 7.2 Cooperative and competitive influences

Organisation	Form of cooperation	Form of competition

Intra-organisational influences

Politics within an organisation take many forms, from inter-departmental rivalries to personality clashes and disagreements. They are often related both to the organisation's own *formal* power structures and to the *informal* exercise of power. These provide two headings under which sources of power can be listed and areas of potential or actual conflict identified (*see* Table 7.3). As marketing frequently provides areas of political conflict (Pfeffer, 1992), it is important to understand the nature of these in order to determine strategies for dealing with them.

Organisational audits

Two types of audit or analysis seem appropriate.

An audit of organisational type

Systematic methodologies are generally available, but many appear to be motivated by the desire to appear 'scientific'. It is, arguably, more important to be clear about the implications of the organisational structure that exists, than to try to 'fit' the organisation into a single specific category. Most organisations have models of responsibilities and line management. It is important to understand the structure of the organisation in order to grasp the implications of power and authority at work within it. The typology offered by Handy (1985) (*see* earlier in this chapter) is a useful starting point, but there is a danger in trying too hard to categorise an organisation in this way. Most organisations will possess characteristics from different categories at the same time. It is more important to identify the specific means by which power is exercised within the specific organisation – for example, via its 'chains of command', lines of management and allocations of responsibilities.

An 'organisational profile' exercise was proposed many years ago by Likert (1967, pp. 197–211), which uses the following 'organisational variables':

Table 7.3 Areas of intra-organisational conflict

Source of power and influence (formal/informal)	Area of actual or potential conflict

- leadership
- motivation
- communication
- decisions
- goals
- control.

Under each heading a number of questions are asked, eliciting scaled responses. These enable an organisation's 'climate' (now more commonly referred to as 'culture' – *see* Chapter 11) to be categorised into what Likert called 'systems', but which may also be described as modes of exercising power. These were:

- exploitative authoritative
- benevolent authoritative
- consultative
- participative.

The exercise can be done once using the perceptions of the existing organisation, and once using ideas about an ideal organisation (the one that would be most effective in your own opinion). Differences between the results can be used to identify the nature of desired changes.

An 'influencing style' audit

This is usually designed to help individuals develop greater awareness of the ways in which they relate to others and the nature of their own personal influence in an organisation. This is a useful way of assessing one's own style of management and ways of exercising power. There is often some discrepancy between how the managers see themselves and how others see them. Salaman (1995, p. 115) points out that, although styles of management are apt to change according to situation, individuals are likely to have personal preferences for particular ones. An awareness of one's own management style is an important step in the learning process. 1979 research, cited by Pfeffer (1992, p. 73), indicated that the ability to be articulate and sensitive rate most highly of those personal traits which are considered to be characteristic of managers deemed to be politically effective. Pfeffer (1992, pp. 165–85) lists six characteristics which he considers particularly important:

- energy and stamina;
- the ability to focus energy;
- sensitivity to others;
- flexibility;
- the ability to tolerate conflict;
- the ability to 'get along' with others.

ISSUES FOR DISCUSSION

The following issues for discussion are presented in the form of questions. Examples from specific public sector industries should be incorporated into responses. Case studies can be used to provide some illustrations of the issues raised.

1 Why has competition become an increasingly important consideration for public sector organisations?

2 What are the most common sources of power within public sector organisations, and how does this impact on customer satisfaction?

3 What personal conflicts of interest may be experienced by those working within public sector organisations?

4 What are the advantages and disadvantages of bureaucracy and the consequences for marketing in public sector organisations?

References

Albrow, M. (1974) *Bureaucracy*. London: Macmillan.

Argyris, C. (1960) *Understanding Organizational Behavior*. Homewood, Illinois: Dorsey Press.

Audit Commission (1991) *The Road to Wigan Pier? Managing Local Authority Museums and Art Galleries*. London: HMSO.

Berthoud, R. (1985) *Challenges to Social Policy*. London: Gower Press.

Bolman, L.G. and Deal, T.E. (1991) *Reframing Organizations*. San Francisco: Jossey-Bass Publishers.

Clarke, J., Cochrane, A. and Smart, C. (1987) *Ideologies of Welfare*. London: Hutchinson.

Clode, D., Parker, C. and Etherington, S. (eds) (1987) *Towards the Sensitive Bureaucracy. Consumers, Welfare and the New Pluralism*. London: Gower Press.

Cohen, M., March, J.G. and Olsen, J.P. (eds) (1976) *Ambiguity and Choice*. Oslo: Universitetsforlaget, cited in Lane, J.-E. (1987) *Bureaucracy and Public Choice*. London: Sage Publications.

Cooke, S. and Slack, N. (1984) *Making Management Decisions*. Englewood Cliffs, New Jersey: Prentice-Hall Inc.

Dahloff, U., Harris, J., Shattock, M., Starapoli, A. and in't Velde, R. (1991) *Dimensions of Evaluation in Higher Education*. London: Jessica Kingsley Publishers.

Department of Education and Science (1989) *Shifting the balance of public funding of higher education to fees: a consultation paper*. London: Department of Education and Science.

Dickenson, V. (1994) 'The economics of museum admission charges' in Moore, K. (ed) *Museum Management*. London and New York: Routledge and Kegan Paul.

Elcock, H. (1994) *Local government. Policy and management in local authorities* (3rd edn). London and New York: Routledge and Kegan Paul.

Emery, F.E. and Trist, E.L. (1965) 'The Causal Texture of Organizational Environments', *Human Relations*, 18, 21–32.

Fisher, R. and Uri, W. (1981) *Getting Yes*. Boston: Houghton Mifflin.

Gerloff, E.A. (1985) *Organizational Theory and Design*. New York: McGraw-Hill International.

Handy, C.B. (1985) *Understanding Organisations*. Harmondsworth: Penguin Books.

Harrisson, T. and Madge, C. (1986) *Britain by Mass-Observation*. London: The Cresset Library.

Hindess, B. (1987) *Freedom, Equality and the Market*. London and New York: Tavistock Publications.

Howarth, A. (1991) 'Market Forces in Higher Education', *Higher Education Quarterly*, 45 (1), Winter, 5–13.

Hutton, W. (1996) *False Economy: The Price of Power*. London: Channel 4 Television, 18 June.

Johnson, G. and Scholes, K. (1997) *Exploring Corporate Strategy* (4th edn). Hemel Hempstead, Hertfordshire: Prentice Hall International (UK) Ltd.

Kanter, R. (1983) *The Change Masters: Innovations for Productivity in the American Corporation*. New York: Simon & Schuster.

Kast, F.E. and Rosenweig, J.E. (1979) *Organisations and Management, A Systems and Contingency Approach* (3rd edn). New York: McGraw-Hill.

Kavanagh, G. (ed) (1994) *Museum Provision and Professionalisation*. London and New York: Routledge and Kegan Paul.

Lane, J.-E. (1987) *Bureaucracy and Public Choice*. London: Sage Publications.

Likert, R. (1967) *The Human Organization*. New York: McGraw-Hill.

Morgan, G. (1986) *Images of Organisation*. London: Sage Publications.

Plant, R., Lesser, H. and Taylor-Gooby, P. (1980) *Political philosophy and social welfare*. London: Routledge and Kegan Paul.

Pfeffer, J. (1992) *Managing with Power*. Boston, Massachusetts: Harvard Business School Press.

Pugh, D.S. (1990) *Organization Theory*. Harmondsworth: Penguin Books.

Rhodes, R.A.W. (1987) *The National World of Local Government*. London: Allen & Unwin.

Salaman, G. (1978) 'Towards a Sociology of Organizational Structure', *Sociological Quarterly*, 26, 519–54.

Salaman, G. (1995) *Managing*. Buckingham: Open University Press.

Self, P. (1993) *Government by the Market?* London: Macmillan.

Smith, P.B. and Peterson, M.F. (1988) *Leadership, Organizations and Culture*. London: Sage Publications.

Stewart, J. (1986) *The New Management of Local Government*. London: Allen & Unwin.

Warner, J. (1995) 'Take-over frenzy that blew the fuse', *The Independent*, 19 September.

Warwick, D. (1974) *Bureaucracy*. London: Longman.

Price, value and exchange

It is often asserted that 'if costs go up, prices go up too, and that's a fact'. This connection between price and costs is well-established in the private sector, and absolutely entrenched in the public sector, largely as a result of seeking to achieve 'fairness' and to avoid cross-subsidy. In reality, cost often bears little relationship to the perceived value of the goods or services on offer and, as a consequence, pricing has become one of the most vexed questions within the marketing 'toolbox'. In the public sector, the issue of price is further complicated by the fact that much of the public sector is publicly funded from taxation and many services are free at the point of delivery. These issues differentiate public sector marketing from private sector marketing.

This chapter examines the issues of price, value, and costs and looks at the influence of taxation on user perceptions. There is a lengthy discussion of some of the weaknesses of using costing systems for establishing price, and it is argued that using cost as a benchmark can lead to flawed decisions. The chapter also examines some pricing concepts, including the effects of non-monetary prices.

**KEY LEARNING
OUTCOMES**

By the end of the chapter, you should be able to:

- **appreciate how price and value are attributes *given* to something by a market;**
- **understand that public sector marketing usually operates within a number of constraints affecting the perception of price;**
- **explore ways in which the management of volume, price and cost are particularly important in a fixed revenue context;**
- **examine and assess the limitations of using costs as a basis for setting price; and**
- **consider how perceptions of price include the influence of quality.**

Introduction

Earlier chapters have discussed in some detail issues which relate, in one form or another, to the marketing mix. While these issues are important, and despite the need to recognise the increasing importance of non-price factors which influence buyer behaviour, many commercial organisations still give priority to pricing considerations in determining market share and profit performance. This is because, as many writers, including Kotler (1988), have pointed out, only price has the potential to generate revenue without incurring investment costs. Indeed, such is the impact of pricing decisions that, when inappropriate, they can destroy otherwise well conceived marketing plans.

Commercial organisations, operating in both consumer and organisational markets, have considerable difficulties in setting prices, and theoretical models of pricing are demonstrably difficult to put into operational practice. Given the real differences between marketing in the public sector and in the private sector, the issues of pricing are even more complex. In this chapter, the discussion will first focus generally on issues of pricing as a component of marketing strategy and tactics. Issues relating more specifically to the public sector will then be developed. It will be demonstrated that pricing decisions which are determined by reference to costs carry a high risk of generating sub-optimal organisational performance, unless they also reflect the competitive conditions present in an organisation's external environment. The quest for optimal performance also requires that pricing decisions must not be taken in isolation, but should form part of an integrated marketing strategy which *explicitly* recognises both the interdependence of other elements of marketing variables and the need to vary their relative emphases over time.

Defining price

Price may be defined as *the value* (measured by whatever means is appropriate) given to a product or a service by a market. The price of a product or a service refers to the terms by which it can be acquired, and may be expressed in monetary or non-monetary terms. Perceptions of desirability and worth are apt to vary, because they are subject to a large number of influences, as has been demonstrated in the discussion of buyer behaviour (*see* Chapter 4). They are also subject to price sensitivity, sometimes described as 'market forces', where a reduction in the availability of a sought-after article is likely to raise the price asked and obtained for it. A reduction in demand, or an increase in supply, may lower price in the marketplace.

Price is, therefore, an important influence on the nature of any organisation's exchanges with its environment. Price certainly influences the customer's perception of the product. High price is often equated with high quality and vice versa. It can also be argued that anything given for free is unlikely to be perceived as having 'value' for the user in the same way as something will be seen as having value if an exchange has taken place.

The relationship of price to *cost* also needs to be considered. The very existence of an organisation creates costs of operation. These costs are essentially 'input prices' from suppliers of goods, labour and services. An organisation must consider its costs in its pricing policies, as input costs have to be covered if the organisation is to survive in the long term (*see* Fig. 8.1). The relationship of cost and price is very complicated, however, and the source of considerable debate.

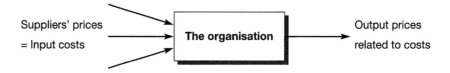

Fig. 8.1 Input costs and output prices

In the public sector, there are a number of additional issues which need to be addressed.

- In many instances the public sector has a monopoly or near monopoly of supply.
- Public sector provision is often largely funded by taxation, which influences the level of acceptable additional prices.
- There is the issue of fairness, equity and equality.
- There are issues of rights, needs and wants.
- There are issues of internal markets.
- In addition, there are issues relating to private sector contributions to the funding of public sector activities.

The desire to achieve 'total quality', by meeting the requirements of the customer or user, necessarily involves a strategic use of pricing. Quality (*see* Chapter 6) is itself a market-driven concept, but it is also one which is high on the UK political agenda.

If we accept the (commercial sector) definition of marketing that believes that marketing's purpose is to identify consumer needs and satisfy them at a profit (Baker, 1985, p. 274), then the nature of demand must be the primary marketing concern of any organisation, influencing the relationship between quantity of supply and price. It can also be argued that the price of a product determines the demand for it. Very highly priced products can assume a small, select or specialised level of demand.

Unfortunately, marketing has many other factors to take into consideration, and marketing objectives are unlikely to be as straightforward as maximising profits, especially in the public sector arena. Indeed, as Pitt and Abratt (1987) pointed out, if profit-making is not a goal, there is a temptation to think that pricing hardly seems important. In organisations where there is no direct charge to the client or end-user, pricing may not be seen to have any obvious role. This idea is usually incorrect, however, since the public sector's need to satisfy multiple markets invariably means establishing a price which can be seen to provide value for money to, for example, the resourcer market.

Some concepts of market pricing

At this stage, it is important to examine some basic concepts of pricing. They are initially easier to understand if the profit-making sector is used as a starting point. It is then possible to explore how the concepts can be related to non-profit and public sector operations.

In spite of the acknowledged importance of price as a key determinant of organisational performance, Winkler (1983) suggests that, in most companies, pricing policy is diffuse and in many cases chaotic. Several departments may contribute their views to the pricing process. In most cases, prices are set at different levels in the organisation and are often set with little account taken of market conditions. This is often because the organisation has no effective information system for gathering market information.

In the absence of market information, a high proportion of organisations resort to using rough-and-ready, 'rules of thumb' methods of practical price setting, the most common of which involve cost–plus procedures. Conversely, many studies have shown that where organisations use good market information, and set prices according to market conditions, then there is a relation between financial success and pricing policies. This theme has been developed further by Winkler (1983).

Furthermore, the issues of pricing need to be considered in the context of two types of problems: *optimisation* (how to achieve the best performance) and *equilibrium* (how to achieve a balance of activities). Hirschleifer (1988) proposes that optimisation problems pose the question: 'Is it better to take this or that action?' While the equilibrium problem poses the question: 'What would happen to prices or demand if some event, such as price increases, changes in levels of taxation, or limitations of supply, were to take place?'

The most important pricing concepts are discussed below.

Price sensitivity

Although a universal and ideal pattern of pricing behaviour is illusory, a good starting point for the discussion of pricing is the economist's 'neo-classical' model of the supply and demand curve. Despite its conceptual and 'abstract' nature, it is used extensively in accounting literature and is a useful prescriptive framework for identifying some of the basic requirements for optimal pricing.

The concept has been developed from three core assumptions:

1 The organisation is viewed as a unified decision-making unit, capable of having objectives and pursuing them.

2 It operates in an environment of complete and certain knowledge about its current and future costs and revenues.

3 Its sole behavioural objective is that of short-run profit maximisation.

If these assumptions do not hold (*see* Cooke and Slack, 1984, p. 56), the concept of optimisation is really invalid and should be replaced by that of '*satisficing*'. In such a situation, organisational pricing decisions will reflect the minimum level of performance acceptable to dominant stakeholder interests, rather than yielding maximum performance. In other words it is a device for establishing equilibrium, identifying 'what will be the effect if ...?'.

The diagram of supply and demand shown in Fig. 8.2 is familiar to many managers and is widely cited in the current UK political climate. The horizontal axis of the diagram represents the quantity of output. The vertical axis represents price, in this case expressed in monetary terms. Given that a price is a ratio of quantities – for example, pence per litre for petrol, price per prescription for medicines, interest rates for mortgages and so forth – the vertical axis is shown in the price per unit of quantity.

The demand curve shown in the diagram is not a straight line for the reason that demand curves measure the percentage change in demand against a percentage change in price. The curve also shows a negative slope – that is, with an increase in price, demand declines; with a fall in price, demand increases. This is generally the case in pricing, as is evidenced by the price cutting seen so extensively in the 1990s, where price discounting is used as a tool to move finished goods. However, there

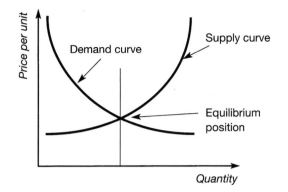

Fig. 8.2 The curves of supply and demand

are some notable exceptions to this phenomenon (which will be discussed later). This change in demand related to price is known as *price elasticity*.

However, the supply curve shows the reverse situation. As price increases, so suppliers will put more into the market. Thus, for example, in pre-Christmas periods, prices tend to be high because there is a shift in price perceptions as demand is driven by the need to give presents, and hence supply increases as well. Equilibrium conditions occur when supply and demand are in equilibrium. Current conditions, which include a plethora of brands and alternative suppliers, mean that direct comparisons between supply and demand cannot be made. As Hirschleifer (1988) maintains, the supply and demand curve is a *model* of reality, not reality itself, and the model needs to be used only as a means for understanding reality and trying to predict the consequence of change.

Price elasticity and inelasticity

Price elasticity occurs where the demand for a product or service decreases, as the price rises, and increases as the price drops. It is not always negative in its effects. These exceptions are often used by monopolies and public sector organisations.

Price inelasticity occurs where the demand for a product or service is not discretionary but essential – for example, where there is a fundamental basic need for a commodity such as water, or a need which has essentially become basic out of habit – for example, smoking – or as a consequence of revised lifestyle – for example, electricity. In fact, it is not wholly true that such products are inelastic – that is, demand does not fall as price increases – but the fall is very slight. Where 'black markets' develop, prices can increase dramatically, as supply falls. The shape of the supply and demand curves change significantly. Very often, in the case of essentials, there is a user expectation that these should be supplied at the lowest possible price to the consumer.

The concept of price inelasticity is often used by organisations to increase prices beyond the expectations of users and, in the case of private organisations such as privatised public utilities, regulatory bodies have to be set up to monitor and control prices.

Some examples of situations in which organisations have discovered price inelasticity are:

- taxation on petrol, alcohol and cigarettes;
- mains water supplies – a fundamental survival need;
- mains electricity;
- prescription charges;
- airport taxes – essential for foreign travel;
- interest rates;
- commuter rail fares, as opposed to leisure fares.

All of these items are, in one form or another, non-discretionary goods and services, assuming that they are incorporated into the user's individual lifestyle. They do exhibit price elasticity, in that everyone would like to get the products for as little as possible, but because of their essential nature, in current market conditions they have become price inelastic.

Interestingly, while consumers complain most vociferously about the cost of water from the water utilities, the same people will often pay very high prices for 'lifestyle', branded water products, such as Perrier. Often they pay more for mineral water than they do for petrol. Another example is where electricity is provided at very high cost – for example, in batteries. It can be seen from these examples that the whole issue of pricing is not about the slavish application of mathematical models but is about an understanding of buyer behaviour as related to the organisation and its products at any given point in time. It is for this reason that pricing perceptions become very important.

Price elasticity and the effect of the environment

A very interesting example of how changes in the business environment can affect price elasticity is shown in the changes in the UK housing market between 1989 and 1996. In the late 1980s the UK housing market demonstrated almost *positive price sensitivity* – as prices went up, so did demand. More houses came onto the market and builders were buying land to build on at very high prices. These circumstances lasted for two or three years, culminating in a virtual collapse of the market in 1989.

Until 1996, the housing market remained almost static, even where those needing to sell houses have dropped their prices significantly. This collapse in the real and notional value of houses caused real anguish and in many cases hardship. For over six years, house sales were effectively immune to reductions in price. Only in 1996 were the first glimmerings of a return to 'normal' seen.

Price elasticity and competitive forces

Competitive forces can affect demand curves. In spite of some of the drawbacks in the use of the demand curve, the approach does emphasise that the behaviour of any profit-orientated organisation is constrained both by its internal cost environment and, more critically from a marketing perspective, by the competitive forces operating in its relevant product market(s). Porter (1980) identifies these competitive forces as:

- *the relative power of buyers and suppliers* – the number, size and distribution of both buyers and sellers;
- *the threat of substitutes and potential entry* – the number of substitute products/services competing for the same consumer expenditure; the extent of barriers to entry for potential rivals, for example patents; the degree of actual or perceived product differentiation; the extent of economies of scale and experience effects; and the unit cost penalty of sub-optimal output levels;
- *the extent of rivalry amongst existing players* – the rate of market growth; the extent of excess capacity in the industry and barriers to exit.

The key importance of assessing market competition derives from the fact that it directly affects the responsiveness of buyers to variations in pricing decisions. Only in the extreme case of an absolute supplier monopoly, where no competitive substitute exists and market entry is completely blocked, will buyer demand be perfectly price inelastic so that purchase volume is unaffected by price changes.

In all other cases, the price–value perceptions of target consumers, as reflected in the demand curve concept, are critical to determining both a company's profit-maximising output and in assessing the likely impact of price changes on its sales revenue. If demand is price elastic, a price increase could generate an increase in revenue, provided the gain in revenue from charging retained customers a higher price more than outweighs the results of a lower sales volume. The level of profits will need to be established using sensitivity analysis.

Price and the product life cycle

Price is also dependent on time, not only in terms of seasonality but also in terms of the appropriate pricing policy to be adopted at a particular point in the product life cycle (*see* Chapter 4). The product life cycle has four stages: introduction, growth, maturity and decline. While the product life cycle was initially devised as a forecasting method, its use is now more relevant as a descriptive tool. At each stage an appropriate marketing policy can be devised. Inherent in that marketing policy is the need to consider fully the combination of price, volume, costs and other marketing activity.

Pricing policies for the commercial enterprise

The clear implication of the preceding argument is that the existence of a comprehensive marketing information system is a prerequisite for achieving optimal pricing within an integrated marketing strategy. This system should properly identify the organisation's relationship with its markets. A marketing information system should be capable of providing data which is relevant to pricing issues, particularly to price sensitivity.

Hughes (1978) and Kotler (1988) suggest that, in order to approximate the characteristics of optimal pricing discussed above, practical pricing procedures should follow an iterative process. By considering key issues sequentially in what amounts to a learning process, optimal price can be achieved by a progressive narrowing of the range of acceptable prices.

From the outset it is essential to establish a range of price alternatives consistent with corporate values, objectives, and policies. As argued earlier, the simultaneous maximisation of both profit and market share is not possible. They are mutually conflicting. Figure 8.3 summarises the relationship between trade-offs that have to be made regarding corporate image, objectives, and the organisation's approach to distribution channels. The horizontal arrows indicate a continuum which exists between the extremes of large market share and small niche market positions.

Given the nature of the company objectives, the pricing policies may be perceived differently by the marketplace. Table 8.1 shows the probable perceptions of the user in the price–quality relationship. Of course, the reaction of the user to different pricing policies will depend upon segmental and behavioural variables.

In summary, we can therefore argue the following points.

1 To be successful, pricing must be market-led rather than cost-driven.
2 The relationship of prices and costs is dependent upon the degree of competition and the price elasticity of demand for a product, its stage in the life cycle and the prevailing conditions in the marketing environment. Cost-induced price increases could incur the penalty of a decline in revenue – unless counteracted by a change in the pattern of buyer preferences in favour of the product, reflecting willingness to purchase larger volume, caused by developments such as an increase in disposable income, a relative increase in the price of competing products, or a change in promotion and advertising.

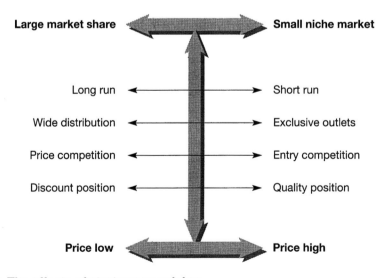

Fig. 8.3 The effects of strategy on pricing

Table 8.1 Relationships between price and perceived quality

	Low price	Medium price	High price
High quality	Excellent value	Market penetration	Premium
Medium quality	Good value	Middle of road	Image
Low quality	Cheap value	Commodity brand	Rip off

3 As a weapon in an organisation's competitive strategy, price is the easiest element in the market mix for competitors to replicate. The use of non-price elements can avoid the profit attrition effects of overt price wars, particularly in oligopolistic (controlled by a few) markets where there is recognised interdependency between players whose mutual interest lies in developing a perceived differentiation between product attributes via promotion, as a barrier to competitive market entry.

Pricing in the public sector

The preceding sections have identified the issues of pricing in the private sector where there is considerable organisational freedom in setting prices. Of course, there are exceptions, not least in the privatised utilities, the reasons for which should now appear obvious. Public sector markets experience particular problems in relation to pricing.

Price and multiple markets

One of the key characteristics of the public sector is the presence of multiple markets. In the private sector, marketing strategy usually needs to consider one market – that is, the primary customer. Where there is a regulatory body (the legitimiser) then that market is also very important. In the public sector, all four markets – primary, facilitator, resources and legitimiser – need to be considered. Conflicts can arise between them.

Price and resourcer markets

In the public sector, price is often linked to the amount of public subsidy from taxation injected (from the resourcer market) into a particular industry or activity. It would, perhaps, be somewhat naive to assume that a non-profit-making organisation is one in which no difference is necessary between the cost of doing something and the revenue obtained or funding provided. Nor should it be assumed that price is always measured in financial terms. Organisations are goal-oriented (*see* Gerloff, 1985, pp. 145–65). Profit-making organisations usually seek to maximise profits for the owners of the organisations' capital. Non-profit organisations – that is, many public sector organisations – have rather different priorities. (*See* Minicase 8.1.)

The goals of non-profit-making organisations are often directed at social, educational, philanthropic or cultural activities, which cannot be measured solely in terms of revenue (*see*, for example, Laughlin and Gray, 1988, p. 59) as can be seen from Minicase 8.1 which examines the UK Arts Council.

MINICASE 8.1

The Arts Council as a non-profit organisation

It can be argued that the Arts Council in the UK is a good example of a public sector organisation which was never conceived as a profit-making organisation. When it was founded in 1945, with many of its personnel inherited from the wartime Council for the Encouragement of Music and the Arts (CEMA), the Arts Council was intended to provide state support for the arts in an environment where private support was unlikely to be substantial. The Council has subsidised a variety of cultural activities over the years, with three main objectives:

● to develop and improve the knowledge, understanding and practice of the arts;

● to increase the accessibility of the arts to the public throughout the UK;

● to cooperate with government departments, local authorities and other bodies in order to implement those objectives.

Most of the Council's work is concerned with the disbursement of funds from parliamentary grants in aid, and the Council publishes an annual income and expenditure account (as distinct from a profit and loss account). It is worth noting, however, that the services rendered by an organisation like the Arts Council cannot solely be measured in terms of grants received and distributed. Unlike a commercial organisation, for which receipts have a direct relationship to their economic objectives, much of the Council's activities have qualitative results which defy purely economic definitions.

However, this does not mean that, for example, pricing is unimportant to the activities the Arts Council supports. It is increasingly common for funds to be raised by selling tickets to specific events. The prices paid frequently involve some concept of exchange. The public support of the arts is increasingly reliant on sponsorship, for which some incentives need to be given in return. Since 1995, the Arts Council (in effect) has been one of those organisations benefiting from profits from the National Lottery.

Other organisations have relied literally on tokens of exchange. Visitors to the Victoria and Albert Museum are invited to make a contribution to the running costs of the museum, in exchange for which they receive a small adhesive badge (although it seems inevitable that charges will be introduced). Some people obtain a sense of pride by contributing to a charity which gives them some visible token in exchange – for example, the Poppy Day buttonhole. The price actually paid in these examples may be left to the donor's discretion. All marketing transactions must involve some element of satisfaction for the purchaser in order to provide an incentive.

In their efforts to safeguard their viability, most non-profit organisations are moving towards a position where they can no longer rely upon individual willingness to share, the generosity of the wealthy, or the largesse of the State. As a result, pricing strategies have become extremely important. The only fundamental differences between marketing in profit-making and non-profit-making sectors often concern the differing nature of their objectives.

Non-profit-making status does not, however, obviate the need for either marketing or pricing strategies. Even an organisation which has goals primarily concerned with the disbursement of funds to support certain kinds of activities will need to engage in pricing – for example, in tickets for a 'charity dinner' or opening night performance – so that some contribution can be made. Without such a contribution, the organisation has to pay all its own fixed and overhead costs from its budget or allocation. It can be argued, therefore, that a non-profit organisation has a positive incentive to raise additional funds in order to maximise the proportion of its funding which can be directed at its primary goals, and thereby maximise its activities. However, much resistance to engaging in income generation comes from a fear that monies received may be used to replace, rather than supplement, the budget revenue. Increasing income generation targets inevitably attract the criticism that they divert efforts from the 'core business' of the particular service.

In many instances, funding organisations and legitimising organisations require to see prices developed on the basis of 'full cost' – a process which, as will be described later, completely 'decouples' price from the marketplace.

Price and the facilitator market

A general practitioner may purchase treatment on behalf of the patient which does not meet the patient's perceived needs, and which may incur additional cost to the patient, monetary and non-monetary. It may have been purchased because it is the most economical for the GP.

Impact of changes in price and volume where revenue is a function of demand

Marketing has been defined as the management process whereby customer requirements are identified, anticipated and satisfied profitably. While profit may not always be an end in itself, the long-term viability of a company will depend to a greater extent on profits or surplus which are determined by an exchange of satisfactions between the customer and the supplier. When considering the role of marketing in improving organisational profit or surplus, it is useful to start by looking at the *absolute value* of profits generated and *profitability*, the rate of return in relation to another aspect, for example capital employed. It is also important to note that there is often some confusion between the *total profit* made by a company and *profit per unit of output* of production. This latter point will be developed later.

Value added and profit

An important element in both marketing management and the development of profits is the concept of 'value added'. The *Corporate Report* (1975) defined value added in the following way:

the simplest and most immediate way of putting profit into proper perceptive vis-à-vis the whole enterprise as a collective effort by capital, management and employees is by the presentation of a statement of value added ... In time it may come to be regarded as a preferable way of describing performance.

Good marketing is about the management of value added: value added to the consumer in the purchase of goods and services, and value added for the supplier through the provision of goods and services which meet identified customer need. In other words it is the *value which the supplier adds to the transaction in the eyes of the customers.*

For a manufacturer, value added is the value added to those materials and sub-contract work in the production of saleable goods. For a shop, it is the value added as a result of stockholding, convenience and location. For a service provider it is the provision of resources and expertise which will satisfy a customer need.

Good marketing has a significant impact on the perceived value of a product or a service. For example, a BMW car is perceived as having more value than a Skoda, thus improving its value added. From a consumer standpoint, the value added is often psychological or perceived rather than real – a theme already developed in Chapter 4.

Thus the aggregate value added which a firm derives from selling its products is the sales value of those products less the costs of purchase of the raw materials and subcontract work which the firm has had to buy in order to produce them.

Influences on value added

Value added is influenced, therefore, by the sales activity of the company through volume, price and mix of work, and through the management of materials usage and subcontract. For example, a change with regard to 'make-or-buy' decisions can have a significant effect on purchases. A sales value increase might hide a fall-off in value added. This measure of 'what the company keeps' can be very important; value added, rather than sales, is a true measure of the commercial progress and performance of a company.

Application of value added

The amount of value added created is also important because out of it the firm pays wages and salaries to its employees, overheads to various providers of services, interest to banks, taxes to the government and dividends to its shareholders. Hopefully it leaves something to plough back into the business as retained earnings. The division of a sales value of £5 million by a typical manufacturing company is shown in Fig. 8.4.

Contribution and net profit

The second important, and more widely used, measure is that of *contribution*, which is the value added less the direct wages paid in a company. The use of con-

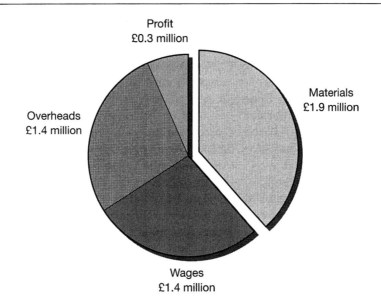

Fig. 8.4 The 'value added cake' for a typical company generating sales revenue of £5 million per annum

tribution analysis is often cited as a good business measure, but its sole use can have disadvantages, as will be shown later.

Net profit is what is left after overheads have been deducted from contribution. The analysis in Fig. 8.5 – a value-added contribution analysis of management accounts – quantifies the 'cake' represented in Fig. 8.4.

(Note: both value added and contribution can be called gross profit, depending upon the accountancy convention. In this chapter, where the term 'gross profit' is used, this is equivalent to contribution.)

	£'000s
Sales	5000
less Materials	1500
less Outwork	400
= Value Added	3100
less Direct wages	1400
= Gross profit (Contribution)	1700
less Overheads	1400
= Net profit	300

Fig. 8.5 Value added and contribution analysis of management accounts

The impact of managing value added

Value added and contribution can also be graphically expressed on a break-even chart (*see* Fig. 8.6). The break-even chart is typically used as a device for cost analysis but it is a very valuable tool for the marketing manager to use in order to identify the financial implications of marketing decisions. It also demonstrates the leverage that marketing activity has on profits.

In Fig. 8.6, the organisation makes a profit at an activity level above the break-even point. Below the break-even point, the organisation will be loss making. It can be seen that as income rises, the value added, that is sales less variable costs, reduces the loss and then increases the profits. With each incremental increase in activity, the profits increase by the amount of value added. It is for this reason that profits are so sensitive to changes in activity.

In Fig. 8.6, the vertical axis measures the value of sales and purchases while the horizontal axis measures the volume of output for the year at 100 per cent, but this does not mean that there is 100 per cent utilisation and in most companies there is often scope for more output above current levels.

The area between the sales line and the purchases line represents value added, which at the year end at '100 per cent utilisation' is £3.1 million. The value added generated goes towards meeting the non-variable costs of the organisation – for example, employment costs and overhead costs. Profit is the level of the value added remaining after those costs have been met.

Direct wages are regarded as a fixed cost, incurred whatever the level of sales during the year, and are plotted with a line parallel to that for purchases. Overheads are also a fixed cost and therefore plotted with a line parallel to the wages line. The area between the sales line and the overheads line represents net

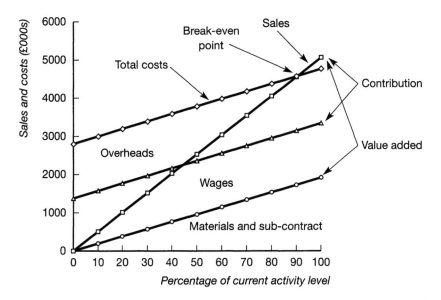

Fig. 8.6 Break-even chart, showing the make up of the cost structure and the make up of value added and contribution

profit. This only becomes positive once the sales line has crossed above the line combining purchases, wages and overheads – that is, at the break-even point. Above that point any value added that is generated goes straight into net profit. It is this fact which makes the management of value added such an important issue in marketing.

The impact of changes in volume, price and cost

The value of using the break-even analysis is that it shows clearly the impact of an increase in sales and prices on the amount of value added and net profit generated.

Table 8.2 shows the changes in profit which can occur as a consequence of focusing on marketing rather than cost management. It should be noted that where revenue is increased as a consequence of price increase, the profit is greater than with a revenue increase of 5 per cent brought about through increased volume. This is because an increase via price does not incur a proportionate increase in variable costs, unlike a volume increase.

The figures shown in Table 8.2 relate to a given set of circumstances. They show the marked differences in profit improvement of revenue management as against cost management. For example, a 5 per cent improvement in volume, with fixed costs held steady, results in a 50 per cent improvement in profit. If wages are reduced by 5 per cent (a familiar cost-management approach), then profits improve by only 23 per cent. In both instances there has been a productivity increase of 5 per cent. These figures are not theoretical. They are taken from actual measures of performance and demonstrate just how sensitive organisational profit is to price and volume. The amplification effect of these two commercial factors is, in the experience of the authors, rarely appreciated by managers.

In the late 1980s and much of the 1990s, the possibility of obtaining price increases in a recessionary climate was often considered to be impossible. However, improvements in value-added performance, essentially price increases, can be obtained through more effective market segmentation and improving the perceived value to the customer of the goods or services offered. This has been achieved by many organisations who have good market penetration and good added value strategies.

The effects on profit of price, volume and cost management will differ according to the particular set of circumstances for a company and the relationship

Table 8.2 Changes in profit caused by increased sales

	Sales (£000s)	Profit (£000s)	Profit (% of sales)
Current budget	5000	300	6%
Increase volume by 5%	5250	455	9%
Increase price by 5%	5250	550	10%
Increase both price and volume by 5%	5512.5	717.5	13%
Reduce wage costs by 5%	5000	370	7%

between fixed and variable costs. In the service industries, where fixed costs are high and variable costs are low, the impact of volume changes in particular is high because of the high proportions of value added per transaction. From a marketing planning standpoint, the development of break-even analysis is crucial to effective marketing planning.

The influence of the mix of products

The example in Table 8.2 is, in effect, taking a look at the results obtained by an organisation over time. As most managers know, companies do not operate in single markets nor do they have a single range of products. Thus, the starting point for break-even analysis and for good marketing strategy is an effective examination of each of the marketing activities, products, markets, sales regions, etc. and their worth to the company. This involves examining the relationships between revenue and costs.

Impact of changes in activity levels where revenue is allocated

In public sector organisations, the situation concerning the generation of income is more complex, not least as a consequence of allocated revenues. In most public sector organisations, some, if not all, of the income is allocated from the public purse. This 'allocation of revenue' essentially reverses the situation which is a norm for commercial organisations.

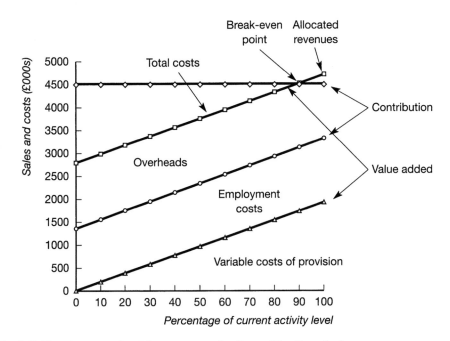

Fig. 8.7 Break-even chart for an organisation with allocated revenues

An increase in activity creates a reduction in surplus

Where the revenue is a fixed amount – that is, the organisation is working to an allocated budget – then the value added in the organisation declines as activity levels increase (value added equals revenue less variable costs). Since the fixed costs, employment costs and overheads change only slightly with an increase in activity levels, it can be seen that below the break-even point the organisation will be in surplus. Above the break-even point, the organisation will be in deficit. In the prevailing economic climate the price paid by funding agencies (resourcer markets) is usually under pressure. In this case, organisations tend to move into deficit earlier. The example shown in Fig. 8.7 reveals a situation prevailing in many public sector organisations. They become loss-making at an activity level of more than 100 per cent.

Possible actions

The problems of managing increases in activity are perennial for such organisations. This is a marketing situation not often faced by private sector organisations, and may lead to a need to ration supply, with all the consequences of managing scarcity, the development of pressure groups and even the emergence of a 'black market'.

Under these circumstances, three alternatives usually face the public sector manager.

- *To manage costs, both variable and fixed, so that more can be done with less.* This is the impetus for efficiency gains. As discussed earlier, does efficiency equate to effectiveness?

- *To introduce some form of charge for the service, which gives additional revenue per unit of output or transaction.* This will give some form of additional revenue. This has many implications in respect of the culture of the public sector and the perceptions of the market which takes the view that tax has already been paid.

- *To introduce some form of real rationing.*

Both of the two latter options mean that an organisation is indulging in marketing activities which will probably be against the wishes of the market. Furthermore, given that the culture of the public sector has a strong cost-management culture, all alternatives will focus on using current costs as a basis for action. The prevailing pressure will appear to be on costs rather than on market forces.

The situation at London's British Museum in the autumn of 1996 may be cited as an example. The strategic options were represented as a simple choice between the imposition of entrance charges or extensive staff redundancies.

Before examining the implications of these issues, it is appropriate to examine the issues of cost-related pricing.

| MINICASE 8.2 | **Cost management in the police force** |

The political desire for increased public sector efficiency is apt to find its most obvious expression in cost-cutting and cost control. Most governments, after all, wish to reduce the Public Sector Borrowing Requirement as much as possible. During the 1980s and 1990s, Conservative governments progressively used 'market testing' and privatisation as means of increasing competition, thereby providing incentives to reduce costs. Inevitably, privatisation has become a political issue as more and more public sector employees see it as a threat to their jobs. Wage bills do, after all, contribute most to the costs of a service.

On 28 December 1993, *The Independent* noted that the Police Federation, representing some 126 000 officers below superintendent rank, had privately warned the Home Secretary about the possible effects of cuts in police numbers and 'semi-privatisation' of jobs. An internal review of police functions was to take place, and would study the scope for transferring some police roles to civilians. These could include desk work, escorting slow-moving loads and monitoring traffic, thereby freeing more officers for policing the streets. This would represent some savings in rates of pay and lengthy training times. The Police Federation saw this move as a cost-cutting exercise to please the Treasury. Privatisation in the prison service, despite Group 4's unfortunate record of escaping prisoners, was already estimated to have saved the prison service some £130 million.

Methods of pricing on cost

The determination of costs is an involved and complicated topic. There are numerous methods in use. However, in the public sector in general, and in the NHS in particular, cost is intended to equal price. As a result, it is assumed that:

- prices are based on actual costs;
- costs are established on a full-cost basis;
- there is no planned cross-subsidisation between activities.

In other words, all activities must stand on their own merits. The term 'full-cost' means that the price must consider all costs involved in the activity, not just the additional variable costs of carrying out the activity. In practice (Howes, 1984), prices need to be set in advance, because in most transactions prices are set on the basis of expected levels of activity and budgeted costs. Furthermore, the NHS National Steering Group on Costing, in June 1993, endorsed absorption costing as a standard basis for calculating contract costs. A brief examination of the 'absorbed costs' method will identify some of the problems of full-cost pricing.

Any organisation has a mix of variable and fixed costs. In practice, the *variable costs* are those which change directly as a consequence of any incremental increases in activity levels. There are also *semi-variable costs*, usually labour, which change indirectly as a consequence of activity levels and generally as a 'step increase'. There are also the *fixed costs* which have to be met irrespective of activity levels. These were shown in the break-even figures in Figs 8.6 and 8.7.

For most managers, these global figures give little guidance for pricing. This is because price is not an absolute; it is a ratio – for example, £2 per kilo. This concept has to be extended into absorbed costs, so that a cost per unit of output or demand can be established. In complex activities, such as medical treatment, a cost for each activity is established and the total cost for the treatment is calculated by summing the individual parts.

To illustrate this concept, a simple example which affects most of us will give some insight into the principle. The costs of running a washing machine are examined below.

Example: the absorption cost of a washing machine

A washing machine has been bought for £300. What is the cost of running the machine? Most of us would say that the costs of running the washer are the variable costs of electricity and washing powder. An absorption costing system would take a different approach, and would need to consider not only the variable costs of running the machine but some of the other attributable costs and the overheads of the house as well.

Calculating the directly attributable costs

First, we consider the attributable costs, which are not variable as a consequence of running the machine, for example, interest payments and depreciation. On a £300 machine there will be:

- interest payments (or loss of interest on cash paid) of say 10 per cent, equalling £30 per year;
- depreciation of the machine over 5 years of £60 per year;
- a maintenance contract of £60 per year.

The sum total of these directly attributable costs is £30+£60+£60 which equals £150 per year.

Calculating the attributable overhead

In addition to these costs the washing machine has to *absorb* some of the overhead costs of the house.

The total overhead costs of the house will be made up of heating, mortgage interest, maintenance, lighting and cleaning costs – totalling, say, £7500 per year. The question is how are these overheads apportioned. The fair apportionment of overheads is one of the key issues in absorption costing. In reality, this apportionment is usually done on the basis of 'best opinion' and can change from organisation to organisation.

In the washing machine case, one of the methods is the use of space utilisation. For an average-size house, with 100 square metres of floor area, the cost per square metre per year is £7500/100 per square metre which equals £75 per square metre per year. The washing machine is one of six items in a kitchen having a floor area of 12 square metres, so it can be argued that the relevant apportioned space is 2 square metres. The reader will argue that this is inappropriate, but this is how absorption costing is done. Thus the overhead allocation is 2 square metres multiplied by £75, which equals £150 per year.

Thus, the cost structure is:

Directly attributable fixed costs	£150
Allocated overhead	£150

Calculating the variable costs

The variable costs of running the machine will in this instance relate to the costs of electricity and consumables (washing powder, fabric softener, etc.).

- The cost *per hour* of a 3 kilowatt washing machine for electricity will be approximately 24 pence.

- The cost per wash for consumables will be approximately 25 pence *per wash*. There are, therefore, two cost ratios which need to be considered for variable costs. Assume an *expected level of activity* of 100 washes per year, for 1.5 hours each, giving a total usage of 150 hours.

Calculating the total cost per wash

The costs of a wash are therefore:

Cost per wash of directly attributable cost	£150/100 washes	=	£1.50 per wash
Cost per wash of apportioned overhead	£150/100 washes	=	£1.50 per wash
Cost per wash of electricity	1.5 hours at 24 pence	=	£0.36 per wash
Cost per wash of powder, etc.	25 pence per wash	=	£0.25 per wash
Total cost per wash		=	**£3.61 per wash**

This cost is of course exclusive of any labour charges which may be attributable. The reader may wish to consider the following questions:

1 What would be the cost per wash if 75 washes per year were done in a year?
2 How would the household expenditure change if 75 washes rather than 100 washes were done in a year?

The determination of full-cost pricing

The use of cost as a basis for pricing is very widespread. A cursory examination suggests that it offers a number of potential advantages over market-related pricing:

- In the absence of reliable data on market conditions, and given that, in the long run, the survival requirement for any organisation is that it must cover all its costs, cost-based pricing seems to reflect a practical means of coping with a complex and uncertain environment by reducing the pricing decision to a routine procedure. Pricing becomes a simple operational rule, rather than a strategic issue, and can be delegated to junior management.

- However, making such decisions into routines is likely to compound, rather than reduce, the risks of sub-optimal pricing. Information about demand is often substituted by cost information simply because it is more difficult to estimate demand accurately and at the right time. Cost actually provides negligible information about demand.

- On ethical grounds, relating price to cost is sometimes thought to be fairer to both buyer and sellers. Sellers are less likely to exploit consumers under conditions of excess demand and yet they still receive a 'fair' return on the use of assets and public funding. Nevertheless, this method tends to protect the inefficient organisation who can always use it to legitimise price increases on the grounds of inflated costs.

Unfortunately, despite the formal adoption of cost classification systems which distinguish between fixed, semi-fixed and variable costs, and the use of standard cost analyses of overheads, direct and indirect, it can be seen that such an approach (bureaucratic in its attempts at standardisation) has its weaknesses. Absorption costing necessarily uses facts about expenditure, estimates of utilisation and opinions on how to apportion overheads. Such costing can only reflect the costs of an activity for a given set of circumstances, on the basis of a number of assumptions. An element of subjectivity and judgement remains.

Cost-plus pricing, a common form of pricing, simply adds a certain amount to the projected cost of making a product or providing a service in order to determine the price. Generally speaking, this can be done in one of two ways.

1 The normal total cost of a year's activities can be multiplied by the desired (target) rate of return in order to produce a percentage mark-up. This is known as *rate-of-return pricing*.

2 Alternatively, *absorption-cost pricing* presumes that all costs, both fixed and variable, are known. Overheads are apportioned to cost centres in a relatively arbitrary manner. A percentage can then simply be added to the unit cost (produced by dividing the sum of costs by units of output) to produce a price.

It has been suggested (Winkler, 1983) that some 80 per cent of British companies were still pricing on the basis of cost-plus in 1983. This concept is now firmly established in the public sector. For example, Howes (1994) states that the fundamental principle for UK National Health Service pricing is 'cost equals price' – that is that prices are based on actual costs, and that costs are established on a full-cost basis. This assumes that:

- actual costs are used as the basis for pricing;
- costs are established on a 'full-cost' basis; and
- there is no cross-subsidy between specialities, procedures and contracts.

While Howes expresses some reservations about the lack of flexibility within cost-based pricing, it is seen as 'a tool to protect services by preventing loss leaders and discouraging providers from offering only profitable services'.

Howes recognises the ways in which differences between patient requirements (we might interpret this as 'between market segments') have significant effects on the costs of treatment. Such differences create complex problems, and might be used to confirm the contention that cost-plus pricing takes little account of the market itself, of any variations in demand that may occur, and of any competition that may be involved. Cost-plus pricing also assumes that costs can be allocated accurately and at the same rate. This is rarely possible, and the results always run the risk of misrepresenting the demands made by different services on an organisation's resources.

Using cost data for marketing decisions

One of the major weaknesses in the application of the absorption costing system becomes evident when it is used to establish the profitability or viability of products, sales activities, etc. Very often, the cost of production of a single unit of output is established, as exemplified in the washing machine calculation, and a decision as to whether to continue with production is often made on the basis of the relationship of this cost to the price available in the market. This level of profit then determines the viability of the activity. However, in view of the fact that absorption costing is based upon *assumptions* and *apportionment*, it retains an element of subjective judgement.

Another issue concerns the manner in which costs tend to be calculated on the basis of cost per unit and price is generally calculated in the same way. Given a price per unit and a cost per unit, then it seems logical that a profit, surplus or loss per unit can be calculated.

To illustrate the point, it is worth taking an example from an area very familiar to the authors: that of pricing and costing educational courses. In a hypothetical case, a new course is proposed for which market research has been carried out. The market research indicates that there is a potential demand for the course, but there is some price sensitivity in the target market. A target price of £1500 per student is suggested. However, the traditional price for courses of this nature is based on organisation-wide cost structures, and a price of £2100 for the course is deemed appropriate by the college's finance department. This price is based on a sum of:

- direct fixed costs of the course – for example, teaching, administration, etc. – of £10 000;
- allocated overheads amounting to £10 000;
- the variable costs per participant: approximately £100.

With an *assumed* intake of 10 participants, the cost per student will be:

(Directly attributable costs + allocated overheads)/student numbers + variable costs.

In the hypothetical example, this amounts to:

(£10 000 + £10 000)/10 + £100 = £2100 per student

In this instance, there are all kinds of assumptions being made about the apportionment of overheads, the number of students and the direct fixed costs of the activity. Most readers will be able to find similar illustrations of costing in other kinds of public sector organisations. Such a method takes little account of the nature of the market itself.

The college's finance department takes the view that, if a fee of £1500 is charged, then for each student the organisation would incur a loss of £600. This would not be considered to be a realistic proposition.

In many instances, the course proposal with a cost of £1500 per student would be rejected on the grounds that it would not satisfy the full-cost criteria. However, such a decision would fail to recognise the 'contribution' the activity would make to the fixed costs of the organisation, its potential for attracting more students, the fact that different products might have different price potential and all the other factors associated with market pricing.

Table 8.3 demonstrates how the costs per student falls with increasing activity levels. Equally importantly, it shows that the cost per student gets proportionately greater as numbers fall. The table also shows how the total financial contribution increases as numbers increase. The figures on the left of the table indicate the projected number of students enrolled (and retained) on the course.

Table 8.3 The relationship of cost and demand on an absorption-cost basis

No of students	Activity fixed cost teaching	Activity allocated cost Overhead	Activity variable cost Materials	Cost per student	Revenue per student	Surplus deficit	Contribution to overheads
1	£10 000	£10 000	£100	£20 100	£1 500	−£18 600	−£8 600
2	£10 000	£10 000	£100	£10 100	£1 501	−£8 599	−£7 198
3	£10 000	£10 000	£100	£6 767	£1 502	−£5 265	−£5 794
4	£10 000	£10 000	£100	£5 100	£1 503	−£3 597	−£4 388
5	£10 000	£10 000	£100	£4 100	£1 504	−£2 596	−£2 980
6	£10 000	£10 000	£100	£3 433	£1 505	−£1 928	−£1 570
7	£10 000	£10 000	£100	£2 957	£1 506	−£1 451	−£158
8	£10 000	£10 000	£100	£2 600	£1 507	−£1 093	£1 256
9	£10 000	£10 000	£100	£2 322	£1 508	−£814	£2 672
10	£10 000	£10 000	£100	£2 100	£1 509	−£591	£4 090
11	£10 000	£10 000	£100	£1 918	£1 510	−£408	£5 510
12	£10 000	£10 000	£100	£1 767	£1 511	−£256	£6 932
13	£10 000	£10 000	£100	£1 638	£1 512	−£126	£8 356
14	£10 000	£10 000	£100	£1 529	£1 513	−£16	£9 782
15	£10 000	£10 000	£100	£1 433	£1 514	£81	£11 210
16	£10 000	£10 000	£100	£1 350	£1 515	£165	£12 640
17	£10 000	£10 000	£100	£1 276	£1 516	£240	£14 072
18	£10 000	£10 000	£100	£1 211	£1 517	£306	£15 506
19	£10 000	£10 000	£100	£1 153	£1 518	£365	£16 942
20	£10 000	£10 000	£100	£1 100	£1 519	£419	£18 380

In determining absorption costs, organisations have to *assume* levels of usage or sales volume. To some extent, such assumptions will remain arbitrary. However, there is an inescapable interdependence between output, cost and price. If this is similarly ignored it produces a paradox.

For example, let us examine an activity in relation to its fixed costs and variable costs. As activity increases, the variable costs associated with the activity will remain constant but the proportion of fixed costs taken by each unit of activity will fall. Thus, as activity levels rise, the 'cost' per unit of output will fall.

Furthermore, costs are also sensitive to the learning curve and to the effects of experience. Thus, in calculating costs, output must be known before a unit cost, on which to base the price, can be calculated. However, demand can also be price dependent, so organisations need to know the price it intends to charge before estimating the level of output on which to calculate unit cost and, thereby, set its price! Thus managers can go round in ever-decreasing circles. Pricing on costs is much easier. In the public sector, organisations have to recognise that different activities in different markets will pose different pricing problems. To expect every activity to accept the same full-cost criteria is to fail to recognise individual behaviour.

There is also a further complication in that, as seen earlier, public sector organisations are usually limited in terms of their financial allocations and budgets. There is, therefore, an arbitrary limit set on levels of output. Consequently cash limits can, in reality, inhibit cost-effectiveness as they place an arbitrary 'ceiling' on levels of activity.

Effect of apportionment of overheads and utilisation factors

The authors' experience of absorption costing systems in industry indicates that the method of apportioning overheads can have an enormous impact on the unit prices charged by organisations. For example, two companies with similar plant, customers, cost structures and facilities, and using the same costing system, can produce costs per unit of output for the same process which differ by as much as a factor of 3 to 1. Factors of 2 to 1 are commonplace. Experience also indicates that similar situations are occurring in public sector organisations. Often such differences are put down to organisational inefficiencies, which in part may be true, but more often than not these are due to the methods by which costs are allocated. These methods are arbitrary, and so they will differ from organisation to organisation, from activity to activity.

Full-cost pricing has a number of effects on marketing planning, and raises a number of important issues. As a consequence of the weaknesses inherent in full-cost pricing on the basis of absorbed costs, the debate has become increasingly fierce in the past few years. Unfortunately, in many managerial situations, issues relating to costs, money and pricing have relied heavily on the expertise of the accountant. Some managers have effectively abdicated responsibility for even attempting to understand the financial consequences of their actions. Thus it is that organisations have become strongly accountancy-driven and decisions relating to price have increasingly been influenced by accountancy and costing departments, often with results that consider customer satisfaction last.

There is considerable concern in marketing and elsewhere about the extent of this trend. For example, Johnson and Kaplan (1987) suggest that arbitrary methods of cost measurement do not really reflect or express the resource demands actually made by a product or a service. If arbitrary data or information is used as the basis of the costs of products or services, there is a strong risk of making poor pricing decisions and, equally, poor ones about the use of resources, mix of products/services and responses to competition.

The consequence of using such distorted financial data can be catastrophic for the marketer. Johnson and Kaplan (1987) consider costing as inappropriate in today's environment, and advocate a search for more objective and useful pricing systems. Roger Schmenner, of the International Management Development Institute in Geneva, argues that the pricing policies of many companies fall into the 'Black Hole' of cost accountancy. Paul Omerod (1994) is also sceptical about the assumptions frequently made with which to evaluate 'efficiency' in a market economy.

In spite of these comments, many governments in Europe and elsewhere, not least in the UK, continue to propound the concept of cost-based market forces. One has only to examine some of the formulae devised for calculating costs for European-funded projects to identify the complexity of calculating costs, and hence prices.

What many organisations fail to realise is the massive leverage that price and volume have on operational surpluses and deficits (profits and losses) which was demonstrated earlier (*see* Table 8.2). However, marketing is about change and modelling is a tool with which to try and address the consequences of change. In the pricing area, marketing concerns itself with matching the customers' perceptions of value with the results of the costing structure used by the organisation. In these circumstances, it is necessary to ask whether or not a method of identifying costs which is based on a set of fixed assumptions is really appropriate for identifying and modelling change. It seems that the answer has to be 'no'.

Absorption costing systems use facts about expenditure, estimates of utilisation and opinions about the apportionment of overheads. Even if such costs are calculated to the tenth decimal place, they remain no more than opinions and only reflect the costs of a particular activity for a given set of circumstances. It is for this reason that the calculation and use of cost rates in organisations causes so much conflict. Yet, in spite of all the reservations expressed by many writers about the validity of such systems, particularly in today's rapidly changing business environment, they are used extensively to provide the basis for fundamental business decisions.

There *are* still situations where the use of full cost is appropriate, and where it is 'better' to use the full-cost approach if required to do so.

Full-cost pricing and compulsory competitive tendering

The introduction of compulsory competitive tendering is requiring public sector organisations to compete in the marketplace with private sector organisations, invariably on the basis of full cost. It has been suggested, in the last two sections, that the use of absorption costs is not always appropriate in a marketing context.

However, some policies dictate otherwise. The rationale for compulsory competitive tendering is based on many of the factors which made *'outsourcing'* so popular in industry during the 1980s. If services can be contracted out to the private sector, it is possible for public sector organisations to:

- convert their fixed costs to variable costs, thereby providing flexibility;
- balance their workforce requirements;
- reduce their capital investment requirements;
- focus their resources on 'core' activities.

Pressured by management fashions, many managers using outsourcing in the 1980s lost sight of the long-term risk associated with outsourcing key inputs. This led to some user dissatisfaction simply because many contract suppliers did not necessarily understand the needs of the market. In addition to the marketing implications, there are also cost implications, leading to what some writers describe as a 'spiral of decline'. This is particularly the case where full-cost pricing has been used. Full-cost pricing using absorbed costs runs the risk of making departments appear inefficient by the inappropriate apportionment of overheads. This is particularly the case where overheads which relate to other parts of the organisation are applied to a single department.

Compulsory competitive tendering can, under such circumstances, result in organisations actually spending more money by seemingly buying a cheaper product or service from outside the organisation. In fact the reduction in actual expenditure to the organisation as a whole is less than the increased expenditure by placing the contract elsewhere, because the apportioned overhead is still incurred. This error in thinking is widespread in both the public and private sector and, indeed, at national level.

Such a situation arises as a consequence of managers failing to think *marginally*. Some writers suggest that one of the most useful ways to succeed in personal and business life is to think and act marginally – particularly important in optimising scarce resources. However, marginal pricing has obtained a very poor reputation among managers because it can lead to indiscriminate price cutting, often a dangerous strategy. In tendering, marginal pricing may also be seen as 'unfair', particularly where a perception exists that public sector organisations are 'feather bedded' – that is, that they have an unfair advantage because they are financed from the public purse.

Very often, public sector organisations withdraw services on the basis that they are costing too much. This has also led to competitive tendering. It has also caused the closure of departments where the rationale for closure is based on the use of fully absorbed costs for decision-making purposes. In reality, the relative savings are often much less than is commonly believed, because much of the expenditure associated with the activity which has been closed is still being spent as an unavoidable cost to the organisation.

Full-cost pricing in internal markets

Similar comments to those concerning compulsory competitive tendering can be made about *'transfer pricing'* in organisations. Transfer pricing causes considerable debate because it is often considered that internal supply departments have, effectively, monopoly markets and can therefore take unfair advantage of the internal customer. However, where internal prices are based on full costs, each part of the supply chain is working under the same constraints. Winkler (1983) proposes that, in transfer pricing situations, costs should be allocated to reflect an accurate measure of efficiency. Good transfer pricing should ensure that the consequences of a transfer pricing policy should not improve the performance of a division or department of the organisation at the expense of the organisation as a whole.

At least two options are available:

● To ensure that the transfer price relates to the 'going rate' for a similar product or service in the market as that supplied by competitive organisations;

● To ensure that transfer prices reflect the marginal costs of production. This assumes the other operational costs of the department are borne by the organisation as a whole.

The effect of taxation on users' price perceptions

The make-up of public sector funding, which enables public sector organisations to meet some of their operating costs, can, in certain circumstances, enable organisations to charge the consumer less than the prices of an equivalent private sector supplier. This leads to some interesting anomalies. For example, where compulsory competitive tendering takes place, the provision of subsidy is seen as giving the public sector organisation a market advantage. Full costing is demanded. In the consumer market, the provision of a subsidy may lead to irrational perceptions on the part of consumers, who are accustomed to equate low price with low quality. In 1988, Greenwich London Borough Council was able to demonstrate that a majority of its residents did not use subsidised public leisure services because of poor perceptions of the quality of Council-owned facilities.

MINICASE 8.3

Pricing, prescriptions and profiteering

In February 1997, several UK news reports carried a story which accused some dispensing chemists of deliberately profiteering from the National Health Service. The NHS prescription charge per item is a standard charge. Dishonest chemists could charge the patient the standard charge and destroy prescriptions for drugs which actually cost the chemists less (sometimes much less) that the NHS charge. No national system existed for recording doctors' prescriptions against the prescriptions actually supplied. Some chemists were accused of making considerable profits.

Conversely, there is often an expectation that, where taxation provides funding for activities, the provision of service should be free. The invariable public outcry after an announcement of rises in medical prescription charges illustrates this phenomenon. If the transactional relationship matrix in Chapter 2 (*see* Fig. 2.7) is considered, some of the anomalies can be explained.

Non-monetary price factors in the public sector

In addition to the financial costs of using the public sector there are often many non-monetary factors cited as costs for the consumer. Such factors include:

- costs associated with the poor image of the public sector;
- waiting times for public sector provision;
- perceived poor transactional service;
- low customer orientation in the service provided.

Such factors emphasise the fact that financial costs are not the only measurements of a product's or a service's value.

The costs of cost-based pricing

In the public sector, adherence to full-cost pricing makes the adoption of pricing as part of a comprehensive marketing policy nearly impossible to achieve. Yet, not only is the attraction illusory, but the reliance on a mechanistic application of cost-plus pricing is inherently flawed on the following grounds.

1 Cost-plus pricing fails to recognise the importance of buyers'/users' perceptions of price/value which are inherent in the demand curve concept. By ignoring the responses of potential competitors, the mechanical application of cost-plus pricing, if demand is elastic and price is raised to attempt the recovery of a cost increase, will seriously compromise user attitudes to public service provision. In recently privatised organisations – for example, some new UK railway companies – the slavish application of cost-based pricing led to high prices, some decline in use and further increases in prices in order to meet required revenue needs.

   This exposes the false logic of cost-plus pricing. It suggests that, faced with a downturn in sales and conditions of excess supply, prices should increase – whereas if sales are buoyant in market conditions of excess demand, prices should be reduced to reflect the decline in unit costs consequent upon increased sales volume. Rigid cost-plus pricing is actually an impediment in situations where margins need to be revised in the light of competitive conditions, reflecting a more flexible approach to pricing.

2 By *assuming* sales volume, the real importance of demand may be ignored. However, output, cost and price are actually interdependent. This can produce the following conundrum; that if costs are regarded as sensitive within the organisation, the organisation needs to know its levels of output before a unit

cost can be calculated. The unit can then be used as a basis for pricing. However, as sales volume is usually price dependent, the organisation needs to know the price it intends to charge before estimating the likely level of output on which to base its unit cost and, thereby, set its price!

3 Not only does cost-plus pricing ascribe an erroneous sense of objectivity and precision to the process of allocating fixed costs. In an organisation supplying a range of products or services, fixed costs are not necessarily the most relevant factors in decision making. The cost-plus method adopted for the recovery of overheads, despite an appearance of rationality, is inherently arbitrary by being dependent upon the subjective judgements underlying the accounting conventions used.

4 Cost-plus pricing assumes a relatively stable market environment, but it is questionable whether this is appropriate in today's increasingly complex and turbulent world with its ever-shortening effect on product (and even service) life cycles.

5 By delegating the role of pricing to an operational level within the organisation, cost-plus pricing can become divorced from strategic objectives and result in conflict between the interests of different parts of the organisation, particularly if pricing decisions are taken without due attention to the other elements of the marketing mix.

In conclusion, it should be emphasised that marketing is intimately concerned with user/buyer behaviours and perceptions, of which pricing is a part. Thus pricing can be profitable but it has to be considered in the context of pricing as part of the cohesive *marketing* policy that understands the behaviours of users and buyers. At the same time, managers within the organisation need a good understanding of money as an organisational resource in order to manage the problems involved. If marketing is to be effective, managers need to understand the financial implications of their decisions.

Summary

1 **Price and value.** Price can be defined as the value given to a product or a service by the market. In the public sector, there is an incentive to demonstrate that price is seen as providing good value for money.

2 **Concepts of market pricing** include price sensitivity, price elasticity, and price inelasticity. These may be influenced by the organisational environment, competitive forces and the product life cycle.

3 **Where revenue is a function of demand** (i.e. in the private sector), the concepts of profitability, value added, and contribution play key roles in pricing policies. The good management of volume, price and cost can have important results for levels of profit.

4 **Allocated income and activity levels.** If revenue is fixed (as in a public sector organisation's budget), an organisation will be limited to a certain level of activity.

5 **Methods of pricing based on cost** are familiar techniques in public sector industries.

6 **Full-cost pricing** needs to be examined in the context of cost-plus pricing, its advantages and weaknesses.

7 **The use of cost data for marketing decisions** presents a number of problems, not least because *assumptions* have to be made, rather arbitrarily, about the apportionment of the costs of an activity.

8 **The effects of apportionment costing methods** can have a powerful influence on price, and there is real doubt about their ability to express the resource demands on an organisation actually made by a service.

9 **Full-cost pricing** is generally used in the context of public sector competitive tendering, but may not always achieve the intended results.

10 **There are, therefore, a number of dangers in using full-cost pricing**, especially in the context of internal markets and outsourcing.

11 **Price perceptions** of public sector industries are influenced by a number of factors, including public associations between price and quality. Some of these perceptions can be related to the transactional relationship matrix discussed in Chapter 2 (*see* Fig. 2.7, p. 42).

12 **Non-monetary considerations.** It is also important to consider the influence of non-monetary costs in public sector provision. Financial costs are not the only measurements of value.

13 **The costs of cost-based pricing** need to be examined within a marketing framework. It is possible to criticise the method on a number of grounds.

Implications for management

All marketers and managers need to understanding the costing and pricing policies of their organisations. The three central questions which need to be answered concern:

- Is full-cost pricing used in this organisation? If so, how are costs attributed, and what are the assumptions on which the attributions are made?

- Is there any use made of marginal pricing? If so, what levels of contribution does it make?

- Are there any advantages to be gained from applying leverage to any of the factors such as volume, price and wages? (*see* Table 8.2).

Furthermore, managers should consider what non-financial costs may influence user/consumer perceptions of their products/services.

ISSUES FOR DISCUSSION

The following issues for discussion are presented in the form of questions. Examples from specific public sector industries should be incorporated into responses. Case studies can be used to provide some illustrations of the issues raised.

1 What non-financial costs are likely to be involved in transactions between customers and public sector organisations?

2 Why is price an increasingly important consideration for public sector organisations?

3 What are the advantages and disadvantages of competitive tendering in the public sector?

4 What are the marketing consequences of public sector organisations having a base source of income which is not related to revenue generating activity?

References

Accounting Standards Steering Committee (1975) *The Corporate Report*. London: ICAEW.

Baker, M.J. (1985) *Marketing Strategy and Management*. Basingstoke and London: Macmillan Education Ltd, p. 274.

Cooke, S. and Slack, N. (1984) *Making Management Decisions*. Englewood Cliffs, New Jersey: Prentice-Hall, Inc.

Gerloff, E.A. (1985) *Organizational Theory and Design*. New York: McGraw-Hill Book Company, pp. 145–65.

Hirschleifer, J. (1988) *Price Theory and Applications*. Englewood Cliffs, New Jersey: Prentice-Hall, Inc.

Howes, J. (1994) 'Costing for Contracting', *Management Accounting*, November, 36–7.

Hughes, G.D. (1978) *Marketing Management: A Planning Approach*. Glenview, Illinois: Addison-Wesley Publishing Co.

Johnson, T. and Kaplan, R.S. (1987) *Relevance Lost: the rise and fall of management accounting*. Harvard: Harvard University Press.

Kotler, P. (1988) *Marketing Management. Analysis, Planning, Implementation and Control*. Englewood Cliffs, New Jersey: Prentice-Hall, Inc.

Kotler P. and Andreason, A.R. (1987) *Strategic Marketing for Non-profit Organizations* (3rd edn). Englewood Cliffs, New Jersey: Prentice-Hall, Inc.

Laughlin, R. and Gray, R. (1988) *Financial Accounting*. London: Van Nostrand Reinhold, p. 59.

Omerod, P. (1994) *The Death of Economics*. London: Faber.

Pitt, L.F. and Abratt, R. (1987) 'Pricing in Non-profit Organisations – A framework and conceptual overview', *The Quarterly Review of Marketing*, Spring/Summer, 13–15.

Porter, M. (1980) *Competitive Strategy: Techniques for Analysing Industries and Competitors*. New York: Free Press.

Schapiro, B.P. (1973) 'Marketing for Non-profit Organizations', *Harvard Business Review*, September/October.

Vladeck, B.D. (1988) 'The Practical Differences in Managing Nonprofits: A Practitioner's Perspective' in O'Neill, M. and Young, D.R (eds) *Educating Managers of Nonprofit Organizations*. New York: Praeger, pp. 71–81.

Winkler, J. (1983) *Pricing for Results*. London: Heinemann.

CHAPTER 9

Communication and promotion

CHAPTER OVERVIEW It had been argued that marketing is far more than just advertising and promotion and that good promotion alone will not achieve the desired results. However, effective communication and promotion is a vital part of any coherent marketing strategy.

In addition the public sector also has a major role to play in changing attitudes towards, for example drug abuse, health education, *etc.* by means of advertising campaigns. Such educational campaigns are rarely used by private sector organisations.

This chapter starts by examining the communication process in general. It relates communication to promotional and selling activities, known as marketing action. The use of segmentation as a means of identifying and selecting appropriate media is also discussed.

KEY LEARNING OUTCOMES

By the end of this chapter, you should be able to:

- **understand the nature of communication;**

- **appreciate that communications are central to promotional strategies and techniques;**

- **consider the need for good promotion in the public sector;**

- **understand the reasons for, and nature of, regulation; and**

- **understand that public sector promotion often targets user groups which are difficult or uneconomic to reach in commercial markets.**

Introduction

Communications have a particular importance for marketing within any organisation. It has already been argued that marketing should be integrated into the organisation and 'owned' by all its members. To be successful, any organisation needs an awareness of its customers', clients' or users' needs. In many public sector organisations, this awareness can easily be obscured by factors, such as operational concerns, despite the fact that its markets provide the reason for the organisation's activities.

Good communications are also essential for any organisation's relationship with its environment. These include the ways in which an organisation markets its products or services. Communications play a very important role in promotion.

Communication

Communication is concerned with conveying, imparting or exchanging data, information, ideas and knowledge. It is impossible to communicate with anyone else without using a form and a channel of communication – that is, by speech, writing, signs or another form of language. Modern, systematic and scientific theories of language and linguistics owe much to the work of the Swiss M.-F. de Saussure (1857–1913) – the father of the 'structuralist' movement – the Russian/American R. O. Jakobson, and the Americans, F. Boas and A. V. Chomsky. In the context of this chapter, however, it is only necessary to understand the simplified model of the communication process represented in Fig. 9.1.

This models the communication process between individuals A and B. Both alternately act as *senders* and *receivers* in a two-way communication. In order for any communication to take place, there must, of course, be some stimulus to communicate, and some motivation to do so. The sender then has to choose an appropriate channel for communication – for example, speech or written memorandum – *'encode'* his or her message appropriately and deliver it. Codes can be found in a variety of forms, including computer operating systems. Language, as a code, uses words in order to communicate. We also use the 'para-language' of speech in our use of tone, speed, volume and emphasis. In addition, we use non-verbal codes, such as gestures, facial expressions, body language and timing. The receiver then has to *'decode'* the message by interpreting its meaning.

Although this may seem pretty simple, the context or frame of reference (Hamilton and Parker, 1990, pp. 8–11) within which the communication takes place can affect the receiver's decoding and understanding of meaning. Every individual has a unique frame of reference formed by a host of variables, including sex, nationality, education, etc. We are all different (*see* Chapter 5), and so we will all react differently to the same experience. This is particularly evident in communications between members of different nationalities, who may have differing interpretations of the same phenomena, and possess different customs and conventions. In some countries, an encounter with a black cat may be considered lucky; in others it may be considered a bad omen.

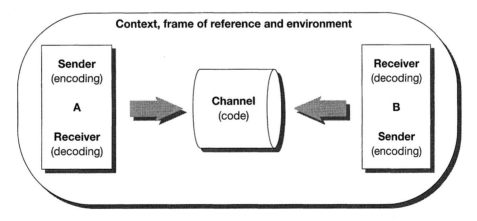

Fig. 9.1 A simple model of the communication process

There are a number of problems inherent in the use of any language. Words can often be ambiguous (Clampitt, 1991, pp. 25–49), and can be interpreted in different ways in different contexts. Meanings are produced by the interaction of content and context. Words often have several different meanings, as a look at any dictionary will reveal. 'Drink', for example, may refer to an intake of liquid, but it is often used, in specific situations, to denote liquid with an alcohol content – for example, when a policeman asks a motorist who has been driving erratically 'Have you been drinking, Sir?' It is, therefore, extremely important to understand the *context* in which a communication is sent and received. The better this is done, the more successful the communication is likely to be.

According to Redding (McPhee and Tompkins, 1985, pp. 15–54), the seminal period in the history and development of communication as a field of study took place in the United States during the years 1942 to 1947, although such studies were not extensively applied to work on organisations until the 1950s. We spend much of our lives in, or in contact with, organisations. Communications hold organisations together. Without communications, an organisation disintegrates and co-ordination disappears. Moreover, communications are essential to organisations' relationships with their environments. These themes need to be examined in further detail.

The organisation as a context and frame of reference

All organisations possess some form of *structure*. McPhee (McPhee and Tompkins, 1985, pp. 149–77) has discussed communication in the context of organisational structures – the ways in which organisations define themselves in terms of constitutions, hierarchies, formal procedures, lines of management and systems. Structures are *established*, usually in a published form.

Organisational structure forms a specific context for a large amount of communication. Inside the organisation, communication, like behaviour, is often determined by the organisation's structure. Importantly, the structure provides some predictability and stability to communication (Rogers and Agarwala-Rogers, 1976). Without effective communication within the organisation, the organisation cannot operate effectively because most of its formal communication systems are designed to obtain *results* and *effects*. In the organisational context, most communications are made to transfer information, instructions and ideas with the purpose of modifying people's knowledge, changing their behaviours, influencing their attitudes and making something happen. In such a context, it is important to identify two distinct, but related types of information within organisations: formal communication and informal communication.

Formal communication

Formal communication is designed to obtain results directly, by informing and instructing members of the organisation. Such communication is designed to effect action, to make or persuade members of the organisation to do certain things. It often serves a control function. It is usually *obligatory* – for example, demanding reports on situations, progress, etc. – and requires or requests some response or 'feedback'.

Feedback is an important aspect of organisational communication, not only because it confirms the receiver's receipt of a message and provides a response to it. It also serves to improve employees' understanding of the organisation and its work. It can contribute to job satisfaction by ensuring that the recipient is actively contributing to a process.

Formal communication can also be *informatory*, in the sense that it communicates information which is selected (it has already been noted that the control of information is an important source of power within an organisation (*see* Chapter 7)) with the anticipation that it will be *used* by the receiver. This is characterised, for example, by communications containing information, rationales, procedures, policies, performance appraisals and motivation appeals. All these help consolidate organisational *culture* (*see* Chapter 11) – that system of beliefs, values and attitudes which is shared by those within the organisation.

Informal communication

Informal communication will occur naturally in any organisation, and will also make an important contribution to the nature of organisational culture. 'Grapevines' will always operate and sometimes informal information is likely to be faster and more accurate simply because it has not been 'filtered' by the procedures and other factors which influence formal communication. Moreover, informal communications are unlikely to depend solely on the vertical (downward and upward) communication flows that characterise many formal communication channels, or on the horizontal communication mechanisms which exist formally between people, usually at the same level within the organisation, to co-ordinate tasks, share information and solve problems.

Informal communications often exist simply because formal channels are in many ways limited in their operation and capacity. They involve rumours and opinions. A statement such as 'I've heard that the University Business Faculty is likely to be amalgamated with Financial Studies and Law' deserves to be taken seriously because rumours circulate extremely fast and, true or untrue, can assume real importance in the perceptions of organisational members. Rumours tend to communicate orally, and thus circumvent formal channels of communication. Despite their vulnerability to distortion, studies have indicated that they normally contain a strong element of accuracy.

Informal communication channels also carry vast quantities of messages. Research indicates (Rasberry and Lemoine, 1986, p. 101) that almost 80 per cent of organisational communications are carried by the 'grapevine' rather than by formal channels. Such communications can, and do, complement formal channels, but they can also threaten its effectiveness, which is why many managers view it with caution and even with distrust. Many try to control its influence, although the best way of doing so is usually to make formal communication systems more effective.

The relationship between formal and informal communications is complex. There is inevitably an area of overlap. Although the degree of discrepancy between them is sometimes represented as an indication of the inadequacy of formal communication and of formal communication structures, it is only fair to emphasise that formal communication is usually slower, more focused on routine, and often less sensitive to detailed issues than informal communication.

There is also a moral and ethical dimension involved in the communication process. Of course, communication can be manipulated in various ways, but it is normally assumed that communications will be 'truthful'. However, given the vagaries of human nature, communication can be used in negative, or even potentially damaging ways. A false message can easily destroy trust or belief in the veracity of its sender. Once trust is broken, the relationship between sender and receiver may be marred. Such behaviour may well have political repercussions within organisations (*see* Chapter 7). Moreover, 'whistle-blowing' communications, which breach confidentiality in the interests of wider concern, can affect relationships both within an organisation and between the organisation and its environment (*see* Minicase 9.1).

MINICASE 9.1

Communication, confidentiality, and censorship

In November 1996, an UK Sunday newspaper reported that the British intelligence service, MI6, had seized copies of a 'sensational' book written by one of its former agents after he had threatened to reveal 'sensitive' information in it by publishing it on the Internet. The author claimed to have been dismissed after protesting that some of the methods used by MI6 were unethical. Fearing a repeat of Peter Wright's disclosures about the British security services, published in his 1987 memoirs, it was argued that publication might damage national security.

Effective communications are important both within the organisation and for the organisation's relationships with its markets. Within the organisation, good communications are essential to personnel managers and public relations managers seeking to improve the relationships between the individual and the organisation. Wilkinson (1989) stresses the point that communication is about people, the ways in which they interact, and about providing the information that they need and want in order to succeed in their work. Good communications contribute to staff motivation, better working relationships, increased productivity, more positive commitment to change and an improved understanding of the markets and the environment. Good communications depend upon truthfulness, openness and plain-speaking. They are essential to the development of an organisational culture which involves all its members.

Communication channels

Channels of communication necessarily imprint their own attributes on the message carried. A telephone conversation has a very different character to that of a word-processed memorandum. All managers should manage these channels effectively. Clampitt (1991) challenges a number of assumptions about communication channels. Most managers will find a use for their waste-paper baskets when confronted with vast quantities of paper messages from which they have to select the most important ones. The increasing use of electronic mail produces the same problem (almost all e-mail programs contain a waste-paper basket) as users proliferate circulation lists and 'shared folders' instead of targeting specific individuals. Some people believe that a written communication is a 'fulfilled obligation' but ignore the fact that there is no guarantee that it will be received or understood in the way intended. Information does not automatically persuade its recipients to act or to take notice. Nor does an increasing number of communication channels or methods increase the level of understanding within the organisation.

A list of communication channels now available is very extensive, and will include the following:

- direct person-to-person conversations
- interviews
- telephone calls and telephone/video conferencing
- memoranda
- reports
- presentations
- letters
- faxes
- newsletters
- notice boards
- audio and video recordings
- helplines
- electronic mail
- answer machines
- 'voice mail'.

Most people will select a communication channel on the grounds of convenience. However, there are a number of considerations which should be borne in mind when choosing a communication channel, particularly:

- *What are the sender's requirements? Is the channel of communication likely to achieve the desired result?* If a carefully considered response is required, it may be better to ask for a written response rather than expect an immediate reply on the telephone. A notice board announcement is unlikely to provide the best channel for communicating a complex issue. All channels have their own characteristics, and it is important to choose the one(s) that serve the function of the message best.
- *Is the channel of communication the most appropriate one for the receiver?* Different groups of receivers will have different behaviours and requirements. A meeting may be a better channel than a memorandum for outlining proposals for new developments. An E-mail may be a more reliable means of confirming the time and location of a meeting than a telephone call.

Difficulties in communications

Clear and good communications can be surprisingly difficult to achieve. The problems of ambiguity have already been mentioned. It is also necessary to discuss the problem of 'noise' or interference, which may disturb the channels of communication and affect the sense and understanding of messages. 'Noise' may be literally the product of the environment within which the communication takes place (machine rooms, busy spaces, etc.), but may also be used as a metaphor for various other factors likely to corrupt the channel of communication. These can include a range of 'distortion factors'. Certain inferences may be made for political reasons. Some senders may simply have a poor awareness of the possibilities of multiple interpretations. Communication barriers may be erected by the sheer size and complexity of an organisation. Bergin (1981) makes the point that complex organisations need to take detailed steps to ensure, for example, that management information reaches all relevant parts of an organisation in the appropriate forms. The more direct the channel between sender and receiver, the more accurately the message will be received.

Communications can easily break down. It may be easy (or tempting) to blame the receiver for misunderstanding a message, but faults can equally well be found with the sender. Managers who are keen to be seen as open, understanding and sensitive to employees may recognise the importance of investing adequate resources in involving personnel and developing their listening skills, as many Japanese companies have done. Unfortunately, many erroneously believe that 'understanding' will necessarily produce agreement. It will not. There are an enormous number of variables in individuals' frames of reference. Many managers are simply not very good at listening to employees. Employees themselves are often reticent, for a variety of reasons, about expressing their feelings or emotions.

The obstacles to good communication are many, and include poor preparation, vague or incomplete instructions, bad memory, narrow focus ('tunnel vision') and defensive attitudes (Hamilton and Parker, 1990). Group influences, emotions, perceptions and attitudes towards the communicator can all affect communication, as can information 'overload' – a real and potential feature of most large organisations. (*See* Minicase 9.2.)

In the final analysis, there is no single or simple criterion for evaluating the effectiveness of communication. Good communication requires the people involved to share good working relationships (not necessarily friendly ones!) and a cooperative culture. This usually involves an element of managerial flexibility in the use of communication channels and a sensitivity to the needs of the users.

Communications also serve a central role in the processes of change. All organisations have to adapt to change if they are to remain healthy, but people can be extremely resistant to change for a variety of reasons. Change can involve some discomfort, disruption of familiar routines and social relationships. It can change people's roles within organisations and even threaten their economic security (Rasberry and Lemoine, 1986), contributing to uncertainties and personal anxieties. In order to manage change effectively, management needs to use good communication techniques to persuade people of the necessities and advantages of change. Hartley (1993) provides an excellent analysis of the characteristics of interpersonal communication and the relevant skills.

MINICASE 9.1

Communication and confusion

Students in one UK university were confused, it transpired, by the way in which some terminology was used inconsistently in the literature published to describe the academic opportunities on offer. The basic teaching syllabus was described as a 'unit'. Units 'belonged' to named degree courses, although it was possible to choose some optional units from named degrees other than the one on which a student might be registered. Named degrees – for example, BSc Information Studies – were linked together into 'programmes' – for example, The Business and Management Studies Programme, which contained BA Business Studies, BSc Information Studies and BA Public Administration and Management.

However, the computerised new Student Management System (SMS) for the university had elected to call all named degree courses 'programmes', and was using this term on published transcript records of the units for which students enrolled. Moreover, students who had chosen a Combined Studies degree route, constructing their own degree courses by selecting a number of units from different degree routes, were being encouraged to use the term 'programme' to refer to their personalised combination of studies, *and* to refer to the 'Combined Studies Programme' as a generic label for their activities as undergraduates.

It was small wonder that students felt confused when asked for unit enrolment details at the start of the academic year. Did a request for the identification of the 'host course', beside one for each unit title, refer to a named degree (called a 'programme' by the SMS), or to a generic group of named degrees defined in some of the literature as a 'programme', to the name of the Faculty within which the 'programme' was located, or to the Combined Studies 'Programme'?

The confusion meant that staff had to spend a considerable amount of time, explaining the system and ensuring that students understood what was expected of them. Had the university taken a clear decision about how such terms were to be used within the organisation, communication would have been much more effective, and considerable time would have been saved.

Promotion and the media

In Chapter 2, we discussed the marketing mix – that combination of elements which, if understood correctly, makes a marketing project effective. We defined promotion as the way in which a product or service is represented, in order to encourage its use. Promotion includes all the activities designed to call people's attention to the existence of a product, a service or an idea and influence them to buy, use or change their attitudes and behaviours. Promotion is, literally, concerned with the advancement of something, its encouragement and active support, publicisation and selling. It seems obvious that people need to know about available products, services or ideas if they are going to use them. This information needs to be communicated to people as effectively as possible.

The development of public communication

Public communication has always been a feature of organised society. The most ancient civilisations developed ways of conveying messages publicly. Before the spread of literacy, signs and public announcements were in common use. Some ancient forms – for example, tavern signs and the office of town crier – survive even today. However, the earliest form of modern mass communication was made possible by the invention in Europe of a method of printing, defined by Steinberg (1955) as 'graphic communication by multiplied impressions'. This was pioneered, using moveable type faces and the 'common' press, by Johann Gutenberg (whose financial backer short-sightedly foreclosed his loan) in the 1440s.

Within 20 years of the invention of printing, the industry had evolved forms of publicity for its products, including the informative leaflet or prospectus, the poster and the list or catalogue. The earliest advertisement for a book dates from about 1466. Printing processes were gradually improved.

Writers, such as Bergin (1981), assert that mass communication, in a modern sense, began with the first daily newspaper, published in London in 1702. The steam-powered press appeared in 1814 and was followed by the development of stereotyped printing, mechanical typesetting, linotype, monotype and the rotary press. Large volume production became possible in the second half of the nineteenth century. By 1861 the British tax on newspapers was abolished and by the early twentieth century the industry was well established. Newspapers fed on the increasing pace of social, political and technological change. Lord Northcliffe's (Alfred Harmsworth's) *Daily Mail* was the first popular newspaper, and took daily sales past the million mark for the first time. Reproductive processes for printing images, such as lithography and the wood-engraved block, had also developed extensively in the nineteenth century, and the application of photography to printing, using the halftone plate, had first been used commercially in the 1880s. Photographic colour printing processes followed.

Wireless communications were pioneered by Marconi in the 1890s, and the first British Broadcasting Company was set up in 1922. From 1927, the British Broadcasting Corporation acted as a monopoly UK public service corporation, funded by receiving licence fees, under John Reith, who held a firm belief in its moral responsibility to inform, educate and entertain, while defending its autonomy (the BBC's charter is periodically reviewed and renewed by government). After the Second World War, television developed dramatically, and by 1954 an Independent Television Authority ensured that some broadcasting could also be funded by commercial sponsorship, as was already the case in the USA. Satellite broadcasting and cable television developments have also extended consumer choice.

The rapid advances which have created the information technology revolution continue to develop forms of mass media and communication. Although many developments owed their origins to military requirements, commercial applications and sponsorship now provide most of the industry's financing. Modern mass media are effectively dependent upon the sale of space and time to organisations which promote their products and services. Forms of information technology, such as the Internet, now exist which permit the user not only to search widely for information, but to place orders for products and services remotely. Telephone systems are now upgraded to integrated services digital network (ISDN) standards in order to facilitate the use of high-volume computerised information services. Melody (in Ferguson, 1990, pp. 16–39) makes the point that access to information and communication is now an essential public utility.

The promotional mix

'Promotion' is the marketing term for influencing and encouraging clients and customers to use products or services or to adopt ideas. This process involves passing from a state of ignorance, through awareness and understanding, to conviction (Wilmshurst, 1984). In the case of social marketing the aim of the exercise is to get as many people as possible to adopt the ideas or values being promoted, and the user is therefore usually termed the 'adopter'.

It is obviously important to realise the nature and sources of likely resistance to promotion. These can include:

1 *Apathy* – a lack of interest in, and an indifference to, the idea or the service being promoted. This phenomenon may even increase as the individual in modern society feels it necessary to be more selective in dealing with the growing number of promotional appeals. Promotion can achieve a saturation level beyond which it is difficult, if not impossible, to go. Resistance grows. Waste-paper baskets have become a necessary feature of modern life, as 'disposal filing', as more and more promotional literature, or 'junk mail', pours through the nation's letter boxes.

2 *Lack of understanding* – an inability or refusal to understand, or to be convinced by, the arguments presented by the promotion campaign. Although this can result from a cynical response, it may also be the product of ill-conceived or badly designed and targeted promotion.

3 *Competition* – the promotional activities of other organisations, services and marketing campaigns which vie for attention, and may be perceived as offering a more attractive or convincing benefit.

We have deliberately referred to ideas, as well as to products and services, because public service marketing, in particular, often seeks to promote certain values deemed to be in the public interest. Anti-drugs campaigns are examples of promotion designed to influence social attitudes and behaviours. In time of war, such promotion takes the form of propaganda – a word originally derived from a sixteenth-century committee of Cardinals in charge of Roman Catholic missions as part of the Counter-Reformation.

Advertising

Promotion is inevitably associated with advertising, because modern, twentieth-century society has seen an unprecedented growth in the advertising phenomenon. The term 'advertising' is related to the French 'avertir', meaning to notify or to warn. Leiss *et al.* (1986) have made the point that advertising has become 'one of the great vehicles of social communication' in modern industrial societies. Never before has any society been inundated with such a volume of visual, written and verbal statements designed to call attention to things, mostly to the benefits to be obtained from specified products and services. In the USA, the first advertising agency was founded as long ago as 1871, and advertising is now a global industry.

Unfortunately, such common usage has also bred a certain cynicism in the potential user. Although advertising exposure may succeed in influencing the gullible, increasing numbers of people appear to suspect that advertising is manipulative, an insult to intelligence, and merely makes products more expensive by adding to their costs. Moreover, much advertising has been criticised for its tendency to emphasise material values at the expense of others. Dyer (1982) argued that advertising manipulates attitudes and values by simplifying the problems of life and now serves a social function that was once met by religion. Although this may appear a somewhat extreme view, we must admit that advertising has become part of modern culture, whether we like it or not. It has contributed a lot to the development of our 'consumer society'. Cashmore (1994) claims that, for example, 'television *is* advertising', because the whole industry (even the BBC, which does not formally accept advertising revenue) depends, directly or indirectly, upon advertising contribution to offset production costs.

Advertising depends upon its ability to influence its audiences in various ways. This involves using communication effects designed to influence behaviours. Communication theory is now a sophisticated discipline (Severin *et al.*, 1988), which is used to understand the relationships between the 'media practitioner' and the 'receiver' or audience. One model of communication effects suggests that advertising seeks to lead a receiver through a sequence of responses designed to end in an act of purchase or adoption (*see* Fig. 9.2; *see also* Figs 3.7 and 3.8). From an initial awareness of the product (*cognitive*), the receiver gains a knowledge of it. This develops into an emotional liking (*affective*), and then into a preference for it. Preference becomes a willing conviction (*conative*) of the superior merits of the product service, or idea, which can then be translated into actual purchase, use or adoption.

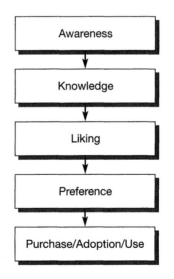

Fig. 9.2 The 'adoption process' model

There may be some doubts about whether the human process is necessarily as logically ordered as this model suggests, but it does identify a number of dimensions which are important parts of the communication process in advertising.

The advertiser, of course, believes that advertising stimulates awareness, demand and consumption. The advertiser is playing an important part in the marketing process. Unless people know about a product or a service, they are unlikely to buy or use it, no matter how much they may have a need or a want for it. Unfortunately, advertising is easily interpreted in the negative way already discussed in Chapter 2. There have been many objections to the methods used by advertisers. Advertising stands accused of attempted manipulation, of trying to influence and interfere with the right of the customer to make up his or her own mind. Authors like Packard (1957) have attacked some advertising methods on the grounds that they can produce conditioned responses at a subconscious level. Galbraith (1958) argued that advertising attempts to subvert the priority of user or consumer 'sovereignty'. Galbraith believed wants and needs should be determined solely by the user. Advertising stands accused, not least by Marxist critics such as Marcuse (1964), of creating false needs. Advertising seeks to attach desirable attributes to products, perceptions of value added which are generated by the producer or provider rather than by the customer. Some writers – for example, Mander (1977) – have even argued that advertising's purpose is simply to create permanent discontent, an insatiable longing which can never be permanently satisfied. As such, it runs the risk of distorting the values of our society, placing undue emphasis upon material satisfaction at the expense of more altruistic concerns. The user becomes victim, not sovereign.

Gilligan and Crowther (1976) assembled a useful list of criticisms directed against the social effects of advertising. Although a society in the 1990s may not be so obviously concerned with, or worried by, issues of 'bad taste' as some writers may have been 20 years ago, there are a number of issues which can still combine to produce a public suspicion of advertising.

- The industry's own regulators have long opposed the use of advertisements designed to mislead or which make false claims. It is certainly morally indefensible to promote the virtues of a product by claiming benefits or satisfactions which the product fails to deliver.

- It is also argued that advertising creates false demands and that it promotes products and services which are not really needed. This accusation might be valid in the context of a subsistence economy, but is hardly appropriate in one dominated by 'consumer capitalism', where many markets serve wants, not needs. However, it may tell us something about the ways in which people's perceptions of needs continue to change over time.

- Another objection to advertising stems from the belief that it is too powerfully persuasive (Packard, 1957; Galbraith, 1958). This view is often adopted by those who see advertising as a manipulative tool of commerce. The criticism does, however, undervalue the intelligence of the individual, his or her ability and desire to choose and use advertising as a means of obtaining information on which to base decisions.

On the other hand, it is possible to maintain that advertising merely helps people match their needs and wants to their opportunities. It increases user awareness. Many in the advertising industry believe that advertising can only develop user/ consumer desires that already exist. It does not create new ones. Leiss *et al.* (1986, p. 33) cite Neil Borden's 'classic' work on advertising, *Advertising in Our Economy* (1947), which argued that advertising can only serve to increase consumption, not create it. The high rate of failure associated with new, unfamiliar products is cited to support this claim.

If advertising functions partly to call attention to the existence of a particular product or service, it might be expected to help users make rational decisions on how best to match their requirements to what is available. Awareness of alternatives enables the potential user to make choices. However, some research suggests (for example, Driver and Foxall, 1984) that this is a highly optimistic expectation. It seems that logical decision-making procedures are the exception rather than the rule. Most people appear relatively indifferent to advertising. Given the high levels of advertising to which anyone living in a capitalist society is now exposed, it would not be surprising to find that much 'information' provided by advertising is automatically 'screened out' in order to avoid forms of information overload. Leiss *et al.* (1986, p. 39) conclude that information is less important a factor than persuasion in advertising. Users may simply want to be persuaded of the merits conferred by a specific product or service, rather than invest time and trouble in a systematic decision-making process comparing similar products or services. For these reasons, therefore, advertising is often used when there is a desire to reach as wide an audience as possible, as quickly as possible, and when there may be some difficulty in locating and targeting users.

Wilmshurst (1985) lists twelve different categories of advertising, related to their function. Nine of these are mainly geared to commercial marketing. *Personal advertising* is placed by the individual who wishes to sell, announce or search for something. *Local 'classified' advertising* concerns items, services and jobs, both wanted and 'on offer'. *Manufacturer's consumer advertising* is familiar to everyone through our exposure to 'branded' products advertised in the media. *Retailer advertising* has become increasingly familiar as retailers establish their own identity in association with specific product ranges – for example, the major supermarket chains. *Trade advertising* and *business-to-business (industrial) advertising* takes place between suppliers, manufacturers, service providers and wholesalers, usually through trade publications. *Corporate advertising* seeks to promote the image of a company or organisation, giving its products or services added value. *Financial and savings advertising* include all those annual reports to investors and shareholders which appear at regular times during the year. *Recruitment advertising* is essential to the employment market.

All of these are familiar types of advertising in commercial markets, and some play an important role in public sector industries where, for example, some kinds of National Health Service marketing bears a strong resemblance to industrial marketing. The three remaining categories are more familiar to public sector organisations which are non-profit making.

- *Government advertising* is a very large and high-spending category. It includes recruitment advertising for public services and also some 'cause advertising' – for example, campaigns for public health and safety.

- *Charity advertising*. Since the definitions of a charity include both education and activities beneficial to the community as a whole (*see* Chapter 2), it is not surprising to find a lot of advertising activity in this category, although some promotion is often provided free of charge by, for example, local radio and newspapers.

- *'Cause' advertising* or *'advocacy' advertising*. This is aimed at persuading people to actively support a particular cause – for example, making less use of their cars in order to reduce the amount of atmospheric pollution. Some such advertising may be government or charity advertising, but some can, for example, be political party advertising. The mass media have become important providers of social and political comment (Blumler in Ferguson, 1990, pp. 101–13). The media play important roles in influencing the perceptions of political policies.

Other forms of promotion

Advertising is only one of a number of methods by which people can be encouraged to use products, services or ideas. The other principal ingredients in what can be termed 'the promotional mix' (*see*, e.g. Wilmshurst, 1985) can be listed as:

- *personal selling*, involving a person-to-person conversation between the seller and the prospective customer or user;

- *sales literature publications* (also including radio, TV, film, video and Internet publicity) and *demonstrations*;

- *sales promotions*, such as exhibitions, demonstrations, competitions, 'special offers', etc.;

- *public relations*, often in the form of the 'free' publicity which can be obtained from media stories about an organisation and its activities. This, of course, can prove negative, as well as positive, and highlights the advantages of maintaining 'good' public relations.

Although this list is obviously composed with private sector marketing in mind, all these techniques can be relevant to the public sector. They can be used to influence how the product or services are perceived by those who need them.

Promotion in the public sector

As might be expected, the public sector also needs to use promotion to develop both an awareness and use of its products and services. Some public sector industries have long used promotion techniques, especially advertising, as commercial marketing tools. For example, the history of railways promotion saw the railways in competition with canals, road transport, and other railway networks. For certain purposes, rail may be promoted in co-ordination with other transport services – for example, London's rail service to Gatwick Airport, or to the ports and shipping operations – but in the absence of a political will to co-ordinate transport policy, many transport systems seem locked into competition with each other.

Competition is an inevitable consequence of introducing choice. One result of increasing the participation rate in higher education and incorporating the poly-technics as 'new' universities in the early 1990s was to increase perceptions of competition as the new institutions began seriously to vie for student numbers and the funding they attracted.

Competition is seen either as:

- *generic*, as in competition between different forms of transport – for example, train competition with bus, lorry or tram; or

- *internal*, as illustrated by competition within one form of transport – for example, between bus companies after deregulation.

The energy industries (which have also been subject to privatisation on the prin-ciple that competition increases efficiency and saves costs) may be in generic competition with each other – for example, gas with electricity or with solid-fuel for heating. As well as external competition, however, some of them may have to manage internal competition in the 'value chain' – that is, in the sequence of value-added processes which, for example, transform raw materials into usable products and eventually deliver them to the user. Electricity provides a good illustration of this. Coal, gas, nuclear fuels, water and wind can all provide sources of power for the generation of electricity. Although a co-ordinated policy and the existence of a national grid permits all of them to make a contribution to the generation of elec-tricity, economic, resource and ecological considerations are sources of competition in the industrial market.

The public sector, of course, still includes a number of areas in which there is no generic competition, because the users have no effective choice. Those who cannot afford private health care are dependent upon state (NHS) provision. Those in poverty, those who are out of work or those who are disabled depend upon the State for benefits. Charities hardly see themselves in competition with state agen-cies, although many of them make important contributions to relieving hardship. The role of promotion in this context increasingly involves competitive advertising, and the media carries many appeals for charitable donations which effectively compete for public attention and donations.

Public relations are, of course, concerned with establishing and maintaining 'mutual understanding between an organisation and its publics' (from The Institute of Public Relations definition). Public relations are concerned with goodwill and public perceptions of an organisation. It is all the more important, therefore, that public sector organisations recognise the importance of public relations. In North America, the public relations director, or director of external affairs, is usually known as a 'communicator', precisely because the work involves both internal and external organisational communication processes.

Promotion, especially in those public sector areas which are not engaged in a competitive search for custom, usually relies mainly on forms of information and public communication. If the task of any organisation is to identify the needs, wants and interests of target markets, and to deliver the products or services which

Promotion and image in the public sector

One of the most obvious areas of work to benefit from privatisation, and the increasing application of commercial techniques to public sector organisations, has been corporate identity consultancy. Denationalised industries were obviously keen to change their image. Their cultures needed to become profit-making ones. They needed to influence public awareness and encourage the sales of their shares. Potential new owners, the users of their services and those who provided them needed a 'message of change'.

Developing the corporate image of an organisation is an established method of changing its culture – the body of beliefs, attitudes and values which characterise the organisation's behaviour. A corporate image helps define an organisation's identity, makes it easy for members to identify with it and, it is hoped, encourages individuals to internalise the values of the organisation – its organisational culture (see Williams et al., 1989, pp. 80–81). Indeed, Morgan (1986) has written about organisations as cultures which express key systems of beliefs and values, and which influence the organisation's actions through language, symbols, rituals and other practices. Organisations try to develop their corporate images by changing their cultures: involving their employees, publicising successes, and using corporate symbols for both internal and external communications.

Corporate identity consultants see themselves as catalysts of change, enabling organisations to restructure and manage developments. Visual symbols can be particularly obvious and significant ways of communicating a new focus and a desired position in the marketplace. In an article in *The Independent* of 20 October 1993, Paul Gosling looked at ways in which the perceptions of organisations can be influenced by corporate identity. This is as true for public sector organisations as it is for those in the private sector. British Rail's InterCity division was a client of Newell and Sorrell when it promoted the train as a relaxing mode of travel.

When NALGO, NUPE and COHSE merged to form the UK's biggest union, UNISON, there was an obvious need to bring together three different cultures and traditions. Their use of an external consultancy helped them through that process. There is, here, a firm indication that management consultants and corporate identity consultants can have a close and effective relationship in implementing change, and in producing real, credible results. Unfortunately, the products of corporate identity are still often thought of as simply cosmetic. In reality, visual symbols can be very powerful influences on the way in which services are perceived.

answer them most effectively, public sector organisations must also make certain that both the user's and society's interests are satisfied at the same time. On this level, much public sector promotion can effectively be termed 'social marketing'.

Solomon (1989) traces the origin of the concept to the early 1950s, when it was first realised that social campaigns were in many ways similar to marketing programmes. The concept has been developed by writers such as Kotler and Roberto (1989). Social marketing is concerned with designing and implementing programmes to expand the numbers of those prepared to accept a social idea or practice. It is, therefore, concerned with much more than advertising campaigns, and involves the whole marketing process. Social marketing requires a careful balance between user satisfaction and public interest (Wells *et al.*, 1992, p.62). Society and the advertising industry would like to believe that this balance is guaranteed by the various regulatory controls, both internal and external, which exist to ensure that conflict does not arise between these demands.

The regulation of promotion

Wilmshurst (1985) stresses the point that the acceptability of advertising depends much upon its perceived truthfulness. It is the dislike and fear of false and misleading claims, and of 'preying on the vulnerable' – for example, children – which have led to the general adoption of controls on promotional advertising. These controls usually take the form of *legal regulation, voluntary self-regulation* processes, or a combination of the two. Jefkins (1992, pp. 355–404) points out that legal control and self-regulation differ in their practices. A law is designed to deter or punish offenders. A breach of the law is subject to penalties, often financial ones. A voluntary code of practice cannot exact such kinds of retribution, although it is not without some sanctions. However, the law can take a long time to bring offences to court and is a fairly cumbersome process. Voluntary controls have the advantage of being applied quickly – for example, by requesting the immediate withdrawal of an advertisement – even if the system is designed primarily to protect the good name of the advertising industry. Jefkins (1992) considers self-regulation a form of public relations for the industry, whereas the law seeks to protect the consumer. Advertising therefore needs to be aware of both forms of control.

Legal controls include both *common law* and *statute law* provision. Common law centres upon civil wrongs for which redress can be sought through the courts. These may involve contracts (misrepresentation can invalidate a contract) and defamation. Statute law refers to parliamentary laws and statutory orders, regulations or instruments. A large number of laws relate specifically to advertising, and are primarily designed to protect customers' interests.

Self-regulatory or voluntary controls usually have no legal force, but operate codes of practice. In the UK, the Advertising Standards Authority (ASA) and the Committee of Advertising Practice (CAP) actively try to ensure that advertisers comply with the British Code of Advertising Practice, which is updated from time to time. Additionally, there are a large number of more specialised, industry-specific codes of practice.

Special considerations for public sector promotion

It is important to recognise how major differences between the public sector and commercial business affect promotion. Solomon (1989) and other writers have identified a number of distinctions between social and commercial marketing.

1 *The political dimension.* We have already noted (in Chapters 2 and 7) that the public sector is particularly vulnerable to political considerations. Public support is essential to the success of social marketing. A political element is likely to

appear as soon as attempts to secure wide public support encounter forms of vested interest. In recent years, commercial marketing itself has become more and more aware of the importance of the political dimension. 'Issues management' has joined the list of business school topics for those concerned with public relations and controversial policy issues. The term seems to have originated with the work of Chase (1977) and has been developed by writers, such as Heath and Nelson (1986). As an example, the importance of being environmentally responsible and friendly has assumed an increasingly high profile. 'Green' issues are seen more and more as important to the quality of human life (Jenkins, 1992, pp. 31–2). Social accountability has even gained recognition in the accountancy profession.

Promotion therefore needs to be aware of issues which may be politically sensitive in any interpretation of 'public interest'. The political arguments surrounding UK road-building proposals in the 1990s provide a good illustration of the problem. The conflict between the 'environmentalists', seeking to protect nature and wildlife from the ecological damage of new roads, and those who simply want relief from an ever-increasing volume of traffic passing through their towns and villages is complicated by a wider debate about the country's ability to sustain a growing level of car ownership and use which threatens the very quality of life in the twenty-first century.

2 *Different target markets.* Public sector promotion has frequently to be directed at the market segments – that is, those social groups – which are hardest to reach. Unlike commercial organisations, public services cannot afford to ignore the least economically profitable sections of the population. Their main function may well be to help them. The identification of these segments requires the same segmentation skills discussed in Chapter 5, but the organisational aims will be very different from those of private sector organisations. This calls attention to a number of other factors with which we are already familiar.

3 *Inability to pay.* The users of many public sector services do not pay for them directly. The commercial conventions of exchange between seller and buyer do not apply. Indeed, some services actually function to provide those in need with financial support. It has been argued that the lack of real purchasing power – that is, the ability to pay according to preference – simply inhibits the growth and development of an efficient market in the public sector. Consequently, there has been some support for the idea of replacing the concept of 'entitlement', for example, with vouchers. The UK Government's 1996 pilot schemes for nursery education vouchers, over which the users have more 'visible' control, are an example of this.

4 *User resistance.* The products or services may not actually be wanted by certain users, who may see them as demands imposed by a culture or a government alien to their own cultures and value systems. This can be illustrated by reference to, for example, 'new age travellers' – a social group which does not wish to subscribe to the dominant social or economic culture.

5 *Limited resources.* Resource constraints often mean that increased demand is not the aim of promotion for public sector organisations. Many of them are actually

in the business of rationing demand to meet the available resources. Some communication campaigns therefore simply seek to raise awareness – for example AIDS and safe sex campaigns. This may be linked to the following point.

6 *'Demarketing'*. Some campaigns seek actively to discourage certain activities in the public interest – for example, drug abuse. Kotler and Roberto (1989) see this as 'marketing in reverse', discouraging use and consumption.

7 *Definitions of profit*. Many public sector services do not, or cannot, measure success simply in terms of financial gain. A strong element of 'social accounting' – the need to acknowledge benefit in terms other than purely financial ones – differentiates many public services from commercial ones. Unfortunately, this characteristic of much public sector marketing can make it very difficult to measure costs and benefits. If financial profitability were to be used as the most important criterion of success, many social services activities would not be considered viable at all.

We can thus conclude that, although public sector marketing can use the basic concepts and techniques of commercial marketing, including that of promotion, there are a number of important differences. Solomon (1989) is convinced that most differences between the sectors result from the fact that the public sector cannot always accept the commercial proposition that marketing facilitates *exchanges* between buyers and sellers.

A public sector marketing mix

The public sector use of the marketing mix therefore establishes emphases which often differ from those common to commercial marketing.

- *Product*. We have noted that public sector products are most often services, with their own generic characteristics (*see* Chapter 4).
- *Price* cannot always be measured simply in money terms, but includes a host of other elements. For example, a candidate's 'price' of entry into a university will include the A-level qualifications first obtained at school or tertiary college.
- *Place*, normally used to refer to distribution channels, is commonly associated with certain institutions, including those offices (or bureaux) typical of many services and which have been discussed, in general terms, in Chapter 7.
- *Promotion* can involve raising awareness, frequently of social and not merely personal concerns, and can even be used to try and discourage certain practices.

Despite such differences, however, public sector promotion techniques still have much in common with those used in the commercial markets. They both need to identify and target the appropriate market segments. However, it should be noted that some public sector services find segmentation something of a foreign concept. Those services which have, historically, been founded upon an ideal of equality and egalitarianism (*see* Chapter 4) may still be resistant to the idea that different groups of people have different wants and needs (*see* Chapter 5).

Social marketing is, arguably, altruistic and diverse in its aims. Much social marketing does not deal with target groups which are likely to provide the biggest profit, but with those who are often the least affluent and hardest to reach. It may even be trying to discourage certain behaviours. As a result, the marketing concepts need sensitive adjustment if they are to be used in the public sector. Where this problem has been examined in the context of specific case studies – for example, in Tomes' and Harrison's (1991) exploration of how to find permanent jobs for people with mental handicaps – it has been found that marketing concepts are very valuable. Promotional tools may need to be relatively low cost, in view of restricted budgets, but promotion is an important part of the marketing mix, raising awareness and communicating messages.

MINICASE 9.4

The importance of good communications

William Wells, the Chairman of South Thames Health Region, gave the 1994 David McCullough memorial lecture (reported in *The Guardian* of 13 July 1994). He looked at the problems associated with National Health Service changes. In his opinion, the NHS was providing greater access for more people at lower relative costs, and at higher quality than ever before. However, he highlighted the public's apparent lack of confidence in the service. Changing technologies and management skills had produced their own results. Even NHS property use was often changing. Understandably, some people were inclined to interpret these changes as threats to their (public) ownership of the health service.

Wells put the blame for many of these problems on the NHS's poor record of communicating its plans and explaining the rationale behind them. Failures to disseminate information and implement change well had created a sense of unease, both among those who work within the NHS and among the general public. In the preceding years, most information about the NHS had come from the centre, but in Wells' opinion the frequently quoted statistics, beloved by the politicians in front of the media, were no longer believed and were having a negative impact. Patients who had just had their operation postponed found it difficult to see why it was claimed that the NHS had 'too many beds'.

Often, the NHS had appeared reluctant to explain its plans at local level, even though people's perceptions of the service were formed by local experience. Moreover, like most organisational cultures, the NHS had developed a jargon of its own, far removed from everyday language. The Conservative government had taken too much responsibility for communications. The NHS planning strategy was too complicated, boring and increasingly bureaucratic. Wells also expressed his reservations about the implementation of marketing in the service. While not doubting the improvements which could be derived from competition, he was suspicious of competition for competition's sake – a 'slavish adherence' to the dogma of marketing principles at the expense of the primary market – the patients.

The increase in the amount of glossy promotional material produced in the name of communication was actually achieving little. The public was becoming increasingly disillusioned with what it saw as a waste of public money. The 'natural' civil service bureaucratic culture, requiring ever-increasing amounts of data in the name of accountability, was likely to offset any desired decrease in the numbers of administrators. Wells maintained that it should be the job of local management to communicate with the public, and the public should be much more closely involved in NHS planning.

Crompton and Lamb (1986) take the view that marketing has a very important role to play in public sector operations for a number of very practical reasons. Not only does a marketing perspective aim to improve the levels of user satisfaction, but by doing so it has the potential of both attracting public support, thereby creating political goodwill, and earning approval and backing from a legitimiser market evaluating outcomes on the basis of effectiveness. Despite the fact that marketing was, for a long time, relatively unfamiliar to many managers in the public sector, such managers have increasingly been trained in business and marketing skills, which are proving their usefulness. Moreover, a commitment to marketing provides an important framework for decision making. A marketing approach tries to ensure that an organisation co-ordinates its activities in order to meet its objectives. The marketing mix, for example, offers a systematic way of analysing an organisation's products or services in relation to its markets.

Crompton and Lamb (1986) are of the opinion that much private sector marketing knowledge can usefully be transferred to the public sector, bearing in mind that much needs to be 'tailored' to the specific demands and the different aims and objectives of public sector organisations.

Marketing and communications techniques

The purpose of communications in marketing is to tell people about a product or a service in such a way that they may become sufficiently interested to buy or use it.

Wilmshurst (1984) rightly stresses the point that there is no 'best way' of communicating with potential clients, users or adopters. There is a range of communication methods available, the most common of which are: word of mouth; personal selling; meetings (of various sorts, including seminars); advertising; sales promotions; and public relations. This list is, of course, based on commercial marketing practices, and for the purposes of public sector marketing we probably need to concentrate on those aspects Kotler and Roberto (1989) refer to as 'personal communication', 'selective communication' and 'mass communication'.

Personal communication

This is particularly important for 'social products', not least because of the way services are often inseparable from the people that deliver them (as discussed in Chapter 4). The quality of interpersonal communication and interaction is essential to the promotion of a 'social product' (Kotler and Roberto, 1989, p. 221). Such communication is often informal – 'word of mouth' is often a very influential means by which ideas are communicated. Messages can be 'cascaded' by means of an ever-expanding circle of contacts. However, this technique does run the risk that the message may become distorted, especially if it is a contentious issue. It is also a very expensive form of communication and promotion.

Moreover, although the 'word of mouth' message is usually perceived as being relatively trustworthy, it is essentially an unstructured form of communication. Promotion campaigns generally prefer techniques over which they feel they have greater control. There is always a risk that 'word-of-mouth' communication can result in an unfavourable, critical response. The models of personal communication techniques described by Kotler and Roberto (1989) are essentially selling techniques. They are designed to form relationships with their markets or adopters. However effective they may be, the majority of public sector services are unlikely to use such techniques to address their primary and secondary markets, simply on the grounds of cost. They are more likely to use such an approach with advantage when approaching a resourcer or legitimiser market.

Selective communication

Selective communication targets specific segments of the market that are identified as possessing particular needs. In Chapter 5, we discussed the importance of segmenting users into groups. Selective communication relies on this technique, for example, to identify possible recipients of direct mail communications, 'telemarketing' and similar techniques. It is noticeable that experience of these techniques in the UK is more familiar in the context of commercial marketing for double-glazing and insurance, but an increasing number of charitable organisations are also using such techniques. Yudelson (1988) once described the 'Four Ps' of non-profit marketing as:

- *performing* – using some activity, for example, an auction, charity dinner or charity performance, as a way of raising revenue;
- *pleading* – asking people to make donations, for example, for a good cause;
- *petitioning* – seeking sponsorship or grants from another organisation (Yudelson sees some analogy between this process and industrial marketing);
- *praying* – hoping for unsolicited contributions.

All such techniques will involve identifying a specific market segment to target.

Mass communication

This addresses the largest possible audiences and usually uses the media. Some theories, such as the 'Hierarchy-of-Effects' model used by Kotler and Roberto (1989, pp.191–3), maintain that mass communication initiates a process whereby some of those exposed to it move through stages of awareness, remembering, favourable response, intention, trial adoption to adoption. At each stage the numbers affected decrease. However, there are a number of arguments which suggest that the use of the media for mass communication programmes has its limitations.

The extent to which social marketing attempts to effect social change by promoting awareness and information might imply that mass-communication techniques are the obvious promotional tools. There is an established belief that mass media can provide information, influence public opinion and encourage change (for the better). Unfortunately, it appears that the mass media are really rather better at reinforcing existing cultural values and ideologies (Swingewood, 1977, pp. 73–92). More recently, Wallack (1989) has asserted that mass media are better at supporting the *status quo* and providing entertainment than at stimulating change.

Wallack (1989) believes that the role of mass media is often exaggerated and even inappropriate to many public sector problems. There is indeed a faith in the ability of a correctly targeted message to effect change. The mass media can indeed reach large proportions of a population. They can increase the 'visibility' of an issue and even lend a kind of legitimacy to a topic through media exposure. However, although the media can cultivate certain beliefs, there is a danger of mis-representing issues by the use of over-simplification, stereotyping, etc. Media representation always runs the risk of distortion simply because it is concerned with re-presentation and interpreting. It is suggested, for example, that, by virtue of television's own (cultural) nature, health issues are seldom treated in sufficient depth. The result could be that such programmes (especially in the USA) actually hinder campaigns designed to improve health. Moreover, they could even foster the impression that ill-health can always be cured by modern medical progress, thus discouraging the adoption of preventative health care techniques like adequate exercise.

The mass media may provide convenient ways of getting information to large audiences. However, it may be unrealistic to assume that the mass media can be effective in promoting social change, especially as audiences themselves grow ever more critical of the information industry.

Summary

1 **Communication** is concerned with the sending and receiving of data, information, ideas and knowledge. Communications are made via channels, and involve encoding and decoding processes. Meanings are produced by the interaction of content and context, the frames of reference within which communication takes place. Organisations themselves function as frames of reference.

2 **Promotion and the media.** Promotion techniques have a long history. Promotion functions to represent the product or the service in such a way as to encourage its use. It is often associated with our society's pervasive use of advertising.

3 **Promotion in the public sector.** Promotion has become an important tool for the public sector. Public sector industries increasingly face competition, whether generic or internal in kind. Promotion, especially in the context of social marketing, needs to ensure that the interests of both the user/customer and those of society are satisfied.

4 **The regulation of promotion.** Advertising is controlled by both laws, civil and statutory, and by voluntary codes of practice.

5 **Special considerations for public sector promotion.** Social marketing is concerned with campaigns designed to increase the numbers of people adopting a social idea or practice. This feature highlights a number of distinctions between the public and the commercial sectors.

6 **A public sector marketing mix** has, as a result, emphases which differ from the commercial sector. There is, however, evidence to support the contention that commercial marketing concepts can make successful contributions to the public sector.

7 **Marketing and communication techniques** are designed to tell people about products/services and encourage their use. Personal communication can be very effective, but it is expensive. Selective communication targets specific market segments. Mass communication addresses large audiences through the use of the media. Our faith in the mass media may be somewhat optimistic, especially as audiences grow more critical of the media.

Implications for management

Managers should consider the following questions:

What is your personal communication style?

Hamilton and Parker (1990, pp.74–102 and 420–36) use four categories of communication style: non-communicators (*closed*), blind communicators (*authoritarian*), hidden communicators (*disguised*) and open communicators (*communicator*). These categories are not usually used exclusively, but can be used successfully in some situations, and less successfully in others. The Manager Tendency Indicator (MTI) test and the Employee Tendency Indicator (ETI) tests can be used to identify which styles most commonly characterise an individual. A more simple diagnostic test is given by O'Connell (1979, p. 159 ff.). Self-awareness is an important step in self-development.

What are the communication channels and styles within your own organisation?

An inventory of those communication chanels and styles most commonly used in any organisation can be made.

Harrison (1995) categorises communication styles into *instructional, informative, consultative, involving* and *participative*. It will be noted that these range from the top-down communication style, commonly used to issue directives about jobs and tasks, usually from the top of an organisation, to the bottom-up style designed to enable all staff to contribute to making decisions. The extent to which certain communication styles may be more common than others within a particular organisation is usually an indicator of the nature of that organisation's culture (*see* Chapter 11). However, communication styles are also the products of a number of related variables: the individual, the individual's role, and the context or culture in which he or she works.

What are the aims and objectives of promotion?

It seems that promotion strategy works best with short statements that define a campaign's intent and the desired communication. Promotion is also obviously constrained in its choice of media by budget, cost-effectiveness, the character of the media, timing, etc. Not least, it must acknowledge the perceptions of its users/audiences. As a first step, managers need to ask the following questions in relation to their specific promotional needs:

● Which customers/users are being addressed?

● Which needs are we seeking to meet?

● How do we satisfy them?

- What information do we need to provide?
- What appeals do we make?
- How best do we communicate them?
- How do we communicate with the various markets?

Furthermore, managers should ensure that promotional campaigns are well planned. One of the most familiar techniques which has been established to model the 'hierarchy of effects' (Wells *et al.*, 1992, p.217) is the AIDA (attention, interest, desire, action) model of advertising. This is one of the models closely related to the communication theory sequence and to marketing communications strategy (Wilmshurst, 1985, p. 59). It can be used in the planning process to ensure that any campaign clearly:

- identifies its objective (the task it sets out to accomplish);
- determines the resources to be used (budget available);
- establishes its message and target market segment(s);
- co-ordinates all the promotional activities involved;
- establishes the appropriate means of monitoring its effectiveness.

This process clearly stresses the function of promotion as part of the marketing strategy to which it is related. Its effectiveness depends upon its ability to meet the AIDA criteria and to improve user understanding and awareness. As a result, much market research (*see* Chapters 10 and 11) is conducted with the intention of identifying and collecting data on market attitudes towards, and perceptions of 'the product'. This research is an essential component of any promotional campaign.

ISSUES FOR DISCUSSION

The following issues for discussion are presented in the form of questions. Examples from specific public sector industries should be incorporated into responses. Case studies can be used to provide some illustrations of the issues raised.

1 What are the most common sources of 'noise' in the communications of public sector organisations?

2 What are the main functions of advertising in the public sector?

3 What is the relationship between 'truthfulness' and advertising? How does this affect the public sector view of advertising and promotion?

4 How important are interpersonal skills in organisational communication?

References

Bergin, F.J. (1981) *Practical Communication* (2nd edn). London: Pitman Publishing.
Cashmore, E. (1994) *... and there was television*. London and New York: Routledge and Kegan Paul.
Chase, W.H. (1977) 'Public issue management: the new science', *Public Relations Journal*, 33, October, 25–6.
Clampitt, P. G. (1991) *Communicating for Managerial Effectiveness*. London: Sage Publications.

Crompton, J.L. and Lamb, C.W. (1986) *Marketing Government and Social Services.* New York: John Wiley & Sons.

Driver, J.C. and Foxall, G.R. (1984) *Advertising Policy and Practice.* London: Holt, Rinehart and Winston.

Dyer, G. (1982) *Advertising as Communication.* London: Methuen.

Ferguson, M. (ed) (1990) *Public Communication. The New Imperatives.* London: Sage Publications.

Galbraith, J.K. (1958) *The Affluent Society.* London: Hamish Hamilton.

Gilligan, C. and Crowther, G. (1976) *Advertising Management.* Oxford: Philip Allen.

Hamilton, C. and Parker, C. (1990) *Communicating for Results* (3rd edn). Belmont, California: Wadsworth Publishing Company.

Harrison, S. (1995) *Public Relations. An Introduction.* London: Routledge and Kegan Paul.

Hartley, P. (1993) *Interpersonal Communication.* London and New York: Routledge and Kegan Paul.

Heath, R. L. and Nelson, R.A. (1986) *Issues Management. Corporate Public Policymaking in an Information Society.* London: Sage Publications.

Kotler, P. and Roberto, E.L. (1989) *Social Marketing. Strategies for Changing Public Behavior.* New York: The Free Press (Macmillan, Inc.).

Jefkins, F. (1992) *Advertising Made Simple* (5th edn). Oxford: Butterworth–Heinemann.

Leiss, W., Klein, S. and Jhally, S. (1986) *Social Communication in Advertising.* London: Methuen.

Mander, J. (1977) *Four Arguments for the Elimination of Television.* New York: William Morrow.

Marcuse, H. (1964) *One-Dimensional Man.* Boston: Beacon Press.

McPhee, R.D. and Tompkins, P.K. (1985) *Organizational Communication: Traditional Themes and New Directions.* Beverly Hills, California: Sage Publications.

Morgan, G. (1986) *Images of Organisation.* London: Sage Publications.

O'Connell, S.E. (1979) *The Manager as Communicator.* Lanham, New York and London: University of America Press.

Packard, V. (1957) *The Hidden Persuaders.* New York: D. McKay.

Rasberry, R.W. and Lemoine, L.F. (1986) *Effective Management Communication.* Boston, Massachusettts: Kent Publishing Company.

Rogers, E.M. and Agarwala-Rogers, R. (1976) *Communication in Organizations.* New York: The Free Press.

Severin, W.J. with Tankard, J.W. Jr. (1988) *Communication Theories. Origins, Methods, Uses.* New York and London: Longman.

Solomon, D.S. (1989) 'A Social Marketing Perspective on Communication Campaigns' in Rice, R.E. and Atkin, C.K. (eds) *Public Communication Campaigns.* London: Sage Publications.

Steinberg, S.H. (1955) *Five Hundred Years of Printing.* Harmondsworth: Penguin Books.

Swingewood, A. (1977) *The Myth of Mass Culture.* London: Macmillan.

Tomes, A.E. and Harrison, B. (1991) 'The Marketing of a Community Service', *Journal of Marketing Management*, 7, 157–65.

Wallack, L. (1989) 'Mass Communication and Health Promotion: A Critical Perspective' in Rice, R.E. and Atkin, C. K. (eds) *Public Communication Campaigns.* London: Sage Publications.

Wells, W., Burnett, J. and Moriarty, S. (1992) *Advertising, Principles and Practice* (2nd edn). Englewood Cliffs, New Jersey: Prentice-Hall.

Wilkinson, T. (ed) (1989) *The Communications Challenge. Personnel and PR Perspectives.* London: Institute of Personnel Management.

Williams, A., Dobson, P. and Walters, M. (1989) *Changing Culture.* London: Institute of Personnel Management, pp. 80–81.

Wilmshurst, J. (1984) *The Fundamentals and Practice of Marketing.* Oxford: Butterworth–Heinemann.

Wilmshurst, J. (1985) *The Fundamentals of Advertising.* Oxford: Butterworth–Heinemann.

Yudelson, P. (1988) 'The Four Ps of Nonprofit Marketing', *Nonprofit World*, 6, November/December, 21–3.

CHAPTER 10

Information and the learning organisation

If organisations are to be adaptable and arrange themselves to meet the needs of their various markets, action has to be taken on the basis of sound information. Throughout this book it is assumed that managers can only act effectively if they have good information on which to base their actions and in this regard, the public sector is little different from the private sector. Furthermore, organisational development through an organisational learning process can only be achieved if information is acted upon to change the organisation to the necessary extent.

This chapter examines the roles of market intelligence, including market research, and information technology in evaluating data and making information more accessible to managers. However, the chapter is not only concerned with the mechanics of data gathering and information processing. The organisational issues concerned with using information to the benefit of both the organisation's markets and the organisation itself, are discussed.

**KEY LEARNING
OUTCOMES**

By the end of this chapter, you should be able to:

- appreciate that information is essential to the innovative marketing process;
- understand that information needs to be constantly updated to take account of the changing business environment;
- understand that information concerns the *interpretation* of data;
- consider the importance of intelligence gathering as marketing research;
- explore the impact of information technology (IT) as a useful and essential tool; and
- consider the advantages of continuous learning.

Introduction

If good communication skills and techniques are essential to the marketing process, so too is information – its interpretation and use. If marketing is about identifying needs and finding ways to meet them, any organisation needs relevant information about its environment and its markets. Various dimensions of the environment have been examined in previous chapters, and methods of identifying market segments were discussed in Chapter 5. We now look at the forms this information can take, and how the organisation can use it most effectively.

Marketing intelligence

Many conceptual models are represented either as static constructions – for example, models of organisational hierarchy – or as step-by-step processes – for example, the model of the 'adoption process' discussed in Chapter 9. Many models fail to acknowledge the fact that processes are often iterative – that is, they need to be repeated over and over again as they have to respond to changing situations. Just as communication often depends on 'feedback' to confirm and clarify a message, so information needs constantly to be updated in response to changes in the environment and in the market.

The processes involved may be compared with the functions of weather stations, which constantly monitor changes in the physical environment and provide data which is collated, analysed and interpreted in order to produce patterns of probabilities and predictions. Weather data is used in two ways: it is interpreted to provide a picture of a current weather situation, and it is used to update existing historical data that is used for forecasting purposes. Any organisation is dependent on its environment, which includes its markets, for its very existence. Like the weather, these are constantly changing.

An organisation therefore needs information in order to reduce risk in decision making and to be able to respond to its markets in effective ways.

- It needs information about its own, *internal environment*, its resources, its performance, abilities and competencies which enable it to operate effectively.

- It needs information about its *external environment* to identify problems and opportunities which will shape its strategies (Oliver, 1990, pp. 173–9).

As in weather forecasting, market intelligence is not an exact science. It still requires elements of art and judgement. Information can be misinterpreted. The wrong assumptions can be made. The hurricane that hit the South of England on 16 October 1987 was not forecast to cause the disruption and damage that actually occurred. Weather forecasters had been adamant that there would be no hurricane that night. Their admission that they had been wrong was interpreted by many as an admission of failure. However, the exceptional mistake does not diminish the importance of gathering information, or reduce the value of learning by mistakes. On the contrary, it emphasises the importance of obtaining good information in order to ensure that an organisation is as sensitive as possible to changes in its environment and to trends in its markets. All organisations need information about their environments and their markets if they are to develop successful strategies for achieving their goals.

The nature and importance of information

Information is never a neutral concept. It is very rarely objective. Although it can be argued that data are 'facts', those data do not become useful information until they are interpreted in some way. We are all familiar with the tiresome way some politicians frequently state that 'the fact is ...', when they really mean that 'my belief or interpretation is ...'. Interpretation inevitably involves some subjectivity, the exercise of some judgements and opinions about the criteria used to select data, and about their significance. Even a computer 'expert system' that interprets data will only be as good as the judgements which were made when it was programmed with the criteria it first uses, even when 'intelligent systems' are used. The heuristics, or rules incorporated into such systems, are first obtained from human experts in the relevant fields.

Wilkinson (1989) makes another important point in emphasising that simply giving people information is *not* communicating, because people are only interested in what they perceive as relevant and understandable. The organisation that faithfully circulates copies of most departmental and committee meetings to all its staff is making a serious contribution to the flow of waste paper, or is in danger of overloading the file-servers on its electronic mail systems.

The expression 'information is power' is well-worn. Information can endow organisations and individuals with a great deal of power. It can be manipulated, used selectively or even withheld. Those 'gate-keepers' who control information can exercise considerable influence. Information is an important and valuable commodity. It provides the tools with which to monitor the performance of an organisation, the means of establishing the organisation's 'best fit' with its environment, and a way of determining strategy (*see* Chapter 12).

Any organisation can affect the nature of its operations and of its environment by the information it produces itself. Some of this information is obviously needed for the purposes of control (*see* Chapter 6) and accountability. Hopwood and Tomkins (1984) noted the way in which, for example, public accountability can be defined as a statutory obligation to provide information and justification of activities for scrutiny and debate. The idea of accountability involves interpretation, evaluation, responsibility and, where appropriate, the use of sanctions. Accountability is concerned with probity (honesty), legality, efficiency (no waste of resources), good administration, justice and equity. Most public bodies are expected to meet these 'bases of accountability' and the standards set for them.

In the UK, the National Audit Commission, established by the 1982 Local Government Finance Act, but responsible to the Secretary of State for the Environment, has a responsibility both for regulatory and inspectorial audits and for operational audits of public sector organisations. Public accountability extends beyond financial probity and legality. It also involves processes and policies which are much more difficult to measure by pre-set standards, and therefore involves public sector accountants using information, criteria of judgement and languages other than, or in addition to, the traditional ones of financial accounting (Hopwood & Tomkins, 1984, pp. 29–33).

Information, therefore, has a central role to play in public sector organisations. It is also an important aspect of the organisation's marketing activities.

The quality of information is important to all managers, because the quality of decisions and problem solving will in part depend upon the quality of the information available. Top management has a number of high priority tasks (*see*, for example, Garratt, 1987). Senior managers need to provide employees with a clear sense of purpose and direction in order to ensure that they work effectively. They

Information and interpretation

Access to information is regarded as an essential ingredient of openness and as a means of raising levels of public accountability. There are, however, occasions when the publication of information, especially that which could be seen as having a promotional function, may appear counter-productive.

The Sunday Express's 1994 'Golden Fleece' campaign encouraged its readers to 'blow the whistle' on any departments of government which could be said to be 'squandering' public money. On 13 February 1994, the paper took the NHS to task for its annual spending of some £5 million on glossy annual reports for hospital trusts and district health authorities. Quality printing, colour graphics and pictures of celebrities were included in literature which many busy general practitioners admitted to binning, unread. The then Shadow Health Minister, Dawn Primarolo, was quoted as saying that there should be less waste on public relations and more meaningful consultation with the public. The Department of Health at the time was said to have issued no guidelines on the production of reports. Since trusts and health authorities are competing for contracts, such reports are likely to serve both a promotional and an informative function.

are also responsible for making decisions, planning organisational activities and monitoring the environment within which the organisation operates. These last responsibilities rely heavily on the availability of good quality information.

If the organisation is going to be effective, and in order to make decisions about how best to satisfy users' needs, the organisation must have information about itself, its environment and its markets. Most people in organisations, particularly organisations in the public sector, are familiar with the role information plays internally – for example, in the processes (sometimes very bureaucratic ones) which are used to monitor performance. However, the organisation's relationships with its environment are also essential to its function and effectiveness. Unfortunately, members of most organisations spend most of their time involved with operational matters, and so may not realise the real importance of information about the organisation's environment.

Sprague and McNurlin (1993) categorise information used by any organisation under two headings: *information based on data*, and *document-based information* in the form of reports, memoranda, etc. The sources for each of these can be either internal or external. The growth of demand for external market information has contributed to the rapid growth of on-line database services. The external environment contains the organisation's most important markets. If an organisation is to identify its markets' needs and find ways of satisfying them, it needs to be able to collect data about those markets which can form the basis of decisions and judgements.

Moreover, these data will be modified constantly as situations change. They need to be monitored regularly. The effective organisation usually needs to research its markets continuously, seeking both new facts and evidence of trends.

Market information (*see* Crimp, 1985, p. 3) has two main purposes:

● to reduce uncertainty in the planning process; and
● to assess the results of the strategy once it is implemented.

Market information can be assembled from various sources, and the process of collecting and interpreting it is usually termed 'market research'. It can make a vital contribution to how an organisation functions, enabling the organisation to analyse its markets and identify existing and developing needs. It helps the organisation plan its activities, improving the services it provides and developing new approaches. It provides the data with which the organisation measures and controls its performance (*see* Chisnall, 1991, pp. 4–5).

The nature of marketing research

The marketing concept is about identifying customer needs and wants, and finding the best ways of satisfying them to the benefit of both the organisation and the customer. A Chartered Institute of Marketing definition defines marketing as the 'management process responsible for identifying, anticipating and satisfying customer requirements profitably (Hannagan, 1992, p. 53).

The concept of profitability must be modified for non-profit and for many public sector organisations, and usually then means 'using resources most effectively for the best user/client/customer satisfaction'. It follows that marketing needs information about customers, clients and users. It needs information and intelligence about their environment, their situations, values, attitudes, habits and preferences. Virtually all organisations, private or public, need more and better information about their markets (Aaker *et al.*, 1995). Marketing research is an intelligence-gathering activity, which involves collecting relevant data systematically and interpreting them. It provides information on which decisions can be based. Baker (1991) agrees that there are three main categories of decisions involved:

- determining marketing goals which are realistic and attainable;
- developing effective marketing plans and putting them into practice;
- evaluating the results and effectiveness of the process.

Marketing research has developed by adapting methods from a broad range of other disciplines.

- It uses *statistical techniques*, such as sampling, in assembling quantitative data.
- It uses *economic models* to describe the production and distribution of wealth.
- It borrows from *sociology, anthropology* and *psychology* in its examination of human groupings, culture and behaviour, qualitatively as well as quantitatively.

It is therefore not surprising to note that Mass Observation – a late 1930s experiment in collecting data about how people lived and thought in 1938 (resulting in a fascinating archive of material on British society and attitudes, which is now stored at the University of Sussex) – found its eventual role as a marketing research organisation.

There are enormous amounts of data available, so much so that deciding which data are important and which are not has become an important skill. Marketing research needs to be focused. Managers need to decide which kinds of data are going to be required for the particular kinds of decisions they have to make. They are usually not just seeking information about the environment; they need feedback about the markets' response to their own activities. For these reasons, marketing research needs to be undertaken only if it is *relevant, accurate* and *timely* (Aaker *et al.*, 1995, p. 2). It must genuinely be *needed*, if it is to contribute to ongoing decision-making processes, and to produce good quality information at the right time. Managers must be convinced that it represents a real cost benefit to the organisation.

The marketing research process

We have already made the point that the marketing research process borrows liberally from the social sciences, statistics, anthropology and psychology. The methods available to marketing research can generally be classified under the headings of *survey, observation* and *experimentation* (Baker, 1991).

The marketing research process has been modelled in various ways – for example, by Baker (1991, p. 39), Chisnall (1992, p. 25), Aaker *et al.* (1995, p. 44) and Gilligan and Lowe (1995, p. 60). The essential elements of the process are represented in Table 10.1.

Once again, it should be emphasised that a 'feedback loop' is involved. The process needs to be an iterative process in which the understanding of the problem can continually be improved and refined. Steps 5 and 6 in Table 10.1 also highlight the existence of two categories of data available: *secondary data* and *primary data*.

Secondary data

Secondary data are available from published sources which have already collected and collated it. They include the results of research programmes by all sorts of agen-

Table 10.1 The marketing research process

	Aims	Tasks
1	Strategic plan	Decide what goals are being sought
2	Problem recognition, specification and definition	Decide what problems and opportunities are involved
3	Cost benefit of research	Assess whether the benefit is likely to be greater than the cost. If so, continue
4	Research plan	Decide how research is to be conducted
5	Collection of data 1	Use secondary sources. If adequate, go to Step 7
6	Collection of data 2	Design and implement use of primary sources
7	Preparation and analysis of data	Interpret and identify implications
8	Production and circulation of report	Make recommendations
9	Decision making	Implement decisions
10	Evaluation	Draw conclusions from experience and feed back into process at Step 1.

cies which provide statistics and trends on areas of interest, such as demography and consumption (*see* Baker, 1985, p. 205). Government publications include both census and statistical material. Chambers of Commerce and Trade Associations publish information about business conditions and specific industries. The press (especially papers with sections devoted to specific subjects) regularly provides certain kinds of data. Commercial marketing research organisations, such as Gallup, sell information on a vast range of topics. Academic institutions and journals publish the results of various research programmes.

It is obviously an advantage if these secondary data can be obtained 'off the shelf' and conducted as *desk research*. Information of this sort can be relatively easy to collect and collate on a regular basis for the organisation's marketing system. Such secondary research can provide essential market information. It uses readily accessible sources of information – for example, from libraries, universities, business schools, information centres and government publications (the UK Government Social Survey started operating in 1941).

This type of information can often be used to identify trends, and can be relatively cheap. However, it cannot act as a substitute for (usually expensive) *field research*, although it is useful in forming hypotheses which can then be explored using primary data.

Primary data

Primary data are acquired from self-initiated and/or commissioned programmes of research, such as consumer studies targeted at specific products or services and their consumption or use. Primary, or field, research uses observations of behaviour, experimentation (such as attempts to understand the probable responses to changes in the marketing mix), sampling and opinion polls. Opinion polls have become increasingly familiar, whether through postal surveys or in the form of those somewhat predatory figures clutching clip-boards who seek to ambush the unwary pedestrian in every public concourse.

The *questionnaire* is a common marketing research tool in many public sector organisations. It could be argued that the questionnaire has become far too ubiquitous, and increasingly attracts only those voluntary respondents who actually enjoy completing them, or who consider their completion a responsible act of citizenship. The questionnaire is a means of obtaining specific responses to a problem which has already been defined. It seeks to obtain valid and reliable information with a minimum of bias and distortion (Chisnall, 1992, pp. 109–38). Its preparation and design requires a high level of expertise, a fact which is sometimes not appreciated. Questionnaires need to be worded clearly and unambiguously, and the instructions for their completion need to be clear and precise (Baker, 1991, pp. 132–58).

Interviews function to obtain information about how respondents interpret phenomena and may be conducted on either a one-to-one or a group basis. *Focus groups* use simultaneous interviews with small groups of people, generating discussion and eliciting views. (The advantages and disadvantages of such techniques are discussed, for example, by Gill and Johnson (1991).)

Interviews can use either *fixed-option questions* or *semi-structured questions*. Fixed-option questions can produce quantifiable, comparable results, but they can be relatively insensitive in the way that standardised (*pro forma*) questions impose their own restraints on the way in which they may be answered. Semi-structured questions can obtain much more sensitive results and a better depth of understanding, but are expensive on time and produce data which may be difficult to compare.

Focus groups (Churchill, 1995) can be used to obtain information on complex issues, can obtain more spontaneous responses to questions and generate information for self-completed questionnaires. However, they are expensive in time and can be easily dominated by certain individuals in a group. They can be difficult to interpret and they are susceptible to researcher bias.

It is not always easy to conduct market research. There is always a danger that it is only possible to obtain data from those who are prepared to give it, and there seem to be increasing numbers of people who are loath to give responses to questionnaires and interviews.

Both secondary and primary research can be conducted in order to obtain data which is useful in developing products/services, finding out more about customer/ user needs, or about the effectiveness of promotions. It should be borne in mind, however, that primary research is usually much more expensive than secondary research, and needs to be evaluated carefully in terms of its opportunity costs.

It is also useful to distinguish between two broad categories of data: *quantitative data* and *qualitative data*.

- *Quantitative data.* These are concerned with size, volume, frequency and other measurable aspects of use. Some writers (for example, Baker, 1985, pp. 203–4) have focused on the fact that some managers seem frightened of dealing with quantitative analysis, but in our experience, many managers are inclined to regard quantitative information favourably because it is seen as 'scientific', and measurable. Its 'factual' nature often gives managers confidence because they believe it can reduce uncertainty. Quantitative data of this sort are sometimes referred to as 'objective facts' (Wilmshurst, 1984, pp. 124–5). Unfortunately, although the manager can use quantitative data to *identify* patterns and trends, he or she cannot use them to *explain* such features and to identify values and opinions. Quantitative data always require interpretation.

- *Qualitative data.* These are sometimes described as 'psychological data' (*see* Oliver, 1986, pp. 128–31), or even as 'subjective facts', and are concerned with users' perceptions, motivations and attitudes. These are often measured, using tools such as questionnaires and panels, but may also involve semi-structured and even unstructured individual interview techniques. 'Subjective data' often involve so-called 'non-rational factors' (Chisnall, 1985, pp. 12–13) which may serve to qualify the belief that decisions are always rational by nature.

Although quantitative data are often regarded as the source of 'hard' information and qualitative data as producing 'soft' information, both forms are necessary. There are numerous examples of organisations, both commercial and public sector, misunderstanding or misinterpreting the nature of demand. Marketing research should be capable of providing the appropriate information, although there are always instances when demand will not behave in the way predicted – for example, in the case of a new product launch. When Euro Disney, near Paris, first encountered financial problems after its launch, there were many suggestions that its managers had failed to appreciate the differences in the cultural habits of Europeans, especially those of French customers who, for example, were relatively unaccustomed to 'browsing' burgers and were more inclined to take 'eating out' as a serious, and more time-consuming activity. Such information was available. Its significance may not have been realised.

Uses of marketing research

Marketing research can be used to define and measure a wide range of items, all of which can provide data and information for marketing decisions. Allowing for the market differences between private and public sectors, these categories can include:

- *Patterns of use.* These are the ways in which clients use products/services, and any changes or trends in those uses over time.
- *Perceptions of products/services.* These range from beliefs and cultural attitudes towards them, to expectations of benefits that are thought to derive from them.
- *Attitudes towards products/services.* Attitudes are dispositions towards things or ideas, developed as the result of experience and which influence behaviour. They determine the ways individuals interpret and respond to experiences. They reveal feelings and are usually difficult to change.
- *Motivation for using products/services.* Motivation is concerned with the relationship between needs and their satisfaction. A motivation can be instinctive or learned (*see* Chapter 2).
- *Types of users.* The classification of users into various types or market segments was discussed in Chapter 5.
- *Competition.* This involves an exploration of any market competition, actual and potential.

(For a comparable analysis of private sector areas of measurement, *see* Chisnall, 1991, p. 33.)

These are important to all marketing processes in that they provide information about the consumers/users and their needs and wants. Whereas the first and the last categories are essentially quantitative, the others listed are qualitative. Attitudes are particularly important because they indicate likely behaviour – the readiness to do certain things in certain circumstances. Attitudes are strongly related to beliefs – essential components of value systems and cultures. As such, they are powerful influences on the way in which people understand things, their emotional (or 'affective') response to things, and the ways in which they behave in the relevant situations. These aspects are discussed under the headings of 'cognitive', 'affective' and 'conative' by, for example, Williams (1981, p. 99), using the basic model of the adoption process described in Chapter 9, Fig. 9.2.

Sampling techniques

It has long been recognised (Cooke and Slack, 1984) that our concepts of rationality are limited and 'bounded' in various ways (a point originally made by Simon in

1976). A perfect decision would, in theory, require all data to be available. This is never possible in practice, and the individual usually makes decisions and choices on the basis of a limited, personal and approximate model of the situation. There is much evidence to suggest that rationality has its limits, and, moreover, that many decisions are only rationalised after the event.

In theory, it would be interesting to obtain *all* the information that might have a bearing on a marketing problem, consulting all the factors and all the people involved. Although it would be theoretically possible to ask questions of all the population, the task would certainly not be cost effective and, in any case, would take far too long, even if all its members agreed to respond. A census usually takes many months or years to prepare and publish, whereas a survey can produce results relatively quickly.

Faced with the need to look for specific data, the marketing researcher usually needs to identify a sample of the population he/she wants to study, selected in such a way that it can confidently be expected to *represent* the characteristics of the whole population. The *population* refers to the totality of people or items involved. In some cases – for example, national census surveys and electoral registers – it may be possible to obtain some information about the whole of a population, but in view of the fact that a large population is likely to be changing all the time, a carefully selected sample of the population may be more accurate, and certainly easier and cheaper to research.

We have already made the point (*see* Chapter 5) that 'the market' is not homogeneous; it is composed of a number of different groups. For this reason, researchers have to decide which populations – that is, which market segments – they need to examine, and the best way of sampling them. Obviously, a population can only be regarded as accessible if it can be identified and defined. Market segmentation is a useful tool in the process of identification.

It is important that the information obtained is both reliable (free from bias and errors) and valid (accurate and specific). Sampling can never be 100 per cent accurate, but distortion can be controlled. The researcher uses a *sampling frame* – a carefully defined population from which the sample is drawn. There are two main types of sampling used in marketing research:

1 *Quota sampling* – or 'purposive sampling', in which the sample is defined in advance, using categories such as socio-economic groups, age, gender, etc. Quota sampling is often used when there is a need to keep costs down or to obtain results relatively quickly. Using published sources, such as census data, research workers are given the task of finding a quota of respondents who fit the definitions required by the quotas they are given. Unfortunately, quota sampling is open to criticism on the grounds that it is open to bias. Research workers who target a shopping complex on weekdays, for example, may find it relatively difficult to interview people who are in work. There is also the danger that researchers can inadvertently introduce elements of bias if they fail to follow their procedures with sufficient rigour.

2 *Random sampling* – or 'probability sampling', using a defined population. Probability sampling is based on the probability that a group of randomly selected members of a population will represent the population as a whole.

Random samples are constructed in such a way that every member of the chosen population has an equal chance of being included in a survey. This is usually considered to be a more objective method, and is commonly used for social surveys. However, its effective use depends on accurate listings of populations (the sample frames), which are not always easy to find or determine.

Random, or probability sampling, is the only type of sampling which can produce statistically valid results, because every member of a population has a chance of being chosen for the survey. In some ways it is also the most difficult technique. It requires the identification and numbering of every sampling unit used, all of whom have to be contacted directly in order to obtain measurements and responses.

Measurement

For marketing research purposes, we usually need data on variables which can be expressed numerically, in terms of percentages or proportions of populations. Even qualitative attitudes can be measured with the use of scales which allow us to give numerical values to events. There are at least five scales of measurement in common use: *nominal, ordinal, interval, ratio* and *rating* scales.

- *Nominal scales.* These are simple forms of measurement which describe classification by attributes such as gender (male or female), or region. Nominal scales cannot meaningfully be subjected to arithmetical operations, because they only record differences of categories.

- *Ordinal scales.* These have the properties of nominal scales, but also rank categories along a continuum. Socio-economic groups and social classes, for example, are usually considered as ordinal variables.

- *Interval scales.* These have many characteristics in common with ordinal scales, but, unlike ordinal scales, interval scales define their categories in units of measurement. However, an interval scale has no absolute zero point. A point can be established anywhere along a continuum. Temperature measurement is sometimes cited as a good example of an interval scale, because the zero is fixed in an arbitrary way on the Fahrenheit scale, for example. On such a scale temperatures can rise or fall, but the term 'twice as cold' would be fairly meaningless.

- *Ratio scales.* These have the characteristics of interval scales but also have absolute zero points. They are therefore obviously useful for measuring variables such as age, income, etc.

- *Rating scales.* These use a scale of categories from which the respondent chooses one of, perhaps, five responses to a statement: strongly agree, agree, neutral ('uncertain' or 'neither agree nor disagree'), disagree, strongly disagree. If numerical values are assigned to the response categories, high and low scores can be interpreted as positive and negative attitudes. Likert's scale is an example of a rating scale (Likert, 1932).

    One technique which uses a rating scale is the use of *semantic differentials.*

    Originally devised in 1957 (Osgood *et al.*, 1957), this technique asks respondents to judge an idea on a seven-point scale between two descriptive adjectives at opposite ends – for example, 'strong' and 'weak', or 'good' and 'bad'. It may be necessary to conduct some preliminary study to determine the most appropriate adjectives to use, and they are best presented in a random order. It is worth bearing in mind that, as with any use of scaled questionnaire, respondents can only rate the attributes that the questionnaire presents them with. It is important to emphasise that questionnaires need to be designed carefully in terms of length, complexity, layout and wording in order to obtain meaningful results while retaining the interest of respondents. Moreover, perceptions of qualities, such as 'good' and 'bad', may differ between respondents.

It remains important to ensure that the method of measurement is *appropriate* for the task in hand. In order to collect relevant information, the marketer must be clear about the nature of the problem and about the objectives of the exercise. This is not always as straightforward as might be thought. In Minicase 10.2, the researcher encountered initial problems in defining the nature of the 'product' itself, because the concept of 'a primary-care led National Health Service' was not only relatively new, but there was no apparent consensus about the definition of the term. Was the concept about structure, process, efficiency, effectiveness, innovation, a combination of all of these or of just a few? In view of this situation, it was apparent that simple questionnaires were unlikely to produce useful information about whether or not people thought that a 'primary-care led NHS' would address the real patient issues. The methodology actually used involved both interviews and focus groups. Qualitative questions were analysed, using a Likert scoring method, and some useful results were obtained.

MINICASE 10.2

Who wants a primary-care led National Health Service?

A Sheffield Business School 1997 MBA dissertation by D. Sloan (to whom the authors are indebted for permission to use some of the material) examined responses from both general practitioners and patients to the concept of a 'Primary-care led National Health Service'. This term had first appeared in a UK Department of Health circular in April 1995 (NHS National Executive, 1995) but there was no official or prescriptive definition of the term. In order to obtain information about how general practitioners (doctors) and patients viewed possible developments in this direction, observations and surveys were carried out using semi-structured interviews with representatives from the majority of GP practices in one locality and patient focus groups from two towns in the same area.

The results of these particular surveys were interesting. They suggested that GPs see the concept of a 'primary-care led NHS' in terms of providing increased value for money, improved quality, primary health care purchasing and a stronger primary health care team. However, they did not see it as a way to give patients more power to take choices about their own health. They were keen to improve the quality of their services and to be responsible for the resources which they and their patients consumed. Patients, however, despite protestations that they believed in health promotion and taking responsibility for their own health, were more in favour of secondary care which could provide the 'high' technology medical services for serious illnesses and pain reduction.

The impact of information technology

Information processing and communication systems have revolutionised the quantity and the quality of information available to organisations (Lenk, 1982). Management is now the largest user of information technology (IT). Since the 1960s, IT has been an area of major economic growth. The development of personal computers and networks have moved computing from its early dependence upon mainframe machines to the use of network communications and laptop machines, and to much greater accessibility. This has complemented changes in the traditional work environment which Ralph Sprague and Barbara McNurlin (1993) characterise as including more team working, greater accessibility to information, and less hierarchical organisational structures.

Blattberg *et al.* (1994) highlight the way in which information has its own value chain, with five discrete elements: *data collection and transmission; data management; data interpretation; models;* and *decision support systems.*

- *Data collection* has now reached the stage where the sheer amount of data available can threaten to overwhelm the user. IT has contributed to reductions in the cost of collecting data. IT has increased both the speed of 'capture' and the volume of data available. All the more important, therefore, to ensure that the data are *managed* effectively, interpreted and processed in such a way that they become relevant and valuable to the users.

- *Database management.* Database management systems are therefore essential if data are to be used in the most effective ways. Any information system depends upon the selection of *relevant* data.

- *Data interpretation.* The growth of 'expert systems' is the result of developing computer programs to search, analyse and report on data, allowing managers to concentrate on those problems and possibilities which are determined as important. They have the advantage of producing interpretations which are easy to understand.

- *Information modelling* uses statistical models to summarise data, which can then be used as the basis of decision making, adding further to the value of the data. Pie charts and bar charts have become everyday management tools.

- *Decision support systems* (DSSs). It has been suggested by writers, such as Hoch (Blattberg *et al.*, 1994, pp. 253–69) that the most effective use of systems is to combine the results of the technology – for example, the information models – with the intuition of the human experts. Marketing decision support systems (MDSSs) have been in use for some time. These depend largely upon their use of models to test various theories regarding how the markets may work in specific contexts and conditions, and upon optimisation – that is, techniques designed to improve performance by identifying or developing alternative ways of doing things. Although MDSSs provide ways of organising and accessing data, however, the real value of the data can only be understood as a result of data interpretation.

One of the most important consequences of the IT revolution is the development of more interactive information flows between providers and users, producers and consumers. In this situation, marketing's role will concern itself more and more with managing the relationships between them (Blattenberg *et al.*, 1994, p. 29).

Information processing and technology has become critical to many business and public sector operations. Since information technology is a high-expenditure activity, these developments represent major investments. Earl (1989) calculated that in large, leading European organisations, the information technology budget was growing at the rate of between 20 and 40 per cent each year. Some public sector organisations have made an even greater investment. In recent years, the information technology function is one of the few areas to have continued its growth.

As Lenk (1982) pointed out, however, the use of IT – for example, automated data processing in public administration – did not lead automatically to innovative ways of doing things. It merely provided ways of handling existing procedures more effectively. It has obvious advantages for routine processes concerned with employment services, taxation, benefit entitlement, and administrative functions (especially in the National Health Service). This has resulted in many public sector industries using IT in three main ways:

1 *large-scale operational systems* designed to perform standard calculations on variables such as utility services consumption or income tax assessments, etc.;

2 *data base systems* designed to support routine operations – for example, a student management system for a college or university, which may contain data on student names, genders, ages, addresses, registrations, sources of fees, module enrolments, assessment results and academic credits, years of study, library borrowing status, financial standing with the institution, award classifications, graduate employment, etc.;

3 *information systems* designed to provide data of a statistical kind for 'intelligence' purposes, such as trends, in forms which can be useful for decision making.

One consequence of the development of centralised information gathering has been an increased ability to centralise control. The issue of power remains a sensitive one in areas such as data protection, privacy, and the power of bureaucracies. In many, if not most public sector industries, IT can often be seen as merely another (and often more efficient) form of control, even if its users see it primarily in terms of an enabling tool. However, its advantages are increasingly obvious in many areas. For example, universities are seeing marketing information systems applied to undergraduate recruitment (*see* Gabbot, in Chapman and Holtham, 1994, pp. 255–74), because the political pressure to increase the participation rate in higher education has created a real need to improve the universities' understanding of their markets.

At the heart of marketing systems using IT is the creation of the database – a collection of information on customers, users and clients, structured in such a way that it is most useful to the organisation (*see* Baker, in Chapman and Holtham, 1994, pp. 25–39). We must stress again, however, that data have to be *interpreted* if they are to be useful. An information system must serve the needs of its users, not the interests of the IT specialist. Information is a means to an end, not an end in itself. It has been a common experience to find that many organisations have been persuaded to buy software programs 'off the shelf' because they have invested insufficient effort in defining the problems they really need to address. The real benefits of IT, as a means of collecting, distributing and using information in any organisation, will depend in the find analysis upon the particular requirements and characteristics of the specific industry and organisation. Applications will always need to be tailored to the demands of a given situation.

Some database marketing methods are proving extremely useful to public sector organisations. One such example is 'postcode geography' (*see* Rickman's paper in Chapman and Holtham, 1994, pp. 191–201). UK postcodes were introduced in the 1960s, specifying areas, districts, sectors and units. The Royal Mail now produces and markets products based on its Postcode Address File (PAF). Among the public sector organisations which currently use postcode data are central and local government, health authorities, the armed forces and the police, utility companies, emergency services, environmental agencies, museums and academic institutions. Their marketing applications depend upon user segmentation. The postcode has become an important source of marketing information. However, the development of geographic information systems (GISs) again require careful definitions of the strategic problems organisations seek to address.

Information systems have a huge potential input to any organisation's marketing functions. Marketing needs as much relevant data and information as possible about the external environment, about users, customers and clients. IT is, therefore, a powerful marketing tool. It is surprising to find that, in 1996, the UK public sector was, apparently, still not using its benefits to the full (*see* Minicase 10.3).

MINICASE 10.3

Computer specialists earning high salaries in the public sector

Roger Trapp, in an article in *The Independent* of 12 June 1996, commented on the results of a survey carried out by Binder Hamlyn and *Internal Auditing* magazine. The survey revealed that a significant proportion of public sector audit departments did not use computers to handle many tasks which were routinely handled by the use of IT in private sector organisations (some 70 per cent of internal audit departments employed no qualified computer specialists).

There was such a high demand in both sectors for computing expertise – for example, in systems security and operations, disaster recovery procedures, etc. – that demand for good specialists was outstripping supply. The major reforms in public sector organisations, including the National Health Service, and in local government had created a need for 'proper' accounting systems and controls, despite the fact that some 55 per cent of internal audit departments were, apparently, still not involved in IT procurement or systems development. The demand was so great that good IT specialists, including short-term 'contractors', were commanding high salary premiums.

The need for continuous learning

Once marketing research has produced and interpreted data, the information is available for use. The effectiveness of that use depends upon the ability of the organisation to learn from it. In recent years, the realisation has finally dawned that organisations *need* to learn in order to keep pace with their changing environment.

Morgan (1989) stressed the increasing importance of recruiting people who enjoy learning. Garratt (1987) sees learning as the key to survival and growth.

Learning, in some form, is usually a life-long process for all individuals. In a modern world, it would be foolish to assume that a basic school education will suffice for a single lifetime. It seems increasingly unlikely that the traditional equation of one life equals one career will be maintained as a norm in the twenty-first century. The increasing pace of technology and change demands that individuals continue to learn. 'In-service training' and 'staff development' have become necessities and norms for many within both the private and the public sectors. Moreover, learning has many benefits. It is often undertaken by people of all ages as a leisure pursuit, not merely as a vocational need. It can increase people's sense of personal worth, and contribute to job satisfaction and motivation. Since organisations consist of people, who create synergy, we can also talk of *organisational learning*.

The learning organisation

Once information has been gathered, it needs to be used. If it is to be effective, it needs to contribute to the organisation's pattern of learning. An increasing number of writers have considered that it is the responsibility of management to improve the quality of their organisation's operations – that is, the quality of the work done by people inside an organisation. This 'enabling' function of management is, for example, the focus of Salaman's (1995) book on management. Peter Senge (1990a & b) of the MIT Sloan School of Management was one of the first to popularise the idea of 'learning organisations'. Senge sees learning organisations as creative institutions, in that they are skilled at obtaining knowledge and modifying their behaviour in the light of experience. Such abilities include (*see* Garwin, 1993):

- *Learning from experience*. Any organisation needs to review and evaluate its own performance, to recognise its successes and failures. Unfortunately, many of us live in cultures where failure is usually deemed unsatisfactory, or even an indictment of ability. In fact, a great deal can be learned from failures, which make an important contribution to the learning curves of all individuals and organisations.

- *Learning from other organisations*. Information from the experience of others often provides useful ideas, some of which can be 'borrowed' to advantage, and can be used for the purpose of benchmarking.

- *Trying out new ways of doing things*. This involves deliberately seeking out new approaches through experiments and projects.

- *Spreading new ideas*. This is seen in how quickly and effectively an organisation communicates new ideas and persuades people to adopt them.

It is therefore important to understand something about the processes through which learning takes place.

The learning process

One of the best known models of learning is the Kolb (1979) learning cycle. In this model (*see* Fig. 10.1), learning is represented as a cyclical process which repeatedly, and ideally continuously, proceeds from abstract conceptualisation through active experi-

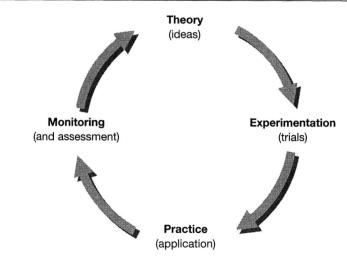

Fig. 10.1 A learning-cycle approach
(after Kolb *et al.*, 1979)

mentation, hands-on experience and reflection, and back to abstract conceptualisation again. Argyris (1991) maintains that most people 'do not know how to learn'.

This model, based on the work of Kolb *et al.* (1979), has been used extensively. The cycle does not necessarily have a fixed starting point. Moreover, different individuals learn most from different stages in the learning cycle and have distinct preferences for certain kinds of activities. As a result, individuals can be said to have different *learning styles*. These styles can be broadly categorised under four headings, each of which bears a relationship to a stage in the learning cycle (Honey and Mumford, 1992).

- *The theoretical style* is used by people who feel more confident in learning when they feel that they can establish a theoretical or conceptual basis for understanding experience. They have a liking for *conceptual models* of understanding, and are relatively rational in their approach to learning. They tend to subscribe to the idea that it is necessary to understand the principles of something before they can understand its practice. They enjoy analysing situations and problems.

- *The pragmatic style* is adopted by people who are very practical and prefer to judge theories and ideas primarily by the extent to which they work in practice. As a result, they are inclined to be sceptical about new ideas because they are always looking at the practical problems of implementing them. They tend to inhibit those who prefer the next style of learning.

- *The active style* of learning is adopted by people who prefer to 'throw themselves into' new challenges and experiences. These are people who are more inclined to take risks and who look forward to new developments. They can also become easily bored by routine and repetition.

- *The reflective style* of learning is preferred by those who like to weigh up any new developments, ideas and experiences as carefully as possible before reaching any conclusions. They are good at observing situations but may take quite a long time to 'own' a new idea because they like to think through all its implications before deciding how useful it might be.

Categorisations of this sort owe a great deal to the 'classic' learning-cycle model illustrated in Fig. 10.1.

Of course, organisations are generally staffed by adults and adults' learning has a number of characteristics which need to be taken into account (Rogers, 1986; Salaman, 1995, p. 80). It usually takes place within short, fairly intense periods of time, and tends to be directed at very specific, practical outcomes, which may be relatively short term. Individuals also tend to have more fixed, particular styles and approaches to learning. Rogers (1986) suggests that managers usually have a need to learn actively, and find it easier to relate their own experiences to concepts, rather than relate abstract concepts to experience.

Argyris (1991) uses the idea of 'single-loop' and 'double-loop' learning to differentiate between two kinds of learning.

- *Single-loop learning* may be thought of as problem solving – the ability to respond to a set of circumstances.

- *Double-loop learning* involves the ability to reflect on behaviour, learn from the results, and use the experience to find better ways of meeting goals. This is necessary if learning is to become a useful and continuous process.

Argyris agrees with Garratt (1987) that many managers, a large proportion of whom have become managers by nearing the top of their professional career paths, are very good at single-loop learning, but are often quite poor at learning by reflecting on their own experiences and mistakes.

Argyris points to the way in which many professionals behave defensively in the face of failure. They have usually been successful in their own academic achievements, and are unaccustomed to experiencing and dealing with failures. Failure can be an important part of the learning process if it is used in the right way, and feedback from failure can be used constructively.

However, many professionals need to learn *how* to learn, how to evaluate their own performances critically and benefit from the process. The same is true for any organisation. An organisation which cannot learn from experience is likely to remain inflexible and relatively unresponsive to its markets. Since those markets will always be changing, the organisation itself needs to be capable of learning.

Improving performance through learning

Learning plays a key role in achieving good performance. If management has a responsibility for improving the organisation's performance, it also has a responsibility for ensuring that the organisation learns. The learning-cycle concept can be applied to the *process* of improving performance, including marketing performance. This process usually involves four stages (*see* Fig. 10.2). The cycle may be repeated again and again as the organisation continues to strive for improvement. Salaman (1995) uses a similar approach, which also owes much to the learning-cycle concept. Many organisations have a number of 'natural' cycles based upon the nature of their work. For example, schools, colleges and universities have 'academic years' and regular cycles of inspection. Local authorities have annual budget reviews which demand planning cycles.

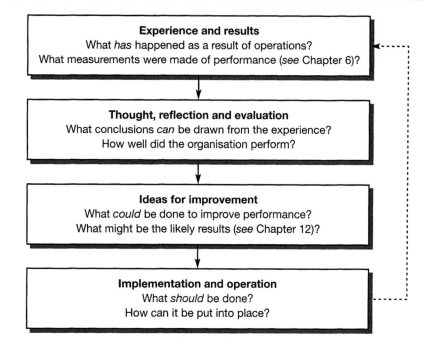

Fig. 10.2 Steps in improving performance

Barriers to learning

The need to learn may involve revising well established patterns of thinking. Garratt (1987) refers to Mant's (1983) concept of the 'binary manager' – the one who has a tendency to think in terms of good or bad, right or wrong. Some reflection will reveal that most issues are far from black and white, and involve a large range of 'grey' areas. In Garratt's opinion, binary thinking is crude and dangerous, especially at policy-making and strategic levels. It encourages the use of excessive simplification and the polarisation of attitudes. This can severely inhibit more flexible and creative thinking which is, increasingly, needed in a turbulent environment.

There are, indeed, a number of factors which can inhibit an organisation's ability and/or willingness to learn. Some managers still seem to find it difficult to encourage personnel to take full responsibility for the jobs that they are doing – a problem which can be very obvious in organisations dominated by bureaucratic systems of control and authority. Hierarchies often expect a high degree of conformity with established norms. Any challenge to accepted practice – for example the suggestion that there might be a more productive way of doing something – may even run the risk of being interpreted as insubordinate behaviour. In some organisations, information may be jealously guarded as a source of power (*see* Chapter 6), either for the individual or for a particular department or section of the organisation. Organisations themselves can thus create barriers to learning.

Organisational culture plays an important role. For example, if some cultures have a tendency to apportion blame when fault-finding, small wonder that their

MINICASE 10.4

Problems with the learning cycle

An effective organisation will benefit from its mistakes by reflecting on them and using the results to modify and improve its behaviour. Unfortunately, some organisations, especially large ones, seem to find this difficult.

This can be illustrated by the attempts of one university to design and implement a student management system. A system of this kind is essentially a database for maintaining records of student details, courses of study, assessments and any other appropriate data that both the university and the student need. In this particular case, the initial specifications were obtained from faculty managers. Although these managers were interested in identifying individual students and 'tracking' their enrolments on specific courses and modules, it seems that little attention had been paid to finding out what data academic staff thought essential for monitoring student progress. Nor had the consequences of the imminent change from a three-term academic year to a two-semester academic year been thought through. As a result, a group of academic staff had to become involved in discussions before a modified database could be put on trial.

Eighteen months later, academic staff heard that a new system, intended to replace the first, appeared to be in the process of development, again without any adequate consultation with some of the most important groups of end-users – in this case, academic staff and students. The consultation should obviously have included registry staff, faculty administrators, academic tutors and the students themselves. (For example, the students wanted to make sure that they had accurate transcripts of what they studied and what their results were in a form which was easily understandable for the benefit of both students and prospective employers.)

Inadequate consultation was all the more surprising since experience of the original system had produced a relatively sophisticated understanding of what was actually needed. In this case there was some real feeling that the administrative computing unit was trying to 're-invent the wheel', and that the organisation appeared to have learned very little from its past experience, and from previous attempts at implementing a student management system.

members react defensively to anything that they interpret as criticism. Such defensiveness will make the individual even less receptive to feedback, less able to reflect on it and use it constructively, less able to learn. Defensiveness is often also a feature of organisations which possess essentially conservative cultures, once seen to typify UK cultural values (Salaman, 1995, p. 92). This conservatism takes pride in traditions, values, stability and security, and gives the appearance of emphasising rationality at the expense of any flexibility which can encourage new ways of doing things. Such values and their associated behaviours are increasingly counterproductive. All organisations, especially public sector ones, need to learn in order to survive and develop. The term 'continuous development' has been used to refer to the process of ongoing learning from experience at work (Wood, 1988).

For some time, organisations have been using Organisational Development (OD) consultancy to help them develop solutions to specific problems. The best OD will always *help the organisation develop itself*, both by providing an 'external' diagnosis of its problems and by helping it develop a culture of learning. The latter most commonly involves changing the culture of the organisation (*see* Chapter 11) – one of the most difficult, but arguably most important, tasks if an organisation is going to develop the appropriate learning skills to improve its operations.

Summary

1 **Marketing intelligence.** Information is essential to the marketing process. Unfortunately, many conceptual models ignore the fact that the environment is constantly changing. Information, therefore, needs constant updating if it is to be useful.

2 **The nature of information.** Information is never objective. Data and facts do not become information until they are interpreted. Information provides management with tools which are used to monitor the organisation's performance and to make decisions.

3 **The nature of marketing research.** Marketing research is an intelligence gathering activity, involving assembling and interpreting data. It uses statistical techniques, economic models, sociological methods and techniques from, e.g. anthropology and psychology.

4 **The marketing research process.** There are several models which describe an interactive process, which can involve the use of either primary or secondary sources of data. Primary sources include questionnaires, interviews and focus groups. Research must represent real cost benefits to the organisation in order to be worth while.

5 **Uses of marketing research.** Marketing research can be used to define and measure a wide range of items, including patterns of use, perceptions of products/ services, attitudes and dispositions, motivations for using them, types of users and market competition. Marketing research uses both quantitative and qualitative data. Quantitative data is measurable, and is often seen as 'factual' and 'scientific' as a result. Qualitative data is more often concerned with motivation and attitudes. Both types of data are important in understanding the nature of demand.

6 **Sampling techniques.** Data are usually collected via representative samples of a population. Generally, there are two types of sampling system: quota sampling (defined in advance, for example, using census data) and random sampling (in which everyone stands an equal chance of being approached). Random sampling produces more statistically significant results.

7 **Measurement.** Various techniques exist for measuring both quantitative and qualitative data. Nominal, ordinal, interval, ratio and rating scales are used, according to their purposes.

8 **The impact of information technology.** The impact of IT, especially of Management Information Systems, on the public sector has been great. Many organisations have invested hugely in IT. Marketing's role is increasingly concerned with the relationships between providers and users, and is therefore a beneficiary of information technology.

9 The need for continuous learning. Learning should be a continuous process, both for the individual and for the organisation. Increasingly, organisations are becoming aware that management has a responsibility to enable members of an organisation to improve the quality of their work through learning.

Implications for management

It is important to define the objectives of any information gathering exercise – that is to decide on the tasks that are necessary in order for the aims of the research to be attained. Once the goals are set, management needs to consider how to design the marketing research process (*see* Table 10.1) by:

- defining the sort of information needed;
- deciding on the potential cost benefit of research and determining the required budget;
- designing an appropriate strategy (for example, by identifying the possible ways of obtaining the information required and choosing the most appropriate methods);
- collecting data;
- interpreting and evaluating the data;
- feeding the results back into a marketing strategy.

Managers should consider how well their own organisations use this approach. Furthermore, the following questions should be addressed:

1 *As a manager, what is my own learning style?* Using the categories listed in this chapter, the manager should assess the extent to which his or her style 'fits' one or more of the categories: theoreticals, pragmatic, active and reflective. In doing so, it is advisable to consider *how* he or she usually responds to, and uses, information.

2 *How can I ensure that my organisation learns?* What strategies are employed by the organisation to encourage and develop a learning culture? What mechanisms and systems exist, or should exist, for making sure that useful information is collected and distributed? To whom is it distributed? How is it interpreted and used by the organisation in order to ensure that a learning cycle takes place?

3 *How effectively does my organisation use information technology?* What role(s) does it play in producing internal information and external information. How accessible is it? To whom?

ISSUES FOR DISCUSSION

The following issues for discussion are presented in the form of questions. Examples from specific public sector industries should be incorporated into responses. Case studies can be used to provide some illustrations of the issues raised.

1 What are the main difficulties associated with 'capturing' and using qualitative, as opposed to quantitative, data?

2 What sources of information are most commonly used for public sector market research purposes? Should market research be aimed at identifying potential demand for existing services and products or be aimed at identifying market need so that provision can be adapted to satisfy that need?

3 What are the main advantages of IT systems in public sector management? What sort of limitations do systems impose on their users?

4 How can an organisation best use the experience of its mistakes?

References

Aaker, D. A., Kumar, V. and Day, G. S. (1995) *Marketing Research* (5th edn). New York: John Wiley & Sons.

Argyris, C. (1991) 'Teaching Smart People How to Learn', *Harvard Business Review*, May–June, 99–109.

Baker, M. J. (1985) *Marketing Strategy and Management*. London: Macmillan.

Baker, M. J. (1991) *Research for Marketing*. London: Macmillan.

Blattberg, R.C., Glazer, R. and Little, J.D.C. (1994) *The Marketing Information Revolution*. Boston, Massachusetts: Harvard Business School Press.

Chapman, J. and Holtham, C. (1994) *IT in Marketing*. Henley on Thames: Alfred Waller.

Chisnall, P.M. (1985) *Marketing: A Behavioural Analysis*. London: McGraw-Hill.

Chisnall, P.M. (1991) *The Essence of Marketing Research*. New York and London: Prentice-Hall.

Chisnall, P.M. (1992) *Marketing Research* (4th edn). London: McGraw-Hill.

Churchill, G.A. (1995) *Marketing Research, methodological foundations*. London: Dryden.

Cooke, S. and Slack, N. (1984) *Making Management Decisions*. Englewood Cliffs, New Jersey: Prentice-Hall, Inc.

Crimp, M. (1985) *The Marketing Research Process* (2nd edn). Englewood Cliffs, New Jersey: Prentice-Hall, Inc.

Earl, M.J. (1989) *Management Strategies for Information Technology*. London: Prentice-Hall, Inc.

Garrett, B. (1987) *The Learning Organization and the need for directors who think*. Aldershot: Gower.

Garwin, D.A. (1993) 'Building a Learning Organization', *Harvard Business Review*, July–August, 78–91.

Gill, J. and Johnson, P. (1991) *Research Methods for Managers*. London: Paul Chapman.

Gilligan, C. and Lowe, R. (1995) *Marketing and Health Care Organisations*. Oxford and New York: Radcliffe Medical Press.

Hannagan, T.J. (1992) *Marketing for the Non-profit Sector*. Basingstoke and London: Macmillan.

Honey, P. and Mumford, A. (1992) *The Manual of Learning Styles* (3rd edn). Maidenhead: Peter Honey.

Hopwood, A. and Tomkins, C. (eds) (1984) *Issues in Public Sector Accounting*. Oxford: Philip Allen.

Kolb, D.A., Rubin, I.M. and MacIntyre, J.M. (eds) (1979) *Organizational Psychology: a book of readings* (3rd edn). Englewood Cliffs, New Jersey: Prentice-Hall Inc.

Lenk, K. (1982) 'Information Technology and Society' in Friedrichs, G. and Schaff, A. (eds) *Microelectronics and Society, A Report to the Club of Rome*. Oxford: Pergamon Press, pp. 273–310.

Likert, R. (1932) 'A Technique for the Measurement of Attitudes', *Archives of Psychology*, 140.

Mant, A. (1983) *The Leaders We Deserve*. Oxford: Martin Robertson.

Morgan, G. (1989) *Riding the Waves of Change. Developing Managerial Competencies for a Turbulent World*. San Francisco: Jossey-Bass Publishers.

NHS National Executive (1995) *An Accountability Framework for GP Fund-holding – Towards a Primare-Care Led NHS*. London: HMSO.

Oliver, G. (1990) *Marketing Today*. Englewood Cliffs, New Jersey: Prentice-Hall International.

Osgood, C.E., Suci, G.J. and Tannenbaum, P.H. (1957) *The Measurement of Marketing*. Urbana: University of Illinois Press.

Rogers, A. (1986) *Teaching Adults*. Milton Keynes: Open University Press.

Salaman, G. (1995) *Managing*. Buckingham: Open University Press.

Senge, P. (1990a) *The Fifth Discipline*. New York: Doubleday.

Senge, P. (1990b) 'The Leader's New Work: Building Learning Organizations', *Sloan Management Review*, Fall, 7–22.

Simon, H.A. (1976) *Administrative Behaviour* (3rd edn). New York: Free Press.

Sprague, R.H. Jr. and McNurlin, B.C. (eds) (1993) *Information Systems Management in Practice*. Englewood Cliffs, New Jersey: Prentice-Hall Inc.

Wilkinson, T. (ed) (1989) *The Communications Challenge. Personnel and PR Perspectives*. London: Institute of Personnel Management.

Williams, K.C. (1981) *Behavioural Aspects of Marketing*. Oxford: Butterworth–Heinemann.

Wilmshurst, J. (1984) *The Fundamentals and Practice of Marketing* (2nd edn). Oxford: Butterworth–Heinemann.

Wood, S. (ed) (1988) *Continuous Development*. London: Institute of Personnel Management.

CHAPTER 11

Marketing, attitudes and culture

CHAPTER OVERVIEW

It is increasingly accepted that organisations with marketing departments but without a supporting organisational culture are less than halfway to being effective marketing organisations. However, marketing culture is influenced not only by organisational attitudes but also by market attitudes. If the market perceives an organisation as unresponsive, this diagnosis often becomes a self-fulfilling prophecy.

Many public sector industries, and many bureaucracies, are seen as having unresponsive cultures. The problem is compounded by the rigorous legislative framework within which the sector operates. A 'systems rule' approach may often appear to be the most economic and efficient mode of operation. This chapter examines the role of attitudes both within organisations and towards organisations. It looks at the important part played by attitudes in the implementation of effective marketing. The text then analyses how organisational culture can be changed and managed, in light of the constraints prevailing within public sector organisations.

KEY LEARNING OUTCOMES

By the end of this chapter, you should be able to:

- appreciate the importance of attitudes and their effects upon customer/user preferences;
- understand the ways in which attitudes influence our perceptions;
- examine differences in attitudes towards public sector and commercial sector practices;
- define the concept of organisational culture;
- explore ways in which attitudes are an important part of that culture; and
- consider ways in which marketing itself can be described as a culture.

Introduction

In Chapter 10, we argued that people's attitudes towards products or services are extremely important subjects of marketing research and information gathering. Given the nature of the constraints influencing public sector markets (*see* especially Chapters 2 and 3) and limiting freedom of choice in various ways, attitudes are particularly important in the marketing of services. Each of the various markets served is likely to have its own sets of attitudes, or culture.

The formation of attitudes

What is an attitude? Our present society has a number of uses for the word. Attitudes have been defined as learned preferences for responding to certain things in particular ways (Williams *et al.*, 1989, pp. 36–40). Aaker *et al.* (1995) define attitudes as people's ways of structuring their understanding of their environment and their responses to it.

There are at least three components involved in the formation of an attitude:

- *a knowledge-based element* (cognitive – based on what is known about the thing or idea);
- *an emotional element* (affective – based on intuitive and emotional responses); and
- *an intentional or action-based element* (behavioural – based on the determination to apply the attitude).

The individual's attitudes towards aspects of his or her world are thus based upon what the individual thinks and believes (the *cognitive* part of an attitude), feels (the *affective* part of an attitude) and therefore does (the *behavioural* result of an attitude) about them. They are, by implication, also related to our systems of beliefs (*see* Williams *et al.*, 1989, pp. 36–40), values and behaviours.

Attitudes are formed by past experiences, but subsequently influence, direct or determine the individual's responses. Attitudes influence the way the individual relates to the world, and the way in which the individual acts. (For more comprehensive definitions of attitudes, *see* Halloran (1970), DeFleur and Westie (1975) and the Open University (1984).)

However, attitudes are not necessarily restricted to individuals. Attitudes can be shared with others, particularly those who belong to the same culture. Broadly speaking, it is usually useful to distinguish between personal attitudes and beliefs and cultural attitudes and beliefs although, of course, they are closely related:

1 *Personal beliefs.* Kelly (1955) maintained that the individual constructs personal models of reality which he or she then tests against actual experiences of the world. The individual is always seeking to make sense of the next events, and uses 'personal constructs' as a way of trying to anticipate them. Most individuals 'test' their personal interpretations of the world against those shared by the 'reference' group or groups to which he or she belongs.

2 *Cultural beliefs* form part of the way of life of a group of people. They are related to the definition of culture which associates it with the products of intellectual development – for example, art, music and literature. Cultural beliefs can also express the attitudes, 'world view', and 'iconology' or the ways in which, at certain times and in certain societies, human values have been used to represent individuals' vision of the world. Cultural beliefs help define a society's judgements of good and bad, its moral values and standards, and find expression in many different ways.

Beliefs, attitudes, values and behaviour all form part of 'culture' in a wider sense. Culture may here be understood as a whole way of life shared by a group of people – its patterns of behaviour, common ideas, beliefs, technology, history and modes of expression. Any individual is normally a member of a group. In marketing terms, they belong to a specific market segment. Any organisation is essentially a group of people, and tends to produce patterns of basic assumptions which are considered valid enough to constitute the 'correct' and accepted way of behaving and doing things within that organisation (Schein, 1989). This creates a way of looking at things and of behaving which sets the group or organisation apart from others. It is an important aspect of group identity, so we can talk, for example, of national cultures, class cultures and organisational cultures.

Attitudes and marketing

Attitudes affect people's perceptions of ideas, things, activities and events. Frequently, the word 'attitude' is used as an alternative to 'opinion'. Insofar as an opinion is usually a statement about how someone thinks and/or feels about something, it may be understood as the verbal or written expression of an attitude – an interpretation – which is often far more informative than factual data. An opinion may not always be particularly rational, but it can reveal much about attitudes and perceptions, and can have a very powerful influence on behaviour. In marketing, attitudes are key considerations in understanding the behaviours of both users and suppliers. In any marketing relationship, the provider will, or should, be trying to ensure that there is a 'match' between what the organisation *thinks* it is supplying and what the user thinks he or she *wants* or *needs*. It has already been pointed out (*see*, for example, Chapter 4) that any product or service has both tangible and intangible dimensions. The *perceptions* of the benefits provided are dependent upon people's *attitudes* towards them. For this reason alone, the identification of differences *between* the attitudes and perceptions of users and suppliers are essential to the development of marketing strategy. Figure 11.1 provides a simple model of this dimension.

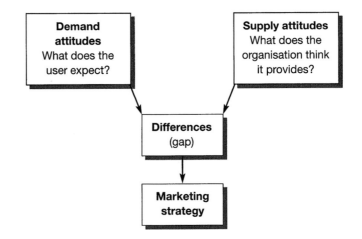

Fig. 11.1 Demand and supply attitudes and perceptions

Attitudes are motivational and influence the behaviour of purchasers and users (*see* Williams, 1981, pp. 147–70). Individuals' attitudes obviously influence their decisions to use certain products and services. For example, if a pensioner regards supplementary benefit as 'charity', an admission of failure and removal of independence, the pensioner may not claim it unless absolutely forced to do so by necessity.

Attitudes are important components of a number of consumer-behaviour models, including the Howard-Sheth model (1969). In the Howard-Sheth model, attitude is central to the learning process. The individual gathers information about a product or a service, forms an attitude towards it, and uses the attitude as a basis for developing an intention to purchase or to use.

Since marketing seeks to identify people's needs and wants, it involves gathering information about people's attitudes, perceptions and opinions, and since attitudes develop selectively (Chisnall, 1985, p. 72), as people make choices according to their needs and wants, it is also important to be aware that attitudes change over time and that the information gathering process has to be a continuous one.

Measuring attitudes

Although we can usually measure the *results of attitudes* to products and services by means of data on adoption and consumption, *attitudes themselves* are less easy to quantify as they are concerned with qualitative opinions and judgements. Considerable efforts have been made to devise a means of measuring attitudes and opinions.

Generally speaking, the ways in which attitudes are measured depend upon the extent to which an attitude or opinion can be scaled. Most techniques try to quantify the extent of individuals' feelings (the *affective* part of an attitude) towards a product or a service, but as we noted in Chapter 10, it is difficult to establish absolute scales of measurement when individuals have subjective and obviously differing criteria for evaluating a product or experience. Attitude scales, such as those of Likert (1932), are usually designed to measure the 'valence' of an attitude – that is, the degree to which a positive or negative feeling is held. It is useful here to consider in more detail some of the techniques described in Chapter 10 and some of the scales favoured by researchers, and generally used to obtain results.

1 *The Likert scale.* This rating scale was designed by Likert in 1932 and is generally well known (*see* Fig. 11.2). Respondents are asked to indicate the extent to which they agree with a carefully worded (that is, unambiguous) statement by choosing one of five categories of response: strongly agree; agree; neither agree nor disagree; disagree; strongly disagree. These categories are scored 1 to 5 for the purposes of collating results from surveys.

It will be noticed that the categories in a Likert scale cannot provide any degree of objective measurement, since they depend upon individual, subjective responses, and cannot claim to be quantitative in a 'scientific' sense. However, the scale can be used to establish some aggregated conclusions on measures, such as the proportion of a sample who have a very favourable response to something compared with the proportion of the sample which does not. Nevertheless, the use of this method will only elicit answers to the questions posed.

Indicate your response to the following statement by ticking the box of your choice.

This organisation possesses a strong marketing orientation.

1 Strongly agree. **2** Agree. **3** Neither agree or disagree. **4** Disagree.
5 Strongly disagree.

1	2	3	4	5
			✓	

Fig. 11.2 An example of a simple Likert scale in use

2 *The Thurstone scale* (Thurstone and Chave, 1929) relies on the collection of a large number of clearly defined statements. A fairly large panel of 'judges' sorts each of these into one of 11 categories, according to the extent to which each statement is seen as representing a relatively favourable, or relatively unfavourable, attitude. The categories are assigned agreed numerical values. This means that the scale is based on current social perceptions of value. The intervals on the scale are, however, determined arbitrarily and subjectively, and the scale is somewhat time-consuming to use.

3 *The Semantic Differential scale* (Osgood *et al.*, 1957) is based on the use of an appropriate collection of oppositional ('bipolar') adjectives, such as 'good' and 'bad', 'high' and 'low'. A numerical scale – for example, from +3 to –3 – is constructed between these bipolar adjectives, and the respondents use it to indicate the extent to which they feel the adjectives are applicable in a given situation. The most obvious weakness of this method concerns the extent to which different individuals and different reference groups may have different interpretations of what constitutes, for example, 'strong' and 'weak'.

4 *Kelly's Repertory Grid* (Kelly, 1955) is a method which attempts to map an individual's personal constructs or beliefs. Since Kelly was a clinical psychologist, the repertory grid was originally designed to map one individual's perceptions of other people, and was first called 'the Role Construct Repertory Test'. In simplified forms, the grid has been adapted for a number of marketing purposes. For example, a number of similar products or services can be compared by asking respondents to identify those that they associate with certain values, or constructs. Thus respondents might be asked to indicate whether they think that a number of different brands of toothpaste are good value for money, have a pleasant taste or have good colours. The results can provide information on brand positioning. Positioning, in marketing terms, is really all about the ways in which a product or service is perceived as distinctive by a purchaser or a user (*see* Fig. 6.5, p. 166).

Attitudes within and towards the public sector

However much recent political developments and the increasing privatisation of state utilities tend to blur the differences between the private and the public sectors, very distinct attitudes persist, for example, towards the very concept of marketing. One important reason for this may be the fact that the public sector has traditionally been seen primarily as having an administrative, rather than a managerial function. In the private sector, marketing has long been accepted as a necessary and integral part of business operations.

We noted in Chapter 7 that attitudes towards public sector services and industries are often characterised by a stereotypical belief in a rigid, impersonal and time-consuming bureaucracy with a permanent level of inefficiency. This stereotype has proved exceptionally hard to change in the context of some public sector organisations.

Stereotyping may be defined as a tendency to make generalisations and simplifications. We can identify two (sometimes interrelated) forms of stereotyping:

1 *Stereotyping in the search for knowledge.* We often look for standard forms or frames of reference which we can use to make sense of the world. The learning process (*see* Chapter 10) actually involves a constant experimentation, testing and modification of such frames of reference, but we often first find such forms in stereotypes. For example, such stereotypes help simplify some of the complexities of social relations (*see*, for example, Halloran, 1970, pp. 55–6). In forming 'first impressions', the individual frequently relies upon his or her existing dictionary of stereotypes. Many stereotypes are culturally established and learned, such as the tendency to identify national groups with certain characteristics and attitudes – a feature which is often extended to the perception of products manufactured in certain countries.

2 *Stereotyping as prejudice.* Over-simplification can also create prejudice, however, especially in conjunction with strong emotions of a negative kind and a lack of open-mindedness. It seems that prejudiced stereotyping is more likely to be found in people who are poor at tolerating ambiguity, who prefer to think 'in black and white'.

These tendencies to simplify and generalise may well be based on relatively limited experience, but can be very powerful in influencing perceptions, as, for example, in propaganda and caricature. They are frequently used in humour. Attitudes within public sector industries can, similarly, be influenced and formed by an organisational culture which regards, for example, adherence to 'the rules' as more important than actively seeking ways of responding helpfully to users' needs.

Many public sector services and industries have inherited a rather negative set of attitudes ingrained in their users' and customers' perceptions of them. 'Bureaucratic consciousness' was one of the major influences on modern life explored by Berger *et al.* (1974). Bureaucracy maintains that 'correct' procedures exist for all eventualities, that all individuals have precisely defined areas of responsibility and specified roles. The individual is seen primarily in terms of his or her function – a tendency which breeds a form of anonymity. This can easily contribute to the sense of depersonalisation experienced by too many clients of bureaucracies, whether waiting in the clinic or 'signing on' for benefit. *The Citizen's Charter* (1991) at least acknowledged the existence of some of these problems. Nevertheless, stereotypes of bureaucratic and officious 'public servants' persist. Unfortunately, it is in the nature of a stereotype to become 'fixed'; they are often very difficult to modify and change.

Stereotyped attitudes towards bureaucracy can produce interesting problems. Take, for example, the need to establish standards for the exchange of computerised data which documents museum collections. The Museum Documentation Association (MDA) is currently seeking to establish minimum standards for documenting museum objects in order to improve the exchange of information between national and international museums and academic communities. Ideally, it should help stop everyone concerned re-inventing the wheel and developing their own individual (and incompatible) systems. Unfortunately, it is still apparent that some members of these communities tend to regard a standard as a (bureaucratic) control to be imposed upon the work they do, rather than as an enabling tool. As a result, one of the MDA's tasks is to develop consensus and encourage the adoption of standards by listening and reacting to the requirements of its 'industry'.

Language

One of the main problems affecting attitudes may well prove to be the language used. Certainly, insufficient attention seems to be paid to sensitivities about language. Language is more than a mere channel of communication. Language is often an important symbol of an organisation's particular culture and identity. It has been developed in an 'industry-specific' manner, much in the same way that a profession will inevitably use particular words, terms and phrases which have specific meanings for its members. 'Specialised' languages and jargon may even serve to exclude those who are not members. References to 'management speak' actually recognise the ways in which power can be associated with the use of a specific vocabulary, and serves to reinforce the identity (and power) of the group which uses it.

Language can be both a source of resistance to change, and a powerful agent for accomplishing it. Maust (1985, pp. 13–21) argued that marketing 'jargon' was generally an anathema to those in the education industry, who would be better served if the proponents of marketing avoided marketing terminology. For example, instead of referring to the 'marketing audit', staff could be encouraged to think of making a systematic review of a school's mission, programmes, enrolments and of the factors which influence them. Instead of talking about the 'marketing concept', staff could consider the need to respond to its various constituencies more effectively. On the other hand, it could also be argued that if the culture of the school could be persuaded to learn, understand and adopt a marketing terminology, it might act as an important stimulus to change and improve effectiveness in an increasingly competitive world.

Such a problem also highlights the potential for a 'clash of cultures' which often exists inside organisations (Raelin, 1985/6). For example, the inherent conflict between managers and professionals is a feature of many public sector organisations where salaried professionals frequently find that their professional culture – for example, as scientists, teachers, doctors, etc., which usually involves a degree of expertise, responsibility and autonomy – can conflict with management and corporate culture, especially in bureaucratic organisations. It is important here to consider a fundamental marketing principle. If marketing is attempting to identify the needs of the users, it should also attempt to use the user's language.

A consideration of language does underline the extent to which the implementation of any management or marketing strategy will, in the final analysis, demand an industry-specific approach. Although the principles of marketing may be discussed in a general sense, every organisation will have its own generic problems, and will demand from its managers its own, tailor-made solutions. The importance of organisation culture is discussed next.

Organisational culture

Organisational culture has been defined as the way in which an organisation develops and learns a set of beliefs, values and ways of doing things which can be seen in its practices and in its members' behaviours (Brown, 1995). The core values of the organisation can be recognised in a range of phenomena – from an organisation's corporate identity, signs and stationery, its use of language, its behavioural norms, myths and rituals to its value systems, ethical codes, basic assumptions and historical sense of identity.

The development of the culture concept

Organisational culture has long been a growing topic of concern in business literature. During the 1970s, the phrase 'organisational climate' was used to refer to the attitudes and beliefs people held about their organisations. There was also a growing interest in the ways in which organisations differed in structure and behaviours from country to country. Human Resource Management (HRM) literature also developed a focus on culture. Traditional approaches had tried to explain variations in performance by considering organisational structures and environmental factors. The new interest in organisational cultures represented a more imaginative approach to understanding such problems. Relationship issues have assumed an increasing importance as it has become apparent that different organisations require different structures and procedures, and that organisations are rarely the predominantly rational entities that management theory once supposed. Social, cultural and political dimensions are important. Methods of studying the ways organisations work, and the theories of organisational behaviour that have been developed, have examined organisations in terms of human relations, organisational structures, systems theory and political power.

Social anthropologists were using the term 'culture' in a modern sense by the end of the nineteenth century. The French sociologist, Emile Durkheim (1858–1917), explored the ways in which beliefs, duties and obligations bound members of a society together. Organisations are themselves like small societies. Each is unique.

The cultural metaphor for organisations has proved useful in understanding the 'basic assumptions' (Schein, 1989) that inform and influence the behaviours of people in organisations.

What is an organisational culture?

Commonly held and relatively stable attitudes form part of any organisation's culture, together with its values and beliefs (*see* Williams *et al.*, 1989, p. 11). The 'routines of everyday practice' are embedded in many aspects of an organisation's culture (Morgan, 1986, pp. 111–40). Morgan believes that the culture metaphor for an organisation has a number of strengths.

- Culture highlights the human aspects of an organisation which are sometimes given less consideration than they may deserve by more traditional approaches which give more emphasis to systems and structures.

- Culture encourages an awareness of the ways in which an organisation depends upon shared systems of meaning, social practices and communication to express the central values which guide the organisation's behaviour and actions.

- Culture is particularly useful in understanding and making organisational changes. In fact, changes in culture are increasingly seen as necessary tools and even prerequisites for making effective strategic changes (Williams *et al.*, 1989, pp. 65–83).

The term 'culture' is therefore used to mean the whole way of life shared by a group of people (Argyle, 1967). It corresponds fairly closely to the historian, E. H. Carr's (1964) definition of 'society'. Culture is not a visible artefact, although a culture may be revealed in part by the use it makes of physical symbols. It is a product of shared meanings, shared constructions of reality and attitudes towards the world. Morgan (1986) writes of 'creating a social reality'. The various structures, goals, rules, policies and procedures of an organisation help its members make sense of their 'world'. In this respect, Morgan argues, every aspect of an organisation is rich in symbolic meanings and rituals through which the culture and the identity of the organisation are reaffirmed.

The history of an organisation (Lessem, 1990) and its founding culture reveal a lot about the organisation's culture. Moreover, the ways in which modern organisations increasingly pay attention to the importance of 'identity' and 'mission statements' acknowledge the importance attached to culture, because a mission statement, in intent at least, will try to expree an organisation's goals in terms of its value system.

In summary, it is worth stressing the following points:

- *An organisational culture is learned* (Williams *et al.*, 1989). It has a frame of reference which is formed and developed over time.

- *An organisational culture is heterogeneous*, in that it is held in common by the members of an organisation.

- *An organisation's culture is subject to its individual identity, its industry and its national culture* (Hofstede, 1980). Different cultures have different expectations, and different frames of reference.

- *An organisational culture, especially one within a large organisation, is not necessarily homogeneous.* There may well exist a number of 'sub-cultures' within it. A university, for example, is likely to have a number of sub-cultures existing within its various faculties or schools, and within the departmental groups within its faculties. In this case, such sub-cultures will be associated with different groups of staff and different groups of subject speciality. Large organisations, especially ones which are divisional in structure, are very likely to experience differences between the cultures of their components. Local authority councils, with their various departments – for example, Finance, Works, Education, Social Services, Museums – usually provide examples of this phenomenon.

The role of organisational culture

Bolman and Deal (1991) discuss the importance of organisational culture and its symbols as providing an important 'frame' or 'lens' through which organisations can be analysed and understood. They argue that culture has a central role in determining effectiveness, although there are a number of differing views of the management and culture relationship. Does an appropriate organisational culture contribute to better management and leadership, or does good management and leadership create organisational culture? Does a strong organisational culture contribute to success, or does success shape the culture of the organisation?

Bolman and Deal (1991) believe that an understanding of organisational culture improves the effectiveness of management. Many members of public sector organisations would agree. Managers who are appointed 'from outside' and gain a reputation for failing to understand 'the way we do things here', and who fail to 'walk around' and develop a 'feel' for organisational culture, are generally less respected than those who do. Their decisions may be regarded with suspicion, and even with contempt. They may even fail to fully understand the generic differences between public sector and private sector industries. There appears to be an equation between the degree of respect for management (understanding, appreciation, and even admiration) and the extent to which management appears to understand the organisational culture. Such mutual respect usually contributes to organisational synergy and effectiveness. It may depend upon a number of factors, including good communications (*see* Chapter 9) and the nature of relationships within a organisational culture. A successful learning organisation (*see* Chapter 10) largely relies upon openness, honesty, discussion and flexibility.

The 'symbolic frame' is indeed a useful way of analysing an organisation (Bolman and Deal, 1991). This perspective looks at ways in which organisations use *systems of knowledge* to create meaning and to understand what they are doing. Any organisational culture uses myths, stories, metaphors, language, rituals, symbols and humour to make sense of what it is doing.

Ernst Cassirer (1953), a Neo-Kantian philosopher, devoted much of his work to analysing how people use myths, language and symbols to make sense of the world. In many ways we see and understand the world *through* the myths that we use. Myths and symbols are full of the meanings which we give them. They are used to explain experience and to maintain a sense of certainty.

**MINICASE
11.1**

Problems of efficiency and culture in the Civil Service

In July 1994, the UK government published a White Paper on the Civil Service. Its proposals were inspired, it is said, more by a desire to increase competition and efficiency than by any new manpower targets. However, the public services minister, William Waldegrave, indicated the government's intention (reported by Andrew Marr in *The Independent* of 14 July) to reduce civil service staffing levels by some 50 000 jobs over a four-year period.

At the same time, the government was also re-stating the view that controlling staff numbers was not necessarily a 'particularly effective' way of reducing costs. Privatisation sometimes led to substitution of staff, which could be even more expensive. The proposed cuts were simply intended to promote competition and thereby increase efficiency. Departments and agencies would now take the responsibility for drawing up their own three-year plans, showing how they proposed to meet their budget targets. National pay agreements would be replaced by 150 units, bargaining at departmental level.

These developments were interpreted by some as a climb-down – an end to the government's addiction to market testing. Such a hope proved to be optimistic. However, market testing provided a focus for some union–employer conflict and political accusations of 'privatisation at all costs'. Yet market testing had been used to examine £1.3 billion of civil service activity, and savings in excess of £150 million had been made. The 14 500 job cuts made at the same time included some 12 200 achieved by contracting work out to the private sector.

There remains some scepticism about such faith in competition. On a very practical note, Sir John Bourn, head of the public spending watchdog, the National Audit Office (NAO), pointed out in 1993 that market testing actually made his job more difficult, because the NAO was not entitled to examine the affairs of private companies that won public service contracts, and thereby measure the efficiency of their operations.

Andrew Marr was also critical of Mr Waldegrave's attempts to reform the Civil Service. The reforms would attempt to keep the 'best' features of public service, altruistic, bureaucratic culture, while at the same time introducing competition and performance-related pay. This represented a major cultural change for the Civil Service.

Mr Waldegrave, Marr thought, was going to change the service's culture by dividing the head – the mandarins – from the body of the service – an apparent reversion to a 'gentlemen and players' hierarchy. By creating a new elite of some 3500 senior civil service posts, presently held by those at grade 5 or above, Mr Waldegrave seems to have suggested that the service would be split in two: those enjoying individual contracts and greater pay, and those lower echelons still subjected to market testing. The new elite was likely to be rewarded according to its ability to 'squeeze' the rest of the system. The politicians' desire to reduce costs and the self-interest of the mandarins would coincide. The 'players' were likely to face more competition, less security and lower pay.

We use *myths* quite frequently to explain certain phenomena. For example, our understanding of 'the Oedipus Complex' depends upon some knowledge of the original Greek myth. Oedipus was the man who killed his own father, unaware of his identity, and then unwittingly married his mother. When he finally learned the truth, Oedipus blinded himself and his mother committed suicide. Not all myths are so tragic. Many organisations maintain a number of myths about their historical successes and failures, or about their leaders, charismatic or otherwise. However, myths can also be dangerous. They can, in fact, contribute to organisational failure. Many organisations cling tenaciously to the myths that they have created – for example, the myth of the friendly British policeman, unarmed and working with his community, protecting its interests and representing justice. Myths often serve an important social purpose. They can be extremely powerful.

Organisational rituals are even maintained when their real usefulness may be debatable. For example, performance appraisals rarely appear to produce learning outcomes, but many organisations continue to use them as expected rituals, and ones which consolidate members' feelings of 'belonging'.

One school of thought believes that management training seldom improves management skills, but may be quite useful as a process of 'socialising participants into management culture' (Bolman and Deal, 1991, p. 265). Some maintain that cultures define the meaning given to their managers' and leaders' actions by organisations. This implies that managers have an important function in creating and managing culture (Smith and Peterson, 1988).

It is important not only to realise the importance of culture to an organisation, but also not to underestimate the power of organisational culture in providing cognitive and emotional security for the individual (*see* Wuthnow *et al.*, 1984). Indeed, it has been argued (for example, by Vaill (1989)) that culture, as a system of attitudes, actions and artefacts, produces in every organisation a 'unique common psychology' (UCP) which influences the very decisions managers make about the cultures of their own organisations. It is, therefore, difficult, if not impossible, to describe the kind of culture an organisation ought to have when the description itself is subject to the existing 'unique common psychology'. For this reason, Vaill believes that most attempts to change organisational cultures are relatively superficial.

Culture is, therefore, the key factor determining attitudes in the marketplace. If demand in the public sector is going to be managed effectively, the culture(s) which support it need to be understood, and if necessary changed.

Cultures and change

In Chapter 2, we likened the organisation to a wild animal. Like a wild animal, an organisation must adapt to its changing environment in order to survive. Hedgehogs, for example, are unable to adapt their behaviours sufficiently fast to avoid large numbers of them being crushed by cars on roads. Kestrels, on the other hand, may frequently be seen hunting for prey beside roadways because small rodents are more easily seen in such environments. Like successful wild animals, organisations may need to adapt their cultures for a variety of reasons, and many need change in order to survive and create competitive advantage in a turbulent environment. Organisational cultures do change, evolve and adapt, sometimes slowly or incrementally, sometimes relatively fast and radically.

Models of change

Brown (1995) reviews a number of models of change.

- Lundberg's (1985) model is, in effect, a more detailed learning-cycle model (*see* Chapter 10) where, given the right conditions (external and internal), 'precipitating' pressures can influence changes in 'cultural visioning', developing a strategy for cultural change which can be implemented and can result in a reformulation of, or modification to, the organisation's culture. Like some other models of change, Lundberg's requires some event or crisis to mobilise the process.

- Dyer (1985) also uses this idea. A crisis may lead the organisation to question some of the values and structures which hold a culture together as a relatively stable entity. A crisis can lead to changes in leadership, and the introduction of new ideas with the power to influence and change cultural patterns within the organisation. This process can also be a cyclical one.

- Schein (1985) uses a biological life cycle model of the organisation, in which different mechanisms can operate at different stages of an organisation's life.

- Gagliardi's (1986) model assumes that survival strategies always modify an organisation's culture incrementally by making it expand its range of options and incorporate new values into its culture as a continuous process.

'Business Process Re-engineering' or 'business process re-design' works from the premise that business structures need to be re-designed organically to meet the changing needs of the environment. Some writers suggest that radical change needs to be integrated into a continuous process of improvement (for example, Total Quality Management). However, there is much evidence that almost all organisational restructuring takes place in response to inward-looking management policies, and is rarely determined by the needs and wants of those who really 'drive' a business or a service – its customers and users.

Lewin (1951 developed a three-stage model of change, which is still in common use in many organisations. It involves *'unfreezing'*, *'change'* and *'refreezing'* and is an approach often used by Organisational Development (OD) techniques, whereby a consultancy will, after exploration and diagnosis, attempt to facilitate organisational change in this way, even making interventions to act as an agent of change.

Levers on change

The reasons why organisations seek to change cultures are usually strategic. Either a new opportunity or some critical event causes an organisation to review its activities and reform its policies and/or its objectives. This usually involves adapting the organisational culture – that is, changing members' attitudes, beliefs and even values, *in addition* to introducing new objectives, structures, methods and training.

This usually means identifying a number of 'target' areas (Williams *et al.*, 1989, pp. 67–83) (*see* Fig. 11.3). Attitudes and beliefs can only be altered by convincing *people* of the need for change. The (now somewhat tired) joke asks how many psychologists are needed to change a light bulb. The answer: 'Only one, but the light bulb has to feel that it needs to be changed'. The right people are needed for the right job, and this may mean moving personnel around. Their beliefs and attitudes may be influenced by using managers to provide the desired role models, and by increasing the opportunities for participation, discussion (*see* Chapter 10), and counselling. Behaviours can be changed by training in new skills. New structures and systems, including technologies, can be introduced. The corporate image can be changed in many ways.

Resistance to change

Inevitably, there is going to be some *resistance to change*. Change is most frequently associated with threats to individual security. Many public sector industries have experienced cost cutting and redundancy policies which contribute to feelings of insecurity. Recipients of letters inviting personnel to apply for voluntary redundancy are initially more likely to respond emotionally to the sight of the word 'redundancy' than to consider the opportunity to volunteer in a rational way.

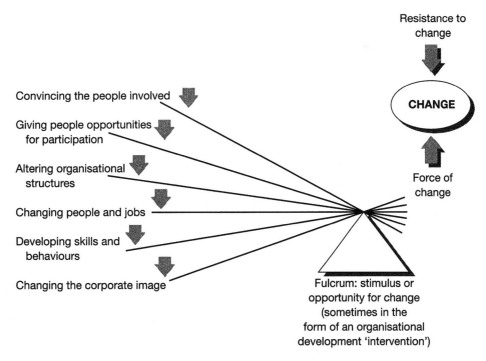

Fig. 11.3 The mechanics of change
(*Source*: Adapted from, for example, Williams *et al.*, 1989)

| MINICASE 11.2 | **Conflicts of cultural attitudes** |

The Independent of 10 September 1993 reported on how the UK government's adviser on efficiency, Sir Peter Levene, had direct experience of the ways in which the public sector was finding private sector ways of working difficult to accept. As one of those responsible for developing 'market testing' as a device for improving efficiency and reducing costs, by insisting on competition for the provision of public services, Sir Peter had been accused of having a primary mission: to cut jobs.

The unions opposed many of the then Conservative government's reforms. One of the main reasons for such hostility to Sir Peter's changes in the Civil Service was a clash of cultures. Many civil servants seemed terrified of moving into the private sector world. To many, the concept of competition was quite alien. Traditionally, their work practices had involved the principle, if not always the reality, of altruistic service to the community. They functioned within a task-oriented bureaucracy, within clearly defined roles, responsible to, and monitored by, a hierarchical system of control. Self-interest could be satisfied by the intrinsic nature of the work, by job security, or by a clearly defined promotion ladder. To those who had grown accustomed to such a culture, competition appeared very threatening.

Cultural attitudes are key elements in the management of change. Thanks to human conservatism it is also one of the most difficult to manage successfully. The needs for change have to become accepted and 'owned' by all the members of an organisation if change is going to be implemented successfully. Although Sir Peter Levene could suggest that there were 'very few' senior civil servants who insisted that services had to be provided 'in-house' at all costs, it seemed that large numbers of civil servants were much more resistant to the concept of 'market testing'. This is in itself an illustration of the extent to which such concepts as 'the market', 'tendering' and 'competition' are still resisted by a culture which originally rarely used them. Organisational culture is formed historically, and is often resistant to changes demanded in a hurry. Changes to culture usually demand realistic time scales.

Given the likelihood of negative reactions to proposed changes, management needs to understand the resistance likely to be encountered. Lewin (1951) once proposed a way of modelling and identifying these 'restraining forces' by what is now generally known as a *'force field analysis'*. The forces which drive cultural change are listed in one column; those which act as restraints in the next (*see* Fig. 11.4). This can be a useful tool when trying to identify the reasons for opposition to change.

Due to marketing's long association with private sector competition and with the selling concept, it often proves relatively difficult to integrate the principles of effective marketing into public sector, non-profit organisations. Its adoption usually requires changes to the cultures of those organisations which have previously seen little use for marketing. Public museums can be used to illustrate this point.

Example: the introduction of marketing to public museums

The UK Museums Association definition of a museum is that of 'an institution which collects, documents, preserves, exhibits and interprets material evidence and

For change	Against change
Users' behaviours have altered	Provider is insensitive to market changes
Political priorities have changed	Organisation culture is conservative
Technology has changed	Out-of-date expertise

Fig. 11.4 A simplified example of analysing conflicting forces
Source: After Lewin (1951)

associated information for the public benefit.' The UK system of support for the arts makes a distinction between private museums and those funded by the State. The latter are either national institutions funded from national taxation, or those supported by municipal local authorities. Since the late 1980s, an increasing emphasis has been placed on improving policy and management in the interests of 'good practice' and public accountability. In 1990 there was also a shift towards greater funding devolution from the Arts Council in favour of Regional Arts Council Boards. More emphasis has been placed on raising commercial sponsorship to support activities, and in 1995 money from the National Lottery started to be used for arts funding, despite the difficulties arising from the necessity to 'match' funds from other sources.

The pace of such developments has increased. Museums need to use marketing techniques, both to increase perceptions of their accountability to their publics, and to attract funding. Research indicates that museums and galleries reach more of the country's population (between 31 and 39 per cent) than any other arts activities. In terms of a multiple-market model, the museum markets can be represented as follows:

The primary market	Visitors and users
The secondary/influencer market	Social and cultural structures and institutions
The legitimiser market	Statutory provision, control and political decisions
The resourcer market	State, local authority and Arts Council funding; income generation and sponsorship.

Unfortunately, the pressures to change created problems within the museums culture. An obvious conflict emerged between many who saw their work as collection-related – that is, concentrating on the objects themselves, their maintenance, research and related scholarship – and those who saw their objectives as primarily user-related – that is, concerned with the display and interpretation of artefacts and marketing them for the benefit of users. It can be argued that the first category of museum people held to a belief that their primary responsibility was to the collections themselves, rather than to the needs, wants and interests of their visitors. The cultural conflict between these opposing attitudes was illustrated during Elizabeth Esteve-Coll's years as Director of the Victoria and Albert Museum, London from 1988 to 1995. As she fought successfully to restructure the museum in a way which was to increase its attendances by 23 per cent and create eight new galleries, she encountered much resistance and criticism from a collection-focused culture which accused her of following a policy of 'popularisation' to the detriment of scholarship and research.

Lewis (1994) highlights the way in which museums have tended to react to the marketing concept with considerable prejudice, equating it with crass commercialism and interpreting it as a threat to professional standards. In fact, as Hudson (1987) has pointed out, successful popularisation is, in reality, dependent on good, sound scholarship to provide the information and interpretation which can attract many visitors. The two cultural perspectives are not irreconcilable, but in order to work together a change in culture is necessary.

In many ways the museum or gallery is in the information business. The artefacts in the museum may be regarded as data. They achieve meaning only through interpretation. Exhibitions are themselves interpretations of their contents. The museum can usefully produce a range of information for the user, from titles and labels, interpretative panels, exhibition guides, videos and catalogues inside an exhibition to publications and teaching materials which can be used outside it. All these forms of information contribute to the 'extended product'. They enhance the nature of the experience for the visitor and user.

As public funding becomes increasingly restrained, there is an increasing pressure to develop additional sources of income. The UK Business Sponsorship Scheme was set up with government encouragement in 1984. In return, sponsors usually require a 'package' of incentives and benefits – for example, the use of the museum or gallery for corporate entertainment, publicity in related publications, etc. UK museums' sponsorship rose from £13 million to £287 million between 1985/6 and 1988/9. Income generation is not exactly a *new* feature of museum management. The Museum of Modern Art, New York, has had a museum shop since 1939. Many art galleries and museums have developed both restaurants and museum shops. The Victoria and Albert Museum, London, has been promoted as 'a good restaurant with a museum attached'. Museum merchandising has grown considerably in many countries, and is now far more sophisticated than the traditional postcard stall in the entrance hall which sold reproductions and a few publications.

In the 1990s, many factors combine to force museums into more marketing-conscious activities. Lewis (1990) recognised the fact that, historically, public subsidy of the arts had created an emphasis upon the producer, the artist and the intrinsic value of the product, leaving the needs of the visitor only to be considered last. This situation is changing dramatically. Hooper-Greenhill (1994) is convinced that, throughout the world, museums and galleries are 'at a point of renewal', needing to grasp the opportunities to develop a clear social function. Bradford (1994) provides a good analysis of the problems of transferring marketing concepts into a public sector, non-profit organisation. The findings of his research indicated that museum curators have to manage relationships in three areas:

- the museum itself;
- the museum's patrons; and
- the museum's reputation with its users.

He concludes that museums cannot accept marketing methods derived directly from a commercial context uncritically. Museums need to integrate a marketing philosophy into the management practices of their organisations. Few museums have established a post of marketing officer as a discrete function. The philosophy of marketing needs to be adapted and 'owned' by the organisation as a whole. This need for an industry-specific adaptation of marketing is supported by a number of recent writers who have made pleas for a more museum-specific approach to marketing.

It can be seen that cultural change usually takes place in response to changing conditions, stimulated by events and managed by effective leadership. The example does, however, stress the importance of considering marketing developments in a sector-specific and in an industry-specific way. Not only does the public sector have characteristics, demands and constraints which differ fundamentally from those in the commercial sector, but different industries have different marketing needs and ways of adapting the marketing concept.

Marketing as a culture

Is marketing a culture? The approach used in this book suggests that it is. In the private sector, there may be an obvious expediency in adopting a marketing culture. Any profit-making organisation depends upon its ability to satisfy markets in order to survive. Only by satisfying its customers' and clients' wants will a business generate enough sales.

In the public sector, including those services, industries and 'agencies' which are increasingly being privatised in many countries, it is necessary to reconsider the importance and function of altruism as a principle – service to others, an unselfish concern for their welfare (*see* Chapter 1). Such a concern was, in large measure, a creation of the State in the nineteenth century, when a number of democracies progressively accepted the need for the state to 'intervene' in order to provide an acceptable standard of living and the amenities considered necessary, or at least desirable, for the maintenance of a 'civilised' society. In the final analysis, such decisions are inevitably political (*see* Chapters 1, 2 and 7) because they are essentially *ideological* – that is, they express the belief system of a nation, political system or even social class.

The history of marketing as a culture in the UK since 1979 has often been related to the history of a political ideology. Driven by a belief in the efficacy of a 'free market', and by an economic policy and need to reduce public sector expenditure and borrowing requirements, the UK has adopted policies designed to improve public sector efficiency, for example, by introducing competition into the sector. Other countries are following suit. However, there are obvious difficulties in trying to change traditional and existing public sector organisational cultures in this direction. To be effective, such moves need to integrate marketing successfully into organisational strategy, as well as culture. (*See* Minicase 11.3.)

On the other hand, there are those who maintain that the emphasis on marketing in the public sector represents a better understanding, ethically and democratically, of social responsibilities and public sector functions. The traditional tensions between perceptions of the public sector as an imposition of the State

Political problems of privatisation

The French lorry drivers' strike of November 1996, which was resolved by securing government support for 'acceptable' working conditions and financial rewards, was followed by the repercussions of a Paris bomb at the Port Royal railway station on 3 December. Politicians were quick to turn this threat to national security to advantage, as reported in *The Independent* of 6 December by Mary Dejevsky. Political parties momentarily ceased criticising each other and called for national solidarity. The trade unions, eager to represent themselves as socially responsible organisations, called off a number of strikes and demonstrations which had been planned.

The apparent accord which had been created was dissipated, however, by an announcement that the French commission on privatisation had vetoed the proposed privatisation of the major national technical group, Thomson, which had defence, technology and media interests. The proposed sale of Thomson Multimedia to the South Korean company Daewoo, for a nominal 1 French franc, raised the political temperature again once the deal was declared 'off'. The French Prime Minister, Alain Juppe (who had, with heavy irony, been thanked by a French lorry driver on a British TV channel when the lorry drivers' dispute had been resolved) stated publicly that the Thomson Group would still be privatised. The French public was understandably confused. A buyer had already been found, and the French Government had supported the deal. The privatisation commission had then rejected it on the basis that there was no guarantee that jobs would be saved, let alone created in France.

which must be paid for by compulsory taxation, and those which see a healthy public sector as a social necessity in a modern world, will inevitably continue to fuel political disagreements.

It is important, however, to reiterate the principles of marketing in the context of the public sector. Marketing is concerned with the identification of people's needs and wants, and with the ability to satisfy them. In the public sector industries, those needs which are considered socially (and politically) 'essential' to protect public interests have been provided by the State. The provision has been made on the basis that it is in the country's interest to provide minimum levels of support for those members of the population who need them. In the past, most democracies have accepted that the provision of such public services has a strong ethical justification. An historical illustration of this can be provided by a brief analysis of the socio-economic 'middle classes' in the UK.

The use of the terms 'the middle class' or 'middle-class values' often disguises the complexity of the middle classes. Traditionally, in the UK, the label in its plural form recognised the fact that there was once an obvious distinction to be made between those 'in trade' – that is, in business and private sector industries – and those in 'the professions', characterised by some sort of public service. The origins of the nineteeth-century British public schools were rooted in this distinction. Public schools were once expected to provide their country with 'professionals' – those who by education and vocation would serve their country as diplomats and civil servants, teachers, lawyers, military personnel and even as clergy. The motivation of public service was considered, culturally, as both important and honourable. Public servants were thought to have a genuine responsibility to society.

It can be argued that, after 1979, experiences in the UK blurred these traditional distinctions. The encouragement of a market culture (which may not be the same thing as a marketing culture) has led to accusations that the dominant 'Thatcherite' ideology privileged notions of self-interest and produced a 'yuppie' generation. Increasingly, there have been accusations of political 'sleaze' and of impropriety, especially directed at those in public services and public office as well as against those who have been seen to benefit from privatised public utilities and companies. Conflicts of interest issues have arisen in a number of privatised industries where the interests of management and shareholders sometimes appear to compromise organisations' responsibilities to their customers and users. There are obvious ethical dimensions in such situations. Accusations of corruption have often been the result.

There is also a wider dimension to be considered. It may be illustrated by reference to a UK BBC Radio 4 *Analysis* programme by Bob Tyrrell, *Shop 'Til You Drop*, broadcast on 6 February 1997. The programme argued that the end of the twentieth century was dominated by a 'consumer culture', in which the extension of the commercial into the political, ethical and social spheres has produced the ultimate 'one-stop shop'. Increasing competition and the ability to create 'product' variants and better 'added value' appear to have increased the range of available choice. Self-fulfilment has become the leading idea of the century, even changing concepts of personal identity. Increasingly, people define themselves less by reference to traditional groupings – for example, class, occupation, etc. – and instead define themselves by what they possess – we are what we buy. However, an increase in the general standard of living does not automatically create a 'better' quality of life for all. Unfortunately, the principle of choice, which is a feature of this consumer culture, requires both *adequate resources* with which to exercise choice and *adequate information* on which to base it. Many public sector industries provide for users who do not, or cannot, always obtain such resources or information. Openness and 'transparency' become political issues. It was argued on the programme that a public spotlight on the processes of decision making has become the best public defence against regulators getting 'too close' to the thinking of the supplier industries and of trying to ensure that the consumer/user really benefits.

The fact that we now appear to have a dominant 'business civilisation' has, in theory, given more power to consumers and users. In a time when unemployment has become a 'normal' feature of life, corporations have, increasingly, had to take notice of their customers' desire to see them contributing to communities in ways other than simply providing employment. Customers are increasingly anxious to see corporations take issues such as ethics, trust and ecology into account. Unfortunately, in the private sector, there is always the danger that the recognition of such issues is token and cosmetic, especially when profit making still provides the 'bottom line'.

This situation does not, however, diminish the real benefits to be gained from adopting marketing as a culture, a set of attitudes, customs, beliefs and behaviours which can be 'owned' by a public sector organisation. Many believe that such a culture is indeed democratic, in that it legitimises the practices which pay due attention to the needs and wants of a society and its members. The very existence of a non-profit sector is based upon a recognition of social responsibility to others. Marketing provides a means of better ensuring that social needs are met more effectively. Some dissent from this opinion is inevitable. The existence of dissent, however, does not necessarily compromise the advantages, that is, public benefit, to be gained from a marketing culture in the public sector. Indeed, if the concept of public benefit is to be maintained as a basic mission of public sector activities, marketing is a *sine qua non* ('without which there is nothing') of its operations.

Summary

1 **The formation of attitudes.** Attitudes represent learned preferences for responding to things in certain ways. They are based upon ways of thinking and believing (cognitive) and feeling (affective) which predispose the individual to act in certain ways (behavioural).

2 **Attitudes and marketing.** Attitude is sometimes used as an alternative to the word 'opinion', and both attitudes and opinions are often expressed in terms of positive or negative responses. The nature of perceptions and responses is of particular interest to marketing research. Attitudes are difficult to quantify, but a number of scales have been developed to help with this task. The attitudes and perceptions of users and suppliers are particularly important in marketing.

3 **Attitudes towards the public sector.** Attitudes are often related to stereotyping, tendencies to make simplifications and generalisations. The private and public sectors have very different attitudes towards marketing. Business has long accepted marketing as a necessary function. Many public sector organisations are still prone to see it as an alien intrusion.

4 **Language.** Language has an important influence on the formation of attitudes.

5 **Organisational culture** is the expressions of an organisation's value and belief systems. Organisations can usefully be described as cultures, emphasising the human and interpersonal aspects of the ways they work.

6 **Cultures and change.** Changes are often implemented by concentrating on people, changing personnel roles, attitudes and beliefs, behaviours, structures and systems and corporate image. Public sector organisations have experienced considerable difficulties in adapting marketing perspectives to their own cultures.

7 **Marketing as a culture.** This book suggests that marketing can itself be understood as a public sector culture. A marketing culture can be interpreted as vital to organisations which democratically seek to serve people's needs.

Implications for management

Mapping the culture of an organisation is not easy. Many aspects of culture, especially those at the deepest levels, are intangible, unwritten, and take the form of habits, behaviours, assumptions and myths. However, understanding organisational culture is one of the most important tasks for the manager. There are many examples of organisations in the public sector, particularly large organisations, where individual managers and groups of managers easily appear 'out of touch' with the perceptions of personnel. They can be accused of failing to appreciate the importance of culture and relationships within the organisation.

There are a number of methods which have been suggested for mapping and understanding organisational cultures – often the first task of good organisational development. Andrew Brown (1995) divides them into two basic approaches:

- those using survey techniques, often involving questionnaires; and
- those based upon interviews and direct observation.

Questionnaires can be said to have only limited usefulness. They only elicit responses to the questions actually posed, and they cannot address information such as the myths, stories, rituals and behaviours of organisational members.

All methods of mapping organisational culture are actually very time-consuming, so it is not surprising to find that systematic and comprehensive attempts to map organisational culture are rare. However, the individual manager will inevitably need to develop a 'feel' for an organisation's culture, and the following approaches can be useful tools with which to form some picture of it. Again it is necessary to make the point that culture is never static. It changes, and as a result, it may be necessary to initiate reforms if the organisation is to survive and develop.

A checklist for mapping organisational culture

Lessem (1990, pp. 149–67) describes Edgar Schein's (1985) approach to obtaining a picture of a culture. It is based on a stage-by-stage, rational sequence of practical steps. Although this approach was obviously formulated in the spirit of an organisational development exercise, reflecting the needs of an 'outside' consultant going into an organisation, it provides a useful checklist of questions. These can be summarised and adapted as follows:

1 What are the physical impressions of the organisation? What patterns of behaviour are physically evident?

2 What surprises the incomer? What atmosphere seems to exist? What degree of formality/informality exists? What sense of conflict or harmony seems to prevail? What personnel policies are evident?

3 What information can be obtained from a 'motivated insider' who can help provide views on, and information about, the organisation?

4 What theories or hypotheses can be formed about the organisation's culture? For example, what seems to be the working atmosphere, the perceptions of the organisation's profile, the effectiveness of communications, the degrees of internal conflict, and the adequacy of the organisation's structure?

Interviews with personnel at various levels of responsibility can be used to check the evidence obtained by this method. Schein (1985) groups the assumptions of an organisation's culture under five headings:

- the organisation's historical and developing relationship with its environment;
- the nature of the organisation's decision-making processes and their patterns;

- the organisation's heroes and villains, concepts of success and failure;
- the organisation's ways of responding to problems;
- the ways in which power is exercised within the organisation.

The original hypotheses formed should be refined; the organisational culture can then be described.

The manager should also consider the following questions:

1 *How strong is the organisational culture?* It has been suggested that organisational cultures tend to be strong in relation to their need for certainty and security (Brown, 1990). The strength of an organisational culture may be measured by the degree of consensus among its members – for example, the extent to which they agree on perceptions of it as relatively weak or strong. A number of 'cultural coordinates' may be used on a questionnaire to establish perceptions of strength. Scaled responses to selected statements may be sought – for example, 'the organisation has a strong sense of tradition'; 'the organisation has an organisation-specific vocabulary' and 'the organisation recruits people that "fit" into its culture' (*see* Brown, 1990, p. 74).

2 *What kind of culture has the organisation got?* The manager may also wish to consider using the Organizational Profile Exercise, from Likert (1967). This is designed to compare perceptions of an actual organisation with an individual's 'ideal' organisation. It can be used to suggest a number of areas in which change may be desired in order to make the organisation, in the individual's perception, more effective.

3 *What are the barriers to change in your organisation?* The Lewin (1951) 'force-field' model (*see* Fig. 11.4) can be used to compare the driving forces for change with those which resist it.

ISSUES FOR DISCUSSION

The following issues for discussion are presented in the form of questions. Examples from specific public sector industries should be incorporated into responses. Case studies can be used to provide some illustrations of the issues raised.

1 How important is organisational culture to marketing?

2 Why can organisational culture prove such an obstacle to organisational change?

3 Why does public sector marketing need to consider the roles of both provider and user attitudes?

4 How would you define a 'marketing culture'?

References

Aaker, D.A., Kumar, V. and Day, G.S. (1995) *Marketing Research* (5th edn). New York: John Wiley & Sons.

Argyle, M. (1967) *The Psychology of Interpersonal Behaviour*. Harmondsworth: Penguin Books.

Berger, P.L., Berger, B. and Kellner, H. (1974) *The Homeless Mind*. Harmondsworth: Penguin Books.

Bolman, L.G. and Deal, T.E. (1991) *Reframing Organizations*. San Francisco: Jossey-Bass.

Bradford, H. (1994) 'A new framework for museum marketing' in Moore, K. (ed) *Museum Management*. London: Routledge and Kegan Paul, pp. 41–51.

Brown, A. (1995) *Organisational Culture*. London: Pitman Publishing.

Carr, E.H. (1964) *What is History?* Harmondsworth: Penguin Books.

Cassirer, E. (1953) *The Philosophy of Symbolic Forms*. New Haven and London: Yale University Press.

Chisnall, P.M. (1985) *Marketing, A Behavioural Analysis* (2nd edn). London: McGraw-Hill.

DeFleur, M.L. and Westie, F.R. (1975) 'Attitude as a Scientific Concept' in Liska, A.E. (ed) *The Consistency Controversy*. New York: John Wiley & Sons.

Dyer, W.G. (1985) 'The Cycle of Cultural Evolution in Organizations' in Kilman, R.H., Saxton, M.J. and Serpa, R. (eds) *Gaining Control of the Corporate Culture*. San Francisco: Jossey-Bass, pp. 200–29.

Gagliardi, P. (1986) 'The Creation and Change of Organizational Cultures: A Conceptual Framework', *Organizational Studies*, 7 (2), 117–34.

Halloran, J.D. (1970) *Attitude Formation and Change*. Leicester: Leicester University Press.

Hofstede, G. (1980) 'Motivation, Leadership and Organization: Do American Theories Apply Abroad?', *Organizational Dynamics*, Summer, 42–63.

Hooper-Greenhill, E. (1994) *Museums And Their Visitors*. London: Routledge and Kegan Paul.

Howard, J.A. and Sheth, J.N. (1969) *The Theory of Buyer Behavior*. New York: John Wiley & Sons.

Hudson, K. (1987) *Museums Influence*. Cambridge: Cambridge University Press.

Kelly, G.A. (1955) *The Psychology of Personal Constructs*. New York: W. W. Norton & Co.

Lessem, R. (1990) *Managing Corporate Culture*. Aldershot: Gower Publishing.

Lewin, K. (1951) *Field theory in social science*. New York: Harper and Row.

Lewis, J. (1990) *Art, Culture and Enterprise*. London: Routledge and Kegan Paul.

Lewis, P. (1994) 'Museums and marketing' in Moore, K. (ed) *Museum Management*. London: Routledge and Kegan Paul, pp. 216–31.

Likert, R. (1932) 'A Technique for the Measurement of Attitudes', *Archives of Psychology*, 140.

Likert, R. (1967) *The Human Organization*. New York: McGraw-Hill.

Lundberg, C.C. (1985) 'On the Feasibility of Cultural Intervention' in Frost, P.J., Moore, L.F., Louis, M.R., Lundberg, C.C. and Matin, J. (eds) *Organizational Culture*. London: Sage Publications, pp. 26–38.

Maher, B. (ed) (1969) *Clinical Psychology and Personality, The Selected Writings of George Kelly*. New York: John Wiley.

McLean, F.C. (1994) 'Marketing in museums: a contextual analysis' in Moore, K. (ed) *Museum Management*. London: Routledge and Kegan Paul, pp. 232–48.

Maust, R. (1985) in Kramer, M. (ed) *New Directions for Higher Education*. San Francisco and London: Jossey-Bass.

Morgan, G. (1986) *Images of Organization*. London: Sage Publications.

Morgan, G. (1989) *Creative Organization Theory*. London: Sage Publications.

Open University (1984) *D307 Social Psychology*. Milton Keynes: Open University.

Osgood, C.E., Suci, G.J. and Tannenbaum, P.H. (1957) *The Measurement of Meaning*. Urbana, Illinois: University of Illinois Press.

Raelin, J.A. (1985/6) *The Clash of Cultures*. Boston, Massachusetts: Harvard Business School Press.

Schein, E. (1985 & 1989) *Organizational Culture and Leadership*. San Francisco: Jossey-Bass.

Smith, P.B. and Peterson, M.F. (1988) *Leadership, Organisations and Culture*. London: Sage Publications.

Thurstone, L.L. and Chave, E.J. (1929) *The Measurement of Attitudes*. Chicago: University of Chicago Press.

Vaill, P.B. (1989) *Managing as a Performing Art*. San Francisco: Jossey-Bass.

Williams, A., Dobson, P. and Walters, M. (1989) *Changing Culture*. London: Institute of Personnel Management.

Williams, K.C. (1981) *Behavioural Aspects of Marketing*. Oxford: Butterworth–Heinemann.

Wuthnow, R., Hunder, J.D., Bergeson, A. and Kuzweil, E. (1984) *Cultural Analysis*. London: Routledge and Kegan Paul.

CHAPTER 12

Marketing strategy and planning

CHAPTER OVERVIEW

A widely held view maintains that there is no need for strategy without competition. In the public sector, strategy has been, and frequently remains, limited to extended budgeting. Existing 'recipes', which have served well in the past, are seen to be appropriate for the present and probably for the future as well. However, times have changed. Competition is now an established part of the public sector environment. Even where there is no competition, the need to make continual organisational improvement to ensure user satisfaction requires strategic decision making.

This final chapter brings together all the elements discussed previously in order to develop organisational strategies and plans. The text discusses the nature of strategy; examines how strategy, planning and implementation can be managed; and emphasises the key role of marketing in organisational strategy development. This chapter also demonstrates the need to develop strategic alternatives.

KEY LEARNING OUTCOMES

By the end of this chapter, you should be able to:

- appreciate that strategy is concerned with all aspects of an organisation's activities;
- understand the extent to which successful strategy is dependent upon good marketing;
- examine the ways in which good strategy demands good analysis, the generation of good strategic options, and good choice of option(s); and
- consider the implications of implementing strategy.

Introduction

The preceding chapters have argued that an understanding of marketing is essential to all organisational activities, particularly in the public sector context. This final chapter addresses a key management role in which marketing has a vital role to play: the determination of organisational strategy. It concludes with an assessment of the ways in which all public sector industries and organisations need marketing as a vital tool in a rapidly changing environment.

What is strategy?

Even today, the word 'strategy' still retains a military connotation. In any organisation strategy is concerned with the organisation's future direction and activities. A strategy integrates the main goals, policies and activities of an organisation (*see* Quinn, 1988). The term refers to the ways in which the organisation defines its aims and objectives and decides on the appropriate means by which they are to be achieved and carried out. Mintzberg (1988) believes that strategy can be defined in five ways:

- as a *plan*, a purposive course of action;
- as a *ploy*, designed to gain some competitive advantage;
- as a *pattern* of consistent actions;
- as a means of identifying an organisation's *position* in its environment; and
- as a particular way of seeing the world, influencing and determining an organisation's cultural *perspective*.

Strategy has the potential to influence most of an organisation's activities and relations with its resources, markets and environment. Corporate strategic decisions, as described by Johnson and Scholes (1997) involve the whole scope of an organisation's activities. Decisions often have important resource implications, and will probably affect day-to-day operations, as well as the long-term future of the organisation. Strategic decisions are also often very complex by nature because they are dealing with uncertainty, involve the whole organisation, and may result in major organisational change. Strategy is concerned with the nature of the organisation's 'fit' with its environment. It attempts to achieve a match between the organisation's activities and the resources at its disposal. Strategy will also emerge as the expression of the expectations and values of those who exercise power in the organisation.

Strategic decisions thus have profound effects at all levels of an organisation, and on the various functions within it. A model of public sector marketing appears in Fig. 12.1, in which Stage 3 is assigned to marketing strategy. It is important to discuss the general principles on which the model is designed before discussing its strategy components in detail.

The multiple public sector markets

These are represented by those dimensions of the model which run consistently in a vertical, or near vertical direction. Given the multiple nature of public sector markets, it is necessary to consider these at all stages of the model. This has the additional advantage of encouraging the reader (repeatedly) to consider aspects of his or her own organisation from the (frequently differing, but co-existent) points of view of the various markets it serves – *primary, secondary, resourcer, legitimiser* and in some cases, *internal*.

The horizontal dimensions of the model are presented in groups, or stages. The order in which the elements of each stage are listed is not necessarily intended as a prioritised order of consideration. Most of the processes in each stage are interrelated. However, the stages themselves follow a logical sequence.

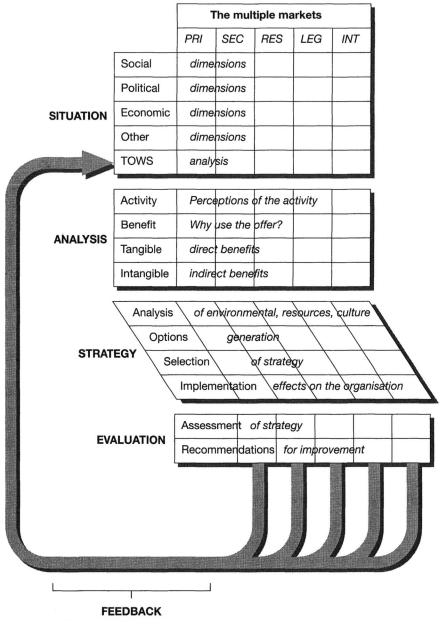

	The multiple markets				
	PRI	SEC	RES	LEG	INT

SITUATION

Social	dimensions				
Political	dimensions				
Economic	dimensions				
Other	dimensions				
TOWS	analysis				

ANALYSIS

Activity	Perceptions of the activity	
Benefit	Why use the offer?	
Tangible	direct benefits	
Intangible	indirect benefits	

STRATEGY

Analysis	of environmental, resources, culture			
Options	generation			
Selection	of strategy			
Implementation	effects on the organisation			

EVALUATION

Assessment	of strategy			
Recommendations	for improvement			

FEEDBACK
into the organisation's learning cycle

Fig. 12.1 Managing marketing in the public sector

Situation

This uses environmental categories to allow each market's relationship with *social*, *political* and *economic* forces to be mapped. In Chapters 2 and 3, we discussed the public sector's relationship with its environment and the particular nature of its general constraints under these three headings.

In Fig. 12.2, an organisation's perceptions of social, economic and political forces are modelled as three sides of a cube. A cube actually has six sides or faces. A minimum of one side and a maximum of three sides can be seen from one viewpoint at any one moment in time. This does not mean that the sides 'missing' from our single viewpoint are not there. Moreover, at different times, and from different viewpoints, the relative sizes of the sides will appear to vary, just as the apparent, relative importance of social, economic and political forces will vary from time to time, according to the manager's perception. This model emphasises three important points:

1 The relative importance of environmental factors changes as the viewer's (manager's) position changes.

2 Since only a maximum of three sides of the cube can be seen at any one moment in time, there are likely to be other dimensions of the environment – for example, technology, culture and the natural environment – which the manager needs to be aware of and to monitor.

3 In order to understand the complexity of the environment, the manager needs to move around it, changing his or her viewpoint frequently in order to maximise awareness.

At this point, it is necessary to return to Fig. 12.1. A further category – 'Other' – has been included in the 'situation' analysis in order to highlight the fact that there may well be additional influences (such as technological developments or cultural changes) which may not readily fit into the first three categories, but need to be considered, when necessary.

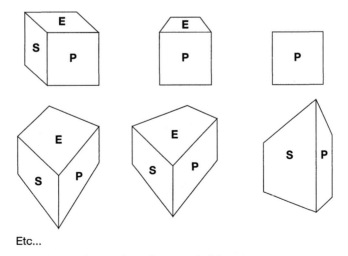

Etc...

Fig. 12.2 Some perceptions of environmental forces

Various techniques have been put forward as ways of modelling organisations' environments. For example, many readers may be familiar with PEST analysis. PEST is an acronym for the **P**olitical (or political–legal), **E**conomic, **S**ocial (or socio-cultural) and **T**echnological dimensions in any organisation's environment. It has been used to provide models of the type illustrated in Fig. 12.3, where aspects of the environment have been related to an organisation which has an obviously functional structure.

Models such as these, however, remain *normative* models. Although they may be useful as frameworks of analysis, they need careful interpretation within the context of specific industries and organisations. Organisations are structured in different ways, and, certainly at the level of the task environment, will differ in their definitions of it. For example, a privatised industry will need to consider its responsibilities to its shareholders. It will be noted that, in Fig. 12.3, the temptation to include marketing as an organisational *function* has been resisted. Marketing needs to be seen as a philosophy which is central to the whole, rather than as a functional department.

In Fig. 12.1, the analysis of the situation/environment provides an opportunity to make an analysis of the organisation's strengths and weaknesses. Figure 12.1 illustrates one widely used method. The acronym SWOT (Strengths, Weaknesses, Opportunities and Threats) is often employed as a guide to making this kind of analysis. In the case of public sector organisations, however, it is more appropriate,

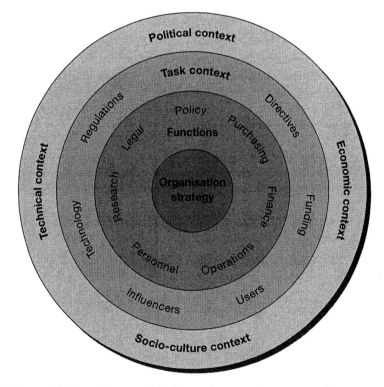

Fig. 12.3 A model of environmental dimensions and components

we believe, to change the order of this familiar formula, and to use the acronym TOWS (Threats, Opportunities, Weaknesses and Strengths). This is because most public sector operations are dependent upon 'external' environmental factors for political sanction and their funding from the public purse, to such an extent that they have to consider their environmental situation before they can identify and evaluate their own weaknesses and strengths. There is, of course, a danger that this argument suggests that public sector organisations are essentially reactive, rather than proactive in relation to their environment. However, in view of the fact that environmental constraints have a particularly strong leverage on public sector organisations, the TOWS model seems appropriate.

Analysis

This provides a matrix with which the organisation's profile and *activities* can be mapped in relation to its markets. It also asks the questions: What *benefits* do its products and services provide? What *tangible* forms do they take? What *intangible* and associated benefits do they offer? These types of questions were discussed at length in Chapters 4, 5 and 6. They need to be considered in relation to all the markets served. Poor decisions – for example about the focus of an organisation's activities ('what business are we in?') – are frequently the result of a failure to analyse adequately the concepts of benefit from user-consumer perspectives (*see* Chapters 4 and 6).

Strategy

This is a framework for identifying the organisation's marketing aims, objectives and resources, its strategic options, its choice of marketing strategy and its implementation tactics in relation to each market. These are discussed in more detail later in the chapter, and use the general strategic framework advocated by writers such as Baker (1985, p. 77) and Johnson and Scholes (1988).

Evaluation and feedback

The importance of evaluation stresses the importance of developing the organisation's learning capability, helping it use the lessons of experience in an approximation to a learning cycle (*see* Chapter 10). The results can be fed back into the model at the appropriate level, a process which needs to be continuous if an organisation is going to maintain its 'best fit' with its environment and markets.

The model in Fig. 12.1 is thus designed to bring together most of the implications for public sector marketing discussed in this book. Once again, however, we wish to make the point that the model is in no way intended to be prescriptive. The actual application of any of the ideas presented will always depend upon the specific demands of the industry, organisation and environment concerned. It is the manager's responsibility to apply the principles involved to his or her own situation.

The role of strategic management

The role of strategic management in the marketing process is therefore concerned with analysing capabilities, identifying options, choosing the preferred option (or options) and making it (or them) work. The basic model of the processes illustrated in the strategy stage of Fig. 12.1 uses four main areas or processes: *analysis, generation of options, choice* and *implementation*.

Public sector and non-profit organisations, such as charities, are, of course, constrained by their particular characteristics. For this reason, the multiple market dimensions of Fig. 12.1 extend through the whole model. The existence of multiple markets certainly complicates strategic planning, and both economic (funding) and political (that is, government policy) influences are likely to loom large in most public sector strategy (*see* Chapter 2). Moreover, we must remember that success/benefit cannot always be measured easily in financial terms (*see* Chapter 8). Nevertheless, concepts of corporate strategy are still relevant to public sector organisations. The Audit Commission, charged with improving the efficiency and effectiveness of public services and acting as a steward for the sensible spending of public money, has achieved considerable success in persuading public sector organisations to adopt strategic management techniques, especially in their approaches to marketing.

Marketing has a central role to play in this process, since ultimately success depends upon the successful planning of marketing activities. Baker (1985, p. 29) argues that general managers and corporate strategists should also see themselves as marketing managers and marketing strategists, because without a market or markets there will be no purpose for their organisations. Kotler (1991, p. 63) sees the relationship between marketing and strategic planning as very close. Marketing information and recommendations contribute to strategic analysis and planning. Market planning is stimulated by the choice of corporate strategy, and marketing implementation provides the results which are evaluated to provide the marketing information and recommendations which inform the learning cycle.

The critical component provided by the evaluation stage is essential for the feedback it provides. Critical evaluation comes most usefully from the user. Kotler (1991, p. 37) reminds us that, in a seminal article, Theodore Levitt (1960) once pointed out that activities should be defined as customer-satisfying processes, because it is the need or want of the customer which provides the demand. Johnson and Scholes (1988, p. 245) make a point of stressing that planning services around the needs of users is strategically important to service providers (and, of course, most public sector activities provide services). However, due notice must be taken of the provider's perceptions and constraints in the public sector context. Perceptions may need to be modified and changed. Constraints will, in most situations, also be subject to changes.

For a public sector organisation to be effective, therefore, strategy, including marketing strategy, must be accepted as a responsibility of all managers within it. Research shows that organisations which are judged 'successful' (*see* Chapter 6) invest adequate time and resources in ensuring that their managers are fully aware of the strategic implications of their work, and can contribute to strategic development. In one sense, this process can be interpreted as extending the 'ownership' of strategy to all those who can contribute to its success. Ideally, this involves all members of an organisation accepting and developing a culture of commitment to continuous improvement. Such a culture is an objective of Total Quality Management. The difficulties of ensuring that such a culture is developed, including the problems associated with changing and managing culture (*see* Chapter 11), should not be underestimated, particularly by those who work in large public sector organisations.

Analysis

The analytical component of strategy normally considers three elements: the environment, resources and the organisation's culture. In the context of Fig. 12.1, we have modified the schema as presented by writers such as Baker (1985).

Environmental analysis

The environmental analysis has already been achieved in the 'situation stage' of the model, prioritised because it has such a powerful influence on the constraints within which public sector organisations usually operate. It is obviously important to collect as much information as possible about the actual and potential influences of the environment (*see* Chapters 1, 2 and 3) – the cumulative result of the 'situation stage' of the model. The organisation's own strengths and weaknesses need to be identified in relation to the environment by making an audit. The results of such an audit will inform the analysis component of the 'strategy stage'.

A marketing audit, according to Kotler (1991), is a comprehensive, systematic, independent and periodic examination of an organisation, undertaken with the intention of identifying problems and opportunities, and recommending improving action. It is important to note that Kotler uses the word 'periodic', highlighting the need to make marketing strategy an iterative process, repeated regularly or continuously in order to keep abreast of developments, and not just as a 'one-off' exercise.

Resources audit

If it is important to establish a relationship (preferably a 'best fit') between an organisation and its environment, it is equally important to be certain that the organisation is capable of sustaining any strategy it wishes to pursue. An analysis of the organisation's resources is therefore needed. Wilmshurst (1984, p. 225) suggests five headings for a resources audit, which are easily adaptable to public sector industries.

1 *Capability* – the experience, expertise and knowledge possessed by the organisation in producing/providing the products or services which are needed. What other potential purposes could this expertise fulfil? In recent years, many organisations, deprived of their original functions by changing environment and circumstances, have looked towards diversification as a means of survival. There are increasing advantages in an organisation's ability to be flexible.

2 *Marketing capability* – the existing experience in delivering and promoting the organisation's products/services. Here the learning curve for many organisations is still fairly steep. The very nature of some public sector industries, such as education, has in the past produced a distrust of the marketing ethos. Demand has been assumed as 'given'. However, this situation has been changing for some time, and increasingly attention is being paid to public sector requirements in this field. Unfortunately, some public sector cultures have, by implication, been guilty of the 'classic', but now largely redundant selling proposition 'we have the product', and have paid insufficient attention to identifying the real nature of demand.

3 *Manpower resources* – appropriate experience, skills and abilities, critical to the success of any organisation. Any organisation is a collection of people. Together, they can achieve more than they could working as individuals (the concept of 'synergy', sometimes expressed as $2 + 2 = > 4$), but their expertise and personal skills need to be balanced if they are to work as successful teams. Increasingly, organisations are becoming sensitive to the advantages of fostering the appropriate interpersonal skills, as well as technical competencies. Leadership styles and team-building are high on the agendas of many organisations. Belbin (1981) was influential in developing this concern in the 1970s, and it has subsequently become central to organisational studies (*see*, for example, Mullins, 1993).

4 *Financial resources.* The availability of resources to finance existing activities, developments and initiatives is, of course, essential. However, as we have already pointed out, most public sector organisations see revenue as the means of achieving their aims, not as the product of doing so. Most are budget-driven, although the increasing development of policies such as internal markets, contract tendering, etc. is modifying this situation a little. So long as there remains some reliance upon funding from central sources – that is, government and taxation – much financing will continue to be budget-driven, with all the political and economic implications that brings.

5 *Image/perception of the organisation.* We have already commented upon certain problems associated with typical public perceptions of bureaucratic public sector organisations. To turn round such negative images of some services (some of which are rehearsed in, for example, the research on 'dependency culture' by Dean and Taylor-Gooby (1992, pp. 85–123)) is very difficult, and will inevitably take a long time.

Resource analysis of product-oriented private sector business can usefully use the model of the 'value chain', as illustrated in Johnson and Scholes (1988, p. 86 ff.). Value-chain analysis owes much to Porter's (1985) work on competition, and seeks to identify resources in relation to an organisation's strategic performance. The extent to which products and services are valued by their users is determined by the ways in which different activities make their own contributions. These value activities can be analysed as a series of operations resulting in the final product or service, supported by the organisation's infrastructure, personnel, and technological resources. However, Porter's model seems much easier to apply to a production-based organisation than to a service organisation without extensive revision.

Culture analysis

The need for an understanding of the culture of an organisation has already been stressed in Chapters 7 and 11. The results of identifying and analysing the organisation's culture form an important part of strategic analysis, not least because they define sources of power, management style, and organisational objectives.

Strategic alternatives and choice

Strategic options need to be generated and evaluated before a strategy, or strategies can be selected. They can then be evaluated by tests on their suitability, feasibility and acceptability. Comparisons with profit-making, private sector business sometimes appear difficult for some public sector industries to make, but in fact many strategic approaches can be adapted.

One of the most basic differences between the two sectors concerns the way in which most business strategies assume that growth is desirable. This is not necessarily the case in public sector industries. Most governments, for example, would prefer to reduce the level of social benefit paid to claimants. Private businesses, however, are essentially competitive, and their strategies for survival and success encourage the idea that growth is normally beneficial to the organisation. Consequently, marketing strategy in the private sector often lists three major categories of opportunity.

- *Market penetration* seeks to increase an organisation's share of the market.

- *Market development* seeks to find new markets with needs for the existing products.

- *Product development* seeks modifications and innovations.

In the business world competition rules, and writers such as Porter (1980) suggest that the three generic types of strategies are overall cost leadership, differentiation and focus.

1 *Cost leadership* aims at achieving the lowest possible costs for making a product, thereby giving the organisation a price advantage and a large market share. Competition is actually one of the ways in which costs are driven down and controlled. It is for this reason that internal markets, market testing and tendering have been encouraged in the UK public sector since the early 1980s. The aims may be rather different from those of the business sector in that low costs will be encouraged as a means of reducing demands on budgets and achieving as much 'value for money' as possible, but price advantages are actively pursued in most public sector industries. For economic reasons alone, it can be seen as a logical strategy.

2 *Differentiation* tries to provide a product or service which is in some way seen by the market as superior to its competitors, literally in the better position. The strategy is essentially a positioning strategy. Any organisation needs to be sensitive to the ways in which its products or services are rated by comparison with those provided by others. This concept is again transferable to the public sector in the context of competition. However, it does raise some problems of a political and even ideological nature in relation to the principle of social equity discussed

in Chapter 5. Additionally, problems continue to exist with those services which remain essentially 'monopoly providers'.

3 *Focus* refers to the potential of concentrating on one specific market segment. We have already argued that different people and market segments will have different needs from others (*see* Chapter 5). It can be argued that some public sector organisations already exist for the benefit of particular segments of the community (for example, the unemployed, those who are 'challenged' in various ways, those who have special needs for education). However, public sector organisations engaged in these markets are rarely in competition, although this is changing as more and more attempts are made to ensure that funding follows demand in the interests of efficiency. Where conflicts can occur between agencies, for example, those jointly involved in special needs education provision, they are as yet usually the result of poor services co-ordination rather than marketplace competition.

At this point, it is worth raising a question about the cost benefits of changing strategies. Although many public sector strategies increasingly involve the principles of efficiency, cost reduction and value for money, it is worth pointing out that the cost of changes are frequently heavy. Cost-benefit analysis is a useful way of assessing the potential value (or not) of strategic changes and developments, although it is not always easy to apportion the full costs of such an exercise (*see* the discussion of costs in Chapter 8), or to assess the probable life span of the benefits expected.

Most generic strategies available to public sector organisations are constrained, even dictated, by the political and economic environment in which they operate. Indeed, strategy is quite likely to be imposed by political direction. Once the goals and strategies have been chosen or established, marketing plans are required to implement them. (*See* Minicase 12.1.)

MINICASE 12.1

The need for marketing to match mission in the NHS

The adoption of marketing principles in public service industries inevitably demands changes. Unfortunately, this sector has traditionally been characterised by organisations which have been both bureaucratic and conservative (with a small 'c'). Research has suggested (as long ago as Miles and Snow, 1978) that an organisation's strategy expresses the dominant culture of its managers, their commonly held beliefs, values and modes of behaviour. If change is going to be implemented effectively, the reasons for it need to be internalised – that is, accepted and adopted within the culture of the organisation concerned. We argue that the benefits of change in public sector industries need to be understood and accepted by *all* participants: the provider, the purchaser and the end-user.

The UK National Health Service changes in the late 1980s and early 1990s provide a good illustration of the validity of this principle. For example, by requiring hospitals to tender for the provision of treatments and patient care, and by enabling certain general practitioners to hold and manage the budgets of their own practices, the NHS effectively separated the provider and the purchaser. If general practitioners were fundholders, they could put their requirements, for example, for the surgical services they require, out to tender. This was designed to encourage competition for the supply of services, thereby reducing costs and increasing efficiency. There are, however, two problems which emerged from the experience of implementing the scheme.

1 There appeared to be some confusion over the identity of the primary market in this situation. For example, hospitals might presume that the general practitioners, rather than the patients, were now their primary market, whereas the direct benefactor of any treatment and the original source of demand is still the patient.

2 The manner in which the funding changes were made offended both some general practitioners within the NHS and many users of the service. Few people would object to changes in the NHS if they were seen as improvements. Although the service is something of a 'sacred cow' in popular perception, it has been traditionally plagued with bureaucratic processes and demand management problems. However, the ways in which the changes were implemented raised many hackles. Many, perhaps a majority of, initial fundholding practices were set up in middle-class residential areas. In some areas it has been admitted that the patients from such practices have been given preferential treatment (such as shorter waiting times) over those from non-fundholding practices. Political capital continues to be made of accusations that the changes are producing a 'two-tier' health service.

These and other criticisms offended people's desire for equity and fairness in a national public service system. After all, the original intentions of the NHS were to provide a service for all 'free at the point of delivery'. Equity was, and remains, a powerful principle, easy to understand and politically sensitive. The way in which fundholding has been implemented seems to have compromised the principle.

We can conclude that, if marketing is going to help increase the efficiency, and perhaps the effectiveness, of public sector industries, its implementation and use have to be *seen* by all those involved to be integrated into the core aims of those industries. Marketing activities must be seen to help implement the organisation's primary function. Public sector marketing must match its mission.

Implementation

Making a strategy work is usually the hardest part of the exercise. The process usually involves the implementation of a marketing plan. A marketing plan will usually contain the following elements (adapted from Kotler, 1991, p. 73):

1 *a summary* of the plan in an easily understandable form, sometimes called the 'Executive Summary';

2 *an assessment of the existing market* situation in the form of relevant environmental information;

3 *an analysis* of threats, opportunities, weaknesses and strengths;

4 *an identification of the aims of the activity/project,* paying particular attention to user perceptions of benefit;

5 *the general marketing approach to be used* (the 'objectives' or specific tasks) as a means of meeting the aims;

6 *a brief summary of what will be done,* by whom, when and at what cost;

7 *some indication of how the activity will be monitored* and evaluated in order to provide feedback.

Successful implementation of the marketing plan will involve many of the ideas and processes described in this book. It will, however, demand specific knowledge of the relevant industry and of the specific situation that only the individual manager is in a position to have. In conclusion, it is again important to stress that there is no 'best way' – that is, no formula which guarantees success. The concepts, ideas and processes discussed are not intended as recipes for successful performance.

MINICASE 12.2

Conflicts of interest in implementation of government policy

It is never easy to know how to put a strategy into effect. There is no 'best way', no infallible 'recipe' for ensuring that a particular course of action will work in a given situation. Organisations and circumstances are all different, so the best that can be achieved depends upon the manager's ability to handle a number of simultaneous variables to obtain the best result. It is for this reason we believe that individual problems demand individual solutions.

A good example of confusion between different policy directions, which apparently 'wasted' public resources, is the UK Government's Urban Policy, launched by Margaret Thatcher in 1987.

A headline in *The Independent* of 17 June 1994 announced that £10 billion had been wasted on a failed policy for the inner cities. A substantial report from a group of independent, university academics, commissioned by the government and agreed with officials in summer 1993, had apparently concluded that the Government's drive to improve the inner cities had failed dismally, at a cost of £10 billion of public funding. A spokesperson for the Department of Environment apparently blamed the failure to publish the report on problems with printing so large a document (all of 400 pages, it was asserted).

It is believed that much of the waste was caused by 'conflicting policy directions'. Some cities that were receiving monies for renewal purposes were at the same time having their revenue support grants cut by capping. Moreover, most of the sums involved seem to have been targeted on building housing schemes and industrial parks, paying little attention to improving other aspects of the infrastructure in order to address the long-term needs of these communities. The report's research apparently supported local authorities' contentions in the 1980s that central government was giving money on the one hand, but taking it away with the other. The Government, it is suggested, should have worked much more closely with local authorities, listened carefully to their needs, and developed a regional approach.

If this is correct, it underlines the importance of understanding all the markets involved. In this case, it appears that there was no strategic framework to ensure a successful implementation of the policy. In particular, the report recommended that long-term partnerships need developing between Government and the cities, and that more participation from local communities and local authorities is needed.

Management, or the 'art' of management, requires skill and judgement. However, the models are seen as useful frameworks to help managers understand and work more effectively in public sector markets.

Conclusions

Strategy is concerned with the ways in which any organisation defines its aims, chooses its objectives, decides on the means by which to put them into effect and carries them out. It has a profound effect on an organisation's relationships with its markets, and on all levels within the organisation itself. This chapter has proposed a model for public sector marketing which recognises its special characteristics, constraints and requirements (*see* Fig. 12.1). The steps illustrated are, however, only intended as a framework, a guide to the elements and processes which need to be interpreted and applied to industry-specific and organisation-specific aims, objectives, environments and markets. It has been stressed that the organisation with a market orientation can benefit from this process, but only if the organisation is prepared to learn. Marketing's relationship with strategic planning is an integral one. The information in Chapters 1 to 11 can be used to contribute to the strategic process. The marketing plan is the result of a proper understanding of marketing, but must still be applied to specific circumstances and to the needs of specific organisations.

MINICASE 12.3

The UK National Health Service and patients' rights

On 1 April 1996, a new complaints procedure was introduced by the UK National Health Service (NHS). It gave patients a number of rights to help them satisfy any concerns they may have about the 'medical service, care or treatment' provided. Hospital trusts publicly invited any suggestions, comments and complaints, with the intention of trying to resolve problems as quickly as possible. *The Patient's Charter* gave patients the right to a full written reply to complaints within a specified time. The services of independent review panels and patient's representatives were made available to deal with complaints.

Such improvements can be regarded as good marketing practice in that they are likely to improve hospitals' understanding of their patients' behaviours, wants and needs. However, they can do little to improve the choices available to NHS patients, who are only able to choose an alternative medical service if they can afford to 'go private'. They can do little or nothing to improve the level of resources which the hospitals can afford to deploy, although they may help improve the *manner* in which it does so. 'Rights', in this example, may be interpreted as procedures to deal with complaints, rather than as rights to choose treatment.

Summary

1 **Strategy** is concerned with analysing an organisation's environment, defining its goals, deciding how best to achieve them, and finding ways of implementing them. It is concerned with establishing an organisation's 'best fit' with its environment. Strategy plays an important part in public sector marketing processes, of which a model is illustrated in Fig. 12.1.

2 **Strategic management** involves environmental and organisational analysis, the generation of strategic options, choice of strategy and its implementation. Public sector organisations have their own distinct characteristics, such as multiple markets, but are increasingly using strategic management techniques. Marketing is central to strategy, not least because it is customer/client needs that generate demand and drive activity. All managers need some market awareness and 'ownership' of strategy if an organisation is to be successful.

3 **Analysis.** Good strategic decisions need good information about the environment, the organisation's resources and its culture. Environmental analysis and organisational culture have been discussed in Chapters 2, 7 and 11. A resources audit will identify the organisation's capabilities, marketing expertise, quality of personnel, financial resources and market perceptions of the organisation. The concept of the value chain may also be a useful analytical tool.

4 **Strategies and choice.** Generic groups of strategic options from the business sector can be adapted for public sector use, although there remain important differences between the sectors. The business sector assumes the existence of a competitive environment. Cost leadership, differentiation and focus are three generic strategies familiar to the business environment, but which have particular implications when applied to public sector operations. However, public sector organisations sometimes have their strategies dictated by political and/or economic constraints.

5 **Implementation.** Making strategy work involves marketing planning and implementation. Marketing plans need to consider: situation; opportunities, weaknesses and strengths; aims and objectives; logistics and monitoring methods. In the final analysis, successful implementation will depend upon the people 'on the ground'.

Implications for management

Strategic analysis, choice, planning and implementation require an effective use of all the techniques discussed in this and earlier chapters of this book. However, the authors wish to repeat again one important, and final point. All the models and techniques included can only be useful if they are applied to the *specific* context in which the manager is working.

ISSUES FOR DISCUSSION

The following issues for discussion are presented in the form of questions. Examples from specific public sector industries should be incorporated into responses. Case studies can be used to provide some illustrations of the issues raised.

1 Why does marketing play such an important role in strategy?

2 What factors demand that marketing is used in a sector-specific manner within the public sector?

3 Why is marketing best regarded as an organisational philosophy or culture rather than as an organisational function?

4 In what ways may public sector organisations encounter conflicts of interest?

References

Baker, M.J. (1985) *Marketing Strategy and Management.* London: Macmillan.

Belbin, R.M. (1981) *Management Teams: Why They Succeed or Fail.* London: Heinemann.

Dean, H. and Taylor-Gooby, P. (1992) *Dependency Culture: the explosion of a myth.* London: Harvester Wheatsheaf.

Johnson, G. and Scholes, K. (1988) *Exploring Corporate Strategy* (2nd edn). New York and London: Prentice-Hall.

Kotler, P. (1991) *Marketing Management* (7th edn). Englewood Cliffs, New Jersey: Prentice-Hall.

Levitt, T. (1960) 'Marketing Myopia', *Harvard Business Review*, July–August, 45–56.

Levitt, T. (1986) *The Marketing Imagination.* London: Collier-Macmillan.

Miles, R.E. and Snow, C.C. (1978) *Organizational Strategy, Structure and Process.* New York: McGraw-Hill.

Mintzberg, H. (1988) 'Opening up the Definition of Strategy' in Quinn, J.B., Mintzberg, H. and James, R.M. (1988) *The Strategy Process.* Englewood Cliffs, New Jersey: Prentice-Hall Inc., pp. 13–20.

Mullins, L.J. (1993) *Management and Organisational Behaviour* (3rd edn). London: Pitman Publishing.

Porter, M.E. (1980) *Competitive Strategy: Techniques for Analysing Industries and Competitors.* New York: Free Press.

Porter, M.E. (1985) *Competitive Advantage.* New York: Free Press.

Quinn, J.B. (1988) 'Strategies for Change' in Quinn, J.B., Mintzberg, H. and James, R. M. *The Strategy Process.* Englewood Cliffs, New Jersey: Prentice-Hall Inc., pp. 2–9.

Wilmshurst, J. (1984) *The Fundamentals and Practice of Marketing.* Oxford: Butterworth–Heinemann.

APPENDIX

Pubton Printing Services Department*

Local context

Pubton Printing Services Department (PPSD) is the in-house printing service of Pubton City Council (PCC). It is part of the council's Supplies Organisation, and is currently managed by George Ponsonby. In spite of an increasing use of modern communications technology in PCC, the demand for printed products remains high, mainly because of the plethora of different systems in use. PCC spends about £3 million per annum on printed material.

Since 1990, a number of external factors have led the Supplies Organisation to examine the effectiveness of PPSD. A reduction in funding from central government has created a financial situation in which PCC is increasingly concerned about the costs of PPSD, and departments using PPSD are keen to reduce their levels of spending on print. In practice, this means that operating deficits will not be tolerated and PPSD sales revenues are likely to fall. However, in spite of these restraints, PPSD is well resourced, with good plant and machinery, and has the potential to become profitable if the appropriate strategy is adopted.

Current trends in the printing industry

A major factor influencing PPSD is the current state of the UK print industry. It is worth examining the trends in the industry and evaluating their possible influence on the department.

Printing is effectively the oldest mass production industry in the country. It has been established for some 500 years and for most of that time the industry has had a monopoly on the storage and retrieval of information. The industry is currently producing in the order of £8 billion of printed goods a year. The industry consists largely of smaller companies, usually employing less than 25 people each, and with an average turnover of some £1 million. The industry has a strong craft history, and its management has tended to develop from those origins. Many companies are managed by their owners, and demarcations between owners and craftspeople are marked. Printed products are widely used in both individual customer and industrial markets. However, most printed products are sold via other companies, and individual customers rarely purchase products directly from printers. The market for printing can therefore be described as an *industrial market*.

*Note: Pubton is an invented town for illustrative purposes. All characters and corporations are entirely fictitious.

PPSD produces offset-lithography material. The introduction of computerised typesetting and desk-top publishing systems, electrostatic copying machines and digital storage and communication systems have forced the industry to pay considerable attention to the management of technological change in the face of technological substitution. The industry has had to develop greater flexibility in order to respond to both changing production technologies and to changing markets.

The market for PPSD

Pubton City Council is an organisation which has extensive dealings with the public. It has a responsibility to work to prescribed procedures, and needs to gather and circulate accurate and systematic information, for both internal and external consumption. All PCC departments, without exception, use printed material. In this situation, there is an obvious rationale for maintaining an efficient and effective in-house printing services department. The current level of sales at PPSD – about £1.5 million – would be an attractive proposition for any private sector printer, since this volume of work is compatible with that of an average size printing company. In addition to existing, in-house production, PCC also purchases a considerable volume of print from external suppliers, particularly marketing and corporate image material where there is a need for specific qualities of work.

The relationship between PPSD and its users is a vital consideration in any evaluation of the department's activities. In 1994, PPSD commissioned an external consultant's report with the following objectives:

1 to examine the extent to which PPSD's resources were being used effectively;

2 to identify the marketing strategies which might help PPSD make good the revenue currently being lost from PCC departments;

3 to examine the nature and effectiveness of existing costing and pricing systems, with a view towards making proposals that better meet changing needs;

4 to identify the organisational structure and operating objectives that PPSD might adopt to achieve its desired objectives.

The report argued that PPSD needed to develop a greater awareness of the real needs of its client departments. An internal research exercise, using a questionnaire, was conducted to determine:

● how many managers in PCC procured print, both internally and externally;

● how managers perceived PPSD's performance;

● what opportunities existed for additional related work (e.g. binding).

Research results

The results of the research are summarised below.

Levels of satisfaction

Levels of satisfaction with PPSD's performance varied from user to user. PPSD obviously found it easier to please some PCC departments than others. Those users who worked in public relations and 'image building' areas tended to express more dissatisfaction than those in more purely administrative areas. The questionnaire invited responses to PPSD's performance using a 'mix' of characteristics: quality of product, ability to meet deadlines and delivery dates, value for money, helpfulness, product specification and ordering systems. An analysis of responses revealed a number of perceptions of PPSD services which needed to be addressed.

- There was some general dissatisfaction with PPSD's services which were frequently regarded as 'expensive'. There was a perceived disparity between quoted prices and assumed costs.

- PPSD was seen as relatively insensitive to changing user needs. A better mechanism for obtaining up-to-date and accurate information about these was required.

- PPSD had apparently failed to communicate a knowledge of existing facilities and capabilities adequately to all its users and buyer groups. There were areas of PCC work in which the purchasers' needs exceeded PPSD's capabilities and resources.

It was clear that there were client departments and services within PCC for which PPSD was producing work very satisfactorily, especially in the areas of administration and technical publications. However, there remained areas of demand which were not being met satisfactorily.

Financial performance

PPSD's financial performance was not easy to measure. Three factors, in particular, contributed to this situation:

1 a very complex system of apportioning costs, making some products appear uncompetitively expensive;

2 an increase in the levels of depreciation as a result of substantial capital purchases made by PPSD;

3 a significant increase in salary levels as a result of a growth in the need for administrative staffing;

4 the provision of a departmental pension fund, which had increased overheads.

Suggested changes

The consultancy report argued that, given relatively low utilisation of resources, PPSD should be in a strong position to handle additional work and be more proactive in both internal and external markets. In order to do so, however, a number of changes were advisable:

Costing and pricing

The existing methods of determining transfer prices involved calculating cost rates for individual machines and processes by apportioning overheads to individual machines on a notional basis. Costs for individual jobs were based on the sum of all the operations for that job – that is, the time taken multiplied by the cost rate. This is often not the most appropriate way of costing in the print industry. Especially in the case of short-run jobs, there is such a high proportion of setting-up cost that any change of batch size, which is not accompanied by a re-calculation of cost, may well give rise to obviously unrealistic prices. This feature was obvious to other PCC departments, who took it as evidence that PPSD did not understand its own cost structures. One painful result has been the tendency of PCC departments to place work with outside printers because it has been cheaper to do so. Moreover, the pressure on purchasing departments to show an operational surplus is an additional incentive to subcontract work out. *PPSD needs to re-examine its costing and pricing mechanisms.*

Value added and wage productivity

One of the options being considered by the PCC's Supplies Organisation is closing PPSD on the grounds that it is insufficiently competitive and somewhat inefficient. However, there are a number of alternative ways of measuring efficiency and performance. The apparent reduction in operational surplus is mainly due to the factors preventing an accurate assessment of the organisation's financial performance (as mentioned above). The *value added* produced by any organisation is the value of the work done (sales) less the cost of the production materials used. Value added is therefore influenced by the sales activity of the department through the volume, price and mix of work produced, and by the management of materials used and work contracted out. Value added is, therefore, a true measurement of the commercial activity of an organisation. Value added also recognises the effects of using different materials and, if it is related to the costs of direct labour (wages), it can be used to measure changes in performance on a period-to-period or on a job-to-job basis. The ratio of value added to wages measures both the effectiveness of the organisation in obtaining the right mix of work and the effectiveness of the organisation in producing that work. It identifies the financial effectiveness of the resources used and measures the productivity of wages. Moreover, it can be used to compare an organisation's performance with that of other organisations. Measured on this basis, PPSD's performance is actually good by comparison with that of the print industry in general, despite a slight fall back influenced by a 'peak' of outwork as the result of a particular contract with low value added. *PPSD needs to reconsider its use of performance measurements in this context.*

Capital employed

New machinery has allowed PPSD to process more work and increase sales. However, the new plant has also required more staff and wages. The sales revenue divided by capital employed (asset turnover) is now relatively low, indicating that the new investment in machinery has not been fully utilised and that PPSD has spare capacity. The department should be in a strong position to handle more work as it has the resources available to handle it. *An improved level of sales would benefit PPSD greatly.*

Marketing opportunities

PPSD is considering three ways of developing additional work:

1 some co-operative activity with another organisation;
2 establishing a sales department to develop a better understanding of the differing needs of customer maintenance and new customer development;
3 providing High Street outlets in the form of franchises.

Existing marketing activity additional to that for PCC relates to five market segments: campaigning organisations; charities; political parties; trade unions; and media organisations. Although PPSD has not promoted its services very actively (its marketing culture would best be described as 'passive'), it does have a distinctive competence in its understanding of the ethos and cultures of these types of organisations. On the other hand, such a competence can also prove to be an inhibiting factor when attempts are made to enter other markets. *In any event, PPSD will need to develop better structures for the administration of client affairs and sales.*

QUESTIONS Given the limited amount of information contained in this case study, the following questions should be discussed:

1 What are the issues which have to be addressed by PPSD in order to ensure that more of the printing contracts from the Council are gained by the department?

2 How might PPSD best develop new clients outside the Council? What is the impact of legislation on this activity?

3 Although many departments perceive that they are saving money by buying from outside suppliers, what are the implications for the Council as a whole? What pricing policy should the PPSD adopt within the Council?

4 How can PPSD persuade PCC of the advantages of retaining an 'in-house' printing service?

Marketing in a hospital trust

Context

Pubton's St. Swithin's Imperial Hospital (PSSIH) is the main provider of National Health hospital treatment and care for the city. Originally an institution founded in the late nineteenth century, it was relocated and redeveloped in the 1960s, and operates as a hospital trust teaching hospital with the Medical School of the University of Pubton. The trust provides services for a Pubton area of about 3.7 million inhabitants. Changes in the UK National Health Service (NHS) have brought about a reconsideration of the hospital's traditional user–supplier relationships, and the hospital is now exploring ways in which its marketing stance and delivery of services could be improved within the current environment.

In order to understand why people in organisations behave as they do, it is necessary to uncover the basic underlying assumptions which are the core of any organisation's culture. In the NHS, traditional concepts of marketing encounter a culture in which until recently, professional judgement has been regarded as sacrosanct, leading to what might be described as a 'provider focus'. Since the inception of the NHS, it has been the medical professionals who have been responsible for identifying and anticipating patients' needs and supplying services to satisfy them. The idea of 'profit motivation' is alien to this altruistic culture. Medical professionals have been accustomed to exercising a high degree of autonomy in making clinical decisions and using their skills and knowledge. They are inclined to resent the degree of management control and accountability which has been imposed as a result of the change to hospital trust status, and many would prefer to be able to retain a greater level of autonomy.

The present situation obviously creates a challenge for marketing. NHS marketing needs to ensure that the medical professionals are providing their users with appropriate services while, at the same time, avoiding the potential dangers that might lead to the organisational bureaucracy conflicting excessively with the professionals' work. At the same time, *Patients' Charter* rights are encouraging the service to take much more notice of the needs and requirements of its end-users.

Despite the need for a marketing philosophy to be adopted and owned by the whole organisation, and the necessity of ensuring that marketing roles and responsibilities are shared among members of the organisation at all levels, the trust has appointed a Director of Corporate Communications and Marketing – a part-time role which is undertaken in conjunction with responsibility for the general management of the trust's directorate. The holder of this post is expected to support the work of the trust by promoting its activities, both externally and internally. This interpretation of the job raises a number of questions. Has the concept of marketing really been understood by the health care professionals and interpreted as merely a glorified kind of public relations exercise? The public relations function in some health care organisations has certainly been given the responsibility for marketing. PSSIHT has not invested in a post which gives one individual the overall responsibility for marketing, a marketing department or specific marketing budget. The marketing function is not represented by any one individual at board level. However, several senior managers within the trust have recognised the importance of marketing and the need for a better level of understanding of marketing among employees. Marketing seminars for senior managers were organised with Dr Pradeep Pundit from the University of Pubton's Business School as early as 1986. A training programme was devised to develop staff awareness of:

- Co-ordination (Stage 1)
- Repositioning (Stage 2)
- Facilitation   (Stage 3)
- Acceleration   (Stage 4)

The next stage was targeted at heads of department, in recognition of the fact that it would be difficult, despite the course's importance, to include all medical staff in the awareness programme.

PSSIHT's marketing stance

An analysis of hospital managers' assessment of PSSIHT's marketing was conducted by an employee on an MBA staff development programme, who concluded that the trust's performance in this area was 'poor'. Although it can be argued that marketing can make 'selling' unnecessary, many NHS managers still tend to see their main function as promoting the 'products' hospitals provide; this supports the existence of a 'we know best' culture. A more productive marketing philosophy recognises that marketing seeks to match the provider's capabilities with the users' needs and wants.

Unfortunately, within the context of the NHS, this may be difficult to achieve simply because, as in many public sector organisations, resources are allocated through political processes whose outcomes may fail to satisfy the level or type of demand. However, there is now a greater level of awareness that users and purchasers are 'driving' the market for hospital services. Providers must be willing to meet the needs and wants of those responsible for purchasing services. Relationship marketing recognises the need to keep customers as much as the necessity of acquiring them in the first place. For these reasons, service delivery and service quality are important considerations. 'Gaps' between provider and customer perceptions and expectations need to be narrowed or closed.

Weaknesses in processes need to be identified. The latter are often the source of serious operational problems at the hospital (*see* Table A.1), and are sometimes described as 'potential fail points'.

The internal markets

It is also important to recognise the importance of internal customers within the new NHS framework. Internal marketing is considered a useful tool with which to improve internal customer satisfaction. There is an important link between external, internal and 'interactive' marketing. Interactive marketing is concerned with

Table A.1 Potential fail points at PSSIH

Event	Consequence
Referral letter not received	GP assumes that the hospital has not responded
Appointment not made	GP assumes that the hospital has not responded
Letter not sent	GP assumes that the hospital has not responded
Patient does not attend	Loss of efficiency
Nurse not available quickly or does not greet patient	Not absolutely essential
Consultation inappropriate or doctor not available	Patient's expectations not met
Inappropriate service	Internal purchaser needs to specify service
Patient fails to return to reception	Outcome not recorded
No appointment made	Loss of income
Staff attitude inappropriate	'Augmented' service non-existent
Doctor fails to send or delays sending outcome letter	GP perceives lack of responsiveness
Patient not added to waiting list	Could have been wrongly prioritised – patient waits longer
WRVS Catering is of poor quality	Catering fails to 'augment' the service

the relationships between customer groups and provider staff. It is an obvious concern for those seeking to address the problems identified in Table A.1. It is useful to emphasise the importance of communicating the mission of the trust to staff in order that they may implement service delivery to achieve the marketing objectives.

There are two important dimensions to internal marketing:

- the notion that every department and every person within the organisation is both a supplier and a customer;
- ensuring that staff work together in a manner supporting the trust's strategy and goals.

Internal marketing has been recognised as especially important in service organisations where there is a close relationship between the production and consumption of the service. It is concerned with both quality management and customer service, and involves co-ordination and process improvement strategies. Any attempt at modelling a customer value chain will reveal that the end-users of the final 'product' or service are still customers (albeit indirectly) of all components in the value chain, although they may only have a 'direct' contact with one (delivery) component of the chain.

Towards a more coherent approach to marketing and operations

In service organisations, cooperation between marketing and operations is vital. Both functions are concerned with how service systems operate. Customers judge services by the efficiency and effectiveness of service processes. The implementation of marketing strategies is the responsibility of the strategic business unit – in this case, PSSIHT's directorate. However, there are dangers in separating the formulation of strategy from its implementation. Some professionals within the trust perceive their operational environment in ways which differ from other employees within the organisation. Any barrier between doctors and marketing managers needs to be overcome because successful implementation depends on the people who carry it out. The trust's marketing strategy may not yet be 'owned' by all its people, yet it is essential that marketing objectives are understood and internalised. In fact, any environmental audit would identify all members and employees of the trust as important stakeholders in the organisation.

Marketing is often perceived as an external activity which organisations need to 'bring in the business', while operational management is an internal activity, often 'behind the scenes'. In many situations, marketing strategies and operational strategies are poorly interrelated. In successful departments within PSSIHT, the senior managers, responsible for marketing and operations respectively, communicate continuously in order to try and achieve a more coherent approach towards marketing and operations. Any changes in the marketing approach may well have an impact on operations. Any modifications to service delivery are likely to have an impact on marketing.

In the final analysis, issues of performance are concerned with the extent to which the organisation as a whole succeeds in fulfilling the aims of its mission and the appropriate strategic objectives. Moving towards a customer-centred approach to performance is a wide-ranging and long-term process. It often involves changing the organisation's culture and modifying members' attitudes throughout the entire organisation, starting at the very highest levels. It may be important to recognise that changes can cause considerable pain, but some level of discomfort is likely to be unavoidable if the organisation is going to find ways of satisfying all its stakeholders, including its customers.

The need for a positioning strategy

PSSIHT's directorate recognised the need to develop its own clear positioning strategy and understanding of market demands. It accepted recommendations that the development of a customer orientation was strategically and operationally essential. A key theme in this process of orientation was the effective development and use of relationship marketing. One of the trust's objectives is to maximise income. An effective way of using relationship marketing to maximise income is to use personal contact methods as a means of marketing health services to customer groups, such as general practitioners, who are directly answerable to their patients for the quality of health services and often act as 'gate keepers' to the services provided by the trust.

As already mentioned, the paradox of marketing is that it often makes life easier for the customer, while at the same time making it more complex for the provider. However, although relationship-oriented marketing can involve higher costs, it also provides an opportunity for giving greater added value, and therefore a higher customer satisfaction with the quality of service. Some writers have argued that the lack of sufficient resources to expand NHS services indefinitely in response to the demand for these services will result in management having to focus more and more on increasing consumer satisfaction through improving existing services. This may involve improvements to the services themselves, the modes of their delivery, and/or changes in the attitudes of NHS staff towards patients. Marketing is more likely to become acceptable to all those involved in health care provision if all are encouraged to see their activities as primarily altruistic or philanthropic.

Quality initiatives are being used as bridges between the development of market-orientated hospitals and the values of the still powerful health care professionals. If this can be achieved successfully, hospital trusts will be able to market appropriately designed, targeted and priced products to satisfy the need of increasingly expert and demanding purchasers. More cooperation is needed between marketers and health care professionals and between marketing and operational management.

QUESTIONS

1 Given the need to develop a customer-driven policy, how can PSSIHT measure customer satisfaction within its markets?

2 What practical steps can PSSIHT take to change its culture with a view towards making itself more responsive to customer needs?

3 What are the most important factors which limit PSSIHT's ability to satisfy all customer demand?

4 PSSHIT is primarily a provider of services. What are the implications of this from a marketing perspective?

Meeting the leisure needs of Pubton's Asian population

Context

Pubton, like many cities in the UK, has a sizeable Asian population. Many families came to the UK during the 1950s to work in the textile and clothing industries. During the 1980s, Pubton invested extensively in sport and leisure facilities, but by 1996 these were not achieving the levels of use originally projected. As a result, Pubton City Council has been exploring ways of encouraging greater use of the facilities, particularly by minority groups. An employee was commissioned to write a report identifying possible strategies which could be used to encourage the Asian community, especially women, to take part in leisure and recreational activities.

Summary of the report

Working with the Asian community involved a high level of sensitivity to Asian cultures. In general, Asian cultures are dominated by the men, and females adopt subservient roles. Considerable efforts were made to obtain information on the attitudes and opinions held by Asian women towards leisure and sport activities, but such research usually involved maintaining a high degree of confidentiality. The evidence obtained from respondents indicated that the Asian community was generally critical of the facilities in Pubton currently available for its use. Most of the respondents maintained that the type of activities available and a lack of facilities which recognise the distinctive nature of their own cultures were the main reasons why they did not make very much use of the public leisure and recreational facilities available.

Pubton's Leisure Services (PLS), in common with the leisure industry as a whole, has an established culture of its own. Assuming that exercise and sporting activities benefit members of the community, it remains essentially a 'provider culture' dedicated to bringing leisure and recreational opportunities to the community, rather than bringing the community to leisure and recreation.

A major concern to the Asian segment of the community was a lack of consultation and communication with Asian people. (Nationally, approximately 4 per cent of the UK population is of black or Asian origin, according to the 1991 census.)

Physically, it can be argued that the recreational needs of Asian women are similar to those of the indigenous female population. The Asian community itself has expressed interest in marketing leisure and sporting activities with an appropriate provision for Asian women. However, most of the activities available take place in leisure centres which are traditionally white, male-dominated areas. It is hoped that perceived problems of this sort can be alleviated by moving PLS towards a more market-oriented approach – for example, by using marketing research interviews with the local Asian community to obtain a better understanding of the specific needs of women and girls.

Information is needed on what kind of services Asian women want, where it could best be provided, at what times and at what prices. It is hoped that bilingual communications and promotion would then encourage the Asian community to make more use of the public facilities which Pubton provides.

In approaching this particular market segment, it is particularly important to identify the cultural barriers to adoption, and make appropriate provision for the segment's needs – for example, by providing women-only sessions and activities. It must also be recognised, however, that the Asian community is not a homogeneous group. It contains a number of distinct cultural traditions and despite the fact that some attitudes may be held in common, in different groups opinions, practices and values will vary. If a comprehensive leisure service is to be offered to the whole Pubton community, it needs to be recognised that there is a variety of cultures contained within it, and a real commitment to equal opportunities, including employment, is vital for the development of PLS.

The needs and wants of each group within the community are different, and they influence the 'buyer behaviour' of the group. The Asian community does not give leisure and recreation the same priority. The report reached the following conclusions:

- The Asian community mainly enjoy passive leisure time activities.
- As the age range increases, participation levels in sports and activities decreases.
- Facilities owned by the Pubton City Council and Asians' own ethnic communities are the most popular places for people to take part in activities.
- The participation of women in activities depends largely upon the approval of their male peers.
- There is a lack of awareness within the Asian community of the provision that is available.

While it would be easy to conclude that Asian culture is the main barrier to Asian women taking part in leisure and recreation, the research indicated that British culture and the existing systems within PLS are in themselves disincentives to the participation of Asian women in leisure and recreational activities.

Market segments

The Sports Council, with its motto 'Sport for All', states that it seeks 'to facilitate opportunities for participation in sport by each and every section of the community'. In this case, it has become apparent that there is an inadequate understanding of what this particular section of the community needs and wants. In the interests of providing equality of opportunity, all service providers within PLS need to consider this problem.

There is evidence to show that the high hopes which the original Asian and black immigrants brought to Britain were not realised. Both Asian and Caribbean immigrants quickly encountered racism and discrimination – attitudes which were further complicated by the nature of the British class structure.

Asian women do not form a simple homogeneous group. The term 'Asian' is used as a racial categorisation of people from Bangladesh, Pakistan, India and Sri

Lanka. The social practices, attitudes and values of Asian women vary considerably between, and even within, their different communities due to original nationalities, social classes, geographical locations, religious faiths, etc. In addition, some Asians came to the UK via African states.

The *'South Asian'* community accounts for over one million people in Britain (1991 Census). They do share certain characteristics: for example, most have strong religious convictions and are bonded to an 'extended family'. While they are generally described as 'black', this does not provide a clear definition as to their origin, nor does it provide any acknowledgement of their unique behaviours and requirements as distinct groups. The majority of Pubton's Asian community can be identified with one of three principal communities.

1 Most of the *Muslim community* in Britain comes from the Mirpur, in Pakistan. There was a large migration of Pakistani Muslims to England in the late 1940s and early 1950s. In order to obtain a clear understanding of these communities and their culture, it is important to understand the society in Pakistan and the role of the members of that society. The Muslims' rules within the society dictate that adult women should not be seen in public places, unless absolutely necessary. This means that some 'basic' activities (as understood by Western society), such as shopping, are carried out by the men of the family. This affects the mobility of Muslim women within their society, and creates additional stress for them when they try to integrate into Western society. It reinforces a strong tendency for Muslim families to form a closed, relatively inward-looking unit around the immediate family. Young people, particularly young Asian women born in the UK, must therefore look to acquire a 'dual cultural identity' that is acceptable to their parents and their community. Members of this community usually continue to use their own languages in their own homes, but are also exposed to English through the mass media, their education and their wider socialisation processes. Strong pressures are exerted upon Asian women to retain their bonds with Islamic culture at all times.

2 Approximately three-quarters of all British South Asians are of *Indian Punjabi* origin (1991 Census) and the majority are Sikhs. Sikh culture is strongly disciplined. From a very early age (11), the Sikh male goes through a form of baptism into the Khalsa – a ceremony which enables him to become a soldier. Women are expected to adopt a subservient role within the family unit and no socialisation is undertaken without the consent of the dominant male member.

3 Many other South Asian women are of the *Hindu faith*. For centuries, Hinduism has built a very rigid system around the concept of caste. The caste into which a Hindu is born into society establishes the duties and responsibilities which are expected of him or her and is understood to be determined by the totality of his or her actions in a previous life.

These three main religious groups account for approximately 98 per cent of the UK Asian population.

It is possible to make some generalisations, however, about the Asian communities in their attitudes to sport and leisure. There are some factors which restrict access to sport at an individual level. Asian cultures give sport a relatively low priority, and certainly place it below work, education, religious duties and family life. The need for modesty among Asian women means that many will only participate in sport in an all-women environment. Unless facility providers within the leisure and recreation industry in England are properly aware of these cultural behaviours and attitudes, they run the risk of being seen to ignore the needs and wants of these communities. There are, in fact, a large number of factors which act as barriers against the participation of Asian women in leisure and sport activities in the forms in which they are currently provided.

The dangers of racism and stereotyping

Unfortunately, over-generalisation can easily lead to stereotyping and prejudice. Racism is to be found in most cultures and has a very long history. Pubton City Council has a legal duty under Section 21 of the 1976 UK Race Relations Act to ensure that it provides equality of opportunity in all its activities and promotes good race relations. Evidence from studies of schools' physical education policies in the 1980s, however, has revealed the continued existence of racial stereotyping, despite the existence of policies designed to prevent it. As an example, Asian girls have been thought to be less capable of adopting certain physical postures compared with members of other racial groups. Many teachers have assumed that all Asian girls were unable to participate in extra-curricular sports, without verification. As a result, some Asian girls have been automatically excluded from such activities. It has been found that some white teachers think that working with ethnic minorities is 'difficult'. The existence of racism inevitably affects social interactions within the community as a whole. Many Asian women and girls do not use sports facilities because they are afraid of racism.

It has been argued that racism has had little impact on sport. However, it is increasingly difficult to deny that racism contributes to the under-achievement, restricted participation and under-representation of the majority of black and ethnic minority people in sport. Those who have achieved success have often done so in spite of the existence of racism in sport.

The UK Sports Council, in 1991, defined racism as any action, policy or practice, deliberate or not, which creates or sustains racial inequality. There are two principal forms of racism: personal racism and institutional racism.

- *Personal racism*. British Crime Survey statistics showed that there were over 130 000 racially motivated incidents in 1992. The common denominator affecting young Asian females in their pursuit of leisure and recreation is this pervasive personal racism, manifesting itself in a host of phenomena, from verbal abuse through offensive graffiti to physical violence.

- *Institutional racism* is most commonly found within the culture of provider organisations. Sports organisations in Britain are dominated by white males. Despite the existence of a number of equal opportunities, the very ethos of or atmosphere within an organisation can act as a barrier to access for Asian women, especially if there is little understanding of the needs of black and ethnic minority communities. Moreover, organisational culture can be particularly difficult to change, and members of ethnic minorities often feel excluded from the relevant decision-making processes. The very structure of the organisations may continue to exclude ethnic minority people.

Attitudes to sport and recreation in Asian communities

Asian communities have few professional sporting role models, either male or female. Many female members of the communities suggest that they do not have sufficient time for leisure activities. Many Asian women are family – and house-oriented. Cultural and religious differences, family and home pressures may lead to the withdrawal of South Asian girls from sporting activities at school. Stories abound of authoritarian parents (by Western standards) wanting their daughters to stay at home – an attitude often supported and reinforced by siblings who 'all say the same'.

The research for PLS relied quite heavily on the use of questionnaires. There are, however, some serious limitations in this method. The Sports Council has recognised that one of the barriers to Asian women taking part in leisure and recreation remains an ignorance of what is actually available for their use. A questionnaire written in the English language can only serve to reinforce this problem. The questionnaires used, therefore, were translated into a number of community languages, which added to the expense of the research.

In order to gain the trust of respondents and obtain reliable data and information, a number of questionnaires were completed anonymously by discussion groups. This was largely done using the help of a number of reasonably eloquent, English-speaking Asian women who met socially and informally at drop-in centres. Considerable care was taken to preserve confidentiality and anonymity.

Of course, the Asian communities themselves are also changing in response to their environmental British culture. More Asian women within the communities are developing the confidence to sustain their own careers and to development without the assistance of their extended families.

The PLS employee conducting the research project was acutely aware of the dangers of introducing bias. The fact that he was male and non-Asian led him to rely heavily on a number of third parties to record primary data. The results he finally obtained indicated the existence of a number of popular misconceptions of the Asian communities. PLS's staff had already been recognised as playing a major role in attracting and keeping customers for leisure and sporting activities in Pubton. It was now found that Asian populations felt strongly that staff from 'our own cultural background' would make the services very much more popular. It was also found that many of those taking part in organised sports felt that sports officials – for example, referees – sometimes discriminated against them. Over 90 per cent of respondents gave high priority to the provision of women-only sessions staffed solely by women. Issues of cost were considered of less importance than issues relating to the ability to obtain more help and guidance.

Asian women were generally very critical of PLS – its promotion, marketing and programming. The communities believed that little had been done previously to acknowledge the variety of cultures present within Pubton as a whole. Furthermore, a majority of respondents were concerned with what they interpreted as an institutional racism present throughout leisure and recreation provision.

The Asian communities believed that changes in policies could only be achieved if the providers recognised the fact that active leisure is not a priority within these Asian cultures. However, it would be possible to provide more encouragement to Asian children to participate in sporting and leisure activities when at school. The benefits of a more active lifestyle needed to be targeted more effectively and promoted more successfully, if more Asian women were to be attracted to activities outside their communities.

Many facility providers consider Asian women a difficult group or market segment to attract and satisfy. This attitude is itself a problem. The findings from the data indicate that, quite often, the reasons given for the lack of suitable leisure services provision for Asian women are the need for additional staffing, suitable transport and publicity in the vernacular languages. These requirements create additional costs and resource implications, and make it easier for local authorities to ignore or marginalise this group in favour of young, white middle-class users. There is, then, an argument for paying greater attention to multicultural issues and awareness training and development. Users from minority communities need to be given confidence that the service delivery and the agencies responsible for them are better attuned to their own needs. Although many young Asian women speak English fluently, it is very important to ensure that the activities available are seen to be relevant to the needs of these communities.

Conclusion

Many local leisure centres are often relatively expensive and are not very accessible to members of the Asian community. Alternative facilities such as community halls and mosques can often be easily and cheaply adapted to provide recreational activities for these groups. However, the community believes that while overt racism remains a problem in many areas, multicultural awareness training can be one useful strategy for moving forward. Organisations like PLS need to reject the stereotypical attitude that 'Asian women do not take part in sports and recreation and that it is not the rightful place of providers to force them to do so'. Policy makers and facility providers must address this very sensitive issue of market segmentation on the basis of race and culture.

QUESTIONS

1 How might cultural changes affect second- and third-generation Asian women's demand for leisure services in the future?

2 What problems are likely to be encountered by marketing research investigating the nature of demand within ethnic minority groups?

3 In aiming to improve utilisation, is PLS trying to find new markets for its existing 'products', or is it trying to identify market needs and organise its resources accordingly?

4 What strategies are open to PLS in its attempts to increase demand for its services within the local community as a whole?

Pubton Local Education Authority – changing from a producer-led to a customer-orientated philosophy

Context

In the 1990s, the UK Department for Education (DfEE) introduced a number of changes that progressively delegated more responsibility and financial control to individual schools and their boards of governors. By 1995, a DfEE target of delegating 85 per cent of the potential schools' budget had already been achieved and PLEA had embarked upon a consultation process designed to determine which other schools services should be delegated to the budgets of individual schools.

The debate was developed under the title of 'Advancing Local School Management' (ALSM) and was given priority by PLEA's Director of Education, Alex Bukovsky, and the Assistant Director Support Services, Archie Trugg. Other factors which influenced the debate were:

1 *the introduction of Compulsory Competitive Tendering (CCT) into certain ('white collar') areas of the LEA's activities*, which could mean that some delegated school budget expenditure could be exposed to competition; and

2 *the continuing existence of financial constraints*, from both government and local council sources, which obviously limit the availability of resources to schools.

Aims

PLEA commissioned an external firm of consultants to conduct research into schools' responses to further delegation. The consultants' terms of reference were:

● to make recommendations to PLEA as a result of the consultation exercise;

● to identify a number of objectives which might address the needs expressed by the schools;

● to help PLEA determine a strategy and form an action plan which could be implemented quickly and effectively given the existing situation – that is, National Curriculum developments, government policies, national school inspection requirements, etc.

Methods

The external firm of educational management consultants, which had extensive experience of working with UK LEAs, conducted a customer research exercise. This was organised around a number of focus groups for the following reasons:

● The required feedback was generally of a qualitative rather than a quantitative nature, and the use of questionnaires was not as appropriate for this purpose.

- The use of focus groups can help clarify meanings and establish the strength of conviction with which particular views are held.
- Schools can be encouraged to articulate their views directly and to assess them against a number of external factors.

A total of 24 focus groups were held: 15 for primary schools; 6 for secondary schools; 2 for special schools; and 1 for nursery schools.

The attendance at these groups averaged overall some 66 per cent, which was considered satisfactory and produced representative and reliable data. However, it is worth noting that one common consequence of using focus groups is a tendency for the groups to express negative criticisms rather than positive points. (Participants often use such opportunities to identify perceived shortcomings rather than existing strengths.) Participants use the opportunity to complain more forcefully than might otherwise be the case. This feature may well explain why some PLEA officers expressed some scepticism about the consultants' report on the exercise.

Results

The results of the consultation exercise can be summarised as follows:

1 A significant majority (over 76 per cent) of school boards of governors passed resolutions opposing further delegation of services to schools. At the same time, a significant number (12 per cent) were only prepared to comment if more detailed proposals and information were made available. Despite the fact that most schools could see that delegation had some advantages in improving a customer/marketing ethos, it was widely believed that the delegation of further funding to schools would achieve little real purchasing power and was likely to add to administrative costs, whereas central provision could maximise the availability of services. There was also some fear that it would be difficult to devise an equitable means of further delegation that would avoid accusations of unfairness.

2 Schools expressed a strong wish to remain part of a cohesive and supportive educational community within the PLEA area. They looked to PLEA to provide strong leadership, strategic planning and management services for schools.

3 However, schools felt that PLEA often failed to provide good and adequate leadership, and that its services needed to be better co-ordinated and planned. Schools wanted to see more equitable and strategic management of resources, and were generally critical of the standards of co-ordination between services.

4 In order to achieve this, schools wished to see PLEA services costed in such a way that informed judgements could be made in value-for-money terms, and that they should be given much clearer information of both levels of entitlement and the standards of service that can be expected from PLEA services.

5 Schools also wished to see PLEA accept the fact that service provision should be customer/user defined rather than defined by the producer/provider. Schools wished to be seen and treated as customers for PLEA services.

6 Both Curriculum and Staff Development and Monitoring and Evaluation services received more support for delegation than other services. There were particular criticisms of in-service courses for teachers. The services of local school inspectors were generally welcomed, although there was some real desire for more support in this area, especially in the context of national (OFSTED) inspections. Of the other services, services to school governors (e.g. training) were highly rated, as were Education Personnel Services and AV/IT Support Services. However, Management Services, Financial Services, Learning and Behavioural Support Services and Works Department Services were strongly criticised. The Works Department was generally felt to be expensive (quotations for repairs and maintenance work were generally much higher than those from private contractors), poorly managed, delivered late or at inconvenient times, and giving poor value for money.

General conclusions

Within the consultation exercise, it became evident that different segments of the market had differing perceptions of PLEA's services and provision. Nursery schools felt that they were relatively marginalised. Primary schools thought that secondary schools were better resourced than they were, whereas secondary schools felt that PLEA tended to favour primary schools. These perceptions could not be supported by verifiable information. However, secondary schools were more articulate in their criticisms of PLEA, and tended to be more acutely aware of the possibilities of acting independently.

As a result of the consultation exercise, the consultants recommended that PLEA pay attention to five main areas:

- *Improving PLEA's strategic management, vision and leadership for schools.* This should involve articulating the authority's vision clearly and communicating all priorities explicitly to all stakeholders. The roles and responsibilities of PLEA senior managers also need to be more clearly defined than they are at present. There is also a need to address the issue of quality directly. PLEA needs to be seen as an enabling authority which is openly accountable to its users.

- *Improving PLEA's planning process.* This involves reviewing its organisational structure, performance standards, accountability, and decision-making processes. This requires the prioritisation of a business plan for the authority.

- *A desegregation of budgets.* This is essential if levels of entitlement are to be resolved jointly between PLEA and the schools in the context of funding decisions and resources. It is also necessary to cost all services on a person-per-day or unit-of-delivery-cost basis if schools are to make best use of their entitlements and judge value for money.

- *Better management of services.* This is needed in order to provide schools with a clear picture of the services available, the extent to which they may be negotiable, their quality and standards and the methods by which provision is accountable to its users, including means of obtaining redress if the users are dissatisfied. These will involve better definitions of the services' use of resources, improved monitoring of performance and greater 'transparency' and openness.

- *Improving the partnership between schools and PLEA*. This can be achieved via better and regular consultation, communications and performance reviews, involving some review of working practices.

Responses

On receiving the consultants' report, PLEA acted promptly and identified a number of key areas for immediate action. The services provided were categorised under a limited number of headings.

- *Directorate responsibilities* included work to satisfy statutory requirements, DfEE returns, and work prioritised by the Director of Education to support schools.
- *Services to schools* included:
  1 Entitlement services – work which schools could expect as a right;
  2 Access services – specialist services which could be provided to specific schools according to specific needs and circumstances;
  3 Income generating services – provided by work which could be purchased by both LEA and grant-maintained schools.
- *Services to other sections within PLEA*. There was some pressure to establish an internal market for such work, but PLEA was resisting such a development at the time.

PLEA agreed an action plan to address the issues and criticisms identified, based on the following developments:

- *The identification and communication of key strategic priorities*. The aim is to articulate PLEA's mission clearly and explain how it is to be put into practice; it is related to available and up-to-date budgetary information.
- *The creation of Service Management Units (SMUs)*. These will develop a cost information framework for all services and monitor the performance of services with the intention of integrating a process of continuous improvement in response to user needs. The services that are provided by PLEA centrally are to be divided into four SMUs:
  1 *Central Services*: Finance, Personnel, IT/AV, Contracts, Repairs and Maintenance, Health and Safety, Legal Services;
  2 *Professional Education*: Curriculum and Staff Development, Monitoring and Evaluation, Management and Governors Support;
  3 *Learning Support*: Special Needs, Educational Psychologists, Educational Social Work;
  4 *Curriculum Enrichment*: Museums and Arts, Music, Outdoor Education.

- *The provision of information.* Within a specified time limit PLEA committed itself to distributing a series of documents to schools which provide descriptions, costs, and targets for all services provided centrally.

In taking this action, PLEA recognised the importance of marketing and customer care. Its interpretation of the 'marketing mix' acknowledged the specific needs of the education service, and involved the following definitions:

- *Product/service* – those services needed to meet current needs, and to respond to future developments;
- *Place* – the need to ensure that services were properly accessible by taking into account constraints of locations, time and information;
- *Price* – the determination of affordable costs to schools compatible with available resources;
- *Promotion* – the provision of accurate information about the services available to schools, both as entitlements and services for purchase.

To do this effectively PLEA also recognised the importance of accurate information on customers, markets, competitors and the services themselves.

QUESTIONS

1 Who are the main stakeholder groups and what are the multiple markets for PLEA?

2 What are the main problems associated with maintaining quality in the provision of services by PLEA?

3 What barriers to change are likely to be encountered in attempting to move PLEA services towards a more customer-led culture?

4 What are the major sources of uncertainty likely to affect the ability of schools to plan their budgets in this situation?

Strategic problems for the Employment Service

Context

This case study focuses on the work of the Employment Service (ES), which is an executive agency of the UK Department for Education and Employment (DfEE).

The aim of the Employment Service is to promote a competitive, efficient and flexible labour market by helping unemployed people into work, especially those who are disadvantaged, and by paying benefits and allowances to those entitled to them. ES operates through a network of over 1000 local offices (Job Centres), nearly 60 districts, 7 regional offices and has offices for Scotland and Wales. The function of the Disability Services Division is to manage the delivery of services and programmes to those in need and to help them into work.

The markets

The ES is charged with meeting the needs of one customer which is both the legitimiser and resourcer market. The Government determines the organisation's responsibilities and the scope of its functions, and also decides its levels of funding. The ES's primary market consists of the unemployed job-seekers, benefit claimants, non-claiming job-seekers and employers who have a demand for employment services. The terms 'customers' and 'clients' can be used to illustrate the fact that the ES uses different marketing approaches depending on whose needs it is attempting to satisfy. This is largely the result of the complexity of its markets and is typical of many public sector organisations. These markets may be summarised as follows:

- *The primary market*. This consists of three main constituencies:

  1 the clients who cannot exercise choice (the unemployed job-seeker or benefit-seeker);

  2 the customers who can exercise choice and are seeking jobs;

  3 the employers who notify the ES of job vacancies.

- *The secondary market*. This includes dependants, relatives and friends of primary clients, as well as all those who believe in the necessity and efficacy of the ES in contributing to the health of society in general. In an environment where levels of unemployment are relatively high, unemployment remains high on both national and local political agendas.

- *The legitimiser market*. This is complicated by the co-existence of a number of important stakeholders:

  1 those responsible for Social Security and employment legislation;

  2 the Department for Education and Employment itself;

  3 the Secretary of State;

  4 the Public Accounts Committee;

5 the Parliamentary Select Committee on Employment and Education;

6 the Ombudsman.

- *The resourcer market* often has a close relationship with the legitimiser market, and can involve:

1 Parliament;

2 the Treasury;

3 tax authorities;

4 National Insurance authorities;

5 the European Social Fund.

In this situation, it is not surprising that the ES pays as much attention to the resourcer and legitimiser clients as it does to the primary client, the unemployed and employers.

The portfolio of services

Over a 20-year period, the ES has built up a strong portfolio of 'products' in the form of 'back-to-work' and re-training programmes, initially as a response to rising unemployment figures and, more recently, in response to the Government's wish to remove more people from the State's 'dependency culture'. This portfolio of products, in conjunction with high profile on the high street, gave the ES a strong brand image in the employment marketplace.

Unfortunately, an analysis of the portfolio reveals that the ES now has relatively few new initiatives. Its traditional function continues through its high-street, Job-Centre services. The 'rising stars' of the portfolio have been the Job Seeker's Allowance, the pursuit of fraud and market testing. Even though the ES has strong environmental scanning systems in place, it has failed to acknowledge competition from other public sector organisations, in particular the Benefits Agency. It has also become preoccupied with a cost-focused business strategy which has demanded time-consuming restructuring and a concentration on quantitative, output-driven targets at the expense of developing products demanded by quality customers (that is, Government).

The majority of the work involved in the Job Seeker's Allowance has already been lost to the Benefits Agency. The ES lost this business because it was unable to demonstrate to Government that it already possessed experienced staff who were capable of developing more exciting and innovative approaches. Furthermore, the ES's 'workhorse' programmes, which demand considerable resources, are operating now in a market of falling unemployment, which inevitably reduces demand. Skills in counselling and in-depth advisory services which the ES once provided have long been sacrificed to a cost-focused, output-driven approach, removing what was once the ES's unique selling point – its ability to provide a high quality, professional service.

The concentration on a cost-focused marketing strategy has been the result of attempts to meet demands from Government to develop value-for-money, cost efficient (rather than effective), and economic services. This has led to the need to develop services that can be easily replicated and delivered in large volumes in order to gain economies of scale.

Product differentiation has been largely neglected. There has been some attempt at market segmentation by developing products to meet specific target groups – for example, the disabled, ethnic minorities, the long-term unemployed and those under the age of twenty-five. However, these have been largely developed with little or no consultation with end-users, and still reflect the orientation of a 'provider culture'. The ES has adopted a defensive approach. It has invested heavily in the development of systems, including sophisticated information technology systems, in order to demonstrate that it is cost effective for the benefit of its major government stakeholders. This has reinforced a product orientation and a dominance of 'systems rule'.

This product, rather than market, orientation, is further reinforced by the fact that the ES has a captive primary market. The ES is required to provide services to a market that, at present, has no choice but to use its services (if benefits are required). In the context of a political climate which seeks to reduce the level of public subsidy involved, customers have no effective choice but to use, often reluctantly, the services available.

Product development is further complicated by the complex functional relationships that exist between the consumer and the product. Many processes of consultation and agreement are required before a service can be made available. This can involve lengthy discussions with representatives from various groups within the ES's multiple markets, especially with the Treasury, lobby groups, government ministers and internal managers. Moreover, once a service is launched, it is subject to scrutiny from many sources – for example, the Ombudsman, the Employment Select Committee, the Public Accounts Committee and taxpayers in general. The net result is that a service runs the risk of being modified and 'watered down' in order to get through the processes involved successfully.

The mode of delivery

The ES operates as a national network. If it were a commercial organisation, this would give it a tremendous marketing advantage over some of its competitors – for example, the private employment agencies. However, this national network is designed more to ensure that the ES can deliver a cost-focused portfolio of services at the same time, in the same places and in the same manner, than to ensure that it can meet the different needs of its end-users. In this way, it can be argued that the ES meets demand efficiently and economically, but not necessarily effectively.

Job Centres are also designed to achieve the maximum throughput at the minimum cost with the minimum of queuing and waiting. To do this, a supermarket-style system, asking customers to pick their own job from a self-service information section, dominates. An information technology system (the Labour Market System – LMS) supports this facility by providing rapid job vacancy updating and benefit calculations.

Economies of scale can reduce the flexibility and range of services or products. This effect is becoming increasingly obvious as more and more of the services the ES is offering are 'contracted out' under franchise arrangements. For example, the majority of Job Clubs, once a very successful concept, are now largely delivered by contractors, which has led to disparate provision, greater difficulty in monitoring quality and equity, and a general decline in the standard of provision.

'Contracting out' has also reduced the power of place that the Job Centres once possessed. Although Job Centres still provide 'gateways' for most of the employment programmes on offer, many of the products are delivered elsewhere. The ES has recognised the inherent problems of this situation and has slowly reduced its presence in the High Street, returning to the cheaper premises in less prominent locations. Benefit and job-finding facilities have also been integrated into shared office accommodation, which can help the end-users. However, while relocation and integration have reduced costs, the ES is losing the brand image it had taken so long to create. This has had the effect that one source of supply for employers' vacancies is declining in a market that is already depressed.

The promotion of services

It can be argued that a 'production orientation' within the ES has, on the one hand, inhibited the development of proper market research aimed at identifying customer needs. On the other hand, the ES actually spends considerable amounts on raising the awareness of its services among the unemployed. The level of advertising is directly related to the success (take-up) of its services and to the levels of unemployment existing. Promotional activity usually adopts a 'chase demand' strategy but, as might be expected, demand exceeds supply. This creates difficult relationships between the ES and Government. Government can be critical of the ES's apparent 'failure to deliver' just at the point at which increases in demand begin to develop. This leads to an alternate switching on and off of resources and makes it difficult to plan their most effective use.

The price of the service

In the desire to reduce costs, the quality of service is likely to suffer. The ES appears to have missed a competitive opportunity to use pricing as a means of generating business. A unit-costing approach encourages high-volume, quantitative output. The pay system and the annual performance agreement for the ES support this approach, and there is little reward to be gained for improving the quality, as distinct from the quantity, of service. It would be possible to consider other approaches – for example, by introducing differential charging for different levels of service, for both job-seekers and job providers. In fact, there are historical precedents for this, for example, the fees charged to employers who once used the now defunct Professional and Executive Recruitment (PER) service. Basic and initial job-seeking advice could be provided free (not unlike the old-style free check-ups at dentists and opticians) with a higher level of service and an appropriate level of scaled charges offered beyond that point.

At the time of writing, there is also no cost differentiation in terms of 'weighting' costs for more demanding and time-consuming job-seekers. There is little incentive for ES staff to deal with what are, perhaps, its most demanding clients. These are actually the very ones who might, in fact, benefit the most from a greater level of support. By default, the existing system encourages staff to choose and concentrate on the 'easier' job-seeker targets. In fact, by concentrating on easier targets, the ES leaves itself vulnerable to accusations that its work could easily be done by private sector organisations and that it is failing to support those people who need the help the most.

Conclusions

This situation has positioned the ES at the high-volume, low-cost end of the employment agency market. Competition is fierce and volatile in this position. Assuming that unemployment continues to fall, or fails to increase dramatically, there appear to be four strategic marketing options the ES could pursue:

- *Do nothing and wait and see how the environment affects the organisation.* Some critics of the ES would agree that this appears to be ES's present strategy, because it seems unable to adopt any other.

- *Go on the offensive and market the organisation more aggressively to the Government,* as the major stakeholder and resource provider. This would involve demonstrating the added value provided by the ES. While there is value to the end-user in terms of the service offered, there is, arguably, an even greater value to the Government if quality of service can be added to the cost value of its investment. This strategy would require the ES to commission extensive market research among the users of its services in order to demonstrate the benefits of such quality added value. It would also require investment in training and development. In some circumstances it could necessitate replacing staff and recruiting new staff. This strategy is fairly long-term and would be staff intensive. In the current environment, where returns on Government investment are required speedily, it might appear to be asking too much, too late.

- *Strategic withdrawal might leave the ES to concentrate even further on honing its cost-focused approach.* This would require investment in the introduction of even more information technology. This could be more attractive in the long term. Initial investment would pay for itself as the result of savings gained from a substantial staff-downsizing (or right-sizing) exercise. The danger with this strategy is that it would make the ES continually vulnerable to internal competition and, more threatening, increasingly exposed to the threat of privatisation of functions and services.

- *The ES could consider a strategic alliance with a competitor organisation or with an organisation that could bring in complementary skills or IT efficiencies that are already well established.* Such an alliance could be formed, for example, with the Benefits Agency (BA), which has already won from the ES the right to deliver the new Job-Seekers Allowance (JSA), albeit operating through the ES Job-Centre network. The difficulty with this approach is that the opportunity may have already been lost.

QUESTIONS

1. What problems for ES management can be identified which derive from the existence of multiple markets for the ES's services?

2. What is the relationship between the demands of the primary and the resourcer markets?

3. What are the advantages and disadvantages of introducing more competition into the work currently undertaken by the ES?

4. Given the information provided, what do you consider to be the most appropriate choice of strategy, and why?

Marketing and the introduction of the Private Finance Initiative into the NHS

The context

The Private Finance Initiative (PFI) is a scheme by which the UK Government is trying to encourage additional, private sector investment in public sector provision. PFI is designed to attract private sector funding into, for example, the National Health Service (NHS) and to encourage the public sector to seek additional means of achieving funding and efficiency by partnerships with the private sector. This will reduce capital costs to the Treasury and, it is hoped, begin to blur the traditional distinctions and boundaries between the private and public provision of health care services. The NHS does indeed need funding for its hospital modernisation programmes. Initially, however, the scheme met with considerable resistance from a wide range of stakeholders, not least from those who fear that any form of privatisation in the context of public sector industries is equivalent to 'selling the family silver' and is ideologically incompatible with their socially altruistic missions.

There is little in the way of a 'true', competitive market in the UK's National Health Service (NHS) or, in fact, in most other public sector industries. Despite the introduction of compulsory competitive tendering in many services, and the development of various forms of internal markets, many public sector organisations, with their traditional cultures, find it difficult to apply a marketing management approach to non-profit activities. Despite, or perhaps because of, their traditions of public service, they have not thought it necessary to make themselves attractive. They can still find it difficult to treat their clients and customers sensitively, particularly if their structures are large and bureaucratic.

The concept and *ethos* of marketing is alien to most public sector workers and this can provoke resistance to both the PFI and to the introduction of competition within organisations such as the NHS. Private investors will obviously seek returns on their investments. They will examine possibilities using marketing feasibility studies. By virtue of their investments, they will acquire influence and control within public sector services. The effects of NHS resistance should not be underestimated. Delays in introducing PFI have already been experienced, despite government assurances (May 1997) that the scheme was still 'on course'. The PFI was reported as having experienced another setback when banks were advised that individual hospital trusts might not be legally entitled to sign PFI agreements without further legislation.

Nevertheless, advocates of PFI continue to argue that it represents a process by which the introduction of a free-market environment will increase competition and, thereby, efficiency. It will provide modern technologies and services to the NHS with minimal immediate cost to public funding. It will reduce the power of some major stakeholders, such as consultants, and improve the quality of patient care within budget.

The stakeholders

An attempt at identifying the stakeholders in PFI within an NHS context uses four main categories:

1 *actors*, or those who control and operate systems and activities;

2 *advantaged customers*, who benefit from the systems and activities,

3 *disadvantaged customers*, who stand to lose in some way; and

4 *miscellaneous other stakeholders*.

Actors include the following categories:

- Hospital consultants
- Doctors, nurses and other professions supplementary to medicine
- Referring GPs and fundholders
- Purchasers
- Family Practitioners' Association
- MPs and Government.

The many categories of customers are listed in Table A.2.

Table A.2 Customers of PFI within the NHS

Advantaged	Disadvantaged	Other stakeholders
• Some patients • The Treasury/Government • Fundholders • Doctors who will get the equipment they want sooner • Purchasers by reducing the cost of services • The private sector • Very large companies who can control the consortia required to fund major PFI projects • Some hospital managers	• Medical consultants who will lose power and will be employed by the private sector with all of the 'rigours' that entails, i.e. producing the output on time to quality standards • Other professions supplementary to medicine • The companies who provide the services or products • The private hospital sector, i.e. BUPA • Small companies who cannot influence the larger members of the consortia • Some patients • Some hospital managers	• Patients and relatives • Foreign suppliers • Builders and project managers, architects, etc. • Hospital managers who can fit into the new system • Taxpayers

Advantages and disadvantages of the PFI

Those who advocate the PFI argue that the initiative can improve the quality of NHS services by allowing a wider range of potential providers to compete in terms of quality standards. The NHS would also benefit from opportunities to use new ideas and better techniques for forging strategic alliances with other organisations. Private finance schemes can also increase cost-effectiveness through the introduction of competition, sharing some overheads with the private sector and thus benefiting from economies of scale, and by taking advantage of the private sector's particular skills and strengths, especially in terms of operational efficiency.

The Government was seeking to minimise risk to the NHS by sharing it with the private sector, using contracts which can include incentives to reduce the likelihood of things going wrong, and benefiting from the private sector's expertise in managing and minimising risk. A more cynical interpretation offered by the *Private Finance Guide* (1994) and other documents, might conclude, however, that the prime objective was to transfer most of the risk to the private sector and to minimise cost to the NHS, with minimal and scant regard to the private sector's ability to derive additional benefits, although it has been argued that the private sector will enjoy both short-term and long-term benefits. Private sector involvement with the NHS should provide more scope for business. Commercial organisations should be able to exploit their expertise to make profits from providing high quality, cost-effective services to the NHS. PFI contracts are expected to give private sector companies opportunities for expansion and the creation of more jobs. In fact, the private sector already derives business from the public sector by supplying the NHS with materials, consumables, capital equipment, etc. It already provides revenue by the use of 'unconventional finance', in the form of capital equipment leasing. PFI will only become really attractive to the private sector, if it can provide an additional source of earnings and profit.

The private sector has not previously made any contributions to the NHS in the areas of staffing provision, management and infrastructure (e.g. buildings). The PFI provides a means by which some of these areas could pass into private sector control, if not ownership. Recent PFI invitations to tender have been restricted to buildings and service facilities provision; medical staffing is to remain within local NHS control.

How can additional profits be made by private sector organisations working with the NHS unless they are able to act as employers and thus control or influence the primary stakeholders, namely the medical staff? It is the medical staff who have traditionally been responsible for controlling most of the spending within the NHS. Unless this group can be influenced, private companies can have very little power in managing resources and budgets.

The NHS marketing mix

The NHS *'product'* is the provision of health care in a market which is characterised by an infinite demand potential and finite ability to resource supply. While technology plays an important part, ultimately it is the 'service contact' element which determines quality and end-user satisfaction. The product is subject to legislation in terms of the quality of provision and the influence of *The Citizen's Charter*, but the requirements of purchasers, such as the fundholding general practitioners, must be satisfied. Hospitals achieve varying levels of excellence.

The *price* of NHS services is influenced by the desire to equate cost with price. Any new initiative such as the PFI must balance the NHS needs for low costs against the desire of private companies and their shareholders for profits. In private hospitals, profits are acceptable and their patients have a choice of providers. In the NHS, profit making would immediately become a politically sensitive issue. The nature of this playing field produces problems for PFI players. Since the current projected level of return on investment for large projects is more than 30 years, this situation is unlikely to encourage many companies to join PFI consortia.

There are severe restrictions on the *promotion* and advertising of professional services, particularly in the NHS field. These may well impact on the PFI by placing constraints on the promotion needed in any competitive market. However, it may well be possible to influence the supply chain – for example, by promoting the advantages of the PFI to fundholding purchasers of the product, much in the sense of industrial marketing. Nevertheless, it will probably be necessary to promote the concept and benefits of PFI to patients and other stakeholders.

The *place or position* of health care provision is changing, irrespective of the impact the PFI may have. There is a current trend away from large district general hospitals towards smaller, community-based units. These have lower running costs, but tend not to be located in prime city locations and therefore do not always meet the geographical needs of patients. It is also sometimes difficult to attract the best senior medical consultants to smaller units. There is also a trend towards creating strategic partnerships with local GP fundholders. Marketing needs to identify such considerations in deciding the appropriate focus for PFI investment.

It is also necessary to consider *people* in the marketing mix. This is perhaps the most difficult area because of the wide range of stakeholders present, most of whom have different objectives. Currently there is massive but silent resistance to any form of privatisation of the NHS by the PFI or any other means. This resistance needs to be overcome by appropriate promotion to explain the benefits to all stakeholders. Training is another means by which people from both the public and the private sectors could collaborate in order to understand each others' needs and cultures. It is fair to say that many organisations within the public sector are trying to 'cross train' their staff in this way, but the private sector appears less willing to train in, and understand, public sector management issues. Unless both parties understand the needs of the other, then neither will satisfy its aspirations.

The concept of *profit* also needs some consideration. Although the NHS is a nonprofit organisation, operating surpluses are permitted. The concept of profit and loss is alien to NHS culture and, historically, most NHS managers regarded 'losses' as the price to be paid for a National Health Service. Overspends would be covered by government finance. Financial discipline was relatively poor. The size and complexity of the NHS makes it difficult to measure in terms of cost, benefit, and profit. If financial profitability were to be used as the most important criterion of success, many social services activities would not be considered viable at all.

PFI consortia

The complexity of PFI consortia demands a well structured market position. So far, most PFI consortia have consisted of a 'Special Purpose Company', formed by a construction contractor, an operator (providing non-clinical services, often termed 'hotel services'), and a funding institution. For a typical multi-department hospital development, the consortium relationship 'map' would take the form shown in Fig. A.1. The relationships between the consortium and the NHS trust (represented by the diagonal arrows) will take the form of development agreements, leases and service contracts.

Conclusions

Few providers have the capability to provide such a comprehensive service as the NHS. The benefits of private sector involvement in NHS developments are difficult to quantify. The creation of consortia to meet these challenges adds to the complexity, cost and time needed to implement such massive projects. Projects such as the Channel Tunnel have encountered a considerable number of serious problems. It may well prove that some public activities are incapable of making profits in conventional terms. It is the responsibility of private sector marketing to evaluate

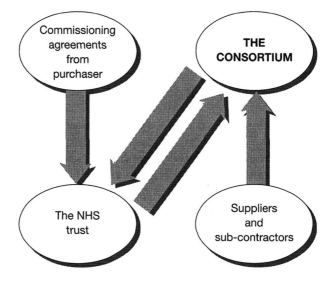

Fig. A.1 The consortium relationship map for a multi-department hospital development

those PFI projects which will minimise the risk to both parties and proceed only when a real profit can be made by bringing added value to the processes involved. Within the PFI initiative, marketing is the responsibility of both the private and public sector partners, and should ensure the provision of the appropriate products and services to the final user at the end of the value chain – that is, the patient.

QUESTIONS

1 What are the main roles marketing can play in the PFI?

2 What marketing strategies might be employed to satisfy the demands of the secondary market in this case study?

3 What are the main sources of resistance to change which are likely to exist within the NHS?

4 What cultural changes may be necessary to effect the outcome of a successful PFI implementation?

Pubton's Sandbags Arts Centre

Context

The Sandbags Arts Centre (SAC) occupies a redundant coachworks on the edge of Pubton's city centre, beside the somewhat polluted waters of the Purton Stream, which flow muddily past on their way to the Spluding Navigation. During the Second World War, the building was used to fill sandbags for defence purposes. Local people make humorous references to 'the modern culture bunker'. Although Pubton possessed a theatre and a municipal art gallery with some good examples of nineteenth- and twentieth-century British painting and sculpture, as well as the Postlethwaite collection of Victorian and Edwardian art, there was little provision for contemporary visual and performing arts in the city until 1978. In that year, a group of individuals got together to form the Sandbags Art Centre, with the aim of providing the city with a venue for performing and visual arts.

Pubton City Council was instrumental in helping SAC obtain the lease of the building, and permission to develop it to provide a 110-seat auditorium, a small gallery, a cafeteria and bar, two printmaking studios, one small meeting room and an office. A total of £127 000 was raised by fundraising events, local business sponsorship and private subscriptions for this purpose, and SAC was officially opened in January 1979. SAC's mission statement states that it aims to provide access to, participation in and promotion of new performing and media arts. SAC is a registered charity and a company limited by guarantee for trading purposes.

SAC's annual turnover increased rapidly, and by 1995 it stood at £310 000, 74 per cent of which was generated directly by the Centre's activities. Unfortunately, as a result of recent trading losses, and an unfortunate franchise agreement for the bar (which was terminated in 1992) the 1995 balance sheet showed an excess of liabilities over assets of £16 246. A successful public appeal was launched which raised £24 262, and SAC committed itself to a new business plan designed to ensure its financial viability and long-term future.

SAC's organisational structure has proved less than satisfactory. The original council of management had up to 22 members and, partly due to the persistence of a voluntary and 'self-help' culture, this often made it difficult to establish clear lines of responsibility. Although the Centre will continue to need the valuable services of its volunteers, it recognised the necessity of developing a more professional management structure even before proposals for structural changes were made in 1995.

An audit of SAC's position in June 1995 identified the Centre's weaknesses as follows:

- regular trading losses and accumulating deficit;
- weak staffing structure;
- lack of good financial control, coherent pricing policy and financial expertise;
- poor public image;
- inadequate marketing information;
- poor building maintenance;
- inadequate technical resources.

The product

SAC provides an annual programme of events involving music, drama, and exhibitions of prints. The print workshops are equipped with two etching presses and an offset lithography press, and are used by local artists and for classes in printmaking. SAC's educational work includes workshops for schools (during term-time and in the school holidays), classes for adults in a number of skills, and training for community arts workers. It provides a venue for ethnic minority cultural groups. SAC has also been successful in obtaining funding for work with disabled people.

Reduced subsidies to drama companies have resulted in a diminishing number of drama and dance events on SAC's programmes. However, it has maintained a lively programme of comedy entertainment, and has a good reputation as a venue for the work of aspiring young comedians. The Centre also collaborates with other organisations, such as Pubton City Council, in organising special events in the city, such as local festivals.

SAC's programme of events (about 150 each year) has introduced modern music, dance, theatre and mime to the city. Additionally, its 1994–5 activities included:

- 68 local community groups hiring the auditorium for stage productions (theatre, amateur opera and musical performances);
- 42 printmaking workshops;
- six exhibitions of prints and graphic work;
- three 'outreach' events with local communities outside Pubton.

It is worth emphasising at this point that SAC's products, with the exception of the sales from the gallery (on which it levies a 10 per cent commission), are generally performances, lectures and workshops. The nature of these products create specific issues for marketing in this context.

Evaluation

SAC's main strengths are mainly in its music and printmaking activities. The Centre has provided much support to young classical soloists, and has a long association with jazz musicians, traditional folk music, especially Irish and Scottish, and with world music. The Centre has excellent contacts with a range of young musicians and music agencies. SAC's print workshops and facilities have an established reputation and artists who use the Centre regularly contribute work to a number of national and international events.

There are only some 17 other printmaking workshops in England, Scotland and Wales, most of which have only existed since the late 1960s. All have membership systems and charge for the use of their facilities, offering between 18 and 70 hours' access per week. They raise revenue through a number of activities, including membership fees, session charges, sales of materials, sales of prints, framing services, teaching, exhibition fees and commercial printing. In the case of SAC's printmaking workshops, there is no competition from similar facilities within a 35-mile radius of Pubton. The processes available also vary widely, from etching (the most popular) to silk-screen and photographic processes. Most workshops run evening classes in printmaking, as does SAC.

The Regional Arts Council Board with responsibility for the Pubton area made a routine appraisal of SAC in 1994. The Board was critical of SAC in three main areas: *core staffing, management structure* and the *building itself*. The core staff then consisted of one full-time director and a part-time publicity officer. It was apparent that SAC needed a full-time administrator, especially to deal with financial matters. It also needed to re-examine the role of publicity and marketing. The management structure had no formal or hierarchical structure; this was essential in order to ensure a clear definition of responsibilities.

SAC's accounts reveal that it uses some of its activities to subsidise others. An analysis of the accounts for the 1994–5 financial year indicates that the Centre was in deficit under three headings.

- The programme of events showed an expenditure of more than £14 000 over income. Losses were particularly high in the area of artists' fees and expenses, many of which had been guaranteed irrespective of the level of box office income.
- The educational activities showed a loss of some £1200.
- The Centre's general expenses (administration, buildings and publicity) exceeded grant income by some £8000.

On the other hand, the visual arts activities made a contribution of more than £1000, and the bar and cafeteria made more than £15 000 in contribution.

SAC's pricing strategy has suffered from a lack of adequate marketing information. This urgently needs more professional development in view of the fact that almost 50 per cent of attendances continue to attract concessionary rates (e.g. students, unemployed and pensioners).

Proposals

SAC produced a new Business Plan in summer 1995 which addressed the problems facing the Centre. Its implementation required major changes to SAC's management structure, financial systems, programming and publicity, and at the same time accepted the need to continue raising funds for the redevelopment of the Sandbags building. The proposed budget accepted the need for some activities to continue to subsidise others.

The new management structure represented a simpler and more hierarchical chain of command and responsibilities. The original council of management was slimmed down to six members of the board. The Centre Manager retained overall responsibility for operations, but was now given a full-time Administration and Finance Manager to co-ordinate the bar and cafeteria activities and those of the volunteers. Each of these areas was given its own manager/supervisor. A Marketing Manager was given responsibility for the box office. A Printmaking Studios Officer, an Education Officer and a Technical Manager (also responsible for maintenance and cleaning) completed the senior management team.

Systems were put in place to improve the control of orders and sales, payments and debts. Computer programs for a new PC machine were bought in to ensure that SAC could produce monthly updates on the Centre's financial position, which would be reviewed regularly on this basis.

The procedures for running the Centre's artistic programme were revised. Fees and expenses were no longer guaranteed, but negotiated separately for each planned event on the basis of agreed percentages. This strategy was designed to reduce the risk of events failing to meet their target audience numbers.

The introduction of a full-time Publicity and Marketing Manager was intended to achieve more accurate sales forecasts. Publicity costs were reduced by the simple expedient of reducing the frequency of programme publications (originally published monthly). Direct responsibility for the box office allowed the Centre to begin to define its primary market in more detail.

A regular review of the bar and cafeteria pricing policies was designed to ensure that the Centre's 'cash cow' could continue to earn a level of contribution which could subsidise some of the other activities. The importance of this should not be underestimated, since this contribution could represent an important percentage of SAC's annual turnover.

It was also recognised that the Centre's volunteers urgently needed proper training, better management and more involvement with decision-making processes. There was also a need for a recruitment and induction programme.

Marketing

Historically, SAC has paid relatively little attention to its marketing strategy, having long prioritised publicity functions at the expense of marketing information. The Centre admitted that it failed to realise its market potential and, at the time of the 1995 Business Plan, had relatively little detailed and co-ordinated information about its audiences and users. This represented a major weakness in its pricing strategies. SAC actually attracts very diverse audiences for its events programme, and without the ability to target specific market segments, SAC has been unable to direct its promotion in useful directions. Although it has clearly established local interest groups for specific types of event, it has never developed a systematic way of identifying them and has instead continued to rely on general poster and leaflet publicity within the Pubton area.

SAC also needs to take care of its other markets, particularly grant aid, which provide much of its regular sources of income other than box office, user and hire charges. SAC depends upon grant aid for some 21 per cent of its annual income, and will be seeking yet more grants and sponsorship to finance its intended capital programme. This requires some real investment of management time, and applications increasingly demand a professional approach to costing and projections.

Implications of change

The proposed changes will inevitably have an impact upon SAC's culture. Having been in existence for some 17 years, the organisation has developed a unique way of doing things, and there will be some members who will find change uncomfortable. Once it was established, SAC developed a particular 'style' of culture which still persists. The building, which now awaits development and improvements, possesses a friendly, but 'worn' atmosphere.

Three wide steps lead to large, glass panelled doors with brass furniture, under a shallow wooden porch which supports the permanent bill board advertising the current programme event. The small entrance hall, with a little booking kiosk directly opposite the main doors, is patently in need of a coat of paint, and the thread-bare carpet pays a visible tribute to the feet of countless visitors. The cafeteria, entered by the swinging double doors to the left of the hall, can seat about 55 people, and has an adjacent kitchen. An attempt has been made to give the cafeteria a somewhat 'bohemian' atmosphere by hanging a large number of old posters and prints around the walls. The bar is situated at one end, and is seriously in need of refurbishment. Next to the bar, a large signpost directs visitors up a flight of wooden, uncarpeted stairs to the exhibition gallery on the first floor, and to 'the office'. The door to the auditorium and print workshops is on the other side of the entrance hall. Due to the weight of the presses, the print workshops had to be installed on the ground floor, next to the West side of the auditorium space which takes up much of the building's volume. Above them are some small dressing rooms, with their own 'back stairs' access to the stage area. The workshops possess a comforting odour of traditional printing ink, and a small glazed unit in a corner of the largest studio extracts the fumes from the acid used to prepare the etching plates. The auditorium has a flexible seating system, whereby tiered seating can be extended from the back of the hall to provide 110 seats in total. When this is folded away, the hall can accommodate a standing audience of 215.

Staff and volunteers operate on friendly, first-name terms. Although everyone assumes responsibility for a particular task, everyone seems quite prepared to lend a hand with any problem as it emerges. It must be said, however, that this contributes to a feeling that SAC is still largely an amateur organisation and, indeed, the time and goodwill of its unpaid volunteers is essential to its survival. Some of them are unemployed young people in their twenties, with a sincere interest in the arts, who are keen to see the Centre encourage young musicians, artists and performers. Others belong to the generation who founded SAC in the 1970s, and manage to convey the impression that they are only too keen to further the cause of 'healthy' modern cultural activities. However, the need for a more focused and professional approach to management and administration at SAC has already alienated some of the volunteers. The proposed developments will inevitably disturb SAC's existing culture.

QUESTIONS

1 How might SAC best influence its culture towards a more 'professional' approach towards the business of its activities?

2 What non-financial performance indicators might SAC use to monitor and improve the effectiveness of its activities?

3 SAC has been accused of providing too wide a programme of artistic events. Would a better focused product range be an advantage to the organisation?

4 What kinds of marketing information does SAC require? Given the limitations imposed by its budgets, how might these best be obtained?

The South Yorkshire Supertram

Context

Over the years, Sheffield has retained a nostalgia for the tram. Sheffield was among the first cities to introduce horse-drawn, and then electric trams in the nineteenth century. It was among the last big cities to get rid of their original tramway systems. The last Sheffield tram ran in October 1960. The tramway system was ideal for Sheffield, a city of many steep gradients on its seven hills. In winter, the trams were renowned for their ability to deal with snow and ice. The costs of electricity were defrayed by cheap electricity generated using the waste heat produced by Sheffield's massive steelworks. In the 1950s the tramway network was comprehensive, reaching out to the limits of the city's boundaries. A journey across the city could be made for as little as one (old) penny.

The decision to phase out the trams was taken for a number of reasons. Trams, running on fixed rails, came to be seen as an 'inflexible' mode of transport. They had become unfashionable with local government professionals. The system could be put out of action quickly, as the 'Sheffield Blitz' had demonstrated in the Second World War. Efficient, diesel-engined buses had been developed. In the late 1950s, buses were increasingly seen as a more appropriate means of transporting people in and out of cities.

From October 1960, the old tram routes were served by buses, despite a persistent cry of 'bring back the trams' which was heard from most sectors of the population. In 1972, the then Department of the Environment suggested that an elevated mini-tram system might be considered for the city. In 1976, the Sheffield and Rotherham land use transportation study team recommended that seven transport 'corridors' leading out of the city centre should be safeguarded for a new, segregated public transport scheme. Sheffield City Council (SCC) supported these recommendations until 1984. In that year, it was decided to prioritise the 'corridors' to Middlewood/Stannington (relatively well established northern areas of the city), and to Mosborough (an area with extensive new housing developments to the west of the city). At this time, the South Yorkshire County Council (SYCC), after exploring new transport policies, expressed itself in favour of proposals for a modern tramway system to use these corridors.

In 1985, the South Yorkshire Passenger Transport Executive promoted a parliamentary bill for a 'light rail' system from Mosborough and Herdings to Middlewood and Stannington (*see* Fig. A.2). In 1988, Sheffield City Council insisted that a second line was also needed to run through the Lower Don Valley to the new Meadowhall Shopping Mall. This line would also serve the new sports complexes built in the area for the World Student Games, and would provide a public transport infrastructure to support the new industrial developments which Sheffield was seeking to attract to an area blighted by the closure of heavy steel and engineering plants in the 1980s.

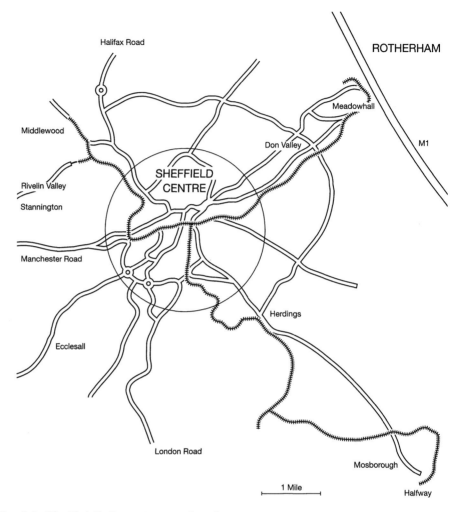

Fig. A.2 Sheffield's Supertram network

Sheffield and cheap transport

In the 1970s, South Yorkshire's transport policies were noticeably different from those adopted by other authorities in the UK. Rather than focus on the development of capital projects, the local Passenger Transport Authority followed the social agenda of the local metropolitan councils. It maintained a policy of low bus fares to attract motorists onto public transport. Fares were maintained at their 1975 levels for almost ten years, which meant a reduction in real terms. At the end of the period, fares were only 20 per cent or less of those in other parts of the country.

During the period of the low-fares policy, bus usage rose slightly from 203 million to 209 million passenger kilometres, against a national trend of declining bus patronage. The evidence suggests that this increase was not due to a large number of short, cheap journeys, but was a result of a policy designed to encourage the use of public transport instead of cars. There was a small reduction in the use of cars at the height of the cheap fares policy. When that policy ended, car use increased between 1981 and 1991. The cheap fares policy ended finally in 1986, and in the period 1984–6 bus fares rose by some 225 per cent. They eventually quadrupled.

Following bus deregulation, the number of bus kilometres (not passenger journeys) rose from 61.2 million kilometres per year in 1981 to 78.2 million kilometres per year in 1991. In effect, there were more buses chasing fewer passengers. A survey of buses entering Sheffield in 1985 showed 10 920 buses passing by, each transporting an average of 24.1 people. In 1991, after deregulation, the number of buses had risen to 13 326 with the average number of people per bus falling to 16.7. This represents a reduction in utilisation of 15 per cent. Furthermore, deregulation had brought onto the roads numerous buses of varying ages and condition – a distinct shift from the policy, originally adopted by the South Yorkshire Passenger Transport Executive, of ensuring that only modern, well maintained buses were in service. In 1996, it was estimated that passenger miles were only half the level they had been at the height of the cheap fares policy.

Information from the South Yorkshire Passenger Transport Executive suggests that there is a relationship between the substantial increases in fares and the failure to increase the quality of the service. The decision to move towards trams was related to a desire to improve the quality of services for passengers.

Trends in car ownership

The South Yorkshire Passenger Transport Executive suggests that, between 1975 and 1985, car ownership nationally grew by 21 per cent. In South Yorkshire, it remained below the national average. Data from the 1991 census indicate that car ownership in South Yorkshire grew over the ten-year period between 1981 and 1991 by over 30 per cent, with most of the growth occurring between 1985 and 1986. In fact, South Yorkshire showed the highest growth of any UK region in the period between 1985 and 1991.

Funding the tramway system

Following parliamentary approval, funding for the tramway project, amounting to £240 million for building the tramway and initiating its services, had to be obtained. It was always intended that the people of South Yorkshire would not be asked to finance the tramway through increases in local taxation, and that the Supertram development would not prejudice other capital projects. These objectives were realised in part under section 56 of the 1968 Transport Act. Obtaining the necessary grant involved meeting the condition that the combined value of revenue and economic benefits would show a surplus over operating costs sufficient to yield an 8 per cent real rate of return on the total investment. The Government also required the development gain to landowners along the route to make a contribution to the cost of the project.

Other non-user benefits identified as part of the grant process included:

- tendered bus savings, i.e. a substitution of trams for buses;
- traffic decongestion;
- a reduction in road accidents;
- amenity improvements;
- better facilities for those with impaired mobility;
- employment benefits;
- city regeneration benefits.

The government grant formed only a part of the funding. Other sources of funding for the project included:

1 a cash grant;
2 credit approvals, for which the cost of borrowing was funded wholly through revenue support grant to the four metropolitan districts of South Yorkshire;
3 credit approvals for which the costs of borrowing were to be funded wholly through operating profits and the eventual sale of the operating company;
4 contributions from developers.

The funding and repayment arrangements are complex.

According to *Modern Tramway* (April 1991), the Government's reasons for supporting the project to such an extent were that:

- Light rail systems provide faster and more reliable systems of public transport.
- There would be benefits from traffic decongestion – for example, from taking more cars out of the city centre and freeing its roads for the more effective use of buses.
- Trams have environmental benefits.
- The resulting economic regeneration of the city would produce more jobs, particularly in the lower Don Valley.
- A reduction in carbon monoxide emissions would improve the air quality of the city.

Management of the project

The management and operating structure of the project is relatively complex, not least because of both political and operational considerations.

The Supertram project is managed by South Yorkshire Supertram Ltd, which has an exclusive operating licence for an initial 30-year period. The company is a wholly owned subsidiary of South Yorkshire Passenger Transport Executive (SYPTE), which in turn implements the policies of the South Yorkshire Passenger Transport Authority (SYPTA), representing the interests of Sheffield City Council and the Borough Councils of Barnsley, Doncaster and Rotherham. It should be noted that the South Yorkshire Supertram operates within the boundaries of

Sheffield. It is the responsibility of the South Yorkshire Passenger Transport Executive to privatise South Yorkshire Supertram Ltd within two years of it beginning its operations.

Implications of constructing Supertram

The Supertram system consists of 29 kilometres of route with 45 specially constructed tram stops (*see* Fig. A.2). Little of the route uses either existing or disused line. In this, the South Yorkshire system differs significantly from the new tramway systems in other cities – for example, in Manchester and in Newcastle. Both the systems in Manchester and Newcastle use fast, existing commuter rail lines to bring passengers directly into the city centre. In other words their city centre tram networks extend existing commuter networks, reducing walking and the need to change modes of transport. About half of the Sheffield route mileage is laid in the traditional form of a tramway – that is within the surface of the carriageway in which it is laid and over which other road traffic is able to pass. In these areas, the tram is subject to delays caused by normal traffic congestion, etc.

During the construction period, the civil engineering works were extensive and prolonged. This caused considerable traffic disruption and, in some cases, spelt commercial ruin for some businesses. Construction of Phase 1 of the project, Sheffield City Centre to the Meadowhall Shopping Mall, was started in August 1991 and opened for operation in March 1994. Phase 2, approximately 4 kilometres long to Norfolk Park, was opened in August 1994. The whole 29 kilometre route, developed in eight phases, was completed on 23 October 1995.

Routes, stops and vehicles

The Supertram network has changed its route structure since it first opened. There are now three designated routes – Yellow, Blue and Purple – two of which pass through the city centre. It can be seen from the map in Fig. A.2 that the lines from the outer parts of the city follow 'dog leg' routes rather than run straight into the city. This can result in extended journey times. For example, the time from Halfway to the city centre is 35 minutes, which is generally longer than an equivalent car journey. The route through the city centre passes the end of a pedestrian precinct, but essentially bypasses the main shopping areas of the city. However, the route is close to the city's two universities, the 'professional' area, and is in close proximity to the railway station and central bus station.

The tram stops are set at approximately 500-metre intervals and all are designed to give high standards of accessibility for all passengers. The platform top is level with the floor of the tram, about 14 inches from the rail level, and all stops have ramps. Most stops have shelters, ticket machines and ticket validators. Signs indicate the name of the tram stop but there is little information about the times and frequency of trams. When asked about this, the operators once stated that 'everybody' knew that the trams ran at eight- or ten-minute intervals.

There are 25 Supertram vehicles, designed and built by Siemens of Germany. The placing of the contract outside the UK caused some critical comment but was not a major issue. The trams themselves are made up of three articulated sections with an overall length of about 35 metres. Large cars were chosen in order to provide good passenger capacity with lower travel frequencies, thus reducing the consequent disruption of traffic as well as operating costs.

The design of the cars is complex, as it has to match the needs of relatively low access levels at the doors, while accommodating the powered bogies which incorporate the wheels and the motors. This results in a multi-level floor layout.

The fittings, colour scheme and general design of the interior of the passenger cars are claimed to be the result of extensive market research. This level of consultation has created an interior which publicity material claims to be as aesthetically pleasing as it is functional, providing a further incentive to car users to change to public transport. Passenger information relating to journeys is given by an LCD 'next stop' display, and announcements are also made via a public address system which has an automatic volume adjustment control.

Overall the tramcar is designed to be structurally strong and lightweight. This gives a high power-to-weight ratio, and enables it to deal with the Sheffield topography, which includes gradients as steep as 1 in 10.

Comparative projects

Research suggests that more than 40 per cent of commuters using the Manchester Metrolink have the option to use cars, but prefer to leave them at home. Patronage has steadily risen from 7.5 million passengers carried on the same lines before the development of Metrolink, to some 13 million passengers at the end of 1993. New markets have been created and the trams are busy throughout the day. Passengers use Metrolink for journeys they would not previously have made. Traders as far afield as Bury and Altrincham, as well as those from the city centre, have all expressed their overwhelming support for Metrolink.

Fares, pricing and use

The pricing strategy of the Sheffield company has changed since the launch of the tram, but pricing had to recognise that Supertram had to compete with bus and rail services. The slightly higher fares reflected the higher quality of the provision which Supertram offered. The Marketing Director, Peter Gross, expressed some optimism in a newspaper article when he stated that 'Supertram had been set up to make a reasonable profit', and that he believed that competition from buses was expected to be minimal, since Supertram would tap new markets in the form of car drivers.

The Supertram system was originally designed as a barrier-free system where tickets are obtained on the platform or from ticket sales outlets. Tickets needed to be validated before entering the tram. In the early period, there was an education system for potential passengers and only a small proportion of passengers were found to be without a ticket. Subsequently, however, conductors were introduced onto the trams in order to act as 'behaviour superintendants' and to reduce the numbers of passengers travelling without tickets.

In spite of the initial optimism surrounding Supertram's launch and the pride in it which many Sheffield people felt, Supertram has not measured up to its financial expectations. Passenger numbers are significantly less than projected, although they continue to grow. Operating losses are substantial, amounting to millions of pounds per year. Thus, late in 1996 and early in 1997, representatives of the Councils involved met government ministers to try to obtain further government assistance in reducing the debt.

Evaluation

During the original planning process, public meetings and exhibitions were held in venues along the proposed routes in order to inform people about the tram project and to contribute to the consultation process. Indeed, in the later stages of development, the process was used to identify appropriate places for tram stops. The company also states (in their information pack) that it was essential that the public was, and continued to be, consulted during the design and construction process so that the layout could accommodate the needs of the local people as far as possible.

The apparent failure of Supertram to meet the targets originally anticipated has created considerable debate and research. One survey asked the public if Supertram should have provided more information about the project during the planning and consultation stage, and 94 per cent of respondents agreed that it should have done. Almost 70 per cent of the respondents knew the Supertram routes but:

- 89 per cent felt that the planned routes would not meet their needs;
- 85 per cent thought Supertram was not the best answer to traffic congestion problems;
- 78 per cent said they would not use the service if it cost more than their present means of transport;
- only 9 per cent of the people surveyed thought that 'quality of service' was the most important feature of Supertram;
- 43 per cent considered the pricing of fares to be the most important feature which might influence their use of the tram.

QUESTIONS

1 Who are the major stakeholders in the Supertram project?

2 Where might marketing research have best been targeted in the initial stages of the project, and why?

3 How does Supertram's market position compare with that of other forms of transport? What dimensions can be used to 'map' perceptions of Supertram?

4 What opportunities exist to use pricing as a lever with which to optimise return on investment?

The student choice scheme at Postlethwaite University, Pubton

The institution

Postlethwaite University, Pubton (PUP) is one of the UK's 'new universities'. Originally, this higher education institution was formed as a local polytechnic in 1969 by the merger of a teacher training college, a school of design and a technical college. During the 1970s and 1980s, its certificates, diplomas and degrees were validated by the Council for National Academic Awards (CNAA). In the early 1990s, the polytechnic was incorporated as a new university with powers to award its own degrees.

After wide consultation, the name Postlethwaite was chosen in honour of one of Pubton's most famous historical figures, Councillor Algernon Postlethwaite (1870–1932), who was a pioneer of mail-order shopping in the UK and a major benefactor to the City of Pubton. He provided the City Council with a number of public buildings which bear his name, a major city public park and a collection of late nineteenth-century British paintings representing young, middle-class ladies wistfully searching for romance, which are generally considered pretty boring, even by ardent and feminist art historians.

PUP has at present three sites near the city centre, and a total enrolment on certificate, diploma, undergraduate and post-graduate courses of 17 247 students. It employs 419 academic staff. The numbers of students rose dramatically in the late 1980s and early 1990s, as government pressures to increase the participation rate in higher education, drives to increase efficiency, and major restructuring within the university took place.

In common with many other universities, PUP has adopted a framework for academic awards which uses a Credit Accumulation and Transfer Scheme (CATS). All named degree courses in PUP consist of a number of syllabuses or modules, which earn students a number of credits for passing them. Most are taught as 20-credit modules, although some subjects, such as some technical skills and practical language modules, are rated as 10 credits. Students need to accumulate 120 credits for each year of a three-year undergraduate course in order to obtain a BA or BSc degree (360 credits). The principle of academic progression is still preserved, and students need to pass a first-year module in a subject before they are permitted to take modules in the same subject in the subsequent year of the course – a system of prerequisites for progression. The university has also adopted a two-semester year, which involves two 13-week teaching blocks, each of which is followed by a three-week assessment and examination period. All undergraduate programmes now also ensure that students are given first-year introductions to PUP's library and IT facilities, to professional and interpersonal skills, and to the core academic disciplines relevant to the named degrees (for example, BA Information Systems) on which they are enrolled.

PUP has eight faculties, with a central policy-making directorate, registry and secretariat which is known, internally, as 'the centre'. The faculties are effectively divisions of the organisation, each with its own senior management team (SMT) and administrative support:

- Hotel and Catering
- Education
- Science and Engineering
- Business and Public Administration
- Architecture, Planning and Leisure
- Social Sciences and Health
- Information Technologies
- Culture and Languages.

PUP has benefited from maintaining a strong vocational focus on its work, and provides a range of 'sandwich' courses in most faculties. It has also been very successful in continuing to attract mature students, who constitute over 20 per cent of its student body. Students are normally recruited through the Universities Central Admissions System (UCAS).

Pubton provides a popular environment for students. Although the South of England is still inclined to regard the Midshires as 'the North', the local culture has a down-to-earth tradition of friendliness. The students form a very specific local community and, in the absence of much university-owned local accommodation, there is an established market for rented student accommodation within the city. Students make a small, but positive contribution to the local economy.

Undergraduate degree courses and student choice

Students constitute PUP's primary market. Most students still apply to named degree courses, but two factors have become increasingly apparent.

1 It was found that students often wish to reconsider the choice of their original degree within the first year of their university experience.
2 It was realised that a significant number of applicants to universities are interested in studying a combination of subjects, rather than making a single-subject specialisation.

In response, PUP introduced a university-wide course structure which permitted first-year students to choose, if they wished to do so, one module from another named degree as part of the first-year programme of study. At the end of their first year they could therefore apply to transfer their registration to another named degree in which they had had some experience. PUP also introduced a Combined Studies Programme (CSP) which permits students to design their own academic courses from modules belonging to (up to three) different named degree courses. This has proved very popular. It provides a broad range of choice and is much appreciated, both by those students who feel that they prefer more flexibility in the combination of subjects that they study at degree level, and by those who feel that they do not wish to commit themselves to a more 'traditional' programme of study or even to a specific career path at an early stage. Each faculty has appointed an academic member of staff to act as CSP Officer. The Faculties of Social Sciences and Health (FSSH) and Culture and Languages (FCL) attract relatively large numbers.

CSP students may be taking modules from more than one faculty, and so the faculties are credited with a relevant proportion of income from CSP students' fees.

The CSP has been greeted as an important agent of change in PUP's development. Its students have achieved very successful academic results. However, it has experienced a number of problems since its introduction. The most obvious one involved the impact of CSP upon PUP's own 'provider culture'. Academic staff were initially inclined to perceive CSP students as somewhat 'second-class' customers, because they did not 'belong' to named degree courses, but were attending modules which formed part of those courses. The culture of the named degree, in which specific cohorts of students followed relatively prescribed pathways of studies, found it difficult to adapt to the presence and importance (that is, the economic contributions) of CSP students who were often, and mistakenly, regarded as 'additional' to those registered on named degree courses.

A number of problems also became apparent as a result of PUP's failure to implement certain standards of practice within all its faculties. The most serious of these was a failure to standardise the university's timetable system. For example, CSP students electing to study modules from both the Faculty of Social Sciences and Health, where the timetable was based upon a division of each day into two teaching 'units', and the Faculty of Culture and Languages, found that the latter's timetable, which divided the day into four teaching units, was incompatible. Such lack of standardised systems created additional restrictions on CSP students' ability to exercise the principle of choice in as flexible a way as possible, and was the cause of some frustration with the system.

The resource problem

When the CSP was first introduced, it proved reasonably easy to accommodate relatively small increases in the numbers registered on modules. However, as staff–student ratios worsened (PUP was looking for increased efficiency in the interests of economy), so the pressure on accommodation – for example, numbers and sizes of teaching rooms, resources (such as technical equipment, language laboratory facilities), staffing (such as staff timetables and availability of additional, regular visiting lecturer assistance) and student support services – increased. Those modules which required a certain level of technical support, such as video skills in the BA Communication Studies, soon found that they could not provide enough equipment for all the students who wanted these modules. The numbers applying to some modules proved too large for existing or available teaching accommodation (lecture theatres and seminar rooms).

Faced with this situation, faculties started to introduce a rationing system. Students were routinely asked for their second choice of options, in case the numbers applying simply could not be accommodated. CSP students were particularly affected because, in some modules, named degree students for whom those modules were *compulsory* elements of their degree courses, were given priority over CSP students, who were *choosing* modules. Moreover, the descriptions of the CSP for publicity and admissions purposes had then to call prospective students' attention to the fact that PUP could not guarantee the availability of all modules advertised. This seriously compromised the *ethos* of the CSP, based as it was on the principle of choice and 'design your own course'. On more than one occasion, embarrassed academic staff had to deal with CSP students who had enrolled on the programme only to find that some of the modules they wished to take, and the availability of which had influenced their decisions to apply to PUP in the first place, were already 'full', and therefore unavailable.

The situation was complicated further when a number of faculties sought to enlarge their student markets by developing new degrees which were 'named', but which combined a number of subjects for which there was a proved demand from CSP students among others. This actually had the effect of segmenting the under-graduate market further but did little to increase the university's total market share of student numbers.

Student perceptions

PUP monitors students' satisfaction, largely by means of its course committees, which include student representatives, and by questionnaires dominated by Likert Scale attitude surveys. CSP students expressed considerable dissatisfaction with the 'cumbersome' nature of the bureaucratic systems surrounding student choice. Since CSP students have to negotiate their individual programmes of study with CSP Officers, and often between CSP Officers for different faculties, before the start of each year's first semester, any delays in the provision of faculty timetables were clearly unfortunate. Ideally, these are required before the student has to make a final choice of university and, while at university, before the end of years one and two. Moreover, the strain on resources meant that choices, once made, could not always be confirmed until the actual start of the teaching semester. From the students' point of view, this situation was obviously unsatisfactory.

PUP, like all other UK universities, is operating in a competitive market. The quality of its work has an obvious impact upon perceptions of the institution in the marketplace, and PUP has its own internal system of quality review. It is also subject to a national system of quality audit. Student feedback and responses form an important part of the processes involved. At the moment, PUP is approaching a point at which some decisions urgently need to be taken in order to remedy any damage that may have been done to the reputation of its CSP as a result of this apparent conflict between demand and resource management. Moreover, the marketing of CSP needs to take account of the resource problems PUP is facing.

QUESTIONS

1   What promotional policies could PUP's CSP adopt to further develop the programme in the light of this situation?

2   Given that this programme was developed to meet an identified market need, what improvements to PUP's operational systems could avoid some of the difficulties identified? What attitude orientations are revealed in the current situation?

3   What impact with failures in administrative and resource management have on students' perceptions of CSP's 'product'?

4   What performance measurements might be relevant to student perceptions of the value and quality of the CSP?

Developments at Ponsonby Road Children's Centre, Pubton

Context

The Ponsonby Road Children's Centre (PRCC) is a voluntary organisation (and registered charity) in an inner city area of Pubton. It aims to benefit the local community, and its management committee has support from Pubton's Young Children's Service. It opened in January 1996.

PRCC's locality has a high level of unemployment and a higher than average number of single parents. The management of PRCC is well aware of the need to attract funding for the nursery facilities it provides. If it can identify a sufficient number of potential sources, PRCC's management intends to develop a marketing strategy to improve the use of the nursery and develop other activities which can be organised by the centre.

Preliminary discussions between representatives of the Local Education Authority and the PRCC's nursery unit produced agreement that the project should identify both short- and long-term objectives. Short-term objectives would concentrate upon identifying a group of stakeholders that could offer some kind of support to PRCC's potential customers. This would help PRCC's management to concentrate its efforts on increasing the number of children at the nursery. The longer-term objectives were to introduce an understanding and awareness of the importance of marketing to PRCC. A marketing approach would enable it to take a more proactive approach to its potential customers and to improve utilisation of the centre's facilities.

PRCC was fortunate enough to obtain a development grant to pay for a short market research project using a local consultancy firm, Evelyn and Bookbinder. The consultants produced a report which is summarised in the following sections.

The approach

Using local sources of information, including the Chamber of Commerce, Pubton City Libraries, and Postlethwaite University Pubton Library, the initial, information gathering exercise focused on:

- collecting and analysing secondary data with the aim of describing the market for PRCC in terms of customer target groups;
- identifying competitors operating on the Ponsonby Road side of the city;
- collecting primary data (by using a questionnaire) on the attitudes of local businesses towards funding those of their own employees with small children, supporting the local pre-school education facilities, and providing sponsorship;
- analysing the financial structure of PRCC with a view towards helping it develop a pricing policy and fundraising activities;
- analysing the existing use of the facilities in order to identify patterns of use and levels of utilisation.

The terms of reference for the project also proposed assessing current perceptions of PRCC, including levels of awareness and perceptions of service quality among both current and potential users. Unfortunately, PRCC decided that it did not wish to proceed with this part of the research, so no data was gathered directly from children's parents.

A short marketing seminar was held for nursery staff and members of the cente's management group. The discussion revealed that PRCC's perceived priorities were:

- fundraising activities to support the base operating costs of the centre;
- the development of differential pricing policies for different user groups.

The consultants believed that the marketing seminar provided the participants with some understanding of the marketing issues facing the centre and would help the management group develop its future marketing strategy.

The markets

There are four main markets which need to be addressed.

- *The primary market* consists of the children who use the centre. However, the design of the centre, the facilities it provides and the attitudes of the staff will influence the facilitator market.
- *The facilitator market* consists of the parents who decide that they want their children to attend the centre. There is also a second facilitator market: the department within the Local Education Authority.
- *The resourcer market* includes all those organisations and individuals who provide finance and facilities (including voluntary help) to support the centre. They include Pubton City Council, sponsors, Pubton College, and paying parents.
- *The legitimiser market* comprises those organisations which enable the centre to operate and whose rules and regulations have to be met (for example for health and safety requirements).

The environment

The consultancy set out to 'map' the environment within which the PRCC operates.

A 1995 review of services for children under the age of eight showed that the area had a particularly high proportion of children younger than four years old. This would indicate that there is considerable potential for the use of the centre, if funding is available. According to the 1991 Census, single-parent households in the area numbered 418, or 22 per cent of all households with children. Households with no employed/earning member numbered 45 per cent of all households with children.

According to a survey carried out during 1991 by Pubton City Council's Housing Department, 46 per cent of respondents in the area received either Housing Benefit, Family Credit, Income Support or Community Charge rebate. Sixty-six per cent of respondents had an annual income under £8000. Twenty-six per cent of respondents had an income between £8000 and £12 000. Eight per cent of respondents had an income over £12 000.

While there is potential demand for PRCC's services, that demand will obviously be limited by the area's high level of unemployment. Unemployed parents will have little requirement for childcare. Local demand will, therefore, be led by the social needs for child development. In spite of this situation, the 'take up' of places at the PRCC has been encouraging. Other providers are active in the area. Any marketing policy needs to take account of these factors.

The competition

The next stage of the process was to evaluate competition within the area. There are two existing nurseries in the area, The Chalk Pits Day Nursery, which is supported and subsidised by the local authority, and the Children's House, which is privately owned and operated. Both nurseries offer their services for children over the age of two years. There are no facilities for infants (six months to two years old).

Each has a different pricing policy. The Chalk Pits Nursery's charges are based on net household incomes. At the time of the research, there was only one parent able to pay full fees. The Children's House has a full-cost pricing policy. Both nurseries were full and had waiting lists. This indicates that demand is not met by existing provision and there is scope for the PRCC to develop.

Private nurseries usually use a fixed scale of charges, regardless of family income. Charges are based on sessions (mornings and afternoons). Fees vary from £1.60 to £3.75 per hour. Discounts are available for some morning or afternoon sessions. Discounts for brothers and sisters are generally available. Discounts are also available for 'full-time' places. Extra-time attendance can be arranged at hourly rates, which are usually high. Any services for children under 2 are also more expensive. Hourly rates offer discounts for booking more than a certain number of hours per week (for example, 15 hours), and there is usually a limit for minimum hours booked per week. Most nurseries charge full-time rate or 50 per cent of full-time rates during school holidays.

The nurseries which are subsidised prefer a sliding scale of charges according to parental income.

The PRCC's biggest potential local demand comes from low-income, one-parent families. There is considerable social need for pre-school provision, but there are considerable economic barriers to the centre's use by many potential parent clients. This barrier may be overcome in part by the introduction of nursery vouchers for children of four years or over, but will remain a problem for children under that age. Other sources of funding need to be developed.

Alternative funding sources

In order to obtain information about potential support from local businesses, a survey was undertaken. This aimed to identify all possible sources of support from commercial organisations in the area. The data source for this was drawn from published listings of local companies. The majority of local businesses are small enterprises employing between two and ten employees. The research focused on the businesses with more than seven employees. From 108 valid addresses there was a 10 per cent response rate – a high rate of return for a postal questionnaire.

- Ninety per cent of respondents employed parents with small children.

- Ninety per cent of respondents thought that there was no difference between the performance of working parents with small children and other employees.

- Sixty per cent of respondents thought that the performance of parents with small children was not influenced by the attendance of their children at a nursery.

- Thirty per cent of respondents thought that parents perform better, a great deal, or markedly better if their children attended a nursery.

- None of the respondents had their own crèche facilities or other resources which could help parents with small children to work, or gave employees any financial support for this purpose.

- None of the respondents was prepared to contribute towards a parent's expenses for pre-school education, and none wished to contribute towards supporting low-income families in the area.

- Only two of the respondents were aware of the existence of the PRCC.

The survey clearly indicated that local employers had little or no interest in supporting local facilities of this nature. If external funding or sponsorship is to be sought, then it will need to be obtained from other organisations.

A personally conducted survey of branches of local banks revealed that banks usually ran their own, pre-school education facilities, but restricted places to children of their own employees. Banks often support charitable activities, but do not usually support individual, local organisations, even those operating in deprived areas.

Conclusions

The research indicates that there is a potential demand for PRCC's services from within the local community. Despite some existing competition, demand exceeds supply. Demand will be very price sensitive because the use of the centre is driven by social needs rather than needs of employed people who need childcare to enable them to work.

There is little local business awareness of the PRCC, and negligible interest in sponsoring funded places. Support from local commercial organisations is unlikely to be forthcoming. Given this situation, the draft marketing plan concentrated on:

- identifying the PRCC's strengths and potential;
- developing a profile of users and potential users;
- determining a pricing policy for PRCC which took account of both the potential market and the centre's operating costs;
- identifying other possible sources of sponsorship funding;
- considering the most effective promotional methods which could be used;
- recommending appropriate systems to keep track of the attendances, utilisation and income.

The management of the PRCC is strongly community focused. Children attending the centre come from many different social, cultural and ethnic backgrounds.

PRCC has the potential to attract a range of users from parents working in local businesses and living outside the area, children in need through the 'buy-in' places available through the Children's Act Funds, parents on training courses (in co-operation with TEC-funded places for parents being trained for work), and disabled children living in the area.

All of these represent different market segments, and will need different marketing approaches. The centre was founded to offer parents in the local community, especially single parents and the unemployed, help in getting back to work. The nursery has the capacity for 23 to 30 full-time equivalent children, although numbers are currently restricted by the numbers of qualified nursery staff needed to look after children of pre-school age.

As an organisation new to the area, PRCC will inevitably take some time to realise its potential. One of the problems invariably encountered in new projects is managers' underestimation of the length of time it takes for demand to develop. This is particularly true of service provision because it is not possible for most users to evaluate the service properly until it has been in existence for a sufficient length of time.

The centre's facilities are capable of being used for a number of purposes and activities in addition to nursery provision, but at present, PRCC's main aim is to provide a high quality of childcare. This is intended to provide the foundation for the development of other activities. It is clear that the physical facilities of the centre are excellent. The building is sound and secure. The staff are actively committed to the centre and well qualified. On the other hand, staffing levels are such that the centre cannot operate extended opening hours. Although it can rely on some further financial support from the local authority, any increase in staffing would have to be met from revenue or sponsorship. One solution to this problem would be to recruit additional staff from unpaid resources – for example, voluntary helpers or using the nursery as a 'training base' for volunteers who wish to train in childcare.

On the basis of existing financial information, there is scope for the recruitment of more children, even at existing staffing levels. Overall utilisation is about 40 per cent (12 children). An analysis of children's attendances, however, reveals a high level of irregularity that can have a major impact on costing. Currently the nursery charges £2.00 per hour, but this is negotiable for parents who cannot afford it. The current average fee is said to be approximately £1.10 per hour per child. Clearly the costs per child will depend upon levels of utilisation. Differential pricing is obviously necessary to optimise demand. It has become evident that user income alone will not provide a secure basis to enable PRCC to meet future costs. Additional funds will have to be raised via sponsorship from other organisations.

Given the existing cost structure, it is suggested that a minimum of £8000 to £10 000 will be required in the first year and in subsequent years. This will enable the centre to develop its potential and additional services as well as providing the low-price nursery provision that the area requires. The PRCC was asked to consider the possibilities of obtaining further funding through targeting:

- childcare allowances for training parents (Pubton College, Pubton TEC, the University and the Health Authority);

- negotiation with other agencies funding nursery provision (for example, Young Children Centres);
- charities;
- sponsorship from commercial companies where there is an interest in children and children's welfare;
- donations.

In addition, income could be generated by the hire of the centre for other local activities. However, every such event has to be carefully prepared in terms of pricing, accountability, delegation, etc. and such activities might prove a distraction from the development of the centre's 'core activity'.

The development of the centre really needs a high-profile campaign to promote the centre and its benefits to parents and children, but this may be too ambitious in the short term. However, public awareness of the centre is crucial to its medium- and long-term development.

QUESTIONS

1 Given the restricted resources available to PRCC, what forms might further marketing research usefully take?

2 In this situation, what are likely to prove the most effective means of promoting the PRCC within the area?

3 To what extent is the PRCC vulnerable to buyer behaviour and segmentation? How do actions of the different markets impact upon the success of the centre?

4 In what ways might PRCC's activities benefit the local community in general?

The Health and Safety Executive and marketing

The organisation

In the UK, the Health and Safety Executive (HSE) is the executive arm of the Health and Safety Commission (HSC). The Commission is appointed by the Secretary of State for the Environment to advise on the need for new or revised legislation, and to make arrangements for its enforcement. Its members include representatives of employers and employees as well as 'independent' individuals. HSE provides the staff resources for health and safety inspection, although some traditionally low-risk sectors of employment, such as offices, are inspected by local authority environmental health officers on an agency basis.

HSC/E is a 'non-departmental public body' (NDPB) and is funded by government with a budget approved by Parliament. It does charge fees for some of the services it provides, such as civil claims work and some licensing applications, but the sums involved are relatively small.

HSE is divided into a number of divisions. There is a single internal management division, an operational division and a research/scientific support agency. This case study concerns the largest single division, Field Operations (FOD), operating in the Midshires area of England. The division is responsible for providing advice, inspection/investigation and enforcement for almost all industrial and service employers in the region. The main exceptions are mines, railways and nuclear plants, which are dealt with by the more specialist operational divisions of HSE.

The work of HSE represents a very wide range of activities, and the advice given by the division includes fielding telephone enquiries, visiting organisations on request, providing factual statements for civil proceedings, providing free and priced publications, lecturing and making presentations, etc. Similarly, 'inspections' range from a ten-minute visual hazard spotting exercise in a two-person dressmaking company to a multi-disciplinary, multi-faceted audit of a large petrochemical company.

Who are HSE's customers and what do they want?

In common with other public sector organisations, HSE provides different kinds of service to different kinds of customer. Sometimes this produces some apparent conflict of interest. In political circles, this might be described as 'responding to different constituencies', but in this situation we can refer to HSE's 'multiple markets'. A clear identification of these is essential to develop an understanding of the different stakeholder groups and expectations.

HSE's *primary market* consists of the direct users and beneficiaries of the service. These can be defined as the owners, managers and employees of the premises that are visited. This is a complex market in itself. There are two considerations of particular interest:

- *Attitudes to inspection.* It might be expected that employers would be relatively reluctant to be inspected while employees would welcome inspections. Research and experience actually indicate that employers generally value 'free consultancy' and that employees are often reluctant to change their familiar routines. There have even been complaints from employers that they do not have enough access to HSE.

- *Attitudes to legislation.* Research has shown that, in general, small firms dislike goal-setting legislation which gives them the freedom to choose solutions to problems. They would rather be told what to do and how to do it.

Clearly, not all employers think in the same way all the time. Their views are likely to change. If asked whether they want more help to comply with legislation they are likely to say yes; if asked whether they want to pay for this through increased taxation, they will often say no.

The main problem HSE experiences with its primary customers is related to the fact that members of this market do not pay for the services they receive and often have what the provider considers to be unreasonable expectations. Industrial customers are usually fairly pragmatic, but members of the public – for example, who have children injured at school or on fairground rides, or elderly relatives killed by incorrectly installed gas appliances – may be less sympathetic. There is always more that could be done if resources permitted, and difficult choices have often to be made in prioritising actions. Any mismatch between resources and demand is likely to increase year by year, as customers' expectations are raised as a result of *The Citizen's Charter* and other government initiatives.

HSE's *resourcer market* is almost exclusively HM Government and the Treasury. Again, this is a complex market to understand, but parliamentary debates on public funding provide valuable insights. The political opposition's offensive has usually been based on the premise that inspection and enforcement are necessary in the public interest, and that reductions in funding lead to a reduction in inspectors and in inspections. Government responses have asserted that advice and encouragement to employers is indeed necessary, that HSE has achieved a noticeable reduction in accidents over its 21-year lifetime, and that it is necessary to preserve a balance between the appropriate safety standards, on the one hand, and industry's ability to function profitably, on the other.

Legislation is, of course, extensive in this area. However there are differing interpretations of how best it should be implemented. The *legitimiser market* is therefore somewhat fragmented in its views. Probably the most influential and closest 'stakeholders' are the Commission and senior management within HSE itself – that is, the very organisations which have the job of 'juggling' the various priorities facing HSE. By virtue of the nature of HSE's work, the professional staff who undertake it might also be included in the legitimiser market. Through self-selection and inculcation they are all critical individuals who know that inspection resource is limited.

What business is the HSE in?

Without quoting the mission statement as an 'easy' answer, the organisation is certainly not in the business of 'pleasing everyone'. The view of staff at operational level is that the organisation is in the business of making quality interventions, including longer term programmes of action designed to realise sustained compliance with legislation. It is recognised, however, that the demand for HSE's services has to be managed, and even reduced – for example, by withdrawing from a public commitment to investigate 100 per cent of gas complaints irrespective of their significance or the remedial action already taken by the industry's suppliers and distributors. Senior management may be tempted to think that the organisation is in the business of survival. It recognises that HSE is on the horns of a resources/demand dilemma. The current approach favours one of relationship marketing rather than service marketing.

Neither of these approaches to the organisation's business is really a consumer perspective. Both are predominantly provider views. This is likely to result from the fact that customers' views are not homogeneous, they are not articulated clearly and they have not been focused on issues of prioritisation. Management has not seriously sought the views of HSE's major stakeholders on these issues. The research that has been undertaken on attitudes to the service was judged inconclusive, although the possibility of further and better focused research was discussed. However, the research already undertaken was more concerned with issues of customer satisfaction than addressing problems of prioritisation.

The current strategy focuses on risk and impact and has moved away from an emphasis on maximising the number of inspections. To facilitate this, HSE has addressed issues of market segmentation. It has devised new categories of premises – for example, 'low hazard/low risk' – and taken these out of the normal inspection programme. The frequency of visits to higher risk premises has been increased. HSE has also changed the 'units of currency' it uses for performance measurement, counting contacts instead of inspections.

Operations management

Operations management can be illustrated by examining briefly the range of inspection and investigative work undertaken by a team of inspectors.

This team had responsibilities for a mixture of manufacturing and service industries. These included engineering, woodworking, plastics, further and higher education, the Health Service and fairgrounds. The territories covered varied with the industry sectors, a rationale intended to balance workloads. For example, health and woodworking were inspected throughout the Midshires area, whereas only fairgrounds in the Pubton City area were targeted. In addition, the team also had responsibility for all miscellaneous premises in Pubton and Artisanville. Staffing in the team varied more than expected throughout the year. At the outset, when operational plans were made, the team had two experienced inspectors, two inspectors just ending their training, and a brand new trainee due to start. The team manager herself had only a limited amount of time for inspection work.

The team manager and the two experienced inspectors undertook audits of a number of NHS trusts, working in pairs. One of the experienced staff led a closely targeted fairground inspection programme over the summer months, using the other and the most senior trainee. The two junior staff were primarily given responsibility for 'keeping the lid on' – that is, dealing with reactive work – and for taking the opportunity to gain as much experience as they could during the year. All members of the team with some experience were given some training and mentoring responsibilities for the new trainee, under the eye of the team manager.

The clients for this work did not commission it. Employers were chosen because of their position on the inspection programme. The NHS trusts were given a schedule for the year and were told what the audit would entail. The team was purposefully attempting to develop better collaboration and cooperation with the trusts. None of the other employers to be inspected were given any prior warning of the inspections unless there were particular local reasons for making formal appointments.

Analysis of the variability in demand proved the most valuable tool for the team's activities when they were reviewed. The team's resources for the year period were basically 50 per cent experienced staff and 50 per cent inexperienced. The trust audits, most of the fairground work and most of the training work fell to the experienced staff. In addition, due to previous experience or intrinsic difficulty, the experienced staff took a larger slice of the reactive work than was desirable. Their workloads therefore became overloaded and the less experienced staff took on new preventative work (which otherwise would not have been done that year) to keep fully occupied. The result was that the team actually worked at a level greater than its theoretical capacity.

The impact of this over-commitment fell almost exclusively on the trust audit work. Reactive demands require a prompt response, and the trainee was patently unproductive if left waiting for assistance. The audit work requires longer blocks of interrupted time for preparation or writing up, and, in consequence, was always being postponed. Ironically, the trust audits were the only activity for which the team had a public commitment. As a result, backlogs of work accumulated and audit reports were typically posted three or four months after an inspection, even if they typically only took a total resource of six inspector days to prepare. The resource pool and the service 'mix' were basically out of alignment. The situation became worse because of unplanned staff moves later in the year.

The team had recognised, at the start of the year, that, if it devoted too much time to considering the uncertainties and problems of the trust audit programme, it would be counter-productive. By the end of the year, it was apparent that there was considerable potential for improvement by:

- designing solutions to the problems posed by the level and differentiation of resources available, the range of services provided, the specialisms required and the geographical area covered; and
- increasing efficiency through planning and undertaking 'blocks' of similar work.

Suggested Improvements

A number of specific improvements were considered, primarily with a view towards improving customer satisfaction. Customers are generally interested in fair treatment, transparency and consistency. Internal customer satisfaction is greatest when the agreed external objectives are being achieved. However, the primary market is made up of a number of different segments, and on the principle of 'horses for courses', audit is the right approach for a complex, diverse, large, multisite employer like an NHS trust, and a ten-minute 'look–see' inspection is the right approach for a small organisation in the 'rag trade'. In other words, an audit does not necessarily imply the provision of an augmented service, it is simply the appropriate form of 'core service' for that particular category of customer, given the limited resources at HSE's disposal.

To achieve an increase in customer satisfaction in a practical way, it is necessary to optimise the way in which staff are allocated to tasks. The creation of a resource-task matrix should enable more experienced and capable staff to take on the most demanding work.

QUESTIONS

1 What kind are the different relationships which exist between the HSE and its clients and how can these relationships be managed within a single organisation?

2 The HSE has considered extending its market research to consider factors other than customer satisfaction. What might be the most useful kinds of information it might look for in this way?

3 What are the issues the HSE needs to consider in determining its pricing policy?

4 What would be the advantages and disadvantages to the HSE of attempting to reduce demand for the service?

The Pubton Water-power Industrial Museum's marketing plan

Pubton's Museum Services supports one major art gallery, built in the 1890s, and five public museums. Two of these celebrate the city's industrial past. The 'flagship' museum – the Pubton Museum of Industrial Heritage – was opened in 1980 on the site of a Victorian cotton mill near the city centre, and was successful in winning the Museum of the Year Award two years later. Three miles away, on the outskirts of the city, the Water-power Industrial Museum (WIM) is a Grade 2, Department of National Heritage site, based around a restored, nineteenth-century paper factory, complete with its original, water-powered machinery, buildings and warehouses. The museum was opened in 1986. It not only illustrates the history and technologies of paper-making, but its displays have been extended to include other examples of water-powered industrial processes, including nail-making, cotton spinning and weaving – all industries which once created the industrial prosperity of the Midshires area. The future of the WIM is now under review by the City Council. The museum is struggling to preserve an acceptable level of local services in the face of continuous pressures to reduce costs, and growing competition from an increasing number of other museums in the county. The future looks less than optimistic. In response to the situation, the museum produced its 1996 Marketing Audit and Marketing Plan, a summary of which appears below.

Marketing audit

History

WIM occupies a historical site on the River Arbiter, one which has been used for industrial purposes since the eighteenth century, and features a mill pond providing power for two large undershot water wheels. These have been restored and one of them is still used to power an early nineteenth-century Fourdrinier (continuous sheet process) paper-making machine. The other runs a number of machine processes associated with the Industrial Revolution, including a small cotton-spinning operation and a machine-powered loom, a trip hammer and bellows for a forge. Some of the paper mill's original workers' and managers' accommodation has been restored, and visiting craftsmen regularly exhibit their skills on regular monthly 'production days'. The museum pays a great deal of attention to providing information and interpretation for visitors, although it has never been able to attract the investment necessary, for example, for interactive video displays and major educational developments. WIM's activities are centred on a programme of special events and exhibitions.

Budget for 1995–6

Income		£
	Admissions fees	37 500
	Merchandising	15 000
	Other	2 000
	Total	57 500
Expenditure	Wages	130 000
	Premises	7 500 CR
	Transport	500
	Supplies and admin.	25 250
	Total	148 250
Net loss		90 750

Staffing

WIM employs eight staff:

- Curator
- Assistant Curator
- Head Attendant
- Engineer
- 3 attendants
- Administrative Officer (clerical)

The museum shares (but does not directly fund) a Marketing Officer with the Pubton Museum of Industrial Heritage.

Facilities and merchandising

The museum operates a gift shop which stocks a range of publications, papers (from the mill) and souvenirs chosen for their relevance to the museum and its displays. It is staffed by the Administrative Officer, when the museum is open. A museum café is run by external caterers on a franchise basis. Income to the museum from the shop and the café combined was some £14 500 in 1993–4 and £12 300 in 1994–5. The kiosk at the entrance to the museum is staffed by an attendant on a rota basis.

Opening hours and events

The museum is open from 10 a.m. to 5 p.m., Tuesdays to Sundays, and is closed on Mondays. A programme of monthly 'production days' attracts a high proportion (about 35 per cent) of the museum's income and visitors.

Education services

The museum welcomes visits from schools, and can usually organise volunteer guides for school parties. Information packs and 'activity' questionnaires are available for children.

Market profile

The existing customer research is based on a survey of visitors one weekend in April 1995, using 142 respondents. Analysis indicated that:

- 65% had visited the museum at least once before;
- 35% were 'new' visitors;
- 95% of visitors came from the Pubton area;
- Information about the museum was usually gathered from local newspapers, local free papers, word of mouth and the museum's own public notice board.

Information from a wider survey on leisure behaviour in Midshires, conducted by the City Council, indicated that WIM was the best known Pubton museum. Of the people surveyed, 49 per cent had heard of the museum, although only 30 per cent of these had actually visited WIM.

Unfortunately, there is little detailed market information available to the museum beyond a simple record of total visitors and the types of tickets sold. The overall trend of annual attendance figures continues to be downward, from a peak of 26 210 in 1987–8 to a low in 1994–5 of 21 177. Visits by schools and colleges account for some 20 per cent of all visitors. WIM's admissions pricing distinguishes between adults, children, family tickets, concessionary tickets, local authority school parties, and school parties from outside the area.

- 41% of visitors are adults;
- 19% of visitors are children;
- 23% of visitors are family groups;
- 2% of visitors are from schools outside the city;
- 8% of visitors are from Pubton district schools;
- 7% of visitors are concessionary (students and Senior Citizens).

Pubton area has approximately 432 000 residents. The local visitors to WIM come mainly from four postcode districts in the South of the city.

Sponsorship and additional sources of income

A number of local engineering and manufacturing companies made a grant to WIM under the National Heritage Arts Sponsorship Scheme. This amounted to some £4000 in the previous financial year. WIM is also made available for location filming (there is a local company which specialises in identifying suitable locations), and has featured in a number of historical dramas and documentaries.

Competition

Museums have proved to be among the most popular leisure venues in the UK, but competition has increased significantly since the 1970s, and competition to create and maintain market share is tough. Research by national organisations indicates that museums attract a majority of socio-economic class groups A, B and C1. Most frequent visitors are likely to be in the 35 to 54 age range (the demographic segment which is forecast to increase significantly in the Pubton area within the next ten years), although some 76 per cent of visitors are between 10 and 16 years old. Most visitors spend less than 30 minutes travelling to a museum.

Marketing plan

Aims and objectives

The marketing plan aims to increase the museum's income to 57 500 for the 1995–6 financial year, representing an increase of some 7 per cent in visitor numbers over those of 1994–5. The museum aims to keep expenditure at a maximum of £148 250. These measures are designed to ensure that the museum can continue to serve future generations of Pubton, and that the museum's unique contribution to industrial heritage is preserved.

Strengths, Weaknesses, Opportunities and Threats

- *Strengths.* This is a unique museum in attractive, listed premises, with a programme of production days, attracting a good level of 'repeat business' from visitors and providing a high level of interpretation and specialist knowledge. It is easily accessible to the public (off one of the main trunk roads into Pubton, with its own parking facilities) and provides café and gift shop facilities. It enjoys a high level of public awareness and the goodwill and enthusiasm of a dedicated group of staff, including the services of a marketing officer.

- *Weaknesses.* The museum faces declining visitor numbers. There is no direct support from the local authority education services, and use of the museum by schools is also declining. The financial performance of the shop and café is dependent upon (increasingly poor) visitor numbers. Pricing is seen as a disincentive to using the museum more by some categories of visitors. The quality of management information, especially marketing information, is seen as poor, and staff morale is at present low. There is no immediate prospect of obtaining increased revenue income. Lastly, WIM is largely dependent upon good weather conditions to attract large numbers of visitors in the absence of good indoor facilities.

- *Opportunities.* Some opportunities may well exist as a result of developments in the National Curriculum for schools, and the development of tourism in this part of Midshires. The general growth in the heritage market may well attract more tourists to the area. Demographic trends indicate that the number of children living in the area will increase, as will the number of residents in the 35 to 54 age range. As a film location site the museum has a number of advantages.

- *Threats.* WIM is obviously threatened by the needs of Pubton City Council to implement further cuts in public services, and the Arts and Libraries budget is particularly vulnerable in the present financial climate. The increasing delegation of school management is likely to result in decreasing support from the local education authority. The development of Sunday opening for shops and supermarkets is likely to reduce WIM's attractiveness to visiting families at weekends, and competition from other leisure venues within Pubton must also be considered.

Marketing objectives

WIM recognises that a sustained marketing effort is needed. WIM's marketing strategy involves increasing the museum's market share and expanding its customer base. This will be achieved by:

1 increasing the level of promotion and advertising, including a trial voucher scheme;

2 better distribution of information, including the use of mailing local hotels, transport companies and special interest groups; better public relations, for example, by using fax;

3 increasing the use of printed material with better targeted distribution;

4 co-ordinating exhibition work with other Pubton museums;

5 improving management and marketing information, including the development of customer research;

6 developing a more varied programme of events;

7 developing a realistic 'product development' programme;

8 exploring new pricing structures and visitor incentive schemes;

9 actively seeking more sponsorship and grants;

10 developing better facilities for schools in the context of the National Curriculum;

11 improving customer care by staff training and development.

Timetable

A calendar of tasks, completion dates and responsibilities for implementing the plan was drawn up.

Unfortunately, in early 1997, a decision was made to 'mothball' the museum in order to save about £90 000. Many visitors to the last production day were critical of the fact that WIM rarely appeared to have produced 'anything new' – one visit tended to be very much like another. Little seemed to have been done to attract new visitors. On the other hand, people's habits had changed, and there was no longer a flood of visitors in the middle of Sunday afternoons after 'Sunday dinner'. The City Council was inviting new ideas to ensure the long-term future of WIM.

QUESTIONS

1 What market is WIM actually in?

2 What kind of management/marketing information is required?

3 How might 'the product' be improved in order to attract more visitors?

4 What strategic alternatives might be possible for WIM in the present competitive environment?

NAME INDEX

SUBJECT INDEX

UNIVERSITY OF LINCOLN